Sexual Violence
in Conflict Zones

Pennsylvania Studies in Human Rights
Bert B. Lockwood, Jr., Series Editor

*A complete list of books in the series
is available from the publisher.*

Sexual Violence in Conflict Zones

*From the Ancient World
to the Era of Human Rights*

Edited by

Elizabeth D. Heineman

PENN

University of Pennsylvania Press

Philadelphia · Oxford

Copyright © 2011 University of Pennsylvania Press

Published by
University of Pennsylvania Press
Philadelphia, Pennsylvania 19104-4112
www.upenn.edu/pennpress

Printed in the United States of America on acid-free paper

10 9 8 7 6 5 4 3 2 1

A Cataloging-in-Publication Record is available from the Library of Congress.

ISBN 978-0-8122-4318-5

Contents

Introduction: The History of Sexual Violence in Conflict Zones

Elizabeth D. Heineman

Revelations of sexual abuse of prisoners by personnel at the Abu Ghraib prison in Iraq and reports of rape in ongoing conflicts in Sudan, Uganda, and Congo have drawn renewed attention to an ancient problem: sexual violence in conflict zones. Information regarding the scale of the phenomenon is imprecise, but estimates point to large numbers. A partial list might include as many as fifty thousand rapes in Bosnia in the early 1990s, between one hundred thousand and a million German women raped by Soviet soldiers at the end of the Second World War, roughly a quarter of a million sexual assaults in the wars in Sierra Leone in the 1990s, as many as half a million rapes in a few weeks in the Rwandan genocide, and perhaps two hundred thousand women conscripted to work as "comfort women" for the Japanese armies in the Second World War.[1] In the early 1990s, rape in the wars in the former Yugoslavia and in the genocide in Rwanda received widespread media coverage, reflecting changed attitudes toward such systematic gendered violence.[2] Although international humanitarian law had condemned wartime rape since the early twentieth century, with some exceptions at the Allied war crimes trials following World War II it was only in the 1990s that international organizations, from courts to the United Nations, took action against conflict-based sexual violence as a violation of human rights and a crime of war.

Yet many millennia of warfare preceded the conflicts in Yugoslavia and Rwanda, and we know relatively little about sexual violence in those earlier wars. Generalizations are based largely on a few recent conflicts, each with origins and aims that may not apply to other conflicts. Equally troublingly, our reliance on recent cases provides few tools for understanding the long-term consequences of such violations as war-ravaged societies struggle to achieve postconflict stability.

The aims of this book are fourfold. First, we add to the body of literature on pre-1990s conflicts, expanding the empirical base upon which scholars theorize sexual violence in conflict zones. Second, by emphasizing pre-1990s conflicts we explore long-term consequences and transitions to peacetime society. Third, by considering a wide variety of cases in depth we hope to analyze the factors making sexual violence in conflict zones more or less likely and the resulting trauma (both social and personal) more or less devastating. Finally, we wish to provide the tools to integrate theories of sexual violence in conflict zones into larger understandings of "public violence," or large-scale state-sponsored or state-supported violence.

The term "sexual violence in conflict zones" sounds like unwieldy bureaucratese for "wartime rape," but the former term is broader. According to the United Nations, "sexual violence" includes (but is not limited to) rape, sexual mutilation, sexual humiliation, forced prostitution, and forced pregnancy. Victims can be female or male, of any age.[3] The concentration camp inmate forced to strip before a row of guards and submit to the shaving of body hair is a victim of sexual violence; so is the man forced at gunpoint to rape his sister, and so, of course, is the sister. An environment of sexual threat may trigger nonsexual violence to contain that threat, for example as fathers kill their daughters rather than risk those daughters' capture and sexual violation.[4]

The term "conflict zone" includes situations of mass armed conflict, or "lethal intergroup violence," whether or not there has been a formal declaration of war, and whether or not state actors play a leading role in the conflict.[5] In some situations, only one side is in a position to wield systematic violence and in so doing creates such an environment of terror that scholars may understand these settings as "conflict zones."[6] Peaceful but militarized settings, such as military bases outside conflict zones and military academies, are also relevant to understanding the phenomenon.[7]

Is there a danger in highlighting sexual violence in conflict zones? Early second-wave feminists emphasized that rape was a common feature of both war and civilian life.[8] Privileging atrocities that occur in the context of events that men and governments recognize as extraordinary could reinforce the invisibility and tacit acceptance of sexual violence in women's everyday lives. Feminists and human rights advocates must thus fight equally against sexual violence in nonconflict settings. Yet mass armed conflict creates an environment with particular dynamics of sexual violence. Rhonda Copelon argues that war intensifies the "brutality, repetitiveness, public spectacle and likelihood" of rape. It diminishes sensitivity to human suffering, intensifies men's sense of entitlement and superiority, and gives social license to rape. Yet wartime sexual violence shares a great deal with sexual violence in civilian settings, from the context of institutionalized male privilege, through consequences such as the denial of reproductive autonomy, to situational detail like the public nature of gang rape.[9]

Further complicating efforts to distinguish "peacetime"- from "conflict"-based sexual violence is the overlap between the two settings. In times of war, nationalist men commit violence in civilian spaces against co-national women whose sexual deportment, they feel, weakens the national effort.[10] Demobilized soldiers, required for years to commit acts of violence but subsequently asked to revert quickly to civilian norms, abuse their wives.[11] Brothels surround military bases in areas where there is no conflict but where prostitutes endure clients' violent outbursts and pimps' economic exploitation to the point of debt servitude.[12] Rather than understanding the study of peacetime and conflict sexual violence to compete, we must remain alert to context-specific factors, to the overlapping and mutual influence of conflict and peacetime patterns, and to opportunities to illuminate the phenomenon of sexual violence more broadly.

Why bring together historical and contemporary study of the problem? Nongovernmental organization (NGO) workers, human rights activists, and lawyers struggle to respond to a phenomenon they know frustratingly little about. Immediate needs such as health care and safe quarters are clear, and activists have scored striking successes in enabling prosecutions of accused perpetrators.[13] Yet to diminish the occurrence of sexual violence in conflict zones, to understand survivors' less obvious needs, and to understand the longer-term impact requires a deeper understanding. Such understanding can come only from detailed research of many individual cases, by scholars with a comprehensive knowledge of the settings in which various instances emerged. Because historians' training emphasizes deep knowledge of particular cultures and eras, and because "many individual cases" can only be drawn from history, historical work must inform contemporary efforts.

Recent episodes of conflict-based sexual violence have spurred increased historical study of the phenomenon over the last two decades. Particular insights gleaned from contemporary episodes, however, have also informed historians' work. If sexual violence had genocidal functions in the Balkans and Rwanda in the early 1990s, for example, perhaps it was worth asking whether sexual violence served genocidal functions in the Holocaust or in the decimation of Native American populations. If captured girl soldiers in recent African wars testified that they performed services like laundering and cooking as well as becoming "wives" of military commanders, then we might reexamine the historical practice of turning captured women into wives or concubines, now grappling fully with the simultaneous economic and sexual functions of the practice.

This volume highlights the potential for historical and human rights research to mutually inform each other. The chapters that follow reveal the impact of recent feminist insights on historical research and an awareness of conflict-based sexual violence as a trans-historical phenomenon. They do not offer a comprehensive overview of the history of sexual violence in conflict zones. Many well-known settings of conflict-based sexual violence are not represented: Nazi concentration camps, Indian partition, the Vietnam War, to name a handful of episodes in the twentieth century alone. Certain types of sexual violence, such as genocidal sexual violence and sexual violence against men, do not have chapters dedicated to them. Yet the chapters span a broad geographic, chronological, and thematic scope, not to argue for constant rules across time and space, but rather to illuminate the ways feminist and human rights perspectives have cast new light on themes that deeply concern historians: colonialism, revolution and counter-revolution, family and community economies, historical memory, state building, and more.

This Introduction, by contrast, accentuates the ways historical research might inform those concerned with human rights in a contemporary setting. Following an exploration of the tensions between the universalist perspective of the human rights framework and history's emphasis on specific context, this Introduction highlights the ways history can help us to understand the relationship between wartime and peacetime sexual violence, the aftermaths of conflict-based sexual violence, the functions of testimonies and legal discourses, and the historical background of the current, feminist-inflected human rights moment. By shedding light on the long history of the phenomenon and of efforts to bring perpetrators to justice, we hope to provide useful information for those committed to understanding the problem today. By revealing the gaps in our knowledge, we hope to spur historians to further work.

Human Rights Universalism, Historical Particularism

The human rights movement is premised on the universalist notion that certain rights transcend time, place, and membership in a social group and thus certain actions are violations at any time, in any place, performed against anyone. Human rights documents thus lean toward a universalist understanding of sexual violence in conflict zones.[14] Reports usually cite such second-wave feminist classics as Susan Brownmiller's *Against Our Will* (1975), which represented sexual violence as a constant in times of peace and war and recognized little difference between one war and the next.[15] After acknowledging that such atrocities are "as old as warfare," human rights literature typically mentions the Second World War and then skips several decades to arrive at the 1990s, perhaps with a stop along the way at Indian partition (1947) or the Bangladeshi war of independence (1971). The recitation of past episodes illustrates the recurrence of what appears as a common phenomenon.

The universal claims of human rights ensure that perpetrators cannot escape scrutiny on the grounds that cultural or circumstantial factors excuse actions that otherwise would be unacceptable. Yet Ronald Dudai has argued that the human rights community's insistence that no contextual factors, such as the other side's aggression, can pardon infringements, has led human rights NGOs to avoid discussion of context more than is healthy.[16] In the case of sexual violence in conflict zones, even feminists associated with universalist analyses of patriarchy, like Catherine MacKinnon, eventually wondered whether such frameworks limited the possibilities of action by equating "business as usual" with extraordinary incidents like the orchestration from above of mass rapes of Bosnian Muslim women for genocidal purposes in the early 1990s. If all sides in a conflict raped, then would it not be prejudicial to prosecute rapes by Serbs without simultaneously prosecuting rapes by Croatians and by Bosnian Muslims?[17]

The universalism of human rights language must be balanced by due attention to the unique features of each conflict. Since the 1990s, historians and anthropologists, disciplinarily inclined toward mastery of native languages and deep study of particular settings, have emphasized context-specific interpretations of sexual violence in conflict zones. A brief examination of specific incidents in World War II will illustrate the value of such work.

In the case of the Asian theater, scholars have discovered a web of long-term cultural factors, medium-term legal conventions, and short-term military contingencies to explain the Japanese "comfort woman" system. A long-standing belief that sex the night before battle provided protection for the soldier led military men to welcome sexual access to women as not simply pleasurable but potentially lifesaving. The ensconcing of a sexual double standard and regimented prostitution in Japan's new civil code at the turn of the twentieth century helped to establish such access as a liberal "right" in the modern age, influenced by Western models. Yet the "comfort woman" system found its immediate origins in concern about the consequences of mass rape (e.g., during the conquest of Nanjing) for the effective military occupation of China. Rather than expanding the system of Japanese brothels in an effort to reduce "wild rape," Korean girls were recruited or kidnapped not just because of their colonized status but also because they were infected with sexually transmitted diseases at far lower rates than Japanese prostitutes. With the expansion of military ambitions in 1937, officers offered their men sexual access to women as compensation for lengthening terms of service (with no leave) under deteriorating conditions and harsh discipline.[18] Even this brief overview reveals cross-cultural factors, culturally specific conventions that transcend particular historical moments, longer term historical developments, and shorter-term historical contingencies. Such an account helps us to understand not simply the fact of sexual violence but its scale and the forms it took.

Turning our gaze to the end of the war in Europe confirms the importance of specificity. With the Soviet advance on Germany, the desire for revenge after a horrifyingly brutal German occupation, permission from above to "let off steam," and Russian habits of binge drinking combined to spark a wave of "wild" rapes of women whose bodies stood in for the German nation as objects of revenge. Yet historically inflected cultural specificity also affected German women's experience of the rapes. Sexual reform of the 1920s and 1930s had, to some extent, dulled older conventions proclaiming a woman morally soiled by rape, enabling some women to interpret their rapes as a physical and emotional injury but not an eradication of self-worth. What constituted emotional and physical harm, however, was itself a product of Nazi-era rationality: raped women assumed that those around them would understand that rape by Slavic or "Asiatic" Soviet soldiers was a particularly serious violation.[19] Historical contingency and local factors, in short, play a great role in determining the scale, form, and effects of sexual violence in conflict zones—even as near-universal conventions of women's subordinate status and men's privilege make *some* form of sexual violence a very common feature of war, regardless of the setting.

How might historical research help us to better understand sexual violence in specific present-day conflicts? Human rights reports on sub-Saharan African conflicts provide some clues.[20] Sections on "historical background" typically identify the former colonial power and the date of independence, then fast-forward to the immediate political and economic history of the present conflict. Yet precolonial- and colonial-era history as well as the longer term history of the independent state might help us to understand the specific manifestations of sexual violence in the conflict at hand, as well as the frameworks in which victims and perpetrators interpret their experience. As James Giblin suggests in Chapter 5, precolonial practices of warfare in East Africa shaped the forms sexual violence took in wars of colonial conquest, with rape and abduction serving the cause of family formation and the building of a labor force. In turn, as Meredith Turshen and Clotilde Twagiramariya have noted, practices of wars of decolonization, such as insurgents' abduction of women to cook, launder, and be available for gang rape in camps, re-emerged in the Rwandan genocide of 1994.[21]

Unfortunately, historical research into specific conflicts is still in its infancy. For many conflicts we have no research at all on sexual violence; for others, a lone scholar, journalist, or activist labors away. Only in a handful of cases do we have enough research to enable scholarly exchange. And most of today's conflicts are occurring in precisely those regions that have long been inadequately studied by historians, and for which historical studies of gender are particularly wanting.

Despite the young stage of research on specific conflicts, enough material has emerged to inspire preliminary typologies. Writing in the early 1990s with access to only a small body of research, sociologist Ruth Seifert distinguished among several functions of wartime rape: communication between male combatants, an opportunity for the military to confirm its ability to enhance its soldiers' masculinity, a tool to destroy an opponent's culture, an effort to deracinate the enemy, and so on.[22] In an effort to consider what makes such violence more or less likely, political scientist Elisabeth Wood addresses well-documented conflicts in which sexual violence does not appear to have played a significant role. She thus takes on a common generalization: that mass sexual violence, in *some* form, is intrinsic to war.[23] In citing these typologies human rights reports acknowledge that sexual violence can fulfill different functions in war, even as they often stop short of inquiring into why specific varieties of sexual violence arise in the particular wars that form the subjects of their study.

Chapters in this book cover episodes in which sexual violence served a range of functions: Soviet revenge against Germans at the end of World War II, maintaining military morale and controlling the spread of disease in the Japanese system of sexual slavery in World War II, capturing women for a lifetime of productive and reproductive service in precolonial and colonial East Africa, rape by both enemy and "friendly" men (that is, men on one's own side) as the community's ability to uphold social sanctions collapsed during Bangladesh's war of independence, punishing women of one's own side who violated sexual norms during a time of imperial intrusion in Soviet Uzbekistan, punishing enemy women who did the same in post-World War I Central Europe. The nature and duration of the violence, too, vary. "Comfort women" endured years in isolated barracks as sexual slaves. East African women lived out their lives integrated into new communities. In Germany at the close of World War II, as in Bangladesh, women suffered a short but intense wave of rapes. German women rarely saw their rapists again; Bangladeshi women might continue to live in the same communities as their rapists. This wide range of experience reminds us that efforts to deal with the aftermath must pay close attention to the nature and purposes of sexual violence in specific conflicts as well as the nature of postconflict transition.

Feminist human rights activists struggled against the belief that because rape in war was ubiquitous it was inevitable, and if it was inevitable there was no point taking action against it. Human rights frameworks reject the notion that a phenomenon's ubiquity makes it acceptable. Yet although prosecution in international tribunals may require universal standards, reducing such violence and ameliorating its effects require an understanding of the particular forms sexual violence might take in an emerging conflict, and the consequences of each form for the victim. Historical work can help us to understand these specifics.

The Long View: Sexual Violence from Peace to Conflict to Peace

In his analysis of male same-sex practices in the Iberian conquest of the Americas, Richard C. Trexler states flatly: "The traditional habit of describing outside conflict as produced by inside civility is problematic. Military formations inspire domestic arrangements rather than vice versa."[24] NGO reports, by contrast, often look to the preconflict subordination of women to explain, at least in part, violence against them during war. Both sides of the debate, however, share one bedrock assumption: we cannot understand conflict-based or peacetime sexual violence in isolation.

Scholars of sexual violence in peacetime settings have paid close attention to rape's function in upholding patriarchy. The mere threat of rape ensures women's second-class status as women limit their movements and seek men's protection in order to avoid danger. Actual rape disciplines women who step out of line, and blame-the-victim practices make it hard for them to gain allies and challenge their victimization. As Sharon Block notes in Chapter 1, in colonial British North America such practices established barriers for women seeking recognition of their peacetime rapes, while making wartime rape more recognizable as a violation.

Explorations of "peacetime" sexual violence have noted that it can be *equally* constitutive of sexual and racial hierarchies. Consider lynching in the U.S. American South, which violently disciplined black men and more subtly disciplined white women by exaggerating the threat of rape. This has not been the case in most considerations of sexual violence in contemporary or recent conflicts. Even gender-sensitive analyses tend to prioritize other categories, for example by noting that mass rape can be a tool of deracination in an effort to demoralize and biologically "contaminate" a racially defined enemy. The central concern remains the destruction of the racial-national-political other, not the impact on gender per se.

What happens to our analyses of conflict-based sexual violence if we remind ourselves that sexual violence is very often a means of constructing gender per se? As Trexler notes, Iberian conquerors interpreted Amerindian men's same-sex activity according to the meanings attributed to such behavior in late medieval Iberia. They thus identified Amerindian men not only as sinners—they were unbaptized—but also as effeminized. The definition of Amerindians as sexual as well as religious others helped to justify their conquest.[25] In his examination of post-World War I Central Europe in Chapter 7, Robert Gerwarth describes counter-revolutionaries who published descriptions of their attacks on enemy women who did not behave in properly feminine ways—who were unkempt, hysterical, Bolshevik. The existence of such women helped to establish the enemy as the enemy. But furthermore, in circulating descriptions of supposedly well-justified violence against them, counter-revolutionaries also reminded their audience of what kind of behavior was beyond the pale for a woman.

Acknowledgment of rape's function in disciplining women can be especially helpful in interpreting "insider" sexual violence in times of conflict. Many observers have trouble conceptualizing such violence as conflict-based events, because the perpetrator and victim belong to the same side and the acts typically occur in civilian space. Yet the backdrop of conflict is essential in understanding this type of violence, which cuts the victim off from her own community. The converse of this interpretive problem is the difficulty in recognizing consensual relationships between conquering men and conquered women—or at least, the difficulty recognizing them as anything other than the woman's traitorous act.[26] The two phenomena—

consensual relations across enemy lines and insider sexual violence—are frequently interwoven, because insider violence may target precisely those women suspected of consorting with the enemy or adopting the enemy's sexual standards.

In Chapter 3, Marianne Kamp analyzes "outsider" and "insider" tensions in the colonized setting of Soviet Uzbekistan. The Soviets understood their deveiling campaign of the 1920s as a drive to modernize a "backward" people.[27] Rather than finding a uniformly "uncivilized" Muslim population, however, they encountered a society divided between reformers, traditionalists, and radical reactionaries. Muslim reactionaries who murdered deveiling women used shockingly violent means to uphold a repressive sexual order. Yet this hardly made the larger setting of conflict irrelevant: Soviet intrusions created the environment in which reactionaries found deveiling women especially threatening. Scholars of other regions have similarly found an increase in "honor killings" during times of foreign occupation or dominance, suggesting the ways conflict with outsiders can exacerbate internal tensions regarding women's proper sexual deportment.[28] Yet the disciplinary function of insider sexual violence extends beyond "honor killings." Women participating in nationalist or revolutionary struggle have frequently found themselves subject to the sexual demands of men in their group—demands that place women's desire for freedom from sexual coercion second to the interests of the group, as defined by its men.[29]

In fact, peacetime and conflict sexual violence mutually constitute each other: peacetime sexual violence can shape the manner of subsequent warfare, and conflict-based sexual violence helps to set the terms of the subsequent peace. Although we usually examine sexual violence as a consequence of war, it can also contribute to its escalation. In eighteenth-century Spanish California, as Antonia Castañeda shows in Chapter 2, sexual violence was a key factor in the escalation of nonsystematic (if frequent) attacks into full-scale conflict. In World War I, as Nicoletta Gullace reminds us in Chapter 6, reports of German-initiated sexual violence motivated Britons to join the conflict.

Given the need to create a stable peace in war's aftermath, human rights specialists must pay special attention to the role of sexual violence in the transition from war to peace. The high level of domestic violence among veterans is well documented and points to problematic aspects of men's transformation from warriors to civilians. Sexual violence can also, however, be a means of redomesticating women who may have taken exceptional roles during a conflict.[30] Larger structural matters include the ways that wartime sexual violence originating in war (but often continuing afterward) lays the groundwork for postwar economies. This, after all, is what happens when captured women become slaves, concubines, or forced brides of the enemy. The woman's property may become the property of her new husband, the woman's offspring become part of her husband's community's labor force, and the woman herself becomes a laborer, not just a vehicle for reproduction, in her new community.[31]

Such scenarios are so common, argues Kathy Gaca in Chapter 4, that they demand a rereading of war more generally. Focusing on the ancient western world, Gaca presents a two-phase model of warfare in which combat between men was preliminary to the equally important stage of capturing women and children for sexual exploitation, labor, and the production of subaltern offspring to be used in various capacities by their conquerors. Captured land was of little use, after all, without populations to labor on it. In addition to exposing the continuity between wartime and peacetime settings, such a framework also warns us against the conflation of "sexual violence" and "war's consequences for women" that has characterized some recent treatments. Forced brides are subject to continuing sexual demands, but these might not be the most important consequence either for the woman, the man, or the community.[32] Yet the exploitation of productive and reproductive labor depends on sexual violence.

Aftermaths: Community and Inner Worlds

History is especially crucial to our understanding of the aftermath of wartime sexual violence; a conflict must be some time in the past to enable an exploration of its long-term impact. In addition to immediate needs like health care, feminists and human rights activists often point to longer-term issues such as the ostracism of raped women and their children. History, however, indicates that the relationship between a sexual double standard and ostracism of raped women is not transparent. In addition, history draws attention to many other aspects of the aftermath of sexual violence.

Activists' concern with women's health and reproductive rights, the common conflation of "woman" and "mother," and the short time frame of pregnancy have made reproductive issues perhaps the most-studied "aftermath" of wartime rape. The story—like a resulting pregnancy—might end quickly with abortion or death during the conflict, or it might continue into the postconflict period as offspring of rape are born and must be raised.

Where sexual slavery has served military or laboring men's needs, as in Japanese "comfort stations" in World War II and in military brothels in the two world wars in Europe, mandatory use of condoms and forced abortions have ensured that women's service would not be interrupted by pregnancy. In genocidal settings the fate of a pregnancy resulting from rape has depended on the attackers' notions of race. Nazi eugenics required "Aryan" genetic heritage from both the maternal and paternal lines, and so a pregnancy of a Polish or Jewish woman and a German military man might result in a forced abortion, or the woman might be left to carry the pregnancy to term, with the understanding that both she and her offspring were slated for elimination anyway. In the wars in the former Yugoslavia, by contrast, Serbian aggressors considered race to be passed by the paternal line. They thus ensured the birth of Serbian babies to Bosnian Muslim women by imprisoning pregnant raped women until it was too late for an abortion.[33] Perceptions of racial heredity have also shaped postwar responses to the reproductive aftermath of rape. Postwar authorities may ease abortion restrictions on the understanding that "half-breed" children of rape are undesirable to the society at large.[34]

"Aftermaths" other than reproductive issues have received less attention or have been conflated into discussions of reproductive issues. An important variable is where victims end up. After her sexual torture, does a violated woman remain with her community of origin, whether in its original location or as a refugee? Or does abduction accompany rape: does she become a wife, laborer, concubine, or prostitute in the community of her captors? In either case, the woman might bear the child of her attacker, but other factors equally shape her postwar fate.

So in late medieval Iberia, enslaved women—including those enslaved as a result of conquest—who bore their owner's child had a legal claim to emancipation. Slaves' disadvantages in the legal system, however, meant they faced an uphill battle in demonstrating paternity.[35] James Giblin suggests in Chapter 6 that in precolonial and colonial East Africa patriarchal norms could actually ease postconflict adjustment—if only because a woman's situation in captivity in many ways resembled the life she would have led had she remained in her home community: marriage without her consent, and upon marriage a life of labor as the lowest ranking member of her husband's household. In both settings the same concepts of kinship-based honor that made the capture of a rival's women an injury to that rival's status simultaneously required fair treatment of women (according to community standards of fairness), including captive women.

What little research we have on women's postabduction lives paints a depressing picture, in part because it suggests that however disadvantaged women's status in their new communities, they might expect even worse if they returned "home." After the Armenian genocide (1915) and Indian partition (1947), efforts were made to gain the release of women in forced marriages or concubinage, some of whom had arrived at that state only after having been passed among many men.[36] Yet in both cases, women often resisted repatriation, fearing that they and their children would be rejected by their communities of origin should they return. The fate of women who *did* return confirms that those fears were well founded. In the meantime, conversion, motherhood, and labor had given many a stable, if low, status in their new communities; some had developed affective ties with family and neighbors. As Justice Teresa Doherty of the Special Court for Sierra Leone notes, women's subsequent choices do "not retroactively negate the original criminality of the act."[37] At the same time, the criminality of the original act does not predict what an abducted woman will consider to be in her best interests years later.

For women who remain in (or return to) their communities of origin, postconflict adjustment can depend on their communities' acceptance of raped women, whether the rapists belonged to the community or were "others," and women's own ability to integrate their violation into a coherent understanding of their experience. Sexual attitudes help to shape both community and personal responses. According to Atina Grossmann (Chapter 8), sexual reform of Germany's Weimar years (1919–33) and the Nazis' approach to sexuality—more clinical, less romantic, less religious—enabled many Berlin women to view rape by Soviet soldiers with detachment, gallows humor, and rational calculation. In contrast to the German women who in some cases described their rapes with an almost cool detachment, Yasmin Saikia's interview partners, Bangladeshi women who had been raped in the 1971 war of independence, could describe the "before" and "after" but not the rapes themselves, which they said they had experienced in a state of unconsciousness (Chapter 9). This nonintegrable experience led some to describe themselves decades later as, quite simply, no longer human.

As Leslie Dwyer demonstrates in her study of Balinese women raped during the Indonesian army's crackdown on suspected leftists in 1965–66, however, we should not attribute women's silence to a generic "trauma" common to women shaped by conservative sexual mores. Political and economic reasons might equally discourage women from speaking of their experience.[38] Thus Bangladeshi women's postwar suffering was compounded by the fact that in this nationalist conflict the rapists had often been co-nationals, not Pakistani soldiers. By contrast, although Balinese rapists and victims came from the same communities, the political divide—raped women suspected of leftist activity, rapists representing a repressive government—enabled women to understand their rape as a violation even as political safety required silence. Cases like Bali and Bangladesh also challenge the thesis that sexual violence is less likely in conflicts in which the combatants expect to live together after the peace.[39] Massive sexual violence may indeed occur in such settings, but continued proximity complicates women's task of integrating their own experience into postwar narrative frameworks.

Even when the rapist is an "other," the messy relationship between sexual and national identity can complicate the ways individuals and communities integrate histories of sexual violence into their ongoing stories. For Polish women interned in the Soviet Union during the Second World War, injuries shared with all captive Poles were easily explained, but the national framework offered little help in interpreting violations that affected women only and that occurred "in private" rather than in the company of other Polish nationals.[40] Specifically female experience was thus excised from "national" experience. In postwar West Germany, by contrast, female experience was appropriated by the nation, as official discourse translated the Soviet rape of German women to the rape of the nation.[41] Both developments made it difficult for violated women to claim their own experience—but for different reasons.

Some problems, such as pregnancy among raped women, are common to postconflict societies. Yet historically specific factors, involving not only the nature of the conflict but also the nature of the peace, equally influence the aftermath of conflict-based sexual violence. The social and economic integration of victims and their children is at play, but so is the victim's ability to make sense of her experience. These histories alert us to the ways that slow, evolutionary processes—such as the development of a postconflict national identity—shape the longer-term aftermaths of conflict-based sexual violence.

Testimony and the Law: Representations of the Enemy, Representations of the Self

Two rhetorical activities have dominated the human rights community's efforts to address sexual violence in conflict zones: collecting and disseminating testimony of atrocities, and reforming and applying international law.

Testimony highlights the victim's voice; the law focuses on the actions of the perpetrators. Both have practical implications. Evidence of atrocity is required before one can demand action, and testimonies often provide that evidence. By enabling prosecution, international law brings at least a small number of perpetrators to justice and publicizes internationally recognized standards for conduct during war. Yet collecting and disseminating testimony, and codifying the law, can also serve other functions, such as helping to constitute the identity of those collecting the testimonies or promulgating the laws.

Even the more transparent functions of testimony, however, form a critical bridge between the human rights community and historical scholars. Starting with the Rwandan and post-Yugoslav genocides, human rights reports have included extensive testimony by victims of sexual abuse.[42] Tribunals have collected evidence by defendants, victims, and witnesses. Testimony is never transparent: defendants' stories may be self-exculpatory; victims may frame their stories in response to questions suggested by interviewers or other interlocutors.[43] Yet such first-person accounts will enable historians of conflicts beginning in the 1990s to write a radically different kind of history from what is possible for earlier wars.

Historians of older conflicts at best have access to oral histories conducted decades after the conflict's conclusion. Frequently such testimonies are collected as part of activist efforts to gain recognition for victims. They must be interpreted not only in light of fading memory but also in light of the effort that prompted the collection of testimony. As Yuma Totani demonstrates in Chapter 13, this is not a purely academic exercise: scholars are not the only ones who evaluate the legitimacy of testimony regarding sexual violence. Even though the Tokyo Tribunal of 1946–48 collected testimony on mass rape and the "comfort woman" system, knowledge of these phenomena had little impact on Japan because the Tribunal was dismissed as "victors' justice" and there was little effort to make its findings accessible for a lay audience. More recently, however, Japanese human rights activists have not only pushed their government to recognize this history but also worked to gain the Japanese public's recognition of testimonies gathered by Korean activists.[44]

Yet testimonies in reports composed during or immediately after a conflict, too, must be understood as products of their historical moment. The exclusion of testimonies of sexual violence until a few years ago, and their widespread inclusion now, reflects the changing concerns of the international humanitarian community, not the changing experience of victims of wartime sexual violence. The precise form in which such testimony appears, too, reveals not only the victims' experience but also the interpretive framework of authors and audiences.

The centrality of first-person testimonies in NGO reports reflects a belief in the transparency of facts in the human rights framework. Confirmed atrocities demand a response. Yet, even given this privileging of description of atrocity, the presentation of sexual violence compared to other types of wartime suffering bears notice. Sexual violence is frequently presented in much more vivid detail, with blow-by-blow accounts of screams, violations of particular body parts, ages of victims, and duration of torture.[45] Of course, the intensely personal nature of sexual violation is one of its hallmarks. Yet German women raped at the end of World War II and Bosnian women raped in the early 1990s do not necessarily recall their rapes as the most painful portion of their wartime experience.[46] Authorship and readership, and not just the voice of the victim, must explain the unique presentation of sexual assault.

As Atina Grossmann demonstrates in Chapter 8, retellings of stories of rape, even by those friendly to the victims, could simultaneously satisfy readers' voyeuristic desires and highlight the virtues of those telling the stories on the victims' behalf. Similarly, for the Bangladeshi war of independence, Nayanika Mookherjee has critiqued the ways journalists present themselves as saviors of raped women by presenting their stories to a larger public.[47] By collecting and disseminating testimonies of both victims and perpetrators in that same war, Yasmin Saikia in Chapter 9 complicates the role of the person bringing the stories to a larger public. No longer solely associated with the victim, she must acknowledge a relationship with the perpetrator and inquire into the humanity of victim, perpetrator, and historian alike.

In addressing gender and violence more generally, Shani D'Cruze and Anupama Rao question the "ethics of redisplaying suffering to a gaze whose politics we assume are valid mostly because they're ours."[48] These questions appear especially pertinent in an age that privileges visual evidence. Written complaints about abuses at Abu Ghraib were not sufficient to prompt action; photographs were. Yet circulating the photographs, even if to excite outrage at the photographers, presented the victims' humiliation to a public gaze beyond the wildest dreams of their prison tormentors.[49] This is a familiar problem to historians of the Holocaust and lynching in the U.S. South.[50] Yet the fact remains that atrocity photographs are, in Karen Strassler's words, a critical "currency" of the international human rights movement.[51]

But D'Cruze's and Rao's unease about exposing suffering on the assumption of sympathetic reception opens a further query: what if politics change? The example of World War I shows how provocative retellings of sexual violations could first excite outrage at perpetrators but then render less credible those making the charges. As Nicoletta Gullace shows in Chapter 6, the difference did not depend on available information regarding the veracity of the charges. Rather, popular reception of reports highlighting sexual violence shifted with changing political sentiment (as the British first sought to stoke hatred of the Germans, then, after the war, took a pacifist turn) and even aesthetics (as tastes turned from melodrama to realism).[52] The effectiveness of charges of sexual violence in demonstrating the enemy's perfidy reminds us of one reason present-day reports offer especially vivid detail regarding sexual violations. Reports are not neutral documents; they constitute demands for action. Gullace's story, however, warns that such reports might be subject to unpredictable interpretive frameworks in the future.

Reports of sexual violence also frequently serve a larger symbolic function: to differentiate the "civilized" from the "uncivilized." In this way, British reports of the First World War distinguished the "barbaric" Germans, who raped, from the "civilized" British, who fought to protect innocent maidens. So closely intertwined are the notions of sexual restraint and civilization that efforts to legally restrain sexual violence in war often reflect efforts to claim "civilized" status. The secularization of Christian prohibitions against wartime rape in late medieval Europe, Anne Curry notes in Chapter 10, was part of states' effort not only to professionalize their armies but also to claim the mantle of civilization vis-à-vis their rivals. Likewise, notes Antonia Castañeda (Chapter 2), Catholic authorities in Spanish California strove to reduce Spaniards' attacks on Amerindian women in part because such acts belied clerics' claims of the superiority of Christianity. In the U.S. Civil War, as Susan Barber and Charles Ritter explain in Chapter 12, the Union's effort to claim a moral high ground included an insistence on military justice for Union soldiers who raped. To be sure, Curry acknowledges, we have little evidence of enforcement of such injunctions in medieval Europe; Castañeda confirms a lack of enforcement in Spanish California. In the American Civil War, Union military justice was not racially blind. Still, as Barbara Donagan argues in her exploration of the English Civil War (1642–51) in Chapter 11, the law's role in fostering a positive cultural identity was significant, encouraging (if not guaranteeing) compliance even when formal enforcement was slight.

Scholars often point to the Lieber Code of the Union army in the U.S. Civil War as the first "modern" effort to prohibit rape in war. Yet, given the long history of legal prohibitions, the notion that medieval and early modern legislation regulating rape in war simply disappeared in Europe, to re-emerge in the United States in the 1860s and elsewhere with the human-itarian and human rights movements of the twentieth century, is implausi-ble. It is more likely that early modern British codes, for example, influenced British-American codes and were reiterated in Britain itself with the Napo-leonic Wars of the early nineteenth century. We might hypothesize about other possible continuities between the early and late modern West, par-ticularly with the Napoleonic Wars serving as Europe's rude introduction to the modern phenomenon of "total war." But we can only hypothesize: we lack research on sexual violence in the Napoleonic Wars.[53] Furthermore, the paucity of research on the regulation of sexual violence in war in non-Christian settings before the modern period leaves open the question of how "western" the association of sexual restraint and "civilization" was.

The division between "civilized" and "uncivilized" has not always run along neat lines, with those arguing for restraint claiming the mantle of civilization while perpetrators' sexual violence becomes a marker of their lack of civilization. Robert Gerwarth's exploration of counter-revolutionary violence in post-World War I Central Europe (Chapter 7) shows how com-plicated the claims could be. On the one hand, enemy women embodied demands of bourgeois civilization—democratization, women's emancipa-tion—to which counter-revolutionaries refused to accede. To commit vio-lence against women was to reject the strictures of bourgeois civilization and thus to be celebrated. At the same time, counter-revolutionaries' char-acterizations of Bolshevik women as barely human helped to justify vio-lence against them. Not enemy rapists but rather enemy women to be raped evidenced the enemy's lack of civilization.[54] Indeed, portraying the enemy as violated can help to establish them as the enemy. Considering the circu-lation of photographs of lynching in the U.S. South and of sexually abused prisoners at Abu Ghraib, Liz Philipose observes the creation of abject racial-ized others who both deserved and needed to be put down.[55]

Such observations about the interplay of sexual violence and the cul-tural construction of the self and the enemy have useful lessons for our own era, with its language of a "clash of civilizations." Mass rapes in Bosnia in the early 1990s prompted suggestions that rape has a particularly disas-trous impact for Muslim women: because Muslim law places high value on chastity in women, raped Muslim women face especially harsh ostracism from their communities.[56] Yet this effort at a culturally sensitive reading of rape's impact had an orientalizing effect. On the one hand, it overlooked the highly cosmopolitan and secular environment of post-Communist Bosnia, instead projecting an undifferentiated sexual conservatism across the Muslim world.[57] On the other hand, it suggested that a sexual double standard that leaves women to bear the shame for their own rapes would be less familiar to "enlightened" Western audiences.

Still, Western reports were hardly invested in creating a flattering portrayal of Serbian culture as more "civilized" than Muslim Bosnian culture. The stakes were different with Abu Ghraib. Journalists and scholars alike, horrified at images of sexual torture of Iraqi men, underscored the depth of those men's injury by emphasizing Islam's harsh strictures against homosexuality. The implication: Western men would not suffer *quite* as much because they live in a more enlightened society. The ironies abound, given not only the sometimes violently homophobic setting of the U.S. military but also the specifically homophobic nature of the torture.[58] In both the Bosnian and Iraqi cases, even voices abhorring sexual violence against Muslims could, along the way, reinforce notions of Western superiority.

Representations of sexual violence in war do not simply occur after the fact: rather, they are often part of the conflict itself. Indeed, such representations help rivals to define themselves against each other. The genres most crucial to contemporary human rights work—testimonies and legal codes— speak to sexual violence even as they help to constitute the identity of the author of the legal code or the publisher of the interview. Yet the long association of universalist human rights talk with the interests of privileged speakers—those who create and control the representations— have created persistent tensions around human rights.[59] This is not a reason to discard human rights talk, but it is a reason to remain alert to the multiple functions that representations of sexual violence in conflict zones can serve.

Uses of History

As this Introduction indicates, the uses of history are overlapping and complex. Research into legal codes regulating rape in war, for example, informs us both about possibilities for prosecution and about states' efforts at self-representation. For ease of reading, however, this collection is divided into five parts.

Part I, "Sexual Violence in Peace and in Conflict," demonstrates the ways historical research can elucidate the relationship between sexual violence in the two settings. The chapters in this section focus on colonial environments, where conflict might take the form of all-out war, or might emerge in other means of dominance. Sharon Block compares prosecutions for rape in peacetime and wartime colonial British America. Antonia Castañeda highlights the role of sexual violence in Spain's extension of colonial authority in California, as violence escalated from frequent but unsystematic attacks to war. Marianne Kamp takes a look at "insider" violence in the case of deveiling murders in Soviet Uzbekistan.

Part II, "The Economy of Conflict-Based Sexual Violence," narrows the focus to examine one of the most notable ways sexual violence bridges conflict and peace. Kathy Gaca proposes a model of ancient western warfare in which rape and capture of women was a central aim of war, because rape and capture created the postwar economy. Examining East Africa in the early twentieth century, James Giblin finds that the integration of captured women into reproductive and productive labor functions survived the transition from precolonial to colonial warfare, even as economic motivations overlapped with the desire to symbolically emasculate enemy men.

Part III, "Tellings of Sexual Violence," considers the rhetorical functions of discourses of sexual violence. Nicoletta Gullace traces British representations of German sexual atrocities in Belgium from World War I to the postwar years, as pacifism brought skepticism about the role of wartime propaganda in motivating Britons and U.S. Americans to join the war effort. Focusing on U.S. American novels' representation of Soviet rape of German women at the end of World War II, Atina Grossmann discovers that U.S. occupation soldiers became the heroes—not only by protecting German women from Soviet soldiers but also by providing a pool of more attractive sexual partners. Finally, by interviewing both victims and perpetrators of sexual violence during Bangladesh's war of independence, Yasmin Saikia reflects on the scholar's role in representing these histories.

Considering the law's normative functions, Part IV takes up "Law and Civilization." As medieval European states sought to establish authority, Anne Curry explains, they incorporated church prohibitions against wartime rape into secular law. Barbara Donagan continues the story in early modern England, when prohibitions against rape during war reflected an effort to professionalize armies in order to limit the damage of the English Civil War. Examining trial records for Union soldiers accused of rape in the U.S. Civil War, Susan Barber and Charles Ritter note both a concern for military discipline and an insistence on enforcing Northern racial practices in the South, most notably by the acceptance of African Americans' testimony in courts.

Finally, Part V takes us "Toward an International Human Rights Framework." Yuma Totani explores the pedagogical function of courts by comparing Japanese responses to information about sexual slavery gathered in the Tokyo Tribunal with revelations culled from more recent legal actions. Rhonda Copelon describes the organizing that made it possible, in the late twentieth century, to hold perpetrators accountable. A major figure in this movement, Copelon focuses on the changing international legal conventions and identifies limitations to current practices.

PART I

Sexual Violence
in Peace and in Conflict

Chapter 1

Rape in the American Revolution: Process, Reaction, and Public Re-Creation

Sharon Block

Rapes occur in wartime and in peacetime. They occur in military conflict zones, in what we might call the social/cultural/political conflict zones of colonial encounters, and in zones without any overt macroconflicts at all—in "peacetime." To what degree can, or should, we distinguish rapes that occur in military conflict zones from those that occur in mainstream society? Are all sexual assaults somehow tied together, as some feminist scholars of rape have suggested? How different are conflict zone rapes from sexual attacks committed in other settings? In other words, what can a study of sexual violence in a military conflict zone reveal, not just about the particulars of the sexual violence committed during a specific military episode, but also about the historic meaning and understanding of rape itself?[1]

As a scholar who has studied heterosexual sexual coercion in early North America from 1700 to 1820, I have devoted significant ink to discussing how early Americans enacted, interpreted, and punished acts of sexual violence. Here I focus specifically on the enactment, prosecution, and representation of rape during the American Revolution. Isolating sexual violence in wartime allows me to test the argument, made by me and other feminist scholars, that sexual power is contingent upon other forms of power. While early American men regularly used the power of their social location as masters, fathers, or powerful authority figures to coerce sex, military personnel relied on their status as warriors to coerce sex. Such different means for sexual coercion should translate into Revolutionary War sexual assaults that were more overt and more violent than other early American sexual assaults.

The first two sections of this chapter detail the commission of sexual attacks during the American Revolution. The many first-person sources that describe these assaults substantiate my claim that rape perpetrated by British soldiers during the Revolution was indeed more violent and more public than peacetime sexual attacks. Unlike sexual attackers in peacetime, military personnel rarely attempted to replicate consensual sexual norms in their assaults on American women. In part because of this more overt nature, assaulted women tended to respond differently to rape in conflict zones: women raped by enemy soldiers often reported their grievances more quickly and with less assistance from intercessors. Ironically, these public and speedily reported attacks more closely matched the archetypal image of rape in early America than did many peacetime rapes. This, in turn, contributed to more successful prosecution and harsher punishment of sexual attackers in wartime than in peacetime.

In the chapter's third section I compare such wartime assaults with discussions of sexual violence in wartime propaganda. Americans virulently condemned the British soldiers (and their Hessian mercenaries) for sexual attacks on Patriot women. As I have discussed elsewhere, such propaganda focused on those sexual attacks that could be constructed to threaten America's Patriot (and patriarchal) politics.[2] Here I expand on that analysis to show how these propagandistic sexual attacks compared to the conflict zone rapes about which we have eyewitness accounts. Ultimately, early Americans highlighted those sexual attacks that best fit their image of an undeniable and uncivilized rape, creating a public image of wartime sexual violence that used rape for political ends.

In the final pages of my chapter I introduce two instances of sexual violence against marginalized members of early American society to complicate the relationship between the commission and representation of sexual violence. While the overt brutality of conflict zone rapes could transcend the bounds of wartime, the public attention that made them into matters of public interest did not necessarily follow. Because wartime rapists neatly fit the image of enemy attackers, the sexual violence they perpetrated became public proof of their illegitimacy. In contrast, rapes against marginalized members of colonial society did not so easily engender a metanarrative of good and evil. These final examples suggest that the public construction of rape, as much as the level of violence or purposeful torture used in the commission of sexual attacks, made an individual attack into a matter for public concern.

Sexual Assaults in Conflict Zones

A variety of historical sources record incidents of sexual assaults in conflict zones. These include military court-martial records, criminal court records of soldiers' trials, personal letters and diaries, and political propaganda. Of more than nine hundred incidents of sexual coercion that I have identified in British America from 1700 to 1820, approximately sixty incidents involved military personnel as alleged attackers. Military courts tried twenty-four of these cases between 1760 and 1781. Not all of these prosecutions involved rape or attempted rape charges; some defendants were tried under more generic charges such as ill using women, conduct unbecoming an officer, attempted murder, or giving a child a "foul disorder." Regardless of the charges, all these documents include an array of first-person testimonies about sexual coercion, sometimes in dozens of pages of detailed trial transcripts.[3]

These records reveal that the presence of large numbers of military personnel during the American Revolution allowed for enactments of sexual violence that were unmatched in peacetime. Soldiers with weapons who patrolled American streets had more direct means for sexual attack than did neighbors or family members in peacetime contexts. Sexual violence in the Revolution tended to be more obvious attempts at sexual battery than covert peacetime assaults that relied on coercion, manipulation, and the replication of consensuality as part of their commission.[4]

Many incidents clearly grew out of the military occupation of the rebelling American colonies, where soldiers used their military authority to force women into sexually vulnerable situations. When Catherine Stone and Isabel Mitchell walked along a Philadelphia street one evening in 1778, two members of the British quartermaster's division stopped them on the pretense of needing to investigate them. Instead of taking the women to a British officer for questioning, however, they dragged Catherine and Isabel away from the street and raped them. That same year in New York City, Thomas Gorman convinced Sarah Willis to open her door to him one night by "saying that he had Authority to press Men for His Majesty's Service"; once inside, he raped her. In 1779 a Sergeant Boswell entered Elizabeth Loundberry's house by saying "he was ordered there by his Officers to look for arms." Once inside, the sergeant insisted she follow him to another room to "shew him where the arms were," locked the door, and raped her. In all of these incidents soldiers received access to women's property and persons via their military position in an occupying army. The Revolutionary War gave them control over Americans and offered distinct opportunity for sexual attacks.[5]

Military status also gave British soldiers an additional means of coercion—weapons. Victims of conflict zone rapes repeatedly testified that

soldiers threatened them with their guns or other arms. Sarah Cain testified that a soldier "presented his Pistol at her & then charg'd his Bayonet
against her Breast & Swore he would Run her thro the Heart." Likewise,
a New Jersey woman told how soldiers swore that if she made noise while
they raped her, "they would Run her thro with a Bayonet." Another New
Jersey victim testified that one of the British soldiers who raped her "swore
he would Blow her Brains out if she did not go" with him. In contrast, the
use of weapons—especially guns—was extremely rare in peacetime sexual
assaults. The Revolution allowed for more violent versions of sexual attacks
than were normally seen in peacetime. Men who might have to rely on
means other than brute force to commit sexual assaults could, as soldiers,
rely on their weapons to coerce sex.[6]

Other soldiers embedded the military conflict directly into their rationale for rape. When British officers confronted soldiers John Dunn and John
Lusty with Elizabeth Johnstone's complaint of rape in 1776, the two Johns
responded by claiming that "she was a Yankee whore or a Yankee bitch, and
it was no great matter." Mary Philips testified that she was gathering wood
near her house when British soldiers saw her and justified throwing her
down and raping her because "She was going to the Damn'd Rebels." And
in 1777 Rebecca Christopher testified that after British soldiers raped her
repeatedly their lieutenant claimed "she harbourd Rebels." In addition to
using the opportunity of occupation to claim sexual license, these attacks
made women's status as Americans into a justification for sexual assault.[7]

Much of this Revolutionary-era sexual violence began in view—or at
least hearing—of family and neighbors. Isabel Mitchell watched British soldiers beat Catherine Stone before they dragged the two women in different directions and raped them. Several men in a nearby room heard Sarah
Willis cry out for help from the British soldier whom she accused of rape.
Two soldiers raped Elizabeth Johnstone in front of her young daughter and
a bedridden older woman. At the very most, soldiers forced witnesses out of
sight before committing rape. A group of British soldiers locked a mother
and another man out of her house so that one of them could rape her disabled daughter. When the mother realized what was happening, she eventually made her way back into the house—only to be raped herself. Soldiers
seemed concerned, if at all, with keeping away people who might physically
assist a victim.[8]

In peacetime, however, sexual assaults were usually committed clandes-
tinely. Masters ordered their servants to distant fields before raping them;

fathers waited until mothers left the house to sexually abuse daughters; neighbors and strangers took women on "shortcuts" through unpopulated woods before attacking them. Indeed, the legal criteria for rape included the specification that the attack had been done in an area where the woman's cries could not have been heard; if others were within shouting distance, the law presumed she had probably not been raped.[9] In reality, however, the lack of witnesses to a sexual attack committed in an isolated location could make a victim's story seem less believable. The Revolutionary era sexual attacks that were witnessed by family members and neighbors often appeared to be more obvious crimes than those peacetime rapes that raised the thorny issue of whether a woman had consented.

The more public sexual attacks in the Revolution were also part of the wartime climate of chaos and plundering. A number of court-martialed British soldiers faced additional charges alongside sexual assault accusations. British soldiers broke into Martin and Christiana Gatter's New Haven house several times, where they beat Martin and raped Christiana. In 1778 two British soldiers were "hanged and Gibetted" in New York for raping a woman and robbing and murdering a man. Two British quartermaster soldiers were charged with ill using women and robbery in Philadelphia.[10]

All these incidents grew directly out of the British military occupation of the American colonies. Soldiers who committed assaults against America's persons and property included sexual violence in their panoply of attacks against their enemy. Unlike many peacetime rapes, these attacks did not grow out of a psychological or economic coercion, and did not attempt to replicate private, consensual sexual relations. They were rapes characterized by brute force and the power of an invading army. As part of their occupation, British soldiers had already disregarded American political and legal institutions; thus, committing rapes with little apparent regard for deniability or possible legal consequence may have seemed more reasonable than it would in individual peacetime assaults.

As enemy invaders, British soldiers' attacks in the Revolution also seemed more likely to involve multiple attackers than other sexual assaults. In more than nine hundred known sexual assaults between 1700 and 1820, attacks committed by multiple assailants account for only about one in ten incidents. In contrast, in the roughly two dozen courts-martial between 1760 and 1781, more than one-third involved multiple assailants. Two British soldiers took turns raping Elizabeth Johnstone in her Long Island home in 1776. Two soldiers did the same to Elizabeth Loundberry in her Stony

Point, New York, home in 1779. Richard Perce and John Pillar were both whipped by a military court for trying to rape an "ould woman" in Rhode Island in 1778. Multiple assailants again distinguished peacetime sexual attacks—many of which aimed at some replication of the normalcy of consensual sexual relations—from sexual attacks in this war zone.[11]

Sexual violence prosecuted in military courts also tended to include more simultaneous victims than those prosecuted in civilian courts. Most non-conflict zone sexual violence occurred against one victim. The small number of cases that involved more than one victim were often child abuse incidents that had occurred over a long period of time rather than a one-event attack against multiple victims. In contrast, almost one-third of the two dozen sexual assault-related courts-martial trials in the Revolutionary era involved multiple victims. In 1776 two soldiers raped one woman and attempted to rape a second woman in her home. Multiple soldiers raped Elizabeth Cain and Abigail Palmer in a New Jersey home in December 1776. In 1778 Bartholomew McDonough was convicted by a British military court for raping Phoebe Coe and her disabled daughter in their Long Island home. William Green and other soldiers sexually assaulted an older and a younger woman in a New York residence. Rather than trying to force women into a version of consensual sex, sexual attackers in conflict zones repeatedly abandoned any attempt at re-creating normative heterosexual relations in favor of the brute force of gang rapes and attacks on multiple victims.[12]

Thus, soldiers used the tools of their trade, the power of their positions, and the claims of an occupying army to sexually assault enemy women. Soldiers committed these rapes as soldiers, not just as random individual attackers. Wartime rapes rarely had to address the complications of defendants and victims who had previous social relationships or of attacks that involved nonobvious or nonphysical coercion. Accordingly, the Revolution's overtly violent and public attacks most accurately fit the archetypal image of rape as an absolutely irresistible crime committed with great brutality.[13]

Reactions to Sexual Violence in Conflict Zones

The differences in the commission of sexual assaults in war and peacetime led to other differences in the aftermath of those attacks. Women subject to conflict zone violence were far more likely to immediately bring their complaints to authorities than were women subject to peacetime assaults. Men relied on more limited defenses to charges of rape in wartime. Partly as a result of these two differences, military tribunals were more likely to convict and harshly sentence soldiers than were civilian criminal courts.

For a peacetime sexual assault to become a matter of public concern, a victim usually had to tell others what had happened to her and bring the matter to the attention of authorities. In civilian cases this usually involved friends and family members who helped the victim bring her complaint to a justice of the peace. The justice of the peace could then decide whether to forward a case to a colony's criminal justice system. Much of the time, women either chose not to bring their complaint to legal authorities (and we learn about these incidents only through letters, diaries, or tangential testimony in other court cases) or delayed making their complaints public until they had talked extensively with trusted friends and family.[14]

In military conflict zone cases, however, women seemed much more likely to immediately notify authorities that they had been wronged. As soon as Isabel Mitchell saw a British lieutenant, she told him about the soldiers who had just raped her. Once the two soldiers who raped Elizabeth Johnstone "let her get up, she went out of the house . . . and meeting two officers she complained of the usage she had received." Unlike in peacetime cases, these women did not doubt that a prosecutable wrong had been done to them, and they immediately notified authorities. A witness-viewed rape committed at gunpoint with significant physical assault fit an archetypal image of sexual violence that was far more common in a conflict zone than in peacetime. As such, victimized women seemed to more immediately report rapes committed by enemy soldiers in the American Revolution than they did during peacetime sexual assaults.[15]

Still, telling officials was not easy for many women even in wartime: when the colonel, seeing Elizabeth Loundberry "crying & wringing her hands," asked what was wrong, only "after some hesitation" did she tell him she had been raped. In 1778 Phoebe Coe did not initially tell the British officers to whom she complained about her daughter's rape by British soldiers that they had raped her too. When asked why, Phoebe said that she "thought it a shocking thing to tell of, she only mentioned the Circumstance of her Daughter, for which alone she thought that he would suffer severely." When Catherine Stone complained to British Lieutenant Robert Douglas about a sexual assault by two British soldiers, he stated that he could see she was ill used, but "he did not ask her as to particulars . . . as she seemed desirous of concealing the worst part of it." Women who had been assaulted by enemy soldiers in the American Revolution might immediately report wrongs to British officers, but telling strangers about such an intimate crime was still not an easy task. Overall, however, the circumstances of many of the sexual attacks in the American Revolution may have made telling their stories easier for these women than for many victims of peacetime assaults.[16]

After women told officials their version of the facts of a sexual assault, the accused then had a chance to defend themselves. In civilian courtrooms, a massacre of the victim's character was the ubiquitous defense to a rape accusation. Establishing that a victim was sexually promiscuous, immoral, or otherwise less than virtuous immediately cast doubt on her claim. But such accusations are noticeably absent from Revolutionary War courts-martial.[17] British soldiers, as outsiders to American communities, were probably unable to rally detractors to American victims' characters. Further, the nature of a woman's character related primarily to a determination of consent; immoral women would be believed to have consented to sex, which negated a rape charge. However, the public nature of many Revolutionary era assaults undermined any attempts to portray the victims as willing participants. Because sexual violence in military zones was often undertaken in front of witnesses through overt physical force, military defendants could not often utilize peacetime defendants' common answer to a rape charge: that while they had indeed had sexual relations, the woman had consented.[18] Thus, accused rapists turned to other rationales for their defense.

As in civilian criminal trials, court-martial defendants claimed that their good character proved they would not commit a rape. One man claimed that his entire regiment knew he "bore a very good" character, and another that his officers could testify that he "always bore a good character." At John Barron's trial for raping a seven-year-old girl in 1763, witnesses claimed that John "has always behaved like a good soldier." Several military personnel attested that William Sanders "generaly [sic] behaved well" when he was charged with attempted rape of a four-year-old girl. By proving themselves good men and good soldiers, defendants hoped to decrease the credibility of a sexual assault charge. But a defendant's general claims to good character proved a rather weak defense—perhaps meant to encourage a more lenient sentence rather than to exonerate themselves.[19]

Given the absence of many standard defense options to a rape charge, it is not surprising that military courts appeared to have a significantly higher conviction rate in sexual assault cases than did civilian courts. Of twenty military tribunal cases in which the verdict is known, eleven led to convictions and one to a conviction of a lesser charge. In contrast, in criminal court cases, the rape conviction rate for white men (all of the military court defendants were white) between 1700 and 1820 was approximately 35 percent.[20] Court-martial conviction rates reflected the very different setting and commission of most wartime sexual assaults.

Punishment under military law was also harsher than punishment under civilian criminal law. Of the eleven convicted defendants, six were sentenced to death. All but one of the remaining convicts were sentenced to corporal punishment. By the Revolutionary era, corporal punishment had begun to fall out of favor as a criminal punishment in America for free and white people. While enslaved people might still be subject to whippings and other bodily mutilations, white men convicted of rape were more likely to be subject to imprisonment by the last quarter of the eighteenth century.[21] In contrast, corporal punishment under military law was exceptionally harsh. Several court-martialed rapists were sentenced to one hundred lashes, and one pair of men, convicted of robbery and sexual assault, was sentenced to one thousand. Thomas Higgins was sentenced to "800 catanine tails." In contrast, corporal punishments in criminal courts were rarely set above thirty-nine lashes.[22]

Rapes by enemy soldiers could be translated into prosecutable sexual violence because they were sudden attacks committed through physical force by obvious outsiders who had a clear motive for the attack that was beyond any individual victim's control. This made such attacks perfect fodder for propaganda publications by American Patriots.

Rhetoric of Rape in the American Revolution

Discussions of sexual violence in the American Revolution appeared in newspaper articles, broadsides, letters, and an array of other publications. These public presentations relied less on reporting actual incidents and more on early Americans' gendered imaginings of power. As scholars have shown in other settings, rape could become a political tool in these public forums to show the brutality of an enemy and the unquestioned innocence of victims, as well as to provide a rationale for, in this case, the Patriot cause.[23]

Some of these published stories overlapped with the ways that firsthand reports discussed sexual violence—such as seeing these sexual attacks as a direct result of war. But most moved beyond detailing individual incidents (indeed, first-person victims' accounts were not published) to emphasize the damage done to fathers, husbands, and the American body politic. To make the biggest impact, publications also emphasized those acts of sexual violence that were the most irrefutable and most heinous. Doing so was meant to leave no doubt that British soldiers were immoral enemies of all civilized people.

As in the firsthand descriptions of sexual violence, many of the print discussions of sexual attacks during the Revolution set those attacks alongside other war-related atrocities. One commentator described how the houses of even Loyalists "were burnt: their wives and daughters pursued and ravished." A newspaper published a letter from a Continental Army colonel, describing the British soldiers' rampages: "almost every species of perishable property, are effectually destroyed, with unrelenting fury, by those devils incarnate; murder, rape, rapine, and violence fill up the dark catalogue of their detestable transactions!" Other reports more generally condemned the "burning, plundering, ravaging and *ravishing*" committed by British soldiers and their Hessian mercenaries.[24]

Patriot publications went beyond just describing rape as part of the booty of war: they used sexual violence by British soldiers as a justification for the Revolution, treating rape as a crime against patriarchs and Patriots. A letter from the Philadelphia Council of Safety asked Americans "to secure your property from being plundered, and to protect the innocence of your wives and children" by joining the Patriot cause. A newspaper article in 1777 told readers that stopping the British military's advance would save "female innocence from brutal lust and violence." In 1778 a minister asked a New England audience how they could "hear the cries and screeches of our ravished matrons and virgins that had the misfortune to fall into the enemies' hands, and think of returning to that cruel and bloody power which has done all these things?" A New England newspaper likewise concluded, "Nothing has more united all the colonies in a strict bond of union, than the brutal cruelty of the British troops . . . they ravish virgins before the eyes of their parents." Such publications set American innocence at the mercy of improperly seized power and made formerly British subjects in America the ultimate victims of the rapes by British soldiers.[25]

Several political commentators made the connections between rape and illegitimate political power even more explicit. As one soldier complained to Thomas Jefferson in 1776, the British "to the disgrace of a Civilised Nation Ravish the fair Sex." Another letter writer added a new twist to the Declaration of Independence's self-evident rights when he condemned the British soldiers' "merciless depredations upon the chastity, property, liberty, and happiness of their vassals." In 1777 a published list of misbehavior by British soldiers paralleled the soldiers' propensity to rape innocent women to the appalling behavior of "persons and bodies of the highest rank in Britain . . . King and Parliament." From the American perspective, the British perverted the empire with their oppressive tyranny just as they perverted the most sacred of bodily interactions with their rapes of unwilling American women. Rape proved the illegitimacy of British rule because legitimate patriarchs, whether as individuals or as fathers of the nation, did not rape. Stories of rape confirmed American determination for rebellion, rhetorically creating a collective body of male resisters to British imperial rule. Even George Washington tied personal morality to legitimate rule: "it is expected that humanity and tenderness to women and children will distinguish brave Americans, contending for liberty, from infamous mercenary ravagers, whether British or Hessians." Rape of innocent women could be used to contrast American heroism to British savagery and illegitimacy. As such, it was a powerful tool for political propaganda.[26]

Much of this rhetoric called for American men to save their wives and daughters from sexual abuse by British occupiers. But unlike the rhetoric where upstanding Patriot men saved their wives and daughters, the testimonies we do have about men's reactions to the rape of their family members and neighbors suggests a more complex and less idealistically heroic picture. While mariner Thomas Gorman raped Sarah Willis in 1778, Sarah called to her neighbor to "take this Man out of my house," but the neighbor admitted that he had been "afraid to interfere." While two women were being raped by a British soldier on Long Island in 1778, one neighbor testified that although they had "pressed him very much" to help, "seeing that there were three [soldiers], he did not chuse to" directly assist them. Instead, he rode to the British camp to report the problem. Martin Gatter testified that he was so afraid of being beaten a second time by British soldiers that he left his family alone in the house and "hid in a Corn Field till Morning" while the soldiers raped his wife. These men's attempts at self-preservation may have been understandable, but they contrast with the public image of noble American men sacrificing or risking themselves to protect American women.[27]

Politically inspired reports of rape also tended to emphasize victims that were unquestionably sexually innocent, and therefore most wronged by the attacks. A disproportionate number of public descriptions of rape by British soldiers focused on those cases involving girls and young women. Of thirty-six sexual violence incidents involving soldiers that were reported in newspapers, political pamphlets, or other politically charged documents, thirteen (more than one-third) involved girls and teenagers as victims. The *Pennsylvania Evening Post* reported multiple sexual assaults of children in a

December 1776 issue—one involving "a child of ten years of age," another involving five "brutes" attacking a "girl of thirteen years of age," and a third involving the (unnamed) "daughter" of a William Smith. A broadside published that year recounted the rape of "a girl about fifteen" by "a *British* officer," and of sixteen "young women" who were taken to the British camp for sexual purposes. In April 1777 the *Pennsylvania Evening Post* again reported the rape of a "young girl." Indeed, all of the newspaper and broadside reports of sexual abuse in New Jersey during the height of the British occupation mentioned that the British had attacked pre- and just-pubescent girls. After the war, Mercy Otis Warren summarized attacks in New Jersey by painting a picture of the "shrieks of infant innocence, subjected to the brutal lust of British grenadiers, or *Hessian Yaughers*." By choosing to emphasize the youth of the victims, Patriots emphasized the British soldiers' unequivocal wrong of taking virginal innocence.[28]

Yet this public emphasis on attacks on young women corresponded neither to the cases appearing before military tribunals nor to all known sexual assaults by soldiers. Only five of the twenty-four incidents prosecuted before a military tribunal involved girls or teenagers as victims, and all of these involved soldiers' sexual assaults on daughters of their ally soldiers, not attacks committed across battle lines. Of the thirty-eight incidents involving attacks by soldiers that were recorded outside of political propaganda, only seven incidents (slightly more than one-sixth) involved girls or teenagers as victims. Some girls and young women were undoubtedly raped by British soldiers. But the unrelenting focus on young victims allowed American publications to emphasize the wrongful violation of unquestionably innocent victims. This provided an appropriate image for a new American nation that claimed its birthright as the innocently wronged subject of the British Empire.

Counterpoint: A Conflict Zone of Colonialism

In 1788, two white men, William Holland and John Pettigrew, held Elizabeth Amwood, a free African American woman, at gunpoint, cut off her hair, and forced an enslaved man to rape her while other men watched. During the assault, Holland shouted degrading comments at her, and after the rape, "Called for Water to wash his hand, saying he had bin puting a Mare to a horse." In Pennsylvania in 1722, James Browne followed a "Squaw" known as Betty or "Great Hills" into a field and had sexual relations with her in front of several Indian girls. James then took another man to the field where

Betty still lay, apparently unconscious, with her clothes up around her waist, and sexually tortured her with a stick of wood.[29]

These two sexual attacks parallel wartime rapes in several critical ways. Soldiers committed rape in ways that marked their military superiority; these rapes of African American and Native American women marked their subservient places in early American society. As in Revolutionary rapes, these men showed no apparent fear of discovery. The multiple witnesses to both attacks served instead to turn the sex into purposeful degradation. But the public and institutional reaction to these rapes differed markedly from wartime attacks. Even though these rapes were two of the most barbaric and purposefully torture filled reported during the entire eighteenth century, none of the attackers were harshly prosecuted. Instead, the men were convicted locally of the crime of assault, not rape, and punished with nothing more than a fine. And neither case appears to have become fodder for public outcry; no newspapers appear to have reported on either case, no broadsides were published about the trial, and their cases have not become part of any local or national histories.

The contrasting outcomes between these cases and Revolutionary War sexual assaults highlight the important work done by sexual violence in conflict zones. The overtly violent nature of Revolutionary War sexual attacks did not alone make those acts seem most like the rapes imagined by early Americans. What one modern scholar has called "real rapes" required not only a particular enactment but a conflagration of the means of the attack alongside a preexisting condemnation of the attacker.[30] A white man who barbarically raped a Native American woman revealed himself as an individual who had committed a wrong, and perhaps criminal, act. But British soldiers who raped American women revealed themselves as the men Americans already believed them to be: enemies of the state and society. Rape was not just created through an act but through the actors. Without a preexisting political narrative into which to fit the horror of the crimes, rapes remained largely un-noteworthy acts between individuals rather than offenses against society.

Conclusion

Wartime sexual assaults clearly differed from most peacetime sexual violence in several ways: the increased incidence of multiple attackers and victims, the association of rape with other assaults and property damage, and the brute force used in lieu of a more diverse array of means to coerce sexual relations. Peacetime rapes involved the messiness of defendant and victims who knew each other; sexual violence committed through psychological, economic, or social coercion; or difficult-to-adjudicate cases without witnesses. In contrast, sexual violence in wartime best fit the image of an incontrovertible rape: an attack committed in front of witnesses, with brutal force, immediately reported, and with an obvious motive. Thus, the prosecutions of British soldiers for rape during the Revolution most resembled the archetypal image of a believable rape in the early American imagination.

But the meaning given to those attacks primarily concerned itself with issues beyond the victims of those assaults. Politically motivated propagandists used these relatively incontrovertible rape cases as an opportunity to exaggerate and condemn the evil nature of its enemy. Rape in the Revolution provided a ready-made motive for the attack (British soldiers were obvious enemies) and ready-made proof that the victim did not consent to the sex (British soldiers were obvious enemies). Such circular logic made enemy status evidence of a believable rape and believable rape evidence of an enemy's evil status. Consequently, rape by British soldiers of unquestionably innocent female victims provided a parallel to the political accusations of American Patriots. Rather than attention to the violation of individual women's bodies, Revolutionary War sexual attacks became publicly valuable as an attack on a body politic.

Instead of condemning rape as (in modern terms) a human rights violation against women, early Americans utilized the harm done to individuals by sexual violence for political purposes. Rather than see rape as a fundamental feature of patriarchies, early Americans publicly discussed it as an affront to proper patriarchal rule. Thus, similarly obvious and violent attacks by white men against Native American or African American women during peacetime did not meet the same standard of importance as did wartime rapes by an identifiable enemy to American society. By making enemy status crucial to the (e)valuation of rape, early Americans gave meaning to the conflict zone of the American Revolution.

Chapter 2
Sexual Violence in the Politics and Policies of Conquest: Amerindian Women and the Spanish Conquest of Alta California

Antonia I. Castañeda

> *In the morning, six or seven soldiers would set out together . . . and go to the distant rancherías [villages] even many leagues away. When both men and women at the sight of them would take off running . . . the soldiers, adept as they are at lassoing cows and mules, would lasso Indian women—who then became prey for their unbridled lust. Several Indian men who tried to defend the women were shot to death.*
>
> —Junipero Serra, 1773

In words reminiscent of sixteenth-century chroniclers Bernal Díaz del Castillo and Bartolomé de las Casas, the father president of the California missions, Junipero Serra, described the depredations of the soldiers against Indian women in his reports and letters to Viceroy Antonio María Bucareli and the father guardian of the College of San Fernando, Rafaél Verger. Sexual assaults against native women began shortly after the founding of the presidio and mission at Monterey in June 1770, wrote Serra, and continued throughout the length of California. The founding of each new mission and presidio brought new reports of sexual violence.

The despicable actions of the soldiers, Serra told Bucareli in 1773, were severely retarding the spiritual and material conquest of California. The native people were resisting missionization. Some were becoming warlike and hostile because of the soldiers' repeated outrages against the women. The assaults resulted in Amerindian attacks, which the soldiers countered with unauthorized reprisals, thereby further straining the capacity of the small military force to staff the presidios and guard the missions. Instead of pacification and order, the soldiers provoked greater conflict and thus jeopardized the position of the church in this region.[1]

Serra was particularly alarmed about occurrences at Mission San Gabriel. "Since the district is the most promising of all the missions," he wrote to Father Verger, "this mission gives me the greatest cause for anxiety; the secular arm down there was guilty of the most heinous crimes, killing the men to take their wives."[2] Father Serra related that on October 10, 1771, within a month of its founding, a large group of Indians suddenly attacked two soldiers who were on horseback and tried to kill the one who had outraged a woman. The soldiers retaliated. "A few days later," Serra continued, "as he went out to gather the herd of cattle . . . and [it] seems more likely to get himself a woman, a soldier, along with some others, killed the principal Chief of the gentiles; they cut off his head and brought it in triumph back to the mission."[3]

The soldiers' behavior not only generated violence on the part of the native people as well as resistance to missionization, argued Serra; it also took its toll on the missionaries, some of whom refused to remain at their mission sites. In his 1773 memorial to Bucareli, Serra lamented the loss of one of the missionaries, who could not cope with the soldiers' disorders at San Gabriel. The priest was sick at heart, Serra said: "He took to his bed, when he saw with his own eyes a soldier actually committing deeds of shame with an Indian who had come to the mission, and even the children who came to the mission were not safe from their baseness."[4]

Conditions at other missions were no better. Mission San Luis Obispo also lost a priest because of the assaults on Indian women. After spending two years as the sole missionary at San Luis, Father Domingo Juncosa asked for and received permission to return to Mexico because he was "shocked at the scandalous conduct of the soldiers" and could not work under such abominable conditions.[5] Even before San Luis Obispo was founded in the early fall of 1772, Tichos women had cause to fear. The most notorious molesters of non-Christian women were among the thirteen soldiers sent on a bear hunt to this area during the previous winter of starvation at Monterey.[6]

The establishment of new missions subjected the women of each new area to sexual assaults. Referring to the founding of the mission at San Juan Capistrano, Serra wrote that "it seems all the sad experiences that we went through at the beginning have come to life again. The soldiers, without any restraint or shame, have behaved like brutes toward the Indian women."[7]

From this mission also, the priests reported to Serra that the soldier-guards went at night to the nearby villages to assault the women and that hiding the women did not restrain the brutes, who beat the men to force them to reveal where the women were hidden. Non-Christian Indians in the vicinity of the missions were simply not safe. They were at the mercy of soldiers with horses and guns.[8]

In 1773 a case of rape was reported at San Luis Rey, one at San Diego, and two at Monterey the following year.[9] Serra expressed his fears and concern to Governor Felipe de Neve, who was considering establishing a new presidio in the channel of Santa Barbara. Serra told Neve that he took it for granted that the insulting and scandalous conduct of the soldiers "would be the same as we had experienced in other places which were connected with presidios. Perhaps this one would be worse."[10]

Native women and their communities were profoundly affected by the sexual attacks and attendant violence. California Amerindians were peaceable, nonaggressive people who highly valued harmonious relationships. Physical violence and the infliction of bodily harm on one another were virtually unknown. Women did not fear men. Rape rarely, if ever, occurred. If someone stole from another or caused another's death, societal norms required that the offending party make reparations to the individual or the family. Appropriate channels existed to rectify a wrong without resorting to violence.[11]

Animosity, when it did surface, was often worked out ritualistically— for example, through verbal battles in the form of war songs, or song fights that lasted eight days, or encounters in which the adversaries threw stones across a river at each other with no intent actually to hit or physically injure the other party. Even among farming groups such as the Colorado River people, who practiced warfare and took women and children captive, female captives were never sexually molested. The Yumas believed that intimate contact with enemy women caused sickness.[12]

Thus, neither the women nor their people were prepared for the onslaught of aggression and violence the soldiers unleashed against them. They were horrified and terrified. One source reported that women of the San Gabriel and other southern missions raped by the soldiers were considered contaminated and obliged to undergo an extensive purification, which included a long course of sweating, the drinking of herbs, and other forms of purging. This practice was consistent with the people's belief that sickness was caused by enemies. "But their disgust and abhorrence," states the same source, "never left them till many years after."[13] Moreover, any child born as a result of these rapes, and apparently every child with white blood born among them for a very long time, was strangled and buried.[14]

The Quabajay people of the Santa Barbara Channel, Font wrote, "appear to us to be gentle and friendly, not war-like. But it will not be easy to reduce them for they are displeased with the Spaniards for what they have done to them, now taking their fish and their food . . . now stealing their women and abusing them."[15] Upon encountering several unarmed Indians on Friday, February 23, Font commented that "the women were very cautious and hardly one left their huts, because the soldiers of Monterey . . . had offended them with various excesses."[16]

At one village, Font noted, he was unable to see the women close at hand because as soon as the Indians saw his party, "they all hastily hid in their huts, especially the girls, the men remaining outside blocking the door and taking care that nobody should go inside." Font attempted to become acquainted with the people of another village on the channel. He went to the door, but "they shut the inner door on me . . . this is the result of the extortions and outrages which the soldiers have perpetrated when in their journeys they have passed along the Channel, especially at the beginning."[17] Font echoed Serra's concern that the sexual assaults and other outrages had severely retarded missionization in California.

Serra and his co-religionists had great cause for concern, because the missions were not meeting their principal objective of converting Amerindians into loyal Catholic subjects who would repel invading European forces from these shores. By the end of 1773, in the fifth year of the occupation of Alta California, fewer than five hundred baptisms and only sixty-two marriages had been performed in the five missions then existing.[18] Because the marriages probably represented the total adult converts means that the remaining four hundred converts were children. These dismal statistics fueled arguments for abandoning the California missions. While various reasons may be cited for the failure to attract adult converts, certainly the sexual attacks and the impact of that violence on women and their communities were primary among them.

Few historians have recognized that the sexual extortion and abuse of native women gravely affected political, military, religious, and social developments on this frontier. In 1943, Sherburne F. Cook commented that "the entire problem of sexual relations between whites and the natives, although one which was regarded as very serous by the founders of the province, has apparently escaped detailed consideration by later historians."[19] Cook tackled the issue in demographic terms and wrote about the catastrophic decline in the Indian population as a result of alien diseases, including venereal diseases, brought in by Europeans, as well as other maladies of the conquest.[20]

Almost thirty years later, Edwin A. Beilharz wrote that "the major causes of friction between Spaniard and Indian were the abuse of Indian women and the forced labor of Indian men. . . . Of the two, the problem of restraining the soldiers from assaulting Indian women was the more serious."[21] In his study of the administration of Governor Felipe de Neve, Beilharz notes that Neve recognized the seriousness of the problem and tried to curb the abuses.

Since the 1970s, the decade that saw both the reprinting of Cook's work and the publication of the Beilharz study, the development of gender as a category of analysis has enabled us to reexamine Spanish expansion to Alta California with new questions about sex and gender. Cook, Beilharz, and other scholars initiated but did not develop the discussion about the centrality of sex/gender issues to the politics and policies of conquest.

It is clear that the sexual exploitation of native women and related violence seriously threatened the political and military objectives of the colonial enterprise in California. Repeated attacks against women and summary reprisals against men who dared to interfere undermined the efforts of the priests to attract Amerindians to the missions and to Christianity. They also thwarted whatever attempts the military authorities might make to elicit political or military allegiance from the native peoples.[22]

From the missionaries' point of view, the attacks had more immediate, deleterious consequences for the spiritual conquest of California, because such actions belied significant principles of the Catholic moral theology they were trying to inculcate. As the primary agents of Christianization/Hispanicization, the missionaries argued that they could not teach and Amerindians could not learn and obey the moral strictures against rape, abduction, fornication, adultery, and all forms of sexual impurity while the soldiers persisted in their licentiousness and immorality. Their actions repudiated the very morality the friars were to inculcate.[23]

Early conflict between ecclesiastical and civil-military officials over deployment and discipline of the mission escort soon gave rise to constant bitter disputes centering on the question of authority and jurisdiction over the Indians in California. The conflict over control of the Indians revolved around the issue of their segregation from the non-Indian population. Rooted in the early conquest and consequent development of colonial Indian policy, the issue has been extensively discussed by other historians. The concern here is to examine it specifically from the point of view of sex/gender and to define a context for explaining why, despite strenuous efforts by church and state alike, there was little success in arresting the attacks on Indian women.[24]

Serra, for his part, blamed the military commanders and, once appointed, the governor. They were, he said, lax in enforcing military discipline and unconcerned about the moral fiber of their troops. They failed to punish immoral soldiers who assaulted native women, were flagrantly incontinent, or took Amerindian women as concubines. In California, he stated, secular authorities not only condoned the soldiers' assaults on Indian women but interfered with the missionaries' efforts to counter the abuse, and thereby exceeded their authority with respect to Amerindians.[25]

To argue his case against Lieutenant Pedro Fages, the military commander, and to muster political and economic support for the California establishments, Serra made the arduous trip to Mexico City for an audience with Viceroy Bucareli. He left California in September 1772 and arrived in Mexico the following February. At the viceroy's request, Serra submitted a lengthy work entitled "Report on the General Conditions and Needs of the Missions and Thirty-Two Suggestions for Improving the Government of the Missions."[26] Serra addressed sex/gender issues as part of several grievances against Fages's command. His recommendations for curtailing the sexual violence and general malfeasance of the soldiers were that Fages should be removed and that Spaniards who married Indian women should be rewarded.

Once the viceroy had removed the lieutenant, Serra continued, he should give strict orders to Fages's successor that, upon the request of any missionary, "he should remove the soldier or soldiers who give bad example, especially in the matter of incontinence . . . and send, in their place, another or others who are not known as immoral or scandalous."[27]

Drawing on colonial tradition established much earlier in New Spain, wherein colonial officials encouraged intermarriage with Amerindian noblewomen so as to advance particular political, military, religious, or social interests, Serra suggested that men who married newly Christianized "daughters of the land" be rewarded.[28] In the second to last of his thirty-two suggestions, Serra asked Bucareli to "allow a bounty for those, be they soldiers or not, who enter into the state of marriage with girls of that faraway country, new Christian converts."[29]

Serra specified the three kinds of bounty to be given the individual: an animal for his own use immediately upon being married; two cows and a mule from the royal herd after he had worked the mission farms for a year or more; and, finally, allotment of a piece of land. Because soldiers were subject to being transferred from one mission or presidio to another, Serra further recommended that he who married a native woman should be allowed to remain permanently attached to his wife's mission."[30]

With this recommendation, which he discussed in more detail in a subsequent letter to the viceroy, Serra hoped to solve several related problems.[31] He sought to curb the sexual attacks on Indian women as well as to induce soldiers to remain and become permanent settlers in Alta California. Theoretically, soldiers would thereby remain on the frontier, and formal and permanent unions with Indian women would allay the natives' mistrust and help to forge a bond between them and the soldiers. These marriages would thus help to ease Indian-military tensions while also cementing Catholic family life in the region.[32]

It was equally important to remove temptation and opportunity for licentious behavior. Thus, in a second memorial to the viceroy written in April 1773, a little over a month after his report, Serra forcefully argued against the proposal that the annual supply ships from San Blas be replaced with mule trains coming overland. In addition to the greater expense of an overland supply line, he reasoned, the presence of one hundred guards and muleteers crossing the country would add to "the plague of immorality" running rampant in California.[33]

The document that resulted from the official review of Serra's memorial, the *Reglamento Provisional*—generally known as the *Echeveste Regulations*—was the first regulatory code drawn up for California. The *Echeveste Regulations* acted favorably on twenty-one of Serra's thirty-two original recommendations, including the removal of Fages as military commander.[34]

Implementation of the new regulations, however, did not stop the abuse of women or the immorality of the soldiers. Serra continued to blame the civil-military authorities. He charged Captain Fernando de Rivera y Moncada, who replaced Fages, with currying the soldiers' favor; moreover, he subsequently accused the newly appointed governor, Felipe de Neve, of antireligiosity and anticlericalism. Thus, in the summary of Franciscan complaints against Neve, which Francisco Panagua, guardian of the College of San Fernando, sent Viceroy Mayorga in 1781, Father Panagua wrote that "another consequence . . . of the aversion which the said Governor [Neve] has for the religious, is that the subordinates . . . live very libidinously in unrestrained and scandalous incontinence as they use at will Indian women of every class and strata."[35] Serra further charged that Neve allowed fornication among the soldiers, "because, so I have heard him say, . . . it is winked at in Rome and tolerated in Madrid."[36]

Serra's charges against Fages, Rivera, and Neve were not well founded. As head of the California establishments, each was fully cognizant that the soldiers' excesses not only undermined military discipline, and thus their own command, but also seriously jeopardized the survival of the missions and the presidios. Fundamentally, the assaults against women were unwarranted, unprovoked, hostile acts that established conditions of war on this frontier. Although the native peoples by and large did not practice warfare, they were neither docile nor passive in the face of repeated assaults. The country between San Diego and San Gabriel remained under Indian control for a long time.[37] It was in this region that the Indians marshaled their strongest forces and retaliated against the Spaniards. Some of the engagements, such as the one at San Gabriel in 1771, were minor skirmishes. Others were full-fledged attacks. In 1775 at Mission San Diego, for example, a force of eight hundred razed the mission, killed one priest and two artisans, and seriously wounded two soldiers. Women participated and sometimes even planned or led the attacks. In October 1785, Amerindians from eight *rancherías* united under the leadership of one woman and three men and launched an attack on Mission San Gabriel for the purpose of killing all the Spaniards. Toypurina, the twenty-four-year-old medicine woman of the Japchivit *ranchería*, used her considerable influence as a medicine woman to persuade six of the eight villages to join the rebellion. The attack was thwarted. Toypurina was captured and punished along with the other three leaders.[38]

Throughout their terms, Fages, Rivera, and Neve were keenly aware that Amerindians greatly outnumbered Spain's military force in the fledgling settlement and that, ultimately, the soldiers could not have staved off a prolonged Indian attack. Neve's greatest fear, expressed in his request to Bucareli for more commissioned officers, was that "if an affair of this kind [disorders caused by soldiers] ever results in a defeat of our troops, it will be irreparable if they [the Indians] come to know their power. We must prevent this with vigor."[39]

Therefore, during their respective administrations, the military authorities enforced Spain's legal codes, as well as imperial policy regarding segregation of Amerindians from non-Indians as a protective measure for the former. They prosecuted soldiers for major and minor crimes, and they issued their own edicts to curb the soldiers' abuse of Amerindians in general and women in particular. Their authority, however, was circumscribed by Spain's highly centralized form of government.[40]

While the governor of the Californians was authorized to try major criminal cases such as those involving homicide and rape, judgment and

sentence were decided at the viceregal level in Mexico City. With the separation of the Interior Provinces from the kingdom of New Spain in 1776, the
commandant-general, who combined in his office civil, judicial, and military powers, became the final arbiter.[41]

A 1773 case illustrates the complexity of legal procedures. This case—
in which a corporal, Mateo de Soto, and two soldiers, Francisco Avila and
Sebastián Alvitre, were accused of raping two young Amerindian girls and
killing one of them near the mission of San Diego—dragged on for five
years. Fages, Rivera, and Neve all dealt with the case, which occurred while
Fages was military commander. Fages received the official complaint from
Mariano Carrillo, sergeant at the San Diego presidio, who had interviewed
the young survivor at that presidio in the presence of four soldiers acting as
witnesses. The girl was accompanied to the presidio by two mission priests
and an interpreter, who was also present at the interview.[42]

Fages forwarded the documents to Viceroy Bucareli in Mexico City
and, on Bucareli's order, subsequently sent a copy to Felipe Barri, then governor of the Californias, at Loreto. When Rivera replaced Fages, he com-
plied with the viceroy's order to bind the men for trial and to send them
to Loreto, the capital of the Californias, in Baja California. By 1775, when
Rivera sent Avila and Alvitre to Loreto (Soto had deserted and was never
apprehended), Neve had replaced Barri as governor of the Californias. It fell
to Neve to hear testimony and conduct the trial, which he opened on October 19, 1775.

The trial, including testimony from six soldiers and comments from
the accused after Carrillo's charges were read to them, produced voluminous documents. Neve concluded the trial on November 22 and sent a copy
of the entire proceedings to the viceroy for final disposition, along with a
statement noting certain discrepancies from proscribed judicial procedure.
Upon receipt of the proceedings, Bucareli turned the file over to Teodoro de
Croix, recently appointed commandant-general of the Interior Provinces,
which included the Californias.[43]

Almost three years elapsed before Croix called in the case.[44] On August
26, 1778, his legal adviser, Pedro Galindo Navarro, submitted his opinion
to Croix. In Navarro's opinion, the accusation of rape and homicide was
not proven. The dead child's body, he argued, was not examined or even
seen; the identification of the soldiers accused was unsatisfactory, because it
appeared to have been prompted by the interpreter; the entire charge rested
on the testimony of a child, "poorly explained by an interpreter." Finally, the
accused denied the charge.[45]

Navarro recommended that the penalty for Avila and Alvitre, who had been detained during the five years of the trial, be commuted to time served and that they should be sentenced to remain and become citizens of California. Croix accepted these recommendations. He issued the order, and the two discharged soldiers were enrolled in the list of settlers at the new pueblo of San José de Guadalupe.[46]

Whether local officials would have convicted the soldiers of rape and homicide must remain a matter of conjecture. In any event, despite laws and prosecutions, the sexual exploitation of Indian women did not cease. The missionaries continuously reported that soldiers "go by night to nearby villages for the purpose of raping Indian women."[47] And while some cases were recorded, many more must surely have gone unreported. Nevertheless, it is clear that the commandants and the governors did prosecute and take disciplinary action when charges were filed against individual soldiers. Contrary to Serra's charges of laxity and complicity, Fages, Rivera, and Neve did exert the full measure of their authority in this and other reported cases of sexual violence or abuse. Abundant evidence details the dual policy of prevention and punishment implemented by the three seasoned frontier administrators in their ongoing effort to check the soldiers' excesses.[48]

Ever concerned that Amerindians would discover the real weakness of the Spanish position in California, Neve sought to prevent the sexual attacks, and thereby to defuse the military and political conflicts they gave rise to, by forbidding all troops, including sergeants and corporals, from entering Indian villages. Only soldiers escorting the priests on sick calls were exempt from this order, and then the soldier was not to leave the missionary's side. Escort guards were strictly admonished against misconduct and were severely punished if they disobeyed.[49]

In the same vein, he prohibited soldiers of the mission guard from spending the night away from the mission—even if the priests demanded it. Neve emphatically repeated this same order in the instructions he left to Pedro Fages, who succeeded him as governor in September 1782. "It is advisable," Neve further instructed Fages, "that we muzzle ourselves and not exasperate the numerous heathendom which surround us, conducting ourselves with politeness and respect. . . . It is highly useful to the service of the King and the public welfare that the heathen of these establishments do not learn to kill soldiers."[50]

Governor Fages was equally emphatic when he issued the following order in 1785: "Observing that the officers and men of these presidios are comporting and behaving themselves in the missions with a vicious license which is very prejudicial because of the scandalous disorders which they incite among the gentile and Christian women, I command you, in order to prevent the continuation of such abuses, that you circulate a prohibitory edict imposing severe penalties upon those who commit them."[51]

A decade later Viceroy Bucareli followed up on Neve's earlier order with his own decree prohibiting troops from remaining overnight away from the presidios, because among other reasons this practice was "prejudicial to good discipline and Christian morals."[52] Governor Diego de Borica, who succeeded Fages in 1794, issued a similar order the following year. These edicts had little effect.

Why, despite strenuous efforts by officials of both church and state, did the sexual attacks persist unabated? Why, despite the obviously serious political and military conflicts the assaults ignited, did they continue? In view of extensive legislation, royal decrees, and moral prohibitions against sexual and other violence, what, in the experience of the men who came here, permitted them to objectify and dehumanize Indian women to the degree revealed by their chasing and lassoing these women from mounted horses and then raping them?

Until recently scholars attributed sexual violence and other concurrent social disorders in early California to the race and culture of the mixed-blood soldier-settler population recruited or banished to this frontier. Institutional historians concluded, with Bancroft, that the "original settlers, most of them half-breeds of the least energetic classes . . . , were of a worthless character."[53] Institutional studies generally concurred with Serra's view that the soldiers were recruited from the scum of society. Serra had repeatedly beseeched Bucareli to send "sturdy, industrious Spanish families" and asked him to advise the governor of the Californias "not to exile to these missions as punishment for the soldier whom he may detest as insolent or perverse."[54]

During the last two decades the conditions that shaped institutional development on this frontier have been reexamined. In addition, studies of the social history of the people recruited to Alta California have been undertaken. As a result, the earlier interpretations have been rejected. Scholars now conclude that the slow development of colonial institutions in California was attributable to limited resources, lack of uniform military codes, and other structural problems—and not to the racial or social class origins of the soldier-settler population.[55]

Instead, the mixed-blood recruits—who themselves derived from other frontier settlements—were admirably able to survive the harsh privations and onerous conditions. In so doing, they established lasting foundations of Spanish civilization in California and the Southwest. Although the *cuera* (leather-jacket) soldiers were indeed unruly and undisciplined, their behavior reflected a particular informality and a "peculiar attitude of both officers and men."[56] According to revisionist studies, the isolation and distance from the central government, a shared life of hardship and risk, and the fact that blood and marriage ties existed among officers and common soldiers—all contributed to this attitude of informality and independence. Oakah Jones, Jr., makes essentially the same argument for contentious frontier settlers and extends the analysis. In this view, the racially mixed settlers responded to the often brutal conditions on the far northern and Pacific frontiers by creating a distinct frontier culture, characterized by self-reliance, individualism, regionalism, village orientation, resistance to outside control, innovativeness, family cohesiveness, and the preservation of Roman Catholicism as a unifying force.[57]

But these revisionists do not address sex/gender issues. The informality of disciplinary codes does not explain the origins or the continuation of sexual violence against native women. Moreover, as the documents for Alta California clearly reveal, Spanish officials enforced colonial criminal statutes and punished sexual crimes to the extent of their authority. However, neither the highly regulatory Laws of the Indies (the extensive legislation enacted to protect the rights of Amerindians), which mandated nonexploitative relations with Amerindians, nor punishment for breaking the laws arrested the violence.[58]

To begin to understand the soldier-settler violence toward native women, we must examine the stratified, patriarchal colonial society that conditioned relationships between the sexes and races in New Spain; the contemporary ideologies of sex/gender and race; and the relations and structures of conquest imposed on this frontier. While rape and other acts of sexual brutality did not represent official policy on this or any other Spanish frontier, these acts were nevertheless firmly fixed in the history and politics of expansion, war, and conquest. In the history of Western civilization writ large, rape is an act of domination, an act of power.[59] As such, it is a violent political act committed through sexual aggression against women.

"The practice of raping the women of a conquered group," writes historian Gerda Lerner, "has remained a feature of war and conquest from the second millennium to the present."[60] Under conditions of war or conquest, rape is a form of national terrorism, subjugation, and humiliation, wherein the sexual violation of women represents both the physical domination of women and the symbolic castration of the men of the conquered group. These concepts and symbolic meanings of rape, as discussed by Lerner, Susan Brownmiller, Anne Edwards, and others, are rooted in patriarchal Western society—in the ideology that devalues women in relation to men while it privatizes and reifies women as the symbolic capital (property) of men.[61] In this ideology, rape has historically been defined as a crime against property and thus against "territory." Therefore, in the context of war and conquest, rape has been considered a legitimate form of aggression against the opposing army—a legitimate expression of superiority that carries with it no civil penalty. In nonmilitary situations, punishment for rape and other crimes of sexual violence against women in Western civilization has, until very recently, generally been determined by the social condition or status of the women violated and by the status of the violator.[62]

In eighteenth-century California, the status of Amerindian women—as members of non-Christian, indigenous groups under military conquest on Spain's northernmost outpost of empire—made them twice subject to assault with impunity: they were the spoils of conquest, and they were Indian. In the mentality of the age, these two conditions firmly established the inferiority of the Amerindian woman and became the basis for devaluing her person beyond the devaluation based on sex that accrued to all women irrespective of their sociopolitical (race, class) status. The ferocity and longevity of sexual assaults against the Amerindian woman are rooted in the devaluation of her person conditioned by the weaving together of the strands of the same ideological thread that demeaned her on interrelated counts: her sociopolitical status, her sex, and her gender.

From their earliest contact with Amerindian peoples, Europeans established categories of opposition, or otherness, within which they defined themselves as superior and Amerindians inferior.[63] These categories were derived from the Aristotelian theory that some beings are inferior by nature, and therefore should be dominated by their superiors for their own welfare, and from the medieval Spanish concept of "purity of blood," which was based on religion and which informed the sense of national unity forged during the reconquest.[64] These ideas—which were fundamentally political concepts that separated human beings into opposing, hierarchical subject-object categories—prevailed during the era of first contact with Amerindians and the early conquests of the Americas.

By the late eighteenth century a different political concept—racial origin—defined place and social value in the stratified social order of colonial New Spain. Race was inextricably linked to social origin and had long been a symbol for significant cleavages in society; it was one primary basis for valuation—and devaluation—of human beings.[65] In the contemporary ideology and society, Amerindian women were thus devalued on the basis of their social status and as members of a conquered group.

Two aspects of the devaluation of Amerindian women are especially noteworthy. First and foremost, it is a political devaluation. That is, it is rooted in and driven by political considerations and acts: by war, conquest, and the imposition of alien sociopolitical and economic structures of one group over another. Second, the devaluation rationalized by conquest cuts across sex. At this level, women and men of the conquered group are equally devalued and objectified by the conquering group. Amerindian women and men were both regarded as inferior social beings, whose inferiority justified the original conquest and continued to make them justifiably exploitable and expendable in the eyes of the conqueror. The obverse, of course, also holds in this equation: women and men of the conquering group share the characterization and privileges of their group. In this instance, the primary opposition is defined by sociopolitical status, not sex.

Although the ideological symbols of sociopolitical devaluation changed over time—from religion to socioracial origins to social class—the changing symbols intersected with a sex/gender ideology that has remained remarkably constant from the fifteenth to the twentieth century.[66] As the term implies, the sex/gender ideology defines two categories of opposition—sex and gender—within which women are characterized as superior or inferior in relation to others.

With respect to sex stratification, women are placed in opposition and in an inferior position to men, on the assumption that in the divine order of nature the male sex of the species is superior to the female. In this conception, the ascribed inferiority of females to males is biologically constructed.

The opposition centering on gender revolves around sexual morality and sexual conduct. This opposition creates a level of superior-inferior or good-bad stratification based on social and political value-centered concepts of women's sexuality. This dichotomization provides a very specific, socially constructed, "sexual morality" category for valuing or devaluing women.

Rooted in the corollary patriarchal concepts of woman as the possession of man and of woman's reproductive capacity as the most important source for her value, this ideology makes woman a pivotal element in the property structure and institutionalizes her importance to the society in the provisions of partible and bilateral inheritance. It also places woman's value, also termed her "honor," in her sexual accessibility—in her virginity while single and, once wed, in the fidelity of her sexual services to the husband to ensure a legitimate heir.[67]

Within this construct, women are placed in opposition to one another at two extremes of a social and moral spectrum defined by sexuality and accessibility. The good woman embodies all the sexual virtues or attributes essential to the maintenance of the patriarchal social structure: sexual purity, virginity, chastity, and fidelity. Historically, the norms of sexual morality and sexual conduct that patriarchal society established for women of the ruling class have been the norms against which all other women have been judged. These norms are fundamentally rooted in questions of the acquisition and transference of economic and political power, and of women's relationship to that power base.

Since the linchpins of these ideological constructs are property, legitimacy, and inheritance, a woman excluded from this property/inheritance structure for sociopolitical reasons (religion, conquest, slavery, race, class), or for reasons based on sexual immorality (any form of sexual misconduct), is consequently excluded from the corresponding concepts and structures of social legitimacy. A woman so excluded cannot produce legitimate heirs, because she is not a legitimate social or sexual being.

The woman who is defined out of social legitimacy because of the abrogation of her primary value to patriarchal society, that of producing heirs, is therefore without value, without honor. She becomes the other, the bad woman, the embodiment of a corrupted, inferior, unusable sex: immoral, without virtue, loose. She is common property, sexually available to any man that comes along.

A woman (women) thus devalued may not lay claim to the rights and protections the society affords to the woman who does have sociopolitical and sexual value.[68] In colonial New Spain, as in most Western societies until the very recent period, the woman so demeaned, so objectified, could be raped, beaten, worked like a beast of burden, or otherwise abused with impunity.

The soldiers, priests, and settlers who effected the conquest and colonization of Alta California in the last third of the eighteenth century perceived and acted toward Amerindians in a manner consistent with the ideology and history of conquest—regarding them as inferior, devalued, disposable beings against whom violence was not only permissible but often necessary. For, despite the Laws of the Indies, the contradictions in the ideology and corresponding historical relations of conquest were great from the very beginning. These contradictions were generally exacerbated, rather than resolved, across time, space, and expansion to new frontiers.

From the very beginning, the papal bulls and scholarly (ideological) debates that affirmed the essential humanity of Amerindians and initiated the legislation to effect their conversion and protection sanctioned violence and exploitation under certain conditions. Loopholes in the royal statutes that were technically intended to protect Amerindians and guarantee their rights, but more specifically protected the crown's interest in Indian land and labor, had permitted virulent exploitation of Indians since the laws were first passed.[69]

More contemporary military and civil laws, such as those enacted by Neve, Fages, and Borica, carried severe penalties for illegal contact with or maltreatment of Indians; but these laws were especially contradictory because they were intended to curb certain kinds of violence by soldiers who were trained to kill Indians and who were sent to California to effect the temporal (military) conquest of this region.[70] Thus, violence against Amerindians was permissible when it advanced the particular interests of the Spanish Conquest but punishable when it did not. Because the sexual violence that occurred in this region was but the most contemporary manifestation of national history that included the violation of enemy women as a legitimate expression of aggression during conquest, it would seem that sexual violence became a punishable offense only when it was the source of military or political problems.[71]

Finally, perhaps the greatest contradictions were those of the greatest champion of Amerindian rights—the Catholic Church. On the one hand, Catholic clergy sought to remove Amerindians from contact with Spaniards, so as to protect them from the exploitation and violence of conquistadors, soldiers, and colonists; on the other hand, Jesuits, Franciscans, and other religious orders relied heavily on corporal punishment in their programs to Christianize and Hispanicize native people. While proclaiming the humanity of Amerindians, missionaries on the frontier daily acted upon a fundamental belief in the inferiority of the Indian. Their actions belied their words.

Accordingly, in his lengthy memorial of June 19, 1801, refuting the charges of excessive cruelty to Amerindians leveled against the Franciscans by one of their own, Father President Fermín Francisco de Lasuén disputed the use of extreme cruelty in the missions of the New California. Force was used only when absolutely necessary, stated Lasuén; it was at times necessary because the native peoples of California were "untamed savages . . . people of vicious and ferocious habits who know no law but force, no superior but their own free will, and no reason but their own caprice."[72] Of the use of force against neophyte women, Lasuén wrote that women in the mission were flogged, placed in the stocks, or shackled only because they deserved it. But, he quickly added, their right to privacy was always respected—they were flogged inside the women's dormitory, called the *monjero* (nunnery). Flogging the women in private, he further argued, was part of the civilizing process, because it "instilled into them the modesty, delicacy, and virtue belonging to their sex."[73]

A key element in the missionaries' program of conversion to Christianity included the restructuring of relations between the sexes to reflect gender stratification and the corollary values and structures of the patriarchal family: subservience of women to men, monogamy, marriage without divorce, and a severely repressive code of sexual norms.

In recognition that the ideologies, structures, and institutions of conquest imposed here were rooted in two and a half centuries of colonial rule, the sexual and other violence toward Amerindian women in California can best be understood as ideologically justified violence institutionalized in the structures and relations of conquest initiated in the fifteenth century.[74] In California as elsewhere, sexual violence functioned as an institutionalized mechanism for ensuring subordination and compliance. It was one instrument of sociopolitical terrorism and control—first of women and then of the group under conquest.

Chapter 3
Femicide as Terrorism: The Case of Uzbekistan's Unveiling Murders

Marianne Kamp

Although a "conflict zone" may be a war zone, many conflict zones consist of situations where the state lacks a monopoly on violence and where, in that absence, various groups try to assert their own dominance through force against agents of the state. Following the 1917 Bolshevik Revolution, the Soviet government and Communist Party struggled against multiple opponents to establish control over most of the territories of the former Russian Empire. The first few years of this struggle, 1918 to 1923, involved open warfare between competing military forces. The civil war's end, when the Red Army defeated the Whites, did not halt conflict in all of the Soviet territories. In Central Asia, armed rebel groups known as *basmachi* (attackers/bandits), fought against Soviet rule, attacking rural communities to supply themselves and to gain cooperation from villagers. The Soviet state, unable to assert dominance over rural districts, sought loyalty from the Central Asian rural poor by offering benefits, while using violence to arrest the supporters of the *basmachi*, the wealthy, and village leaders. In the late 1920s and early 1930s, *basmachi* attacks continued, but rural Central Asia also experienced Soviet state power, as authorities established village councils, initiated land reform, and threatened traditional elites. Those elites tried to mobilize their own resources to maintain their positions.

In this context, one of the Communist Party's initiatives for rapid cultural change opened a new, gendered zone of conflict. From 1927 to 1930, Uzbek men attacked and murdered Uzbek women who had unveiled. The murders were a violent social response to the *Hujum* (attack), a Communist Party campaign to change Muslim women's lives in Central Asia by enforcing legal equality, opening schools and jobs for them, and encouraging them to join the Communist Party. In Uzbekistan, mass unveiling ceremonies became the *Hujum*'s most potent symbol. It is estimated that 2,500 women were murdered in connection with unveiling between 1927 and 1930—during the *Hujum*. The officially atheist Communist Party pushed for a radical social change, one that intervened in Uzbek family and community life. Many Muslim clergy denounced these efforts and called upon fellow Uzbeks to attack and kill unveiled women. Many murderers were from the victim's family; others were neighbors or community members.

For several years the Communist Party regarded the unveiling murders as "crimes of everyday life," a category that included polygyny and minor marriage, and thus as evidence of Uzbek society's need for the party's intervention in family life. Crimes of everyday life violated the Soviet Constitution's guarantees of rights, but unlike other crimes, their motivation was attributed to custom, which both marked their perpetrators as backward and mitigated the consequences of their actions.

Some historians have argued that the party prematurely or wrongly initiated the *Hujum*, thus stimulating a wave of violence against unprotected women.[1] Both the party's regard of murders as "crimes of everyday life," and scholarship that sees the party as provoking the murder wave, assume that in Central Asian society, violence against women, including murder, was natural. Neither party nor scholars question why men would respond to state offenses, or to women's unveiling, by harming women. Anthropologist Shirin Akiner writes: "For Central Asians, [the *Hujum*] was a defeat and a brutal rape; the honor and dignity of the community was suddenly and monstrously violated."[2]

The Soviet state launched radical changes, but to focus on the state's role as provocateur is nonetheless very one-sided. The state did not murder or rape women; Uzbek men did. Rhetorical flourishes aside, coerced unveiling cannot be made the equivalent of rape or murder. The temporal and cultural contexts for these murders help explain them, but even more important are questions about the purposes of the murderers. In trying to deal with the murder wave, one of the state's strategies was to re-evaluate the seriousness of the murders, changing their legal category from "crimes of everyday life," to "terrorism" and "counter-revolution."

The murder wave in Uzbekistan took place in the context of a struggle for control of society between groups whose religious ideas shaped their politics, and a government that forcefully opposed religion. The Communist Party regarded enforcing women's equality as important to transforming the economy, politics, and culture, for the goal of "building socialism." Clergy who spoke in the name of Islam incited religiously sanctioned femicide (the misogynous killing of women by men), a form of terrorism designed to force women to conform to a social order that the religious leaders proclaimed to be divinely willed.[3] Without religious incitement there might still have been murders of women for unveiling in Uzbekistan, but not on such a large scale. Although this chapter examines only Uzbekistan, similar religiously incited, targeted waves of femicide have taken place in other conflict zones as well, most notably in Algeria in the 1990s.[4]

This wave of femicide was clearly gendered. Women were murdered as women, for stepping outside of the bounds that Uzbek society deemed acceptable and because in doing so they became perceived as politically aligned with the Communists, and opposed to Uzbek society. In this conflict, murder was the most extreme form of gendered violence; reported murders outpaced reports of rape and assault. The state's organs of surveillance had enough presence throughout Uzbekistan to collect evidence in murder cases, which evidently were not easily covered up. It cannot be known whether the lower reporting of rape and assault related to unveiling means that these acts were fewer in number, or that the victims were afraid to report these crimes. Murder, rape, and assault of unveiled women all contributed to a climate of increasing fear, and to women's reveiling.

During the *Hujum* many acts of violence against unveiled women were reported, but the focus of this chapter is femicide. Cheryl Benard, discussing rape in war, notes that "Rape inflicts trauma, but fortunately it cannot really lastingly destroy a population."[5] The targeted killing of people because they are part of a group (in this case, Uzbek women who unveiled) has a different intent and impact than rape.

Why did so many men murder women for unveiling during the *Hujum*? I propose several connected answers that involve "honor," political change, and religious incitement by comparing the wave of murders of unveiled Uzbek women with other kinds of violence against groups. This wave of sexist murders (femicide) is comparable with "honor killings" of women in other contexts, as well as with race-based lynching in the United States. While reference to an "honor killing" paradigm may seem more logical, comparison with lynching highlights certain aspects of this murder wave, noting that many murderers were not family members but were political opponents who expressed violent dissent against the state, and that they murdered women as members of a group, for a purpose. The historian W. Fitzhugh Brundage describes lynching as "a drama that helped to cement the entire southern social order. The dramatic spectacle of each lynching taught all southerners, male and female, black and white, precisely where in the social hierarchy they stood."[6] Antiunveiling murders in the *Hujum* served a similar purpose. Several thousand Uzbek women who transgressed the patriarchal social order, defying both family and religious norms, were murdered. Religious leaders incited and validated murder, and murderers, who came from the same communities or even families as their victims, were told that their actions would "restore honor."[7] Brutal murders taught other women the lessons that they should not unveil or join forces with the Soviet state. To murder unveiled women was to attempt to restore a rapidly eroding social order, by terrorizing other women back into submission. Murdering women, while it did not make any change to Communist domination of Uzbekistan, did express religiously framed hostility to the party's fiercely antireligious agenda, and to the Communist Party's efforts to transform society and the economy.

Ultimately, the Soviet state's interpretation of this murder wave changed. As state actors came to recognize that incitement was a factor and that the murders were political in intent, they stopped designating these murders as "daily life crimes" and began to name them as terrorism. My own analysis of this wave of femicide as gender terrorism draws on that change in Soviet law.

A Time of Cultural and Economic Revolution: Tearing Apart the Social Fabric

In Uzbekistan's cities in the early 1920s, a few Uzbek women who were associated with modern education, or with the Communist Party's Women's Division, unveiled as a symbol of their own commitment to social change. Veiling in Uzbekistan was culturally specific in that women wore a head- and body-covering robe, the *paranji*, with a horsehair face veil, the *chachvon*, covering the full face. In 1927 the party appropriated the symbol of unveiling, calling on women to "throw off the paranji," claiming that unveiling would end women's seclusion and change the dynamic of Uzbek family and social life. Some of the women who participated in the party's public unveiling meetings wanted to unveil, but many were coerced. Following the party's highly publicized International Women's Day unveiling meetings on March 8, 1927, a wave of attacks began. Many of the unveiled quickly resumed veiling as murder and assault of unveiled and activist women increased.

The *Hujum* was only one facet of the Communist Party's policy in Central Asia, and it coincided with other party attacks on the economy and culture of Uzbekistan. In 1927 the Communist Party focused on Islam in Central Asia, closing the major religious Islamic institutions: maktabs, madrasas, Sharia courts, many mosques, and shrines. This policy deprived the Muslim clergy of positions, income, influence, and official respect. During the 1920s and 1930s the government arrested, exiled, and executed many Muslim clergy.[8] In land reform, which started in 1925, wealthy landowners saw their property redistributed to the poor. As the *Hujum* continued, the Soviets in Central Asia began agricultural collectivization. These programs threatened the property, social influence, and lives of the wealthy and the religious leaders. While old elites lost their sources of capital, new, pro-Soviet groups took control.

Uzbek society understood the *Hujum* as one element in a huge social upheaval.[9] An OGPU (secret police) study of rural attitudes quoted an ordinary farmer telling his neighbors: "The Soviet government carried out land reform and now carries out reform on the woman question, taking second wives from those who have them and giving them to the landless peasants. Removing the paranji is one of the means of the Soviet government to carry out this reform."[10]

Partly in response to Russian colonial rule (1865–1917), Uzbek communities established boundaries through religious ritual and separation from Russians. Before the revolution, insistence on Muslim women's veiling asserted this boundary.[11] Through land reform, collectivization, closing Islamic institutions, and replacing old elites with new officials who supported the Soviets, the Soviet government set out to rid Uzbek society of the structures that maintained community boundaries. Unveiling women was part of this larger program.

Violence and Unveiling

Before 1927 there were Uzbek women who unveiled individually, and they faced harassment and opposition, but not murder. The murders for unveiling began only after the Communist Party initiated the *Hujum*, which turned unveiling into a political act that seemed to demonstrate women's support of the party. Popular stories associated unveiling with prostitution, rumors of the rape of unveiled women spread, and many clergy members encouraged men to "punish" unveiled women. The state used the OGPU and local authorities to collect reports of antiunveiling violence, and the social attitudes behind violence.[12]

In Bukhara, Muslim clergy who saw women in headscarves—in other words, women who were not fully veiled—said, "Look at how Muslim women have debased themselves. . . . They want the whole people to become infidels. Muslim women are throwing away their religion and turning to another." Some preached that neighboring states would attack Soviet government for the unveiling campaign. A group of unveiled Bukharan women rode in an automobile caravan past a mosque; men at prayer began cursing them, saying that unveiled women became prostitutes. In a village called Tuda-Maidon, a religious leader collected false evidence about the unveiled wife of a village council representative, claiming that she was a prostitute. Under pressure, she reveiled.[13]

Widespread libel mongering had serious implications in Uzbek society. A student at the medical technical school, Pulatova, committed suicide because her classmates called her a prostitute for unveiling.[14] Family members of unveiled women had to endure aspersions. Some men divorced unveiled wives. Some of the murders of women were undoubtedly attempts to restore family honor by killing women who were blamed for bringing shame on their relatives.[15]

One of the first heavily publicized murders of an unveiled woman took place shortly after the March 8, 1927 International Women's Day mass unveilings. In Shahrixon region, in the Farg'ona Valley, a local Women's Division director, Hadicha-xon G'oibjon-qizi, convinced women to unveil on Women's Day. One week later a group of men murdered her. The case received weeks of intensive publicity in the main Uzbek language newspaper, *Qizil O'zbekiston*. Not long after this, the OGPU reported that party members and Communist Youth League (Komsomol) members in Shahrixon agreed at their meetings that unveiled women were prostitutes, and eighteen women who had unveiled now reveiled.[16]

In many villages, social leaders called on the population to oppose this new, unwanted government intrusion by attacking everyone involved. In Andijon, police reports noted that farmers, the wealthy, and the clergy used the same language of opposition to unveiling: "God forbids it," "I forbid it," and "She'll become a prostitute." In Qashqa Darya province, a rich man, Krimjon o'gli, declared: "The government demands unveiling women ever more strongly. We will kill them if they uncover, both our wives, and those who put up to it. And then, finally, we will tell the government not to mess with our lives."[17] Elderly women whom I interviewed, both those who had supported unveiling in the 1920s and those who reported unveil-

ing under duress, remembered hearing clergy members declaring that unveiled women should be killed.[18] This language, advocating killing unveiled
women and their supporters, was widespread and may have made murder
seem normal.

Husbands, fathers, and nonfamily groups murdered women for unveiling and activism. The OGPU collected a long list of murders that took
place between January and August 1928. Usually women were stabbed or
beaten to death. In many cases attacks were public, and news of them spread
through communities.[19] In Xorazm province twelve murders of women were
reported in three months. The police noted that murderers often claimed
that murder was not a response to unveiling:

> It is characteristic in cases of the murder of women that the physical mur-
> derer (husband or brother) presents as his reasons for murder purely fam-
> ily reasons (jealousy, dishonoring the family), rejecting a political element
> to the murder. But the conditions accompanying the murder (in most
> cases the victim was planning to unveil or was unveiled) give reason to
> suspect that not only family and daily life relations played a role in the
> murder. These murders . . . reflect "that work" that is being carried out by
> groups who are our enemies, against the liberation of women.[20]

The OGPU included in their report notice of a letter, signed by eighty people, declaring they would kill the unveiled and their helpers.[21]

Arrests in unveiling murder cases often included accomplices. In a notorious case, an Uzbek actress, Nur-xon, was murdered. Her brother stabbed
her and was arrested, but so also were her father, a mullah, and a local rich
man, for having entered a pact and forced Nur-xon's brother to swear that he
would kill her for the transgression of going on stage.[22]

Although it was evident that some clergy incited the murders of the unveiled and that much of Uzbek male society opposed the party's efforts to
change women's social roles, the murder wave was not solely the fault of
antiparty forces. Numerous Uzbek Communist Party members, police, and
local officials also harassed, insulted, raped, and murdered women. While
a few Communists supported unveiling, others were upset that the party
charged them with enforcing the unpopular *Hujum* campaign. In Bukhara,
Adolat Bukhanova, age eighteen, was murdered four days after Bukhara's
first mass unveiling. Her husband, a party candidate, forbade her to enter
school, but she tried to enroll anyway, and he killed her.[23]

In a Farg'ona valley village, eight women unveiled at a Komsomol meeting. After the meeting the Komsomol secretary told the men at a teahouse

that unveiled women were prostitutes.[24] OGPU records from towns throughout Uzbekistan report that government workers, village chairmen, and party members made indecent proposals to unveiled women and called them prostitutes. Unveiled women saw local officials as enemies, along with the clergy.

Men in public roles preyed on the unveiled—especially on those who turned to the government for help.[25] Women were easy targets; without government representatives protecting women, it almost seemed that rape was acceptable. One police report observed, "Thus, the people say that the Party wants to unveil women so they can rape them."[26]

The *Hujum* Commission relied on party members to unveil their wives and to support unveiling in their communities. Party members' only reward for taking on the task of unveiling women was possible promotion. The party members who planned the *Hujum* campaign, a group that included widely respected Uzbek party members as well as Russians, leaned on men whose motives for joining the Communist Party varied, whose knowledge of Communism was limited, and who often valued their connections to traditional elites. The Uzbek membership of the party increased rapidly in the 1920s, and the party exercised little training or oversight of members.[27] Party members often shared the attitudes toward unveiled women of other men in their communities.

When many of these party members were unwilling to unveil women and—worse still—when some attacked those very women, the party interpreted this disloyalty in the same terms that religious people use to defend their religion against associations with abuse. Just as many Muslims would say that those who attack women in the name of God are not real Muslims, the Communist Party leadership regarded those who did not support the *Hujum* as "not real Communists," but as enemies who deserved dismissal.[28]

The *Hujum*'s leaders neither anticipated that women who unveiled would be murdered nor foresaw a murder wave. They attributed increasing murders to provocation by the clergy and the wealthy. That even party officials attacked women thus calls into question the conditions that created, permitted, and sustained this murder wave.

Stopping Femicide in Uzbekistan

Murdering women terrorized others very effectively. Women who had unveiled, willingly or unwillingly, reveiled out of fear. Unveiling activists tried to convince women to risk not only their reputations but also their lives for the sake of publicly uncovering their faces. Uzbek women activists called for stronger legal protection for the unveiled, but legal protection relied on judges, police, and local administrators who were not proponents of women's equality.

Local law enforcement did not prevent murders, but laws defending victims of unveiling-related violence were enhanced. In August 1928 Uzbekistan's criminal code was amended to declare that "Killing a woman or severely wounding her on the basis of religious and daily life crimes connected with her liberation carries a sentence of not less than eight years severe isolation."[29] Publicity of the law encouraged women who survived to bring charges against attackers but did not help murder victims. The text of the law itself revealed the Commissariat of Justice's indecision about the explanation for these crimes: were they connected with everyday life, or were they expressing opposition to the state's policy of women's "liberation"? The sentence for an unveiling murder was made the same as for any ordinary murder, and harsher than the minor sentences for "daily life" infractions.

In 1928, Women's Division workers proposed banning veiling; Uzbek women activists vociferously supported the ban through demonstrations, petitions, and print media.[30] They believed that if unveiling was legally required, then women would happily unveil, and men would cease holding women individually responsible for dishonor and sin. However, both the republican-level government and the USSR Communist Party's Women's Division rejected a ban on the veil as unenforceable and as a misunderstanding of party policies and goals. In 1930 the party reduced *Hujum* efforts when the struggle over unveiling became a distraction from the party's economic revolution.

Although the party de-emphasized unveiling, the state increased prosecution of the murderers of unveiled women. After April 1929, murdering a woman for unveiling, or for activism, was no longer a "crime of everyday life," with relatively minor penalties. The state's agents had been referring to the murders as acts of terrorism, and in 1929 their legal status changed. Statute 64, which allowed death sentences for acts of anti-Soviet terrorism, could be applied to murderers of unveiled women.[31] In 1930 the USSR government declared that liberation-related murders of women constituted counter-revolutionary crimes.[32] This legal redefinition showed a change in government attitude in that the government defined these murders as acts of defiance against the state, not as family crimes or crimes linked to custom.

The Soviet state's increasingly harsh treatment of its opponents in the late 1920s, combined with an ever-stronger presence of state authority to the

Uzbek countryside, resulted in the state's ability to combat the murder wave. The state savaged both clergy and wealthy Uzbeks through arrest, dispossession, and exile; it intimidated rural communities through collectivization of agriculture; and under "Stalinism" it ruled through fear. Incitement to murder diminished, and murders of women for unveiling and activism decreased (but did not cease altogether), even as unveiling increased. In addition, a larger proportion of the population began to believe that the state would enforce its laws and punish the murderers of unveiled women.

Femicide: Gendered Violence in a Conflict Zone

This femicide wave occurred largely because of commonly held patriarchal assumptions about women's proper place, public discourse from religious authorities who declared the unveiled impure and demanded their suppression, community pressure on men whose wives or sisters unveiled, and a broad awareness of state weakness. During the first year of the femicide wave, prosecution was minimal; the attitude that one could kill a woman and get away with it was pervasive, and there was little to deter rape and murder. Communist Party members acted under the same conditions as nonmembers, faced the same community pressures, heard the same religious incitement, and could use their limited local authority either to support the unpopular campaign or to inhibit women's activism.

To explore the reasons why so many women were assaulted, raped, and murdered for unveiling and activism, I turn to four elements that together suggest an answer: concern for women's purity in a situation of social turmoil; group or mob violence, similar to lynching, which has the purpose of intimidation of a category of people; femicide as an "honor crime" carried out by intimates to restore their social standing; and incitement, meaning active social discourse about, and pressure to carry out, these crimes.

Carroll Smith-Rosenberg's analysis of violent social relations in times of rapid change offers insight into gendered violence. Smith-Rosenberg suggests that, when experiencing rapid change, hierarchical societies that "insist on rigid dress codes and rules of physical decorum" will regard "physical and sexual disorder as particularly threatening." In this context such societies see behavior that disrupts the rules as "sexually dangerous and physically polluting," and make "stern efforts to control" those who act outside the boundaries of the acceptable.[33]

In the first few years after the 1917 revolution, when the Soviet state directed its efforts toward dispossessing Islamic institutions and the wealthy in Central Asia, it stirred up a violent response and fought against the *basmachis* for nearly a decade. The state retreated from this radical program, quelling most of the *basmachi* activity using military means. In 1925, however, the state began again with dispossessing the wealthy through land reform, and in 1927 it attacked the Muslim clergy by closing their institutions. Had the *Hujum* not taken place, many Uzbeks would still have engaged in antistate violence. In 1929 and 1930, when the state initiated rapid collectivization of cotton-growing regions in Uzbekistan, there was a new wave of attacks and murders—this time against activists for collectivization and members of village councils who supported land seizures.[34]

Uzbek society was hierarchical, and Uzbek women's bodies were bounded by the *paranji* and *chachvon*. The *Hujum* was one facet of the rapid, forced changes in Uzbekistan; a campaign against veiling was a state attack on men's authority over women and on Uzbek separateness from Russians. In this context of the state's concurrent attacks on religion, private property, and the wealthy, women's unveiling was magnified as socially polluting. Murders of unveiled women were physical attempts to reassert one social boundary and to enforce at least one aspect of a social order that was under a full-scale assault.

Many of the murders were committed by family members, but the assaults and rapes, as well as the most publicized murders of unveiled and activist women, were carried out by nonfamily groups and were carried out against women targeted for their activities, not for their relationship to the murderer or rapist. Thus, while some of the murders could be analyzed as "honor crimes" (to be discussed below), the broader sweep of violence against unveiled women was connected to political actions and divisions, and played out against women precisely because of social ideas that women should be subordinate, and because of their vulnerability and lack of legal protection. These aspects of the murder wave suggest a comparison with racist lynchings in the United States. Antilynching activists estimated that some three thousand African Americans were murdered by lynching between the 1880s and 1930. Lynchers acted as groups and murdered African Americans, sometimes as known individuals accused of particular actions and sometimes anonymously simply because of their race. Lynchers acted with "the purpose of suppressing either some tendency (in the target group) to rise from an accommodated position of subordination, or for subjugating them further to some lower social status," wrote the sociologist Oliver C. Cox. Cox argued that lynching, and the threat of it, "function to maintain white dominance," and that it would produce "terror among Negroes" because of the absence of "legal power presuming to question the free violence of the lynchers."[35]

The targeted murders of women showed a degree of organization that went beyond individual action. Murders of women for unveiling were not spontaneous crimes of passion; they were premeditated and often involved group planning and action. Uzbek men who killed Uzbek women expressed hostility toward the individual victim and her decision to enter the public by unveiling, going to school, or getting involved with the state's programs. Murders also expressed coordinated opposition to the state and the Communist Party, demonstrating that the local community, not the state, had authority over women's actions and their bodies. These murders were politically motivated, designed to challenge the state and to terrorize other women. Many murders were deliberately gruesome, involving cutting, dismemberment, and the disposal of the body with symbolic dishonor.

The male power structure made a brutal effort to enforce an unequal social order (a gender hierarchy) through violence by terrorizing an entire group. Certain scholars would argue that this use of "terror," meaning "violence intended to instill fear in a large audience," is too broad.[36] However, even in the 1920s those who described the murders of Uzbek women referred to them as "terrorism," and defining it as terrorism was important in stopping the murder wave.

However, many of the unveiling murders were carried out by husbands or other family members. An Uzbek woman activist in favor of unveiling, Saodat Shamsieva, recalled: "The father, husband or older brother of every woman or girl who threw off the paranji in the *mahalla* [urban neighborhood] or village would, having killed her, come to us saying, 'I killed her because I did not want her to uncover and to cause me shame.'"[37] We can be fairly certain that in these cases, no rape was associated with the murder, because rape would have created additional honor issues rather than ending questions about honor as did murder. The murders seem to be "honor killings," which are generally thought of in relationship to social ideologies about male control of women's sexuality, and to other forms of domestic violence, rather than as related to political agendas or situations of conflict.[38] Recent scholarship on honor killings points out that in these cases the murder's "publicly articulated 'justification' is attributed to a social order claimed to require the preservation of a concept of 'honour' vested in male (family and/or conjugal) control over women and specifically women's sexual conduct; actual, suspected or potential."[39] Honor killings can be seen within the context of domestic violence. The notion of honor is based on the relationship between the victim and a family whose honor her actions have been deemed to harm. Purna Sen defines honor crimes as often including other family women in policing women's actions, as well as collective decisions regarding punishment.[40] That is, family members might justify their murder of an unveiled member of the family as restoring lost honor, as was the case in some of the *Hujum*'s murders. But the assaults, rapes, and murders of the unveiled committed by unrelated persons during the *Hujum* do not fall within this explanatory rubric, and the rubric does not account for the sudden, politically based murder wave.

In some Islamic societies and some non-Islamic societies, honor killing is a means of social control.[41] Honor killings are almost always explained as "not part of Islam," but rather "cultural," as if that somehow makes them more acceptable, or at least saves Islam from the taint of association with them.[42] Whether Islam condones or condemns such murders, the discourse that promoted the unveiling murders in Uzbekistan used appeals to Islam to convince men to murder women in their families and communities.

However, "honor killing" is not a sufficient explanation for the wave of murder in Uzbekistan. Men were not acting in accordance with what they thought of as "tradition." Culturally, this burst of violence against women was an anomaly. Although ethnographic sources documented intimate violence against women, I have found no evidence that Uzbeks interpreted codes of honor as necessitating killing disorderly women.[43] In addition, unlike the rewritten law codes of other parts of the colonized world, where Western notions of "crimes of passion" shaped the idea that women's transgressions of the patriarchal order might be mitigating circumstances in murder cases, permitting defendants to use "honor" as a legal justification for killing, there was no similar bias in Soviet law.[44] Legal codes were under constant revision in the 1920s, but the only major mitigating factor in violent crimes was social class. Among Uzbeks, patriarchy ordered gender relations, but the idea that became widespread during the *Hujum* (that women who unveiled should be killed for that sin) was startlingly new and was swiftly propagated. The campaign's initiators did not anticipate this response.

In Uzbekistan, Islam is the religion of the community where the violence occurred, and the religious ideas that promoted and justified that violence were grounded in interpretations of Islam that denied any public roles to women. When the *Hujum* began, most Muslim clergy opposed unveiling, and many incited violence against the unveiled. During the Russian colonial period (1865–1917) the Sunni clergy of Central Asia had developed modernizing and traditionalizing trends. The Jadids, or modernists, advocated rethinking Islam and reforming Islamic education and institutions; they condemned their clergy foes as "qadimists"—essentially, obscurantists. By the 1920s the advocates of a modernized Islam believed that they shared ground with the Communists who called for land reform and women's rights; they thought that the traditionalizers depended on the people's ignorance for maintaining their own authority. The traditionalizers opposed both the Communist order and those who supported it, seeing both as destroying religion. Some of the modernist clergy publicly supported unveiling, declaring that Islamic law did not require women to wear the *paranji* and *chachvon*. Traditionalizing clergy members condemned unveiling as a sin deserving of hell, declared that unveiled women were prostitutes, and began to preach violence against the unveiled.[45] While Islam did not create the context for this wave of femicide, the traditionalizers incited murder by their preaching, thus helping to translate into terrorist acts men's anger over broader social changes and over government intervention into family life.

Incitement plays an important role in lynchings and in honor killings. In accounts of murders in Uzbekistan, perpetrators often had to be convinced to carry out their acts. Even in cultures where "honor killings" seemed to be an accepted practice of social control, murders were incited with killers being under social pressure to restore honor.[46] In Uzbekistan, some Muslim religious leaders played this role, using words to convince other Uzbeks that punishing unveiled women was necessary and right.

This wave of murders was not an enduring cultural phenomenon but instead a burst of political violence that eventually subsided, even as women abandoned traditional veiling. When the incitement decreased as a result of radical social upheaval and government suppression, so did the murders.

Several factors changed in 1930. Far from reducing intervention in everyday life in Uzbekistan, the Soviet government increased its efforts at economic transformation by launching rapid, forced collectivization of agriculture. The dispossession of the wealthy became even more extreme, and the Communist Party deliberately empowered the rural poor to seize the land and goods of those who were more affluent. In the early 1930s thousands of farmers who were seen as prosperous were arrested, exiled, and sometimes shot. The *basmachi* groups were thoroughly suppressed in the early 1930s, and Uzbek society lost its ability to continue any form of armed conflict against the state.

The *Hujum* campaign more or less ended in 1930, when the Communist Party dissolved the Women's Division. But the efforts for unveiling continued, accompanying collectivization, and by the mid-1930s, more women were unveiled than were veiled.[47] The Soviet state and Communist Party ruled Uzbekistan through fear and force during the 1930s. Those who incited violence against the unveiled (as well as many others) were swept away in collectivization-related arrests and in the antireligious crackdown. Incitement to murder women for unveiling decreased, not because the provocation (calls for women to unveil) ended but because the state increased its own means of violent control.

The state took prosecution of unveiling-related murders more seriously in the 1930s than in the 1920s, and consequently imposed on those who were found guilty a greater penalty: death instead of eight years of imprisonment. This was because the state had come to new conclusions about the murder of unveiled women: it was not a "crime of custom" but an act of counter-revolution. Changed law deterred such murders in the 1930s, probably more through the widespread fear of the state that the Stalinist system inculcated than through changed attitudes. That is, Uzbekistan, as a zone of conflict between anti-Soviet and pro-Soviet groups, was the context for sexual violence, rape, and murder of women. During the 1930s open opposition to the Soviet state was crushed; Uzbekistan ceased to be a zone of open and overt conflict, and sexual and gendered violence assumed more "ordinary" dimensions there.

In discussing honor crimes in Iraqi Kurdistan, sociologist Shahrzad Mojab argues that "One cannot expect an end to honor killing in a state which has no respect for citizens' right to life."[48] I would argue that a state's ability to stop honor killing, or lynching, or other forms of violence, may be related more to its intent and its means to do so than to its respect for citizens' rights. The Soviet Union had little respect for citizens' rights in the 1920s and 1930s, but its harsh laws against the murder of unveiled women did have a deterrent effect. While in the ideal world an expansion in state respect for rights would create conditions leading to the outlawing of honor killing, or racist or misogynous murders, nonetheless, the state's ability to enforce the law is related to the state's intent, its reach, its personnel, and its monopoly of the means of violence.

PART II

The Economy of Conflict-Based Sexual Violence

Chapter 4
Girls, Women, and the Significance
of Sexual Violence in Ancient Warfare

Kathy L. Gaca

One compelling social justice concern in the modern day is the practice of armed men at war, adolescent and older, seizing, traumatizing, and subjugating foreign or enemy girls and women through rape, torture, and related debasement, by such methods as subjecting the victims to prostitution, domestic servitude, forced impregnation, and maternity. Many of these women and girls are killed for various reasons after being sexually assaulted— because they resist or fail to please, or because they embody the enemy.

Provoked by such military and paramilitary atrocities in the former Yugoslavia, Rwanda, Darfur, Congo, and elsewhere, numerous scholars, activists, and artists have responded vigorously in diverse fields such as international law, feminist philosophy, medicine, film making, political science, and education. Substantive steps have been taken on a number of counts: Ruth Seifert focuses on such sexual violence in warfare and argues that this practice is a central "weapon of war" in those armed conflicts where the aggressors aim to supplant peoples of a certain cultural identity: "If the aim is to destroy a culture, [its women] are prime targets because of their cultural importance in the family structure. . . . Their physical and emotional destruction aims at destroying social and cultural stability." Claudia Card articulates a few of the more long-term "patterns of intelligibility" to rape in war and peace: "an important aspect of both civilian and martial rape is that it is an instrument of domestication: . . . a breaking for house service . . . utilitarian, recreational, or both."[1] These assessments of wartime rape deepen the more inchoate understandings of the practice first offered in the mid-1970s, when Susan Brownmiller interpreted wartime rape as an exultant postconquest celebration, and Andrea Dworkin saw rape in war and peace alike as a primal act of conquering and colonizing women as a people.[2]

In the more recent wave of studies since the 1990s, however, the task of uncovering the historical significance of heterosexual battery and sexual assault in warfare remains superficial and is overly dominated by twentieth- and emergent twenty-first century examples. The few cited instances from ancient and medieval warfare derive from Susan Brownmiller's watershed but now dated study, *Against Our Will: Men, Women, and Rape* (1975).[3] Historian Gerda Lerner's *The Creation of Patriarchy* (1985), a more ambitious but still preliminary venture to historicize heterosexual rape in ancient armed conflict, is rarely mentioned in such studies.

Furthermore, the incidents of ancient wartime rape drawn from Brownmiller are treated with two different historicizing interpretations. First, they are portrayed as a vague and distant counterpart of the modern phenomenon, a "mirror [of] the wartime sufferings of women through the centuries," as the legal scholar Catherine Niarchos phrases it.[4] Second, they are used to assume a developmental schema over time, in which heterosexual rape and related violence in ancient warfare are a sporadic and small-scale operation that has only in modern times become a weapon of war on a mass scale. As Kelly Dawn Askin puts it in her legal history, *War Crimes Against Women*, "Rape and other forms of sexual assault have thrived in wartime, progressing from an . . . incidental act of the conqueror, to a reward of the victor, to [the] discernible mighty weapon of war" that they have come to be in modern times.[5]

As I argue below, the first interpretation, the "vague and distant mirror," is nebulous but has the right intuition, while the second developmental hypothesis mistakenly interprets Brownmiller's sketchy coverage of rape in antiquity as though it were an exhaustive study indicating that wartime rape then was but a set of isolated and semilegendary incidents compared with the magnitude of the undeniably major problem now.

There is, to be sure, justification in some important respects for the preponderant focus on the contemporary manifestation of the crisis. First, women and girls who are assaulted in the present merit attention because they are able to seek redress under evolving international law, whereas those who are long dead can do no such thing. Second, thanks to this focus on present and still-living memory, a veritable revolution in our documentary sources on heterosexual practices of warfare as sexual violence has taken place since the early 1990s. Surviving women and girls are now providing an abundance of first-person testimonies about their torments for the first time ever in the history of Western and world civilization to international teams of investigators, including physicians, human rights activists, journalists, and lawyers. These testimonies are of incomparable value for grasping the immense violence of the practice and can only come from the living.[6]

Nonetheless, the dominant attention given to current and very recent instances of sexual violence in warfare leaves many pressing questions unanswered, and I will address a few important ones here. Historically speaking, how significant were the capture and subjugation of women and girls to warfare in the Mediterranean region from the Bronze Age through late antiquity? What does this practice mean for our understanding of warfare in its relation to gender, society, and social injustice? In dealing with these questions, I examine Greek sources dating from Homer through late antiquity (the sixth century), also including several medieval Byzantine Greek sources as well as a few Old Testament sources.

The History and Problematic Conception of Warfare

Primary historical sources from antiquity have helped keep the sexualized brutality against captive women and girls an obscure topic since the Greek historian Herodotus (flourished ca. 444 B.C.E.), the founder of Western historiography. Ancient historians in particular, such as Thucydides and Polybius, have generally been at best brief about this dimension of warfare, partly as a matter of historiographic principle. Polybius, for example, criticized other ancient historians who did dwell on the topic, such as Phylarchus, for producing sensationalistic and "womanish" narratives.[7] Moreover, even where ancient Greek sources do deal with the practice, the force of their testimony has not yet been given the sustained attention it merits.

Contemporary historians of ancient warfare largely replicate the ancient historians' ingrained tendency to be cursory about the subject. They acknowledge in brief that the sexual assault of female captives was a regular part of warfare in the ancient world, but they have not ventured to consider the methods, aims, and magnitude of such violence. For example, Pritchett, the most authoritative historian of ancient Greek warfare, states, "Physical violence to maidens and women was apt to occur on the night of the capture of a besieged city." Ducrey, a prominent historian on the taking of prisoners during Greek warfare, similarly gives spare acknowledgment to the practice: "The taking of a community was regularly followed by the reduction to slavery of the women, or in any event, their rape." Harris, a distinguished Roman historian, is relatively expansive in according several paragraphs to suggesting that rape was "commonplace" in Roman warfare.[8]

Furthermore, social historians concerned with heterosexual rape in antiquity have also sidelined the topic of sexual assault in warfare and its aftermath, which is an area where one would expect the subject to be prominent. Heterosexual rape in antiquity is discussed in this scholarship mainly in its function as a civil crime within a community at relative peace, not as a routine part of the widespread destruction of communities or regions through warfare and of the ensuing domination over those female captives who survived.[9] As a result, heterosexual practices of sexual violence in ancient warfare hardly register in our historical consciousness, just like the countless victims themselves, who are mainly nameless and faceless to us.

The challenge, however, runs even deeper than having to counter oversights in ancient military and social history. To put the sexualized brutality against captive women and girls in its rightful place in our understanding of warfare, the predominant present conception of warfare as a matter of man-to-man violence must be transformed from the ground up, because this is only the first half of the story as far as antiquity is concerned.

Clausewitz's early nineteenth-century *On War* epitomizes how the early modern and modern notion of warfare resists any effort to intelligibly relate Western warfare to customs of heterosexual assault and domination carried out both during and subsequent to armed conflict. Often considered "not simply the greatest, but the only great book about war" in Western military theory, *On War* defines warfare exclusively as armed combat among males of fighting age.[10] "War is a duel on a larger scale. Countless duels go to make up war, but a picture [of war] as a whole can be formed by imagining a pair of wrestlers. Each tries through physical force to compel the other to do his will; but his *immediate* aim is to *throw* his opponent in order to make him incapable of further resistance." The element of pronounced male struggle defines Clausewitz's notion of "war as a whole." Furthermore, his wrestling analogy has its limits, because the most effective "throwing" of male opponents in combat means killing them, multiple duels to the death, not pinning them down for the count. This focus on war as an armed lethal contest between armed male combatants has long been and remains the predominant way to conceptualize, narrate, and depict warfare before the advent of pushbutton military technology, as anyone can experience by surveying the military studies section of any library or bookstore. Since antiquity, the vast majority of depictions and writings on warfare, both primary and secondary, bombard us with this view of warfare as "men killing and men being killed," as Homer puts it (e.g., *Il.* 8.64–65).

In this military history, moreover, the objectives of warfare as a lethal contest among men have generally been portrayed as having little or nothing to do with a sexual lust for power, rather than as being motivated greatly by such lust.[11] The aggressors and defenders fight man to man for reasons motivated by anger, strategy, greed, and ambition, but rarely if ever by their militarily indoctrinated libido. The armed men on the offensive seek to avenge an injustice or dishonor; to capture a mountain pass, river crossing, or region; to amass wealth from the plunder of material goods; to ravage land and steal the harvest stores; or to occupy a new land and control its mines, forests, waterways, and other natural resources. Conversely, the male defenders fight in an effort to prevent the aggressors from attaining such asexual objectives and taking the land, harvests, and other resources from them. Thus, seen in this light, warfare in antiquity may have been multifarious, but it was not centrally involved with sexual violence and domination—even if it might have amounted to that on the periphery, where the victors dragged their female captives for their own release and recreation after attaining their retaliatory or territorial goals. From this perspective, consequently, the aggravated sexual assault of captive women and girls through warfare and the resultant subjugation of female survivors can only have been an ancillary byproduct of warfare, and as such of no more interest in elucidating the historical genesis of Western warfare than the production of sawdust is to grasping the practices and goals of carpentry.

In terms of this androcentric paradigm of warfare, consequently, it is almost impossible to see the sexual commandeering and subjugation of surviving girls and women as integral to the emergence of warfare and as one of its most persistent and driving goals over the course of time. In the rest of this chapter I sketch an historically grounded reassessment of Western warfare that places this military objective at the center where it belongs.

The Sexual Subjugation of Girls and Women

Ancient Greek and Byzantine Greek narratives make it clear that girls and women are routinely "andrapodized" (*andrapodizein, andrapodizesthai*) as part of ancient warfare waged by loose bands or more formally structured armies of many ethnicities, including Persians, Greeks, Carthaginians, Macedonians, and Romans. Military practices described with the Greek verb *andrapodizein* and cognate forms are well recognized as a fundamental purpose of ancient warfare, for the verb relates in some sense to the turning of war captives into slaves or subjugates (*andrapoda*).[12] It stands to reason that subordinating conquered captives would be critical to the origins of Western warfare, for to establish dominion over live people was a first step toward extracting the benefits from any regions of land and their natural resources.[13] Regardless of the wealth in resources of conquered areas, their acquisition was of little value without human subjugates to work the locales and to serve their keepers in diverse capacities. Surviving conquered subjects were eminently valuable to exploit for their labor, both productively and reproductively, wherever their conquerors or traders placed them and with whatever postconquest social status they came to be given—be it as formal slaves or other kinds of subordinates, such as spear-prize wives or concubines.

The semantic field of *andrapodizesthai* relates to this creating of conquered subjects through warfare, as understood and conveyed in Greek. In Greek sources, moreover, ancient warfare is routinely characterized as a two-phase procedure of systematic violence that is marked by clear but incomplete distinctions in sex and age: killing the men and andrapodizing their women and children. Proficient male aggressors—adolescents or older but still fighting age—regularly tried to kill as many opposing male defenders as possible. The defenders fought back to prevent the aggressors from ravaging their settlement, village, or city, and then rounding up and driving off the surviving women and children living there at the time, that is, the women and girls as well as boys still too young to be of fighting age. To Herodotus these two phases of warfare are so familiar that he sums them up as "slaughter and andrapodizing (*phonos kai exandrapodisis*)" (Hdt. 3.141, cf. 3.147.1), that is, the killing off of grown males and the andrapodizing of the women, girls, and boys. Homeric epic does not use the verb *andrapodizesthai*, but the two-phase practice is nonetheless a prominent feature of Homeric warfare. "They kill the men, use fire to level the city, and other men take away the children and the deep-belted women" (*Il.* 9.593–94). *Andrapoda*, furthermore, are mentioned once in the *Iliad* as captive war booty whom Greek warriors trade in exchange for replenishing their stores of wine (*Il.* 7.467–75).

This method of warfare as presented in Homer and Herodotus recurs throughout all the centuries of armed aggression and warfare as described in Greek narratives up to the fall of the Byzantine or eastern Roman Empire in 1453. For example, the Athenian military, after besieging Scione and Melos during the Peloponnesian War, "killed off all the males from adolescence onward, and they andrapodized the children and women," as

Thucydides states (5.32.1, 5.116.4, cf. 3.68.2, 4.48.4, 5.3.4). Likewise, Alexander's conquests regularly involved killing the fighting men who resisted and andrapodizing the children and women, such as the taking of Gaza (Arrian, *Anab.* 2.27.7). Similarly, according to Appian, the armies of Mithridates VI Eupator routinely practiced "slaughter and andrapodizing" in Asia Minor and environs (*Mithr.* 251), and so did Roman armies in their conquest zones, such as in a retaliatory attack on the rebellious Celtic tribe of Senones. "They andrapodized the women and children, and uniformly killed the males adolescent and older" (*Gall.* fr. 11). This pattern of military practice persists into late antiquity and beyond, and it continues to be described in Greek narratives with the same pattern of phrasing, such as Goths in Agathias stating that Roman forces "killed most of our people and mercilessly andrapodized the women and children of our wealthy men" (*Hist.* 1.5.6) or the medieval George Acropolites giving a chiastic and sex-specific variant on the phrase "killing and andrapodizing" that goes back to Herodotus: "killing of the men, and of the women, andrapodizing (*phonoi te andrôn gunaikôn te andrapodismoi*)" (*Annales* 4, ed. A. Heisenberg 1903).

Given the recurrent practice of andrapodizing groups of predominantly female war captives (women and girls as well as boys) throughout Western warfare as narrated in Greek, it is critical to grasp what this verb signifies in all such narratives of armed conflict. As I have demonstrated in depth elsewhere,[14] 'andrapodizing' does not refer to the transaction involved in trading or selling war captives, as has long been thought, and it also does not mean simply to 'enslave'. Rather, 'andrapodizing' means to engage in partly lethal practices of premeditated and systematic violence against the remaining inhabitants once the male inhabitants in the community or region have been killed off or sufficiently maimed so that they can pose little resistance or threat of future retaliation.

Central to this violence against the women and girls is aggravated battery and sexual assault or rape. First, the fifth-century C.E. Greek lexicographer Hesychius defines *andrapodizein* precisely as the forceful violence, *biazein*, inherent in taking captives by the spear. Second, Greek sources associate the military mores of andrapodizing with the beating and sexual assault inflicted on captive women and/or girls during conquest. Evidence of this sort is important, because it identifies andrapodizing with aggravated sexual assault and battery (*hybrizein*), and thereby confirms Hesychius's definition.

Third, Greek narratives dealing with the second phase of ancient warfare often simply dispense with *andrapodizein* in favor of its more forthright semantic equivalent *hybrizein*. In these cases the terminology for the two fundamental aspects of ancient warfare is not Herodotus's "killing and andrapodizing (*phonos kai exandrapodisis*)" or Acropolites' "killing of the men, and of the women, andrapodizing (*phonoi te andrôn gunaikôn te andrapodismoi*)," but "killing" and "aggravated sexual assault and battery (*hybrizein*)," as indicated in Greek history, oratory, and early church history, including Appian (ca 95–165, *Hann.* 246), Libanius (314–393 C.E., *Orat.* 17.2, 59.157), and Athanasius (ca 295–373, *Hist. Arian.* 10.1–2). In relation to young female captives, therefore, to be andrapodized commonly meant being subjugated or enslaved through ruthless beatings and sexual assault that frequently followed the killing of their men.

Insofar as andrapodizing is recognized as a widespread custom and purpose of warfare in antiquity, it follows that deliberate, degrading sexual violence perpetrated by armed males against women and girl captives was a habitual objective and practice of ancient warfare. By this means, armies of the Persians, Greeks, Macedonians, Romans, and other ethnic groups regularly commandeered the daughters, sisters, wives, and mothers among the conquered and transformed the female captives who survived this treatment into the spear-dominated subjugates or domesticates (*andrapoda* or *aichmalôta*) of the conquerors. The surviving female captives belonged to the conquerors and were theirs to treat as seen fit by the commanders and soldiers.[15] The warriors themselves would use some of them in army brothel prostitution, spear-prize concubinage, and marriage by the spear afterward, including forced impregnation and maternity, while also exploiting them for nonsexual labor. They would trade or sell off the remainder of the captives to other middlemen or buyers ready to exploit them in similar sexual and nonsexual ways.[16] Thus, sexually specific, and largely female-targeting, violence on the part of warriors has historically been central to warfare and to the creating of enslaved or other subjugated persons in antiquity.

Historical Modes of Warfare That Culminate in Female Sexual Subjugation

Ancient warfare as organized sexual violence against captive women and girls is a complex and differentiated range of aggressive practices, just like its first-phase counterpart of men killing men. The ulterior motives, intensity of cruelty, and the female victims' capacity to survive the violence vary depending on whether the warfare was predatory, parasitic, expansionist, or retaliatory, both across and within ethnic lines and regions, including inter-necine civil war. For the most part, these four modes of ancient warfare are not mutually exclusive in practice, even though they are analyzed separately in my typology for better seeing the centrality of captive female bodies to warfare in antiquity.

Ancient predatory warfare is conducted, as Aristotle states, rather like hunting expeditions largely against groups considered to be ethnic outsiders,[17] and these range from loosely organized private or freebooting ventures to coordinated state-sponsored enterprises. In this mode, the armed men who aim to hunt down and catch girls and women first do battle with, and strive to eliminate, the male defenders who try to stop their female relations and slaves from being abducted. Predatory warfare takes the form of assaults against communities with little or no fortifications, such as Athenian soldiers making raids on rural or village-dwelling Thracian peoples, as well as sieges in cities of Asia Minor on the magnitude of those conducted by Alexander and his Macedonian successors. Over the course of time in antiquity, when a community or area was taken, a violent hunt of this sort routinely took place. The women, girls, and boys in attempted flight were "easy prey (*agra hetoimê*)" to chase down and subdue for the soldiers who seized them.[18]

Most warfare as described in Homeric epic exemplifies this predatory mode, which leads to the forcible removal or "natal alienation" of the captive girls and women once its objectives are reached.[19] In the *Iliad*, as Achilles states, when he and his fellow armed marauders go on war raids in towns near and around Troy, they habitually shed the male blood necessary so as "to get the men's women" (*Il.* 9.325–29) and "to take the women's day of freedom away" (*Il.* 20.193–94).[20] Sexual violence is central to this wartime project of subjugating captive women and girls (*Il.* 2.354–56, 3.301, 22.59–65). Homeric epic also shows that aggressive warriors take the young female captives so as to compel them to sexually serve their masters and to perform other kinds of manual labor by day, such as weaving and grinding. Agamemnon specifies four criteria for measuring the captives' worth: whether the women and girls are attractive, skilled at crafts, and of sound mind and good stock (*Il.* 1.112–15), partly for breeding.

The conquering warriors generally kept choice captives for their own personal exploitation and traded others on a market. Xenophon and his fellow mercenaries, for instance, each kept a select few barbarian captives for themselves and planned to trade away the rest for a profit upon reaching a market. But then, to their financial loss, they abandoned all but their favorite few to virtually certain death in an approaching snowstorm, because the larger group of humans as prospective sale items had become an impediment threatening the mercenaries' own progress and survival (Xen. *Anab.* 4.1.12–15). The Athenian plundering of Sicilian Hykkara epitomizes the profit motive, for the Athenian forces andrapodized, transported, and then sold Hykkara's most marketable inhabitants, its women and children, so as to help fund their imperialistic goal to take over Sicily (Thuc. 6.62.2–4).[21] Included in this group of captives was a young girl whose parentally given name we will never know but who was renamed *Lais*, that is, "Booty" girl, and who came to be a prominent courtesan in Corinth (Plutarch, *Nic.* 15.4).

The Old Testament Song of Deborah, the earliest or nearly the earliest composition extant in the Bible, likewise highlights the targeting of young women through predatory warfare. Had the Canaanite warrior king Sisera not already been slaughtered triumphantly by Jael, unbeknownst to Sisera's mother and princesses in his family, he and his warriors would have been engaged in precisely the second-phase warfare that Sisera's wife and daughters assume must be keeping him away: "They must be finding spoil, taking their shares, a young woman to each man, two young women" (Judges 5:28–30). Deuteronomy corroborates this two-phase norm of ancient warfare in relation to peoples outside the land claimed by the Israelites: "If [the city] does not make peace with you," that is, surrender, "but offers battle, you shall besiege it, and the Lord your God will deliver it into your hands. You shall put all its males to the sword, but you may take the women, the dependants, and the cattle for yourselves, and plunder everything else in the city. You may enjoy the use of the spoil of your enemies which the Lord your God gives you" (Deut. 20:12–14).[22]

Even though the Old Testament and Homeric epic are among our earliest sources for elucidating the forcible removal mainly of young female captives through predatory warfare, the practice goes back to the Bronze Age. To name one example from the sixteenth century B.C.E., a date concurrent with the Mycenaean Greek Shaft Graves, the Karnak stela of Kamose, an Egyptian king of Thebes, celebrates his victory over Asiatic men by declaring, "Oh miserable Asiatic, look, . . . I have cast your wives into the ships' holds," and goes on to list other wealth taken as plunder, such as chariots.[23]

Predatory warfare for the forcible abduction of girls and women can also use stealth or trickery to dispense with, or at least diminish, the risky and labor-intensive first phase of having to fight and kill armed male defenders. For example, as Herodotus notes, when Greek men of Ephesus encountered shipwrecked Greek Chian sailors in their territory during the

Ephesian women's celebration of a festival for Demeter, the Thesmophoria, the Ephesian men immediately regarded the Chian men's presence as predation: "Sure that the Chians were bandits who had come to carry off their women, they came out in full strength to protect their women and proceeded to kill the Chians" (Hdt. 6.16.2, cf. Hom. *Od.* 9.39–42). This "stealth and steal" mode of warfare is often classified as piracy rather than warfare, for its armed practitioners strive to seize the girls and women without first confronting their armed menfolk, and then to make a quick getaway by ship. Nonetheless, by the redefinition of warfare presented here, piracy is predatory warfare in its most direct form, reducing or eliminating as it does the first-phase prelude of lethal male combat and going straight to the second-phase end.[24] Each incident of piratical warfare may have been a small-time operation compared with the siege and conquest of a populous ancient city, but throughout the Mediterranean, the practice made up for its small impact per incident by its sustained frequency and range, which made it a recurrent scourge along the coastal areas that curtailed the freedom of women and girls to go out unattended in these areas.

The next mode of warfare, the parasitic, is similar to the predatory but with a surprise twist. The conquering warriors do not forcibly remove women and girls, but themselves adopt the location of their captives—the victorious enemy moves in and stays, or at least tries to stay. In this mode, the men of a community or area are eliminated and then the conquerors, like wolves dressed up to look like husbands and fathers, take the slaughtered men's place with the surviving female inhabitants. In this case the captive women and girls become the warriors' domestic inmates, subjected prisoners in the very places that were once their homes. Ancient Greek colonizers are known for having deployed this mode of warfare.[25] In the Archaic period, for example, armed male Athenians colonized the city of Miletus by slaughtering the adult male Carians who had inhabited the city and compelling their daughters, wives, and mothers to serve them as live-in domesticates and vehicles for reproducing their offspring.[26] This practice, however, was not unique to armed Greek male colonizers. In the Hellenistic period, Campanian mercenaries similarly killed the adult males of Messene and Rhegium and forced the surviving females in those cities to live with and serve them as subjugated captives, albeit only briefly in Rhegium (Polybius 1.7.1–8).

It is reasonable to think, and has historically proven the case, that predatory warfare is conducive to expansionist conquest. First, as with any predatory hunting of animals, once an area is depleted of prey, it is time to move on to a new untouched habitat. This same circumstance applies to gaining a high yield of exploitable captive women, girls, and boys. Second, because in this case the prey are humans—and predominantly girls and women—the more plundered a region is, the more well defended the remaining inhabitants in the area become in order to protect their youthful sector, who are critical for the survival and well-being of any group. They build city walls and defensive towers, and it becomes advisable, and at times necessary, to have girls and women remain indoors and be constrained by other forms of protectionism that restrict their freedom. Sieges then become necessary, and bands of predatory warriors accordingly will either become siege specialists, like Demetrius Poliorcetes (the Besieger), or move farther afield to "virgin" territory that is both easier to conquer and results in numerous exploitable captives. Alexander's conquests in the Near East and India, his "booty raid on an epic scale," adopts both procedures, and is one of the most outstanding campaigns from antiquity showing the expansionist proclivity of predatory warfare.[27] Parasitic warfare is likewise a part of expansionism insofar as the conquering soldiers, or other male settlers in league with the conquerors (and often of the same ethnicity), take up occupancy in the conquered regions on terms of sustained domestic violence and domination over the surviving female captives compelled to cohabit with them. This is not to suggest that all expansionist imperialism in antiquity was the result only of ambitious predation and parasitic takeovers, for here I am mainly delineating the expansionist proclivities of these two modes of warfare.

The capture, sexual assault, and subjugation of women and girls among the enemy also play an important and distinctive role in ancient punitive or retaliatory warfare. In this warfare mode, aggressive military action is motivated by an ostensible or genuine grievance against another group. In its more calculated and somewhat dissimulating form, retaliatory warfare is a mix of the predatory and parasitic with a thin pretext of vengeance. The targeted peoples have failed to surrender with due alacrity and acquiescence and consequently must be punished, such as when the Athenians slaughtered the young and older adult males of Melos for their refusal to become a subject ally, andrapodized and sold off the Melian women and children, and then resettled the city with their own colonists (Thuc. 5.116.4). The Romans made predatory retribution one of their trademarks of imperialistic warfare: "Spare those who surrender, but fight to the end the arrogant" (Virgil, *Aeneid* 6.853). "The arrogant" were largely non-Roman ethnic groups. What made them haughty to Roman eyes was that they aided Roman enemies militarily, failed to surrender to Roman armies, or tried to change their minds after surrendering, such as by resisting Roman administrative and military occupation.[28]

Punitive warfare can also involve formal truces or alliances between enemies that collapse into intense animosity. In the *Iliad*, for example, the Greek and Trojan warriors swear a solemn oath to Zeus, as part of the suspension of hostilities for the duel between Menelaus and Paris. In their oath they swear that if either side transgresses the pact of the duel, the double-crossing warriors and their sons must have their brains spilled out and their wives must be raped by the warriors on the other side (*dameien* or *migeien*, *Il.* 3.298–301).[29] After the Trojan Pandarus treacherously breaks this truce and wounds Menelaus, Greek hostility greatly intensifies in its punitive force.

Whereas predatory, parasitic, and expansionist warfare mainly targets peoples of a foreign ethnicity, retaliatory warfare in antiquity has two faces. The first is directed against peoples of another community or ethnicity who from the aggressors' perspective are believed to have done something wrong and deserve punishment. The other face is internecine, which is directed against people of the same or similar community or ethnic group. In these local cases the men who take up arms first turn against one another in divisive feuds, strife, and civil war. Regardless of whether the retaliatory warfare is carried out far from, near, or inside the homeland of the aggressors, once the attacking males kill most of the grown males among the opposition, they then consider it their right and even their obligation to exact additional punishment by sexually mauling the women and especially the female children of the losing side, who are often their erstwhile neighbors. Here the lust for vengeance is no skimpy pretext to justify predatory or parasitic aggression against outsiders, but an impassioned force that burns from hatred and anger and fuels these emotions further.

There need not be any formal treachery for one group to erupt into retributive warfare against another, especially in cases of simmering enmity among people who know each other well and specialize in abhorring one another. The internecine strife of Corcyra during the Peloponnesian War is a chilling example of a punitive outbreak. Once the male members of the Corcyrean democratic faction finished systematically torturing and killing the men of the Corcyrean oligarchical faction, their vengeance was only halfway finished. Next it was time to andrapodize the men's women, as they then did.[30]

Punitive revenge may be directed against outside people who live within a traversable proximity, be their ethnicity the same, similar, or altogether different. In Genesis, for instance, when the Israelite Jacob's sons take vengeance against the Hivites for the rape of their sister Dinah, they kill every adult male and carry off "all their dependants, and their women, and everything in the houses" (Gen. 34:25–29). Even more strikingly, as Herodotus observes, the long-standing enmity between the Phocians and Thessalians leads to Thessalian outrage at the Phocians, because the Phocians declined to accept the Thessalians' Persian-backed offer to pay only an indemnity for failing to side with the Persians. In revenge, the Thessalians in league with the Persians burnt their way through the region of Phocis, caught some Phocians who failed to flee in advance, and then gang-raped the women in this group so violently that they killed them—a clear example of women being andrapodized to death (Hdt. 8.32–33). Thus, when adult fighting men defended their communities or social sector from retributive violence, they were justified in fearing that the aggressors would sexually assault their women and girls in a horrific way if they lost and their opponents won.[31]

Consequently, organized sexual violence against the women and girls is fundamental to retributive warfare, just as it is with warfare in the predatory, parasitic, and expansionist modes. But with punitive revenge the goal is not primarily to tame the female captives as though they were wild barbarian animals that need to be beaten, raped, and thereby broken in and made exploitable. This is a primary goal of warfare in the predatory and parasitic modes, and in expansionist warfare that is not mainly retributive. Here, instead, the goal is ruthless punishment. Given this aim, the sexual violence of retributive warfare has a proclivity for becoming especially sadistic, and often fatal for many victims, such as the Thessalian men gang-raping Phocian women to death, or the semibarbarian Pheretime in Barca having the breasts cut off of the wives whose husbands she blamed for killing her son (Hdt. 4.202.1).

Sadism, disfigurement, and slaughter, however, are not necessarily inherent in punitive warfare. In the incident of the Hivites, Jacob's sons are stirred to vengeance because the Hivite Shechem copulated with their sister Dinah without their consent. They seem satisfied taking their revenge as predatory warriors, first killing off as many adult male Hivites as possible and then carrying off a number of female Hivites—sexually brutalized girls and women, no doubt, but alive and ripe for exploitation. Nonetheless, lurid sexual sadism combined with killing off the female captives is consonant with the retaliatory mode of warfare, while lethal torture and disfigurement, such as the cutting off of breasts, is contrary to the predatory, parasitic, and expansionist modes of warfare. In the latter trajectories of warfare, a reasonable number of the bludgeoned, raped, and subjugated women and girls should be kept alive so as to be useful in the sex and other trades of the ancient world.

Conclusion

Predatory, parasitic, retaliatory, and expansionist modes of warfare virtually exhaust the known practices of warfare in antiquity, regardless of how intermingled in their modes historical incidents of warfare have been. Insofar as organized sexual violence against women and girls is integral to the first three modes, and prominent in the fourth, it follows that the violent subjugation of women and girls through sexual assault and torment has been an integral and important part of Western warfare over the two millennia from the Bronze Age to late antiquity.

When warfare is predatory or parasitic, the centrality of taking women and girls as captives is indisputably primary. This is shown with special clarity in the case of raids that attempt to sidestep the messy and dangerous prelude of male bloodshed and to abduct women and girls who are gathered outdoors for religious rituals. In these two modes the sexual violence serves the purpose of turning women and girls into brutalized sex objects and exploitable subalterns. When retaliatory, sexual violence against enemy girls and women is likewise central to warfare, but for a very different reason. No hate-driven retaliatory warfare is complete without gang rape and the like, for the females on the opposing side need to be so maltreated to gain payback. As the solemn Homeric vow to Zeus indicates, the traitors' women *must* be raped and dominated. This aspect of sexual violence is conducive to gruesome sadistic glee on the part of the attackers. When cruelty is activated with this intensity, rare would be the victimized girl or woman who could survive.

Warfare in the expansionist or imperialistic mode is more diverse in its objectives and includes the aggressors' asexual desires, such as to assume control of precious mines and cultivated lands. But when predation and/or retribution still inform the expansionist goals, then the objective of taking captive girls and women as subaltern wives, concubines, prostitutes, and slaves remains central, such as taking them for the purpose of exploiting their indigenous knowledge and their capacity to reproduce and to perform other kinds of labor.

Historical practices of warfare from the Bronze Age through the Byzantine era are a medley of the preceding modes of warfare, in which predation was often one fundamental way to remunerate the victorious rank and file or to fund the war undertaking (e.g., Hykkara), even if the soldiers' generals would have said that their main goal was not predation but to add Sicily to the Athenian Empire. Thus, regardless of the combination of modes involved in any particular historical instance of warfare, I have argued, the armed male aggressors regularly sought, as one driving objective, to commandeer through sexual violence the female bodies among the enemy or outsiders. The mode or mixed modes of warfare through which the aggressors engaged in this commandeering conditioned the kinds of abuses to which they subjected the girls and women. We start to grasp the centrality and variegated import of this female battery, sexual assault, and exploitation in warfare and its aftermath only by seeing beyond the androcentric paradigm of warfare, with its focus on the lethal man-to-man dimension, as though this illuminated side of the moon were all that is worth knowing about Western warfare in our history.

By revealing the dark side, as I have done here in a preliminary way, second-phase warfare against girls and women finally emerges in our consciousness of warfare and its social injustices. With this historical knowledge and awareness, international human rights activists stand to become better informed in their efforts to relegate these persistent norms of second-phase warfare strictly to the past. This aspiration is as daunting as it is noble and urgent, for this human rights goal amounts to an attempt to outlaw one of the most persistent and fundamental purposes of warfare as historically practiced from the Bronze Age to late antiquity and beyond. Its aim is to place freedom and dignity finally within the reach of girls and women in a world where, on a global scale, boys and men no longer allow their socialization into manhood to be militarized in these terms.

Chapter 5
The Victimization of Women in Late Precolonial and Early Colonial Warfare in Tanzania

James Giblin

An eloquent reflection on eastern Africa's recent history of conflict is "Weight of Whispers," Yvonne Adhiambo Owuor's prize-winning short story about the traumatic after-effects of the Rwanda genocide of 1994.[1] As she describes the degradation (and also resilience) of Rwandese women who become refugees in Kenya, Owuor reflects bitterly on the region's history of armed conflict, remarking that "annals of war decree that conquest is not complete unless the vanquished enemy's women are 'taken.' Where war is crudest, the women are discarded, afterward for their men to find. Living etchings of emasculation."

The following pages use a historian's evidence to consider Owuor's insight. The obvious point that emerges is that she is correct in believing that wartime victimization of women has a long history in her region and in saying that in the past, the wartime victimization of women has been an expression of masculinity in the context of rivalry with other men. Yet the evidence cautions against an ahistorical understanding of masculinity as a hard-wired source of brutality but suggests instead that the expression of masculinity in the wartime treatment of women reflects the particular historical context of war. Forms of wartime victimization change along with the changing historical context of war, and I suggest that moral discourses are an important element of that context. The moral norms that define masculinity, I argue below, have shaped the particular forms of victimization of women found in wars of the past.

My evidence is drawn from southern Tanzania, a region that witnessed frequent warfare from the 1870s through the British conquest of German

East Africa during the First World War. Regional warfare in the 1870s and 1880s stemmed from two developments. The first was the rapid expansion of East African slave trade, which drew caravans of slave dealers and chattels to the island of Zanzibar from vast portions of the eastern African mainland. The second was the arrival in southwestern Tanzania of a remarkably militarized people, the Ngoni, whose migration from South Africa began in the 1820s as an attempt to flee the tyranny of the famous Zulu warlord, Chaka. By the 1840s the Ngoni had reached present-day Tanzania, and by the 1870s they had taken control of the Songea portion of southern Tanzania. These twin developments resulted in both militarization and alliance building among military commanders throughout southwestern Tanzania. The most prominent of these alliance builders was Mkwawa, the leader in the modern-day Iringa region called Uhehe, whose increasing power allowed him to defend his subjects against both the Ngoni and coastal slave traders, while also raiding neighboring societies for captives, some of whom he may have sold to slave traders.

European colonialism made its appearance in Tanzania in the late 1880s, when the Germans conquered key port towns along the Indian Ocean coast. When they resolved to extend their authority inland, they found Mkwawa to be a formidable obstacle. He massacred a German military column in 1891 in a battle that remains the most celebrated Tanzanian victory over European invaders. The Germans attacked Mkwawa for a second time in 1894, this time driving him from his capital. A guerrilla war ensued until Mkwawa's suicide in 1898. The Germans fought this war by making alliances with Mkwawa's former regional enemies. Thus, not only did the Germans enter into the same forms of alliance making that had developed among African leaders in preceding decades, but their style of warfare was influenced by the military traditions and practices of their African allies. In particular, they allowed their African allies to reward themselves with captured women. Moreover, German officers looked the other way as their own African soldiers engaged in the capture of women. While the officers in the German *Schutztruppe* (protection force) were white, the rank-and-file soldiers were African, many of them recruited as mercenaries from South Africa and the Sudan.

These same German practices of relying on African allies and using the capture of women as the primary incentive to auxiliary warriors persisted during the next phase of fighting in southern Tanzania, the Maji Maji War of 1905–7. During the Maji Maji, one of the great African rebellions against

European colonialism, again women were captured in large numbers both by African soldiers in the German army and by their African auxiliaries. Moreover, similar practices were also documented during the First World War, when both British and German forces captured and conscripted both men and women to provide porterage and other forms of service to their troops.

Oral histories I collected in southern Tanzania during the 1990s revealed that this period remains well known. Interestingly, the most common genre of oral account about this period places women at the center of this history of warfare. Far more common than stories of men's heroism in warfare are stories of flight by ordinary villagers, particularly women, from approaching armies. Very often these stories portray women as having played a decisive role in saving their families and property from advancing warriors. Thus, the oral record is full of women's agency in wartime, although I know of no stories including women's active participation in conflict either by fighting or by providing supplies and other support to male fighters. Clearly, being forced to flee is perhaps the most common form of women's victimization in wartime. In this chapter, however, instead of dwelling on their wartime experience in flight and hiding, I turn to the scarce evidence concerning what happened to women who fell into the hands of their enemies during warfare.

A Changing Context: Women in Wartime During and After the Slave Trade

The slave trade in eastern Africa reached its peak late. While the Atlantic slave trade from West Africa declined from 1807 when the British declared it illegal, in East Africa the demand for slaves on the clove-exporting islands of Zanzibar and Pemba became most intense in the 1870s and 1880s. As the political histories of many portions of East Africa attest, it was in these decades that the slave trade became most profoundly destabilizing.

When the Germans occupied the Indian Ocean coast of Tanzania in the late 1880s, they, like European colonizers throughout Africa, faced a dilemma. On the one hand, their government and citizenry expected them to achieve the most urgent aim of the European civilizing mission—the abolition of slavery. On the other hand, fearful that the abolition of slavery and slave trading would undermine the economy of their newly won colony and deprive the colonized societies of the social control exerted by slave-owning elites, German authorities acted only haltingly to stop slave trading. As a result, slave trading continued through the 1890s and into the first years of the new century, although it was now only rarely conducted by large caravans of chattels whose arrival in towns shocked humanitarian observers, and more often by small groups that German officials could, if they chose not to look closely, assume to be families.[2] Yet, while the movement of slaves into German-controlled lands along the coast territory became surreptitious, farther inland, in southwestern Tanzania and elsewhere, the capture of slaves through raiding and kidnapping continued. The enslavement of women in these ways was described in stunning detail by Marcia Wright. Her book, *Strategies of Slaves and Women*, utilizes the written autobiographies of women who escaped slavery by entering early Christian mission communities to provide an account of the enslavement of women in areas around the northern end of Lake Nyasa in the last years of the nineteenth century.[3]

If we consider all of the vast area of eastern Africa that witnessed such depredations to have been a "conflict zone," then surely Wright's book provides a vitally important account of what happened to women in such circumstances. Here, however, I restrict the definition of a conflict zone as an area that witnessed not merely raiding and kidnapping in undefended communities but warfare between armies. What can we say about the fate of women during the warfare of the slave trade era? Our chief problem is that we lack a written account of warfare in the region before the Germans became participants in it during the 1890s. The oral accounts of the region's communities shed little light on the experience of women captured in warfare. One type of oral account comprises stories of precolonial battle and warfare. Told primarily by members of chiefly families and courts, they were first recorded in writing in the 1890s by German military officers who were keenly interested in the tactics and military history of their foe. A second type of oral account includes the stories of wartime flight mentioned above. Like the former type, which are chiefly accounts of battle and warriors, however, these stories relate nothing directly about the fate of women whose attempts to flee warriors failed. Of course, they do testify to the dread of capture that impelled women to prepare to take flight at a moment's notice.

Another way of studying the wartime experience of women during the slave trade era is to read the German accounts as evidence not only of the warfare that they witnessed in the 1890s but of war in preceding decades. This is a reasonable approach, because German dependence on African allies ensured that the wars of the 1890s would be fought much as they had been in earlier decades. The German commanders who pursued Mkwawa from 1894 to 1898 were hampered by the small size of their forces and the long distance from their coastal bases. They relied heavily on alliances with chiefs of the Sangu people, who had long been enemies of Mkwawa. The Germans were in no position either to teach the Sangu a new style of warfare (the unfamiliar Sangu tactics sometimes confused the Germans during battle) or to reward their Sangu auxiliaries directly. Thus, it is reasonable to assume that the widespread capture and distribution of women among Sangu fighters that the Germans described in the 1890s was a practice inherited from earlier warfare.

German officers observed many instances of the enslavement of women by their allies. Officer Heinrich Fonck witnessed the capture of hundreds of women, men, and children by Sangu forces in January 1897.[4] Back at German headquarters in Iringa a month later, Fonck learned that one of his own soldiers had slipped out of uniform to sell three "wives" (the Germans required that their soldiers obtain the "consent" of captive women whom they wanted).[5] This was, he commented, part of an "extensive slave trade between, on the one side, Arabs and colored traders, and, on the other, the Hehe and perhaps soldiers and station employees."[6] Other German officials also saw large numbers of captive women. In 1897, Tom von Prince found an "enormous" number of enslaved women in Usangu, many of them captured during raids into the adjoining territory of Njombe.[7] A missionary in Iringa found that German-appointed headmen were distributing captive women to their subordinates.[8] Thus, one of the principal forms of continuity between the German campaigns and precolonial warfare was that commanders rewarded soldiers—including Sangu warriors and other auxiliary forces as well as the soldiers under their direct command—by allowing them to enslave and sell women. These observations from the 1890s lend weight to the occasional references in some oral accounts to enslavement during precolonial war.[9]

One reflection of women's fear of enslavement was the immediate abandonment of villages at the outbreak of warfare. "Settlements were often abandoned," wrote Fonck in 1896. "The people lived in isolated refuges in inaccessible places. The consequence was a dearth of food. . . . Death and murder, robbery, plundering, arson, cattle theft, and attacks on caravans, [military] posts and messengers . . . were the order of the day."[10] The Germans saw roads crowded with slaves, refugees, and herds of stolen cattle, leading past deserted villages reduced to smoking ruins.[11]

Certainly the capture of women as standard military practice did not end with the death of Mkwawa. During the Maji Maji war of 1905–7, German auxiliaries once again captured many women.[12] For the Maji Maji period, a vitally important source is the interviews collected by a team of student researchers from the University of Dar es Salaam in 1968. The interviewers met many elderly eyewitnesses to Maji Maji. They were told that, just as during nineteenth-century wars, many villagers fled into uninhabited woodland during Maji Maji. "Those who were in the villages always ran into the forests to hide themselves from the enemies who attacked their villages," testified one elderly villager.[13] "Oh don't remind me of those by-gone days," said Tuhuvye, an elderly woman in Kidugala, in present-day Njombe District,[14]

> There was not a single time we could say we were in peace. Very often the Sangu came in this area and attacked people. After fighting and defeating the people they took human captives; they took our cattle too. Sometimes they came to the village and did not find people. In this case they took what they could and burned down all the houses and some of our things and our food . . . those were very bad years. Sometimes all the people left the village and we hid in the forest until we heard that there was peace— the enemies had gone away.

The interviewers found that both German and anticolonial forces seized captives in great numbers. Some Sangu men who served on the German side "fought against [an enemy of the Germans named] Mbeyela, taking some of his subjects as war prisoners. Most of those captives were taken to Usangu."[15] The interviewers learned about the tactics of the Sangu forces and the fate of their captives[16]:

> Every [Sangu] leader was instructed to kill every male rebel, cut his hands and bring all the victims' hands to Utengule [the capital of the Sangu chief Merere] before the German authority. The warriors would be rewarded at the end of the Maji Maji suppression according to the number of hands brought. The warriors were not given pay nor food while fighting. They had to depend on whatever they could seize in the areas they passed. Their final pay was the gift of captured women, children, and livestock.

"When they came back [to Usangu]," said Ramadhani Mjengwa of raiders returning to Usangu,[17]

> they brought with them many slaves, mainly women and youths. . . . My father, for example, was given two slave women by Merere. Malanje

was also given slave women and one slave boy who is still alive called Mwakilanji. . . . Many people had been killed on the side of the Maji Maji rebels. . . . Wherever the rebel fighters went they slaughtered all the male villagers in the Maji Maji affected areas, captured women and children and took off all property, especially livestock.

A former soldier of the Sangu chief Merere testified that[18]

we took captured women and children as prisoners. Later on we were to be given them as slaves and wives by the German leaders . . . we had to come back with a cavalcade of war prisoners. . . . On the way back from Ungoni we passed the same route up to Mbeyela's country. Here we took a lot of cattle, goats and sheep. Together with those taken from Upangwa we had a very big herd of livestock, and Bwana Jambo, the German leader, distributed the spoils of war of animals and people to each chief, who also redistributed them to his subjects. Magoti, who was then a boy, and Bibi Mbilinyi, a girl, were among the people taken by us as war spoils.

Bibi Mbilinyi herself testified that[19]

my mother, myself and many other women and children were pushed around by cruel people whom we could neither recognize nor understand their language. Many of those who either could not walk quickly or were sick were killed and left on the road dead. The rest had to carry heavy loads of food for those cruel people. Boys had to look after the cattle which these enemies had taken by force wherever they passed. We traveled a very long distance for many days till we came to this country. I cannot remember much of what I saw, because I was too small. But when I grew up I became used to the life of this country and was then married to my master Malanje.

Another former war captive, Fatma Matumula, explained to the university students in 1968 that during the attack that resulted in her enslavement, "most of our men managed to run away . . . [the Sangu attackers] ordered all of us women to follow them. But one of us who could not walk quickly because of her baby on her back was killed together with her baby. The rest of us were taken into slavery here at Usangu."[20] Captive women from Njombe were also taken to Uhehe, the region adjoining Sangu territory that had formerly been ruled by Mkwawa. "Many Bena and Pangwa captives (mostly women) were brought by force to Malangali and were shared among the residents as servants. Even today there are people in Malangali whose mothers or they themselves were captives."[21]

Thus, there is abundant evidence of women's capture and forced exodus from their homes during Maji Maji. The absence of accounts of the sale of captive women to coastal traders during 1905–7 suggests that, as German efforts to suppress slave trading gradually brought an end to the long-distance movement of slaves, captives were now most likely to be settled in the communities of their captors. The 1968 interviews show that at least some of the captured women lived out their lives in the homes of their captors, long after the institution of slavery had been finally abolished in 1922. As late as the 1950s, women who had been seized as war captives paid visits to their home regions and families.

Why did these war captives remain in place several decades after no court would have recognized the rights of slave owners, and no village authority would have risked appearing to condone the practice of slavery? It seems likely that, while these women had been subjected to capture and forced resettlement, in their new homes they gained the status of wives. To be sure, they were married involuntarily; yet their position did not deny them all rights and status. Like other wives, they possessed opportunities to negotiate their social circumstances and build supportive networks of friends, husbands' relatives, and, most crucially, their own children. Perhaps their most important resource was a moral discourse of kinship, which they used to demand the rights of spouses and mothers. Their own sense of moral obligation ensured, moreover, that unwillingness to abandon their children would also tie them to the homes of their husbands. Indeed, their involvement in forced marriages by no means placed them in a situation of moral and social alienation, for they belonged to a generation of women for whom involuntary marriage arranged by parents was common. My argument here is thus that the norms of propriety attached to relations of marriage and kinship continued to govern the treatment of women after they fell into captivity. A slender piece of evidence supporting my contention comes from the same attack by the Sangu allies of the Germans against their enemies in Njombe that led to the instances of captivity during Maji Maji described in the interviews above. When the Sangu leader, Merere, plundered the home of a prominent enemy of the Germans, Mbeyela, among the women whom he took captive were Sara, a wife of Mbeyela, and Saiyinga, Sara's daughter-in-law. Merere took Saiyinga as his wife but refused to marry Sara. In earlier days, when Merere and Mbeyela had briefly been allies, Merere had visited Mbeyela's home, eaten food cooked by Sara, and come to regard her as his *shemeji*, or sister-in-law. According to Mbeyela's grandson, Merere declared that "to take the wife of my relative [Mbeyela], who used to cook rice for me and look after me when we were fighting the Ngoni, and today make her the wife of someone else, this wouldn't be possible, it's forbidden."[22]

The Victimization of Women and Rivalry Among Men

Although southern Tanzania did not witness open warfare between the death of Mkwawa in 1898 and the outbreak of the Maji Maji conflict in 1905, the capture of women by leaders and armed forces occurred nevertheless. As the following story from an early Christian mission in Njombe District suggests, although norms of proper behavior toward spouses influenced the treatment of women in captivity, women became captives as the result of rivalries among male leaders. It also suggests that, because the control of women was an essential aspect of male authority, the seizure of another man's female dependents challenged not only his political and social standing, but his masculinity as well. Just as Yvonne Adhiambo Owuor suggests, capturing a man's women was a form of emasculation.

During Maji Maji, one of the best-known incidents of fighting occurred at a mission station in Njombe established by German Lutheran evangelists in 1898. Very shortly after the outbreak of rebellion in 1905, the Yakobi mission was besieged by the forces of Mbeyela, the same chief whose women would later be seized by the Sangu leader, Merere. The residents of the mission, led by their German pastor Paul Gröschel, repelled the attack. However, lacking ammunition, they soon abandoned the station, which was plundered and destroyed later in the war.

Around Yakobi, many people believe that Mbeyela attacked the mission not because he was committed to the anticolonial cause but for a far simpler reason. He wished, they said, to seize "Mwangasama," as they called Gröschel's German wife, and to have children with her. This story was first recorded by University of Dar es Salaam researchers in 1968, and I have heard it several times at Yakobi, most recently in 2004 while in the company of a team of Tanzanian scholars and students. Expecting a story of resistance to the German colonial oppression, my colleagues were astonished to hear one of the most prominent moments in the Maji Maji war explained as a dispute over a woman. Elsewhere I have suggested that the persuasiveness of this story in the vicinity of Yakobi may be due to the nature of gender politics in the area.[23] I think that, in a culture where a man's marriage to multiple wives is perhaps the primary source of discord in families, listeners to this story cannot fail to ponder how a man's impetuous decision to seize another man's wife brought ruin upon himself and his entire family.

The story of conflict between Gröschel and Mbeyela over Gröschel's wife takes on added significance when compared with another episode at Yakobi before Maji Maji. Gröschel resided at Yakobi continuously from its founding in 1898 until his abandonment of the station in 1905. During this period, German colonial authorities instituted taxation throughout German East Africa. Taxation thrust missionaries like Gröschel into an awkward dilemma. The German officials expected missionaries to assist in tax collection, but the missionaries were reluctant to do so. While they did not want to alienate the military and civil officials whose permission they required to reside in the colony, the missionaries feared that their African neighbors would perceive them as unwilling or incapable of protecting them. Gröschel knew that Mbeyela had permitted the mission station in his territory because he expected the German evangelists to act as mediators with colonial authorities.

Gröschel was appalled, moreover, by the colonial regime's method of tax collection. During the first years of the century tax was collected by army patrols, consisting of *askari* (the African soldiers in the German army) who were often commanded by African noncommissioned officers. The behavior of these patrols was brutal. They seized the livestock and other property of persons whom they considered liable to tax, inflicted summary corporal punishments, and sometimes burned villages whose residents had fled their approach. An additional racial tension entered the picture when evangelists like Gröschel encountered the African sergeants. Their lack of deference toward the European missionaries grated on Gröschel and his colleagues, who deplored what they regarded as their arrogance, disrespectfulness, and pretension.

The practice that embittered Gröschel's relations with the German military was the seizure of women by tax patrols. In July 1900, after a party of soldiers took captive the two wives of a neighboring village elder during tax collection, Gröschel decided that he "must stand by the husband and help him to obtain justice."[24] Gröschel went to the camp of the military patrol and obtained the release of the women, who were being held by two young servants—"two nearly naked boys"—while the soldiers roamed the surrounding countryside looking for taxpayers. The two boys were beaten by the husband of the abducted women and other villagers. Gröschel's accusations of mistreatment of women by soldiers led to the rapid deterioration of his relations with the German commander in the region, Lieutenant Albinus. Evidently other women were captured and mistreated at this time, for Gröschel complained about the "abominable and brutal ways in which people, and especially women and girls, are treated without good reason by the soldiers."[25]

Similar events occurred in the following year, when[26]

> there was tax collection in Mbeyela's area. This took place without European supervision, and through the injustice of the *askari*, and yes, cruelties were committed. The most hideous thing was that many women were held in the camp of the *askari*, where they were subject to all of their infamies.

An inspector for Gröschel's mission society happened to be visiting Yakobi on this occasion, and he, too, described mistreatment of women by soldiers under the command of a "black sergeant."[27]

> We took the opportunity to ascertain the names of the [abducted women]. About ten women were named as having been captured with whips and disgraced. Some of them we saw ourselves, including a girl, really only a child, and an old woman with gray hair, who had been assaulted by the four boys of the *askari*, one after another. Some men were left—at the moment I can't give the number of weeks, but it was a matter of weeks—in slave yokes, from which they weren't released even at night.

Eventually, relations between Gröschel and Lieutenant Albinus became so acrimonious that it prompted intervention by both the headquarters of Gröschel's missionary society in Berlin and the governor of German East Africa.

Gröschel's African neighbors had their own interpretation of these actions. The context for this reading was the expectation that political leaders should serve as the benevolent guardians of their kin and other dependents, who customarily formed relations of fictive kinship with their chiefs. I have heard an extraordinarily moving oral account of how the greatest of the region's chiefs, Mkwawa, fulfilled this expectation. Describing his final days before he chose suicide as German troops surrounded him, this story portrayed Mkwawa as having acted with affection and solicitude toward the children and women of his family.[28] The story can be understood to mean that Mkwawa chose suicide because he could no longer uphold his duty to protect his wives, children, and other dependents from the Germans.

The expectation that an honorable male leader should act with paternal benevolence and provide protection to his women helps to explain why Gröschel's neighbors believed that the tax patrols seized women from among the missionary's dependents as a way of testing both Gröschel and his male followers. As both they and the Germans knew, seizing the women of rivals was a ploy frequently employed by chiefs who wished to assert their dominance.[29] A son of Mbeyela who lived near Yakobi, wrote Gröschel, said that the African soldiers had acted with an "arrogant" manner because they wished to "bait" Gröschel and "see what the people of the Europeans would do."[30] As the leader of his small Christian community and as patron of the villagers who lived near the mission, Gröschel was apparently held to much the same expectation as other leaders such as Mkwawa.

Seen in light of the treatment of women during the tax campaigns of 1900 and 1901, the explanation given by villagers at Yakobi for Mbeyela's attack on the mission during Maji Maji appears much more persuasive. Historians might be inclined to dismiss the notion that a notable battle during a great anticolonial rebellion was caused by a leader's desire to capture a woman. In attacking Yakobi, however, Mbeyela may well have been using the same means of asserting his dominance as had been employed by the African tax collectors against Gröschel. This was the tactic of seizing a rival's women, while perhaps violating his right to control their sexuality as well. Thus, we have reason to believe that during precolonial and early colonial wars, women were victimized as pawns in rivalries among men.

As our evidence of late precolonial and early colonial warfare in southern Tanzania shows, while war always made victims of women, the forms of their victimization changed with transformations of the larger historical context. In the period of extensive slave trading in the 1870s and 1880s, women captured in war were often sold to traders from the coast. As the slave trade declined from the 1890s, women continued to be captured in war, but now they were increasingly incorporated into the households of their captors as wives. As we have seen, the interviews done by University of Dar es Salaam students in 1968 contain numerous accounts of the assimilation of captured women into Sangu villages.

Both of these practices—either selling female war captives to slave traders or incorporating them as wives into the households of their captors—suggest that a crucial motivation for capturing women in war was material. Victorious fighters benefited either by selling their captives or by using them to increase the size of their households, where women contributed their reproductive power as well as their labor. However, the episodes at Yakobi suggest that a more complex mixture of motivations may have lain behind the capture of women in war. The victimization of women at Yakobi by tax collectors and the subsequent attempt of Mbeyela to seize Mwangasama, the wife of missionary Gröschel, show that rivalry among men continued to make victims of women despite the end of the slave trade. Control over women and the provision of benevolent guardianship to them were basic signifiers of masculine maturity. For this reason, seizing a man's wives and daughters, and violating his right to control their sexuality, were ways in which men made a profound test of their rivals' courage and willpower. To return to the terms of Yvonne Adhiambo Owuor, it was a way of symbolically emasculating one's enemy. At Yakobi, and doubtless elsewhere, women suffered capture and rape as a consequence of such contests among men.

Yet, it is important to remember that such contests victimized women because a strong sense of male honor prevailed among men. Norms of honorable behavior included acting justly toward all women and protectively toward one's own women. An example of honorable male behavior toward women was the refusal of Merere, the Sangu leader, to make a wife of Sara, the "sister-in-law" whom he took from his former ally, Mbeyela. Honorable behavior toward women in no way implied equality between men and women. A man was expected to control many aspects of the lives of his wives, daughters, and other female dependents, including their sexuality in particular.

Of course, the norm of honorable behavior toward women could certainly be violated, particularly by a man who felt that his authority and masculinity were doubted by rivals. Nevertheless, the moral expectation that men would act honorably toward women provided female war captives with space to improve their condition. Probably one reason why many women remained married to their captors even after the colonial government made slavery illegal was that the right to fair treatment that they acquired through marriage (even though their marriages were involuntary) allowed them to make tolerable lives for themselves. Indeed, as some oral accounts show, part of the process of making their new lives tolerable occurred when family members and neighbors discreetly chose to avoid mention of the women's origins, so that eventually young people would no longer know of their former captivity. As their experience of captivity slipped farther into the past, and as they built up networks of support that could assist them in claiming just treatment from spouses, life in their new homes probably appeared to offer more security than did the prospect of returning to former spouses or parents.

My argument here is that, while women were victims in all wars, there existed moral norms on which women could base their demands for just and honorable treatment from men, including their captors. Like moral norms in all societies, they were often violated. Yet, one of the contradictory complexities of East African societies was that it was honor, as a constituent of masculinity, that prompted the capture and sexual violation of women in war.

Tracing the story of the wartime victimization of women in East Africa from the conflicts discussed here of the late nineteenth and early twentieth centuries, to the very recent tragedies described by Adhiambo Owuor, would not be possible in a brief chapter. I would suggest, however, that if we are to achieve a fuller historical understanding of the hideous atrocities perpetrated against women during recent years in places such as northern Uganda and the eastern Democratic Republic of the Congo, we need to consider the transformation of moral discourse over the past century. As we have seen here, a century ago the moral discourse that prevailed in political life was that of kinship. Relations of kinship were the basis of masculine and feminine self-identity, and of claims to justice and charity. Leaders claimed authority over subjects by invoking relationships of real and fictive kinship, while likewise subjects used the same relations to claim protections from their leaders. Over the course of the twentieth century, new moral discourses to a great extent supplanted the discourse of kinship in political life. These new discourses were based upon allegiance to nation-states, upon respect for bureaucratic institutions, and upon world religions. We might wish to ask whether these new bases of morality are any more or less effective than the older discourses of kinship in promoting claims to justice, protection, and succor by the victims of war.

PART III

Tellings of Sexual Violence

Chapter 6

War Crimes or Atrocity Stories? Anglo-American Narratives of Truth and Deception in the Aftermath of World War I

Nicoletta F. Gullace

On April 12, 1927, Gordon Catto of Dunedin, New Zealand, wrote to the *Evening Star* on the subject of German atrocities committed during the Great War. According to Mr. Catto, his wife was a nurse in the Ramsgate General Hospital in England during the period 1914–15 and "actually nursed Belgian women and children refugees who were the victims of Hun rapacity and fiendishness, the women having had their breasts cut off and the children with their hands hacked off at the wrists." On discovering Mr. Catto's letter, "a lady investigator" promptly wrote to Ramsgate General Hospital, seeking independent verification of his account. She received the following reply: "Dear Madam, I am at a loss to know how the information about atrocities to women and children, committed by the German soldiers, could have originated in respect to Ramsgate, as there were no such cases received. Yours faithfully, Sydney W. Smith."[1]

This exchange is one of many recounted in Arthur Ponsonby's *Falsehood in War-Time*, a seminal work in the interwar deconstruction of wartime atrocity narratives. The seemingly simple exchange highlights the cryptic and far from transparent process by which the "war crimes" of one historical moment become the "atrocity stories" of another. This chapter asks why acts of war that impassioned belligerents during the conflict were so thoroughly and swiftly discredited later. It suggests that the imperative to acknowledge masculine suffering after the war shaped—perhaps unconsciously—the will to disbelieve wartime acts of violence against women and children.

While harrowing descriptions of German atrocities in Belgium and France were a mainstay of Allied propaganda during the Great War, such accounts fell out of favor following the armistice. By the late 1920s American scholars such as Harold Laswell and H. C. Peterson had come to accept that accounts of war crimes were lurid fabrications invented—or at best exaggerated—by British propagandists to lure America into war.[2] Work done by pacifist intellectuals in Britain seemed to arrive at the same conclusions. In light of recent work by John Horne and Alan Kramer that suggests German atrocities may have been more widespread than postwar scholars believed, I wish to examine the reasons for the emergence of postwar skepticism and ask why particular information—especially information regarding atrocities and war crimes—comes to be considered believable or unbelievable at particular historical moments. According to Horne and Kramer, as many as 6,500 Belgian civilians were murdered by the Germans in the brutal invasion and occupation of 1914. And Ruth Harris's investigations suggest that countless French women were raped and impregnated by German soldiers during the German assault on northern France.[3] Why, then, did interwar investigators discredit recent events that were still palpable to those living in formerly occupied territories? And why did mass audiences that had voraciously consumed atrocity stories during the war, begin to doubt them later? Scholarly opinion regarding the credibility of war atrocities changed considerably after the war, undercutting public faith in the sexual violence committed during World War I. While a number of factors contributed to this shift in sentiment, I will argue that the masculinization of suffering in the aftermath of war undercut emotional receptivity to narratives of female pain, making accounts of atrocities and war crimes increasingly suspect.

During the turbulent early years of World War I both British and German propagandists vied to capture American sympathy and to represent the merits of their own case to this powerful neutral nation. The British not only deployed hundreds of tons of printed material—including books, cartoons, poems, news reports, and sundry other documents that still clutter the basements of many university libraries—but carefully monitored the American press to ascertain the effectiveness of their work and to gauge the various successes and failures of their German counterparts. In addition to what amounted to a media blitz on America, well-known individuals such as the former ambassador to the United States, Lord James Bryce, corresponded with an array of respected Americans to prepare the ground for the reception of often sensationalistic British propaganda. By 1917 Sir Gilbert Parker, the head of propaganda organization for the United States, directed correspondence with no less than 260,000 such individuals, most of whose names had been culled from the pages of *Who's Who*.[4] In addition to cultivating this "personal propaganda," the British Foreign Office assiduously feted and entertained American journalists while providing them with news from British press sources, which held exclusive control over the transatlantic cable systems.

As postwar observers noted, the British campaign was extraordinarily effective in shaping American understanding of World War I and constituted the moral equivalent of a rout for the Germans, whose own more bombastic and forthright propaganda techniques won little sympathy outside the Middle West. While much British propaganda distributed to the United States addressed complex issues of international law, the British often shaped such discussions to suggest that the meaning and purpose of international law was to protect the lives of innocent women and children.[5] In addressing such issues as the invasion of Belgium, the sinking of the Lusitania, or the shooting of nurse Edith Cavell, the British created a highly sexualized image of German monstrosity and used it to market an evocative, sentimental, and deeply gendered version of the conflict to the wider American public. From the start, the British regarded such images as a potentially powerful way of interesting Americans in the war. "It is remarkable to note how instant is the response in the United States to every fresh German atrocity," the British propaganda administrator Sir Gilbert Parker noted with satisfaction in 1916. "It might have been expected . . . [that] German atrocities would have by this time become somewhat stale. But this is not the case. There seems to be no more certain appeal to the American public than through the medium of such atrocities."[6] Indeed while the Americans had much cause to be irritated with the British over neutral shipping rights and the freedom of the seas, the British carefully used atrocity propaganda to distract American attention from such controversies and to reinforce the idea that Great Britain stood as a bulwark defending the safety of women, children, and family values themselves.[7] In newspapers, pamphlets, posters, and cartoons, the image of the raped woman—and the concomitant endangered child— became rhetorical shorthand for the imperative to support the Allied cause.

Theodore Cook's *Crimes of Germany*, a pamphlet widely available in both Britain and the United States, is typical of the atrocity literature distributed on both sides of the Atlantic. Beginning with a lurid chapter on "Crimes Against Women and Children," Cook promised to reveal "the terrible nature of the crimes it is necessary to expose: the outrages against women and children, the massacres of civilian population, the deportations at Lille and elsewhere, the use of helpless creatures as screens to the German troops, the killing and mutilating of wounded and prisoners. . . . It is an atrocious catalogue, and the evidence supporting it can never be denied."[8]

Published to great acclaim in 1916 and 1917, Cook's summary of atrocity reports was heralded as a throughly documented work that would "doubly corroborate . . . 'Belgian atrocities' of August and September 1914." Weeding out the more bland and mundane atrocities from official compendia, Cook extracts liberally from testimonials notable for their sexual or sadistic content. His first account is the hair-raising story of a "Belgian Soldier," taken from the Appendix of the Bryce Report, Britain's official inquiry on German atrocities in Belgium[9]:

> We were passing the flying ground outside Liege at Ans when I saw a woman, apparently middle age, perhaps 28–30 years old, stark naked, tied to a tree. At her feet were two little children about three or four years old. All three were dead. I believe the woman had one of her breasts cut off, but I cannot be sure of this. . . . The woman's clothes were lying on the grass, thrown all about the place. . . . J. B. cut the cords which held the woman up. . . . The body fell and we left it there.

Pamphlets such as Cook's publicized accounts buried in the Appendix of the Bryce Report and gave a new lease on life to harrowing stories that had captured the news in 1915.[10] Quickly sensationalized, such testimony took on a poetic life of its own. Cook could not resist titillating his readers with the content of his pamphlet, and the language of his preface contrasts markedly with the tone of its evidence. "Artists like Zola or Flaubert or Maupassant never saw the horrors they describe, . . . never suffered through them, the loss of all they held most dear," declared Cook.[11]

> But it is certain that the greatest imaginative writer has never penned a picture so pathetic, so poignant, so unimaginably horrible in all its naked details, as is given in the simple words of these peasants. . . . Never have the tortures inflicted upon whole populations been so faithfully recorded in the exact syllables of the victims themselves. And from the assassination of the Archduke's wife at Sarajevo [sic!] to the shooting of a hospital nurse in Brussels, Prussia and her Allies have concentrated their cruelty upon women.

What are we to make of such assertions? New work by John Horne and Alan Kramer, Ruth Harris, and Larry Zuckerman (who has offered a gripping account of the occupation of Belgium during World War I) all suggest that the German invasion of Belgium and northern France was undertaken with the utmost brutality and wanton loss of life. Harris, particularly, gives credit to the depositions of raped women to suggest that the sexual violence, so summarily dismissed after World War I, was a significant part of the terror meted out by the Germans. While Horne and Kramer, and Zuckerman are somewhat more circumspect in offering wholesale corroboration of sexual crimes that were difficult to verify, their studies nevertheless offer an indictment of German conduct in Belgium and France that leaves open the possibility of widespread abuse of civilian populations. While these authors are inclined to discount some of the more sensational stories that gained credence during the war (particularly allegations that the Germans deliberately chopped off the hands of little children and amputated the breasts of their rape victims to mark their exposure to venereal disease), their accounts lead us to entertain the possibility that mass rape accompanied the invasion and occupation.

In the interwar period, however, accounts of sexual violence during the German occupation were widely discredited. Numerous studies appeared, revealing atrocity stories to be "hoaxes" and laying emphasis on images of sexual violence in war propaganda, rather than on the sexual violence itself. Because ample evidence existed that German outrages were instrumentally repackaged by the Allies for propaganda purposes, scholarly attention shifted from war crimes themselves to the question of public opinion and its malleability.

While it is understandable that this interpretation might have found favor in Germany, why were Allied intellectuals so ready to believe that they had been unwitting dupes and that their nations' sacrifices had been made in vain? At stake was nothing less than the legitimacy of the war itself. Wartime publicists, particularly in Britain, America, and Australia, focused much attention on sexual outrages and crimes against children, fearing, perhaps, that the selective executions of male officials, which made up the bulk of atrocities, might fail to arouse public indignation. Commenting on H. A. L. Fischer's half-hearted defense of the Bryce Report in 1927, James Morgan Read notes—I think rightly—that "If Fisher meant that the Germans distinguished themselves in Belgium by ruthless execution of civilians, he was perfectly correct; but that was not the general impression from reading the report":

The Appendix especially was filled with alleged instances of German fiendishness; one could hardly open the volume without discovering some example of a child or woman or an old man who had been killed, tortured, or mutilated in the most horrible manner conceivable. And yet the Belgian reports of 1922 failed utterly to substantiate the charges made in the Bryce Report. Thus, the report asserted that at Malines "one witness saw a German soldier cut a woman's breast after he had murdered her, and saw many other dead bodies of women in the streets." Another witness testified that at Malines a drunken soldier met a two-year-old child. "The soldier . . . drove his bayonet with both hands into the child's stomach, lifting the child into the air on his bayonet, he and his comrades still singing." The postwar Belgian report on Malines did not mention anything like either of these two cruelties.[12]

In effect, the medium of war propaganda began to compromise the evidence of actual atrocities, leaving interwar investigators with much printed and visual material to analyze, but with little interest in the forensic evidence that might have remained in the occupied territories. The emphasis on literary as opposed to physical evidence in interwar atrocity scholarship reveals a deep-seated suspicion of the motives for war and a strong desire, even among the Allies, to discredit an undertaking that cost so many male lives. As Lloyd George recalled in his postwar memoirs, "there was a growing feeling that war itself was a crime against humanity."[13] Lord Birkenhead advocated placing the Kaiser on trial for war crimes, stating directly that "the ex-Kaiser is primarily and personally responsible for the deaths of millions of young men."[14] Indeed, even at the Paris Peace Conference, where there was little questioning of the justice of the conflict, war itself had become an "atrocity." This change of mood inflected the analysis of propaganda, which was retrospectively read for its falsehood, sensationalism, and sentimentality, rather than for any underlying truth to the charges leveled at the time against Germany.

Nowhere does the melodrama of war come through more clearly than in the famous Liberty Bond campaign and other visual representations of the war that plastered hoardings and walls in those nations most distant from the conflict. While the number of posters depicting crimes against women and children were only a small percentage of the total produced in allied countries, they made a disproportionate impression and remain some of the most frequently reproduced even today. As naturalized American Paul Herberger wrote to his sister in Germany in 1917, "It is ridiculous what kind of parades tramp through the city streets the whole dear long day; Liberty Bond drive, Red Cross drive, recruiting drive, and everything with the

usual American slam bang. Veritable circus parades . . . the most undigni-
fied things are good enough, as long as they bring in the money. . . . Never in
the history of the world has a people been driven into war more lightheart-
edly than these Yankees."[15] Indeed, the more distant from the conflict, the
more flamboyant the images of violence against women used to arouse the
domestic population.[16] The result of displaying such posters was to thoroughly gender the causes of the conflict. If America, in actuality, entered the
war to combat unrestricted submarine warfare, the image most strikingly
proffered to Americans was one of violated womanhood and German rapacity. It is perhaps understandable, then, that as Americans began to doubt
the wisdom of their entry into the war, they began to doubt also those acts of
violence against women, which had proved such a graphic pretext for their
involvement.

While rumors of German atrocities in Belgium had circulated in both
the British and American press beginning shortly after the invasion of Belgium in August 1914, their veracity had been widely questioned until they
were confirmed by a group of eminent investigators appointed by the British
Crown and led by the former ambassador to the United States, Lord James
Bryce.[17] British authorities were delighted with the success of what came to
be known colloquially as the Bryce Report. Charles Masterman, the head
of the British propaganda bureau at Wellington House, wrote a congratu-
latory letter to Bryce in June, declaring that "your report has *swept* America. . . . [E]ven the most skeptical declare themselves converted just because
it is signed by you!"[18]

While the Bryce Report was greeted with widespread approval, not
all those who read it were equally impressed. In the Midwest of the United
States, where large German populations resided, in ethnic enclaves of American cities, and among pacifist intellectuals on both sides of the Atlantic,
some lingering doubts remained. Max Müller, an architect from New York,
wrote to Bryce in January 1917 asking him whether he was "going to give us
a rest with your mud slinging? You are thoroughly soaked with mud, lies
and dirt. Unfortunately you have not drowned in it but there is hope that
when the Germans will land in England they will make you prove your lies
or swallow them."[19]

More troubling, perhaps, were the more measured challenges to Bryce's
integrity appearing shortly after the war. In June 1919 a minister named
Bernard J. Snell wrote to Bryce stating that "As a minister of Religion I
have done my best to guide the thinking of the Church committed to my

care. . . . Many times I have . . . said that we could rely on yourself as utterly trustworthy. Therefore it comes as a great shock to me to read in 'Christian Register' . . . [that] 'the Bryce Report on atrocities has been withdrawn and . . . Lord Bryce regretted ever having signed it, as much of it proved to be unauthentic.'"[20] The report to which Snell is referring was presented at a meeting of the International Congress of Women held in Zurich, Switzerland. As a pacifist organization, the group had a strong stake in discrediting a rationale for war that, as Susan Kent has shown, was difficult for feminists to dismiss. Because violence against women and children seemed so incontrovertible an imperative to fight, the discrediting of the war would, in some sense, depend morally on the discrediting of its victims. If women were *not*, in fact, raped and mutilated, and children were *not*, in fact, bayoneted, eviscerated, or relieved of their hands by angry Uhlans, the morality of the war itself could be contested much less problematically. Pacifists thus had a stake in discrediting sexual crimes that had justified war to a malleable public.

Skepticism about German atrocities congealed in the years after the war. Not only did Lord Bryce receive a small but steady stream of letters from Britain and America questioning the integrity of his 1915 Report, but others seemed inclined to recant their wartime positions. In the *London Magazine* of January 1920, Lord Fisher apparently claimed that England was "fooled into the war," while the former Italian prime minister, Signor Nitti, stated in his memoirs that, "During the war France, in common with other Allies, including our own Government in Italy, circulated the most absurd inventions to arouse the fighting spirit of our people. The cruelties attributed to the Germans were such as to curdle our blood. We heard the story of poor little Belgian children whose hands were cut off by the Huns. Mr. Lloyd George and myself . . . carried on extensive investigations as to the truth of these horrible accusations. . . . Every case investigated proved to be a myth."[21] While a trickle of sources questioning atrocities appeared in the immediate aftermath of the war, it was in the late 1920s that the first wave of publications appeared discrediting or, at the very least, questioning, their veracity. Robert Graves, *Goodbye to All That*, Arthur Ponsonby's *Falsehood in War-Time*, and Harold Laswell's *Propaganda Technique in the World War* each dealt with the circulation of atrocity stories that the authors clearly believed to be patently false. According to Laswell, perhaps the most influential postwar expert on propaganda, "A handy rule for arousing hate is, if at first they do not enrage, use an atrocity."[22] A report prepared for the Serbs regarding Austro-Hungarian atrocities, for instance, placed atrocities against women and children in parallel columns, recording the number of incidents that fell into each of the following categories[23]:

> Executed or otherwise shot, Bayoneted or knifed, Throats cut, Killed, Burnt alive, Killed in massacre, Beaten to death with rifles or sticks, Stoned to death, hanged, Disembowelled, Bound and tortured on the spot, Missing, Carried off as prisoners, Wounded, Arms cut off or broken, Legs cut off or broken, Noses cut off, Ears cut off, Eyes gouged out, Sexual parts mutilated, Skin torn in strips, Flesh or scalp removed, Corpses cut into small pieces, Breasts cut off, Women violated.

Laswell's detached tone, his evenhanded treatment of all the belligerents, and his somewhat sardonic analysis of the technique itself, all belie a certain tone of authoritative skepticism. "Stress can always be laid upon the wounding of women, children, old people, priests and nuns, and upon sexual enormities, mutilated prisoners and mutilated non-combatants," commented Laswell. "These stories yield a crop of indignation against the fiendish perpetrators of these dark deeds, and satisfy certain powerful hidden impulses. A young woman, ravished by the enemy, yields secret satisfaction to a host of vicarious ravishers on the other side of the border. Hence, the popularity and ubiquity of such stories."[24]

An even more significant spate of books interrogating war propaganda and exposing its falsehood appeared between 1935 and 1939, following the investigation of the Nye commission on U.S. munitions. Suspicious that American intervention had been orchestrated by capitalist munitions makers bent on easy profits even at the expense of human life, Americans began to regard their entry into the war as part of a conspiracy between interested parties at home and abroad. The "exposure" of atrocity stories was central to this narrative of American involvement. According to H. C. Peterson, "Sex stories . . . were among the most effective [forms of propaganda] and were given wide circulation by the American traveling-salesmen public." Excerpting from the Bryce Report, Peterson relates the story of twenty girls who were allegedly laid on tables in a public square and gang-raped by twelve German soldiers. "This story is undoubtedly the work of someone's feverish imagination," commented Peterson. "If it were not the work of one of Bryce's clerks or atrocity collectors, it was probably an ordinary barrack-room classic."[25] Peterson's dismissal of the report seems to be based largely on its lack of plausibility, rather than any empirical evidence. By the 1930s the atrocity stories of World War I lacked the ring of truth and found few defenders. Indeed, for Peterson, the Bryce Report was "in itself one of the worst atrocities of the war."[26] The definitive work in this genre of schol-arly literature was perhaps James Morgan Read's influential *Atrocity Propa-ganda, 1914–1919*, first published by Yale University Press in 1941, reprinted in 1976, and still cited as evidence of the fabricated nature of German atroc-ities during World War I. Judicious in tone, thoroughly researched, and inclined to give credence to some accounts, Read's work is perhaps the most cited work on atrocity propaganda to this day. Yet, given the abundant evi-dence of atrocities cited by Horne and Kramer and by Ruth Harris, why did transatlantic skepticism emerge among the victors themselves? And how are such two diametrically opposed assessments of the veracity of atrocity reports possible, coming from well-respected scholars, publishing with the same university press, albeit two generations apart?

The most common explanation has been political. Scholars have noted that isolationist feeling in the United States led to a suspicion of European entanglements and a belief that the United States was somehow lured into war against its own best interests. Pacifist sentiment in Britain functioned in a similar manner. According to Horne and Kramer, "Retrospective disil-lusionment with the war and growing scepticism at war propaganda led to the view that 'German atrocities' were the invention of wartime Allied gov-ernments wishing to prolong the slaughter."[27] Significant numbers of de-bunking works were written by scholars with German sympathies, such as George Sylvester Viereck, or pacifist intellectuals, like Arthur Ponsonby, who wished to vindicate unpopular political positions that they had held dur-ing the war.[28] Self-congratulatory works by propagandists like George Creel in America and Sir Campbell Stuart in Britain did nothing to allay fears that powerful, and possibly corrupt, forces were managing the sentiments of democratic populations unable to make reasoned political decisions.[29]

Indeed, the exposure of verifiably false atrocity stories and the discov-ery of the deceptive techniques employed by even the most respected pro-pagandists led to the questioning of all war crimes, particularly as British documents regarding the intentional manipulation of public opinion were inadvertently made public in America. The Dumfries atrocity hoax, in which a fifteen-year-old Scottish girl claimed that her sister's breasts had been cut off, and the story of a corpse conversion factory, in which the For-eign Office purported that the Germans were turning their casualties into soap and margarine, were discredited quickly and are included in almost all debunking studies. The private correspondence surrounding the prep-aration of the Bryce Report did little to allay fears about its integrity. Let-ters from members of the committee to Bryce made it clear that not all the signatories found the evidence to be reliable and cast doubt on whether the evidence was authentic at all, or rather prepared in the general spirit of other reports, without any independent verification.[30] To make matters even worse, a vast archive of official material documenting the British propaganda efforts in America mysteriously found its way to Stanford University, where outraged American scholars were able to peruse reports suggesting that they had been the unwitting victims of a deliberate and studied attempt to shape neutral opinion.

Postwar gender relations, however, also shaped the increasingly critical examination of "propaganda" by interwar scholars. Both Britain and the United States saw broad expansions of the franchise in the postwar years, with the enfranchisement of women creating deep anxieties about an emotional electorate, which could be subject to sentimental and irrational appeals by powerful demagogues. In a spate of postwar works on "propaganda" even the most reassuring were far from encouraging to those who feared the manipulation of democracy by the press and unscrupulous politicians. According to the theorist Edward Bernays, writing in the 1920s, "The conscious and intelligent manipulation of the organized habits and opinions of the masses is an important element in democratic society. Those who manipulate this unseen mechanism of society constitute an invisible government which is the true ruling power of our country. We are governed, our minds are molded, our tastes formed, our ideas suggested, largely by men we have never heard of."[31] While Bernays believed that such forces were part of the normal working of democracy, many other commentators presumed this "invisible government" to be a malign force and the "propaganda" it spread to be ipso facto false. Such fears were echoed in Britain with the frequently expressed anxiety about the "Americanization" of the British press and an open hostility to the extension of an equal franchise to women, who were presumed to be the most susceptible to this new media. The opposition to an equal franchise for women, however, also had other implications that were directly linked to the issue of masculine suffering in the Great War. The duchess of Athol opposed equal suffrage in 1924, because the preponderance of women on the register would be "largely due to . . . the fact that we lost 740,000 precious lives of men in the Great War. . . . To propose a great extension of this kind looks like taking advantage of the heroic sacrifice of those men."[32] This theme would modulate discussions of the moral of the war and would shape retrospective readings of war crimes themselves.

The masculine nature of suffering was a central trope for critics of propaganda who wished to draw new moral conclusions from the war.

If idealists like Wilson and Bryce had depicted World War I as a crusade to save civilization from the forces of barbarism, the horror of war itself soon took precedence as the moral of the conflict.[33] While Jay Winter and others have argued that idealism over the objectives of the war persisted into the interwar period, such faith certainly coexisted with a more cynical retrospective outlook on the conflict.[34] For those who still believed in the righteousness of the war, its moral and causes were sanitized and masculinized, recalling the heroic public school spirit that had inspired men to stick by their comrades and demonstrated the worth of British soldiers.[35] Far more influential was the angry retrospective on the conflict.[36] For Robert Graves and his cohort, the slaughter of young men—not the rape of Belgian women—took precedence as the locus of pity evoked by the war. "We no longer believed the highly coloured accounts of German atrocities in Belgium; knowing the Belgians now at first-hand," recalled Graves. "By atrocities we meant, specifically, rape, mutilation and torture . . ." Although Graves acknowledged the brutal impact of war on civilian populations, he blamed all sides equally and regarded much of it to be unintentional collateral damage. "French and Belgian civilians had often tried to win our sympathy by exhibiting mutilations of children—stumps of hands and feet, for instance—representing them as deliberate, fiendish atrocities when, as likely as not, they were merely the result of shell-fire," commented Graves detachedly. "We did not believe rape to be any more common on the German side of the line than on the Allied side. And since a bully-beef diet, fear of death, and absence of wives made ample provision of women necessary in the occupied areas, no doubt the German Army authorities provided brothels. . . . We did not believe stories of women's forcible enlistment in these establishments. 'What's wrong with the voluntary system?' we asked cynically."[37]

Discrediting accounts of violence against women was also a convenient way to undermine the moral case for intervention and to shift collective pity to those who fought. When asked by his rector to read war poems at a memorial service in Oxfordshire, Graves rejected Rupert Brooke and instead "read some of the more painful poems by Sassoon and Wilfred Owen about men dying from gas poisoning, and about buttocks of corpses bulging from the mud. . . . I also suggested that the . . . survivors should thank God they were alive, and do their best to avoid wars in the future."[38] Graves's sympathy is reserved exclusively for the young men who fought in the war. The juxtaposition of the meretricious suffering alleged by female Belgian victims with the real suffering of young British men, reversed the order of sacrifice demanded by the war. If men had been encouraged to enlist to help the victimized women and children of Belgium, the discrediting of female suffering highlighted the purposelessness of their sacrifice. Pitting the claims of foreign women against those of British men, writers like Graves discredited atrocity reports for rhetorical, aesthetic, and moral purposes, rather than because of compelling new evidence. Indeed, the shadowy "lady investigator" cited at the beginning of this chapter remains as mysterious as the anonymous sources cited in wartime atrocity pamphlets. The tendency of interwar readers to credit debunking investigations over the similarly underdocumented ones of the earlier Bryce committee, reflects a shift in national mood that emphasized the masculine and civic nature of suffering over the altruistic concern for foreign (and female) victims that dominated the propaganda of the war years.

This shift in the locus of sentiment was accompanied by a parallel aesthetic shift in the language and images used to evoke pity. Writers like Robert Graves, Sigfried Sassoon, and Eric Maria Remarque turned to a gruesome battlefield realism to capture the unadorned horror of male death. This poetic style was developed in explicit contrast to the feminized "newspaper language" spoken by overwrought civilians on the home front.[39] One of the most admired aspects of the Bryce Report was its "dispassionate" and "objective" language, which was a flat, bureaucratic, and therefore apparently truthful style of nonflamboyant narration. Yet much of the more popular atrocity material that drew on the Bryce Report showed no such restraint. A letter from Colonel R. P. Dickerson, of the National Loyalty League in Springfield, Montana, to "William of Hohenzollern" demonstrates the bombastic evocation of female suffering that went out of fashion after the war. As Dickerson wrote to the Kaiser in 1917, "You in the estimation of the world outside of Germany make Timour, Tamerlane, Atilla, Alaric, Xerxes, Napoleon, Nero, Caligula, and Tiberius and other destroyers of human life, honor, soul, and property seem small and puny by comparison."[40]

> Do the stumped arms of little children reach out to you in your dreams? Do the horror-streaked eyes of outraged women haunt you in your sleep? . . . Do the souls of unborn children cry to you at midnight as the souls of their mothers cried when the bayonets of your Prussians pierced them? And do the myriad of souls of little children that might have been born of the multitudes of young that you have killed crowd about you in the gloaming and cry: "Oh Kaiser! But for you we might have had fathers and might have had mothers and might have been born of love and lived in love and seen God."

The rhetorical and visual excesses of atrocity propaganda came to seem almost comical to skeptics, whose ranks increased during the interwar period. "The dear people are so stupid that the papers, which are influenced . . . by the ammunition manufacturers . . . can feed them anything," commented one German-American living in Seattle to his sister in 1917. "Can you imagine that our Ernest could commit such cruelties as the English lies spread to the whole world? Do you believe that he would run his bayonet through small children, and eat them up without pepper and salt, like the newspapers here preach it to the people every day, and which the uneducated masses like to read." Paul Herberger's attitude to such stories went from initial anger to humor and disbelief. "Shortly before I left Seattle, a Belgian countess gave lectures in which she told the people that she had seen with her own eyes how German soldiers threw chocolate to the hungry children, and, when the children tried to grab the chocolate, that the soldiers cut off their little hands. Now, is it not too ridiculous? But the dear people here believe all those things and want to hear more cruelties. . . . The whole slander does not arouse my ire any more; it is funny, and it amuses me."[41]

The exaggerated tone of popular atrocity narratives contributed to the incredulity of interwar audiences. In his preface to *Crimes of Germany*, Theodore Cook could not resist the most extravagant rhetorical flourishes: "The Prussian soldier . . . is admired by the whole German nation . . . not because he is as ready as any soldier . . . to sacrifice his life . . . but because he is ready and willing to kill everything living in his path. . . . In Belgium he was not content with bayoneting babies; he laboriously chopped their little toys to pieces."[42] Such assertions were sometimes illustrated by comic drawings of German atrocities. Indeed, atrocities were far more likely to be conveyed to the public through cartoons than through photographs. A 1917 edition of *Crimes of Germany* is effectively illustrated with photographs, many of them architectural ruins, but others showing the bodies of the dead and wounded. Another edition, however, was illustrated with satirical cartoons by Jean-Gabriel Domergue. Domergue, Will Dyson, Louis Raemaekers, and many lesser known illustrators exhibited and published atrocity cartoons, some of which were extraordinarily influential in creating a visual impression of German rapacity. Yet, while Raemaekers's cartoons had a disturbing realist quality, many others were clearly intended to be sardonically amusing. Because cartoons and drawings were often more readily available and widely reproduced than photographs, skeptics could conclude that atrocities were an imaginative fabrication.

Arthur Ponsonby famously debunked the allegation that Belgian priests had been used by the Germans as bell clappers. According to Ponsonby, Germans had instructed the priests of one occupied town to ring the church bells. As the report was passed from one person to another and from one newspaper to another, it metamorphosed into the gruesome story of the priestly bell clappers, thus becoming another atrocity story. When James Morgan Read investigated Ponsonby's evidence, however, he discovered that no such stories had been reported in the papers Ponsonby cited. Instead, Read found the account in the *Norddeutsche Allgemeine Zeitung* of July 4, 1915, and concluded that it was a piece of German satire, ridiculing the allied press. What Read's discovery reveals is that the perpetuation of the "myth" of atrocities, like the perpetuation of atrocity stories themselves, took on a life of its own. Indeed, narratives made up of an unverifiable concoction of truth and fabrication could seem plausible at one moment and implausible the next.

In the postwar period the overwrought language used to describe atrocities seemed to sow the seeds of suspicion. Hemingway's dislike of "big words" found a parallel in the suspicion of the rhetorical excesses of the penny press and the assumption that such flamboyance was incompatible with truth. In *How We Advertised America*, George Creel dealt repeatedly with the charges by Republicans that he used "bombastic" and therefore untrue language to promote the war.[43] To Creel the work of the Committee on Public Information was to "fight for the 'verdict of mankind.' . . . In all things first to last, without halt or change, it was a plain publicity proposition, a vast enterprise in salesmanship, the world's greatest adventure in advertising."[44] To those unsure of the merits of U.S. involvement in the war, such an appraisal was probably far from reassuring. Once again, words, bombast, and the flamboyant use of untrustworthy information to arouse joy or horror seemed to explain America's slide away from splendid isolationism. In retrospect, the words and images used to inflame passions over even indisputably true events, like the sinking of the Lusitania, seemed meretricious and even deceptive. In such a context, propaganda, rather than war crimes themselves, became the focus of analysis; the Leipzig trials, the intention to "hang the Kaiser," and the search for victims of war receded as international issues outside of the invaded communities.

Yet the changing credence given to such events opens up questions of both historical and contemporary interest. What are the political and cultural factors that shape the tendency to believe or disbelieve in the credibility of remote events? Whether they be weapons of mass destruction or Guatemalan disappearances, our willingness to believe may be dictated more by our political sentiments than by inaccessible evidence. In an age when the propaganda apparatus of the modern state has been used for the purpose of fabricating information as well as publicizing hidden crimes, the remote spectator may lose faith in factuality and begin to believe whatever fits most easily into his or her already forged worldview. Whether it be the severed hands of Belgian babies, the attack on the Maddox in the Gulf of Tonkin, the murder of Kuwaiti incubator babies during the first Gulf War, or the "incontrovertible evidence" of weapons of mass destruction, presented to the United Nations by Secretary of State Colin Powell, the instrumental manipulation of "facts" for the purposes of state-sponsored propaganda has eroded the credibility of even the most liberal states. The consequences have been dire indeed. Mark Wollaeger notes that one of the most important results of the propaganda campaign during World War I was "the transformation of factual enumeration into a form of rhetoric divorced from empirical grounding, and the formation of what Walter Lippman called a 'pseudo-environment' of mediated images."[45]

During the twentieth century, justifications of war have often depended on humanitarian enormities. The importance of democratic public opinion and the ready availability of information, even in relatively authoritarian societies, have meant that emotional appeals to mass audiences have become a primary mode of distinguishing just from unjust wars. In this context even unquestionably true atrocities become politically instrumental, and those in opposition frequently engage in the denial of actual events. Mahmoud Amedinajad thus organized a conference of Holocaust deniers in Iran to relativize the Holocaust and undercut the moral legitimacy of the state of Israel. In its exasperation to preserve the truth of the Holocaust, the European Union has sought to criminalize Holocaust denial, using the law to shore up the failing edifice of historical judgment. Such a debate could only take place in a realm where facts have lost much of their authority.

For those who are remote from the events themselves, news of war crimes invites a leap of faith—the choice to believe or doubt. Whether we, as remote spectators, choose to believe may have less to do with whether or not the reported horrors are true, than with whether or not we find the implications of believing them acceptable or unacceptable. For feminists the challenges posed by the malleability of facts are all the more fraught. On one hand, feminist activists and social scientists have spent much time trying to publicize acts of rape in war; on the other hand, scholars of gender have contributed to the unmooring of "fact" by pointing out the instrumental way that information about gender and biology has been used historically to buttress the oppression of women. The politicization of the modern "fact" has cast empirical evidence into doubt and made the verification and response to atrocities all the more difficult to secure. This analysis is not meant to endorse a postmodern understanding of the relativity of facts. In precisely the opposite way, it is meant to affirm the reality of facts—including barbaric acts—before their manipulation, invention, or embroidering by the twin forces of government and media. What it attempts to highlight, however, is the way the repeated manipulation of facts for the purpose of propaganda has created a relativist environment in which individuals feel justified in regarding truth as "opinion" and choosing, without reference to evidence, what to believe or doubt.

Such discussions must be infuriating to the actual victims of war. For every Anne Frank there are no doubt a million others like her who were not able to tell their stories. Relief workers in Darfur note what seems to be genocide fatigue, when they fail to excite interest or compassion among those able to offer relief to the Sudanese victims of rape. In a context where mass suffering leaves remote spectators unmoved—or, worse still, unconvinced—it is perhaps literature, broadly defined, that holds out our best hope of conveying the truth. The memoir, the novel, and the film offer a personalized narrative of victimhood still able to move the distant spectator to pity, belief, and compassion. After World War I, literature by soldier-writers like Robert Graves, Eric Maria Remarque, and Henri Barbusse did much to make resonant the terrible suffering of men in the trenches. What mass statistics could not convey, personal accounts could. The social scientific amassment of data, while crucial to establishing the truth of sexual violence in conflict zones, may have to be combined with individual stories of suffering and human loss so as to move us to act once again.

Chapter 7
Sexual and Nonsexual Violence Against "Politicized Women" in Central Europe After the Great War

Robert Gerwarth

He handed me a revolver. I took my own, however, and automatically advanced one step . . . her lips did not move: hardly aware of what she was doing she had begun to unbutton the upper half of her jacket, as if I were about to press the revolver against her very heart. I must admit that the few thoughts I had at the moment went out to that body, so alive and warm . . . and I felt pangs of something like regret, absurdly enough, for the children that this woman might have borne, who would have inherited her courage and her eyes. I fired, turning my head away like a frightened child setting off a torpedo on Christmas Eve. The first shot did no more than tear open the face. . . . On the second shot everything was over.

Fictional and embedded within a tragic love story, the killing of the Bolshevik partisan Sophie von Reval by the young German officer Erich von Lhomond during the German *Freikorps*' Baltic campaign of 1919–20 remains one of the most widely known accounts of paramilitary violence against women in the immediate aftermath of the Great War. Written by the internationally acclaimed Belgian novelist Marguerite Yourcenar (the first woman ever to become a member of the Académie française), this final scene of *Coup de grâce* (1939) touches on the use of violence against women in the broader context of the White Terror, which haunted most of East-Central Europe after the end of the Great War. Although scholars have recently paid more attention to the Great War's Eastern front than has traditionally been the case, we still know relatively little about the civil wars and paramilitary campaigns that occurred in the post-World War I combat zones of East-Central Europe after the war officially ended in November 1918.[1] As this chapter demonstrates, "politicized women," including women with "revolutionary" family ties, were a primary target group of the paramilitary violence that haunted Central Europe after 1918. The torture and killing of Rosa Luxemburg in January 1919 may be the most prominent example of violence against women in the period, but it was by no means an isolated event. Apart from accounts of Bavarian and Austrian *Freikorps* soldiers shooting captured Communist women "for target practice" after the crushing of the Munich *Räterepublik* (Soviet Republic), activists fondly remembered having whipped a captured working-class woman "until there was no white spot left on her back."[2] Another paramilitary involved in the 1920 fighting in the Ruhr proudly reported in a letter to his family. "We even shot ten Red Cross nurses. . . . We shot these little ladies with pleasure—how they cried and pleaded with us to save their lives. Nothing doing!"[3] The British Joint Labour Delegation, which published a first-hand account on *The White Terror in Hungary* in 1920 after conducting extensive interviews with surviving victims, also listed incidents of murder, gender-specific torture, and enforced sexual intercourse between prisoners committed by men who often emphasized their "moral superiority" over the "Communist enemy."[4]

This chapter examines these rituals of violence against "politicized women" with the aim of explaining the peculiarities of gender-specific violence in Central Europe immediately after the end of the Great War. If the underlying assumption of this volume is that war, rape, and other acts of violence against women are inseparable, this chapter investigates the particular circumstances in postwar Central Europe that led to violence against those women who were considered deviant (from the paramilitary activists' conception of "ideal womanhood") and politically dangerous. Although rapes certainly occurred, one of the peculiarities of this case study is that while the perpetrators happily confessed to brutal torture and the mutilation of female bodies as well as killings of "politicized" women in their published memoirs and diaries, they never mentioned rape. The relative absence of rape in perpetrators', as well as victims', accounts of the White Terror after the Great War suggests two different interpretations: either rape remained the exception in this particular zone of conflict, or it was not mentioned in the autobiographical accounts because it was considered an act irreconcilable with their military "honor" (by the perpetrators) or an act that exposed them to social stigmatization (by the victims). While the former officers who formed the backbone of paramilitary fighting units considered the killing and "disciplining" of "politicized women" perfectly legitimate, rape was seen as a morally unjustifiable act. To understand this peculiar "logic" of violence against women, it is important to reconstruct the moral parameters of the perpetrators and the concrete historical circumstances under which they acted.

This chapter focuses on the three major successor states of the collapsed Central European empires: Germany, Austria, and Hungary. While it is evident that an account of postwar paramilitary violence against women could have included other "related" forms of right-wing activity in Europe, for example in Italy, Romania, Finland, Russia, and perhaps even in Ireland during the paramilitary campaign of the "Black and Tans," there is good reason to believe that the militias in Germany, Austria, and Hungary were shaped by distinct influences that distinguished them from comparable movements in other parts of Europe. After four years of fighting in a common war against the Allied Powers, all three countries experienced the trauma of defeat in the Great War as well as the shock of revolution and democratization in the winter of 1918–19. The relatively bloodless democratic revolutions in Central Europe in November 1918 led to the simultaneous proclamation of republics in Germany (9 November), Austria (12 November), and Hungary (16 November), and the enfranchisement of women in all three countries. The perceived threat posed by Communist women and female political emancipation in the specific context of war, defeat, and revolution triggered a brutal suppression of women involved in, or associated with, the revolutionary upheavals of 1918–19.

The White Terror directed against the perceived internationalist threats of Bolshevism, Jewry, and feminism culminated in the bloody suppression of Rosa Luxemburg's and Karl Liebknecht's "Spartakist Uprising" in Berlin, the crushing of the Munich *Räterepublik* by German and Austrian *Freikorps*, and the violent retribution following the fall of the Communist Béla Kun regime in Hungary in 1919. Violent counter-revolutionary activities continued unabated for years after the collapse of the short-lived Communist regimes of Central Europe, most notably (but by no means exclusively) in the disputed borderlands of Upper Silesia, the Baltic states, the Austrian Burgenland, and Carinthia. Although the exact figure of both male and female deaths, rapes, and mutilations caused by the White Terror is impossible to establish, it is certain that tens of thousands of people fell victim to paramilitary violence in the immediate postwar years.[5] Although the vast majority of the victims were men, killed either in combat or after their surrender, the memoirs, diaries, and letters of paramilitary activists indicate quite clearly that the number of female victims was more than marginal.

Scholarly analysis of counter-revolutionary violence against "politicized women" has traditionally been overshadowed by the attempt to demonstrate the degree of extreme nationalist opposition to the German, Austrian, and Hungarian postwar republics as well as the role of the militias as "vanguards of Nazism."[6] The most widely known exception to this general neglect is, of course, Klaus Theweleit's *Male Fantasies*, a psychoanalytical account of German protofascist "soldier males" first published in German thirty years ago.[7] Drawing on Freud, Reich, Deleuze, and Guattari, Theweleit used memoir literature to analyze the "deformed" psychological structures of the soldier male's mind. His account is particularly strong in identifying passages in the memoir literature that point to incidents of violence against women committed by *Freikorps* men.

In explaining *Freikorps* violence against women, Theweleit emphasizes the dichotomous perception of women by the "soldier males," who distinguish categorically between the desexualized and depersonalized nurse or wife and the threatening and sexually evocative rifle women, or female partisans (*Flintenweiber*). The hard and "disciplined" body of the warrior is contrasted with the soft, "fluid" female body, which the warrior violently rejects and ultimately aims to destroy. Theweleit's investigation places particular emphasis on the origins of these perceptions and psychological dispositions. Using Freudian psychoanalysis of child development, he attempts to explain the disrupted development of the "soldier males" by means of a disturbed mother-child relationship and the activists' paramilitary socialization in Wilhelmine Germany. Despite Theweleit's stimulating analysis, many historians have rightfully criticized his psychohistorical approach, most notably his application of individual psychology to larger social groups.[8]

Apart from moving beyond an exclusively German context of investigation, this account of postwar paramilitary violence will differ from Theweleit's interpretation in two important ways. First, it will be suggested that counter-revolutionary violence against women was not indicative of a "universal" "soldier male" mindset but was peculiar to a specific group of soldiers who shared similar experiences in the defeated Central European empires. It seems important to point out in this context that out of the roughly twenty million soldiers of the Central Powers who had participated in (and survived) the Great War, only a small minority of men participated in postwar paramilitary atrocities. Second, this article will abandon Theweleit's methodologically problematic emphasis on the individual psychology of perpetrators in favor of a greater emphasis on group dynamics and a peculiar "logic" of gendered violence that resulted from these para-military group dynamics. It will be suggested that within the paramilitary units, violence against "politicized women" was not perceived as deviant behavior, but as a "legitimate" response to restore "order" and to "discipline" women whom they considered to be a threat to "healthy" gender relations and society as a whole.

An investigation of paramilitary violence against "politicized women" in Central Europe after the Great War can build on some recent publica-tions on paramilitary violence in Central Europe[9] as well as on a rich body of primary sources; yet, any analysis is confronted with a problem famil-iar to many historians of violence in civil war conflicts, namely, the relative absence of victims' voices—voices that have been silenced by murder or fear of social stigmatization.

Most important for a chapter that explains the paramilitaries' actions and perceptions of a "hostile" outside world in general and "politicized women" more specifically, are the numerous memoirs, diaries, and letters written by former activists, in which the experiences of the immediate post-war period are narrated from a personal perspective. Handled with care and measured against other evidence such as police files, court testimonies, and a few surviving victims' accounts, these personal documents provide illumi-nating insights into the moral framework of the activists and shed new light on the Central European zone of postwar paramilitary violence.

Manifestations of Violence

In the winter of 1919–20, an advancing *Freikorps* unit in Latvia captured a Communist woman named Marja who was accused of having tortured Ger-man prisoners in the embattled city of Mitau. The commanding officer, a man called Pahlen, ordered that the prisoner should not be shot but beaten to death with a whip. When continuing their advance, the troops paraded alongside the publicly displayed body of the woman: "The last body which they ride past seems to be that of a woman. It is difficult to tell, however, because it is a bloody mass—a lump of meat totally cut up by whips—that lies in the red mash of snow."[10]

The brutal murder of a female prisoner of war and the subsequent dis-play of her mutilated corpse testified to a new quality of violence against women in the period largely unseen in Germany and the Habsburg Empire since the days of the Thirty Years' War. To be sure, atrocities against enemy populations, including women and children, during the Great War are well documented, but they were never directed against members of the perpetrators' own national community.[11] Furthermore, violence against women was considered a punishable crime by the military authorities of the Central Powers, and even some of the paramilitary activists of the postwar period were conscious of the "duty of protection of the female gender which a soldier must obey."[12]

The end of the Great War and the partial collapse of state authority in November 1918 changed the situation profoundly, in that it "liberated" those determined to continue their soldierly lifestyle in paramilitary units from the "constraints" of military discipline. Despite the vague distinctions between combatants and noncombatants during the Great War and the tentative observance of the general rules of combat, it was now the paramilitaries who decided which targets were "legitimate" in the embattled regions of the postwar period. The transformation of the war between states war into a civil war had a profound impact on the treatment of enemy soldiers and captives, both male and female.

An example that illustrates the new expression of violence against women is the well-documented case of a Hungarian woman, Mrs. Hamburger, whose brother-in-law had been a People's Commissary during the Kun regime. She was arrested on the charge of "Bolshevik activities" and, apparently at the command of the militia leader István Héjjas, subjected to torture in the Kelenföld barracks in the outskirts of Budapest. The report by the British Joint Labour Delegation on the White Terror describes in great detail her ordeals, which deserve to be quoted in full as a rare example of a victim's account: "Three of the officers who had whips beat Mrs. H with them severely and ordered her to strip. She refused, when she was beaten again and again until she finally gave way and stripped. When naked she was again beaten." Another prisoner, Béla Neumann (a male), was brought from the cellar and

> commanded to rape Mrs. H. He refused, saying that he was an old friend of Mrs. and Mr. Hamburger. They beat him unmercifully, but he still refused. Then two officers . . . took pincers and pulled out Neumann's teeth. . . . Mrs. H. fainted two or three times, but was each time revived by douches of cold water. She says the officers were not drunk. Finally, before the eyes of Mrs. H., they castrated him with a pocket knife. Neumann was then carried away. Another man was then brought up. . . . They stripped him, when Mrs. H. observed that he had been maltreated and one

of his genital organs crushed in some way. He too was ordered to violate her. He was physically unable to do so, but the officers forced him to make advances on her. Next they ordered Mrs. H. to sit naked on a hot stove . . . [and one of the officers] inserted the handle of his whip into her body, twisting it, so that she suffers still from frequent hemorrhage.[13]

Quite apart from being a rare victim's account, the case of Mrs. Hamburger is remarkable because it tells us about the rituals of (sexually charged) degradation employed by the militia men in their desire to humiliate, hurt, and (in the case of Naumann) kill the perceived "enemy." Because of the lack of reliable evidence, it is difficult to determine whether or not it is atypical that she was not raped by the militiamen themselves.[14]

How can we explain these patterns of gender-specific violence in the context of the Central European counter-revolution? Part of a possible explanation for the use of brutal violence against women after 1918 is certainly the dehumanizing experience of the Great War and its effect on gender roles. The often ritualistic torture of "Bolshevik women" and the public display of their dead bodies were partly an expression of a new ultramilitarized masculinity, hardened on the mechanized battlefields of the Great War. Recent research into the Great War as a watershed in gender relations has demonstrated quite clearly that the war had profound implications for ideas of masculinity in Europe, particularly in those countries that were vanquished.[15] George Mosse's work on Germany, for example, has shown how the Great War and the experience of defeat brought about a reaction that recast the stereotype of masculinity as one dominated by the experience of war and wartime camaraderie. This cult of virility, forged in the trenches, spread throughout Europe in the wake of protofascist movements and contrasted sharply with the allegedly effeminate world of democratization, peace and, of course, increasing female political emancipation, which these soldiers experienced when they returned to their homelands in 1918.[16] Many future activists felt that defeat had devalued their lives and careers, but the loss of their uniforms and social prestige made it difficult for them to be reconciled with a world "turned upside down."[17] Such perceptions certainly had repercussions on gender relations. In Joseph Roth's insightful novel about the paramilitary activist Theodor Lohse, *The Spider's Web* (1923), the protagonist is severely traumatized by the loss of his lieutenant uniform, with which "his belief in his own power" to approach a woman "had gone":

What inkling had he now of women? His were the cheap little girls, the hurried minutes of cold love in the darkness of a vestibule, or in some alcove, haunted by the fear that the neighbors might come home unexpectedly, the pleasure which died away at the sound of an unexpected footstep and the glow of warmth which cooled off, raw and wet. His was the barefoot simpleton from the north, the woman with the angular rough hands and the crude caresses, chill to the touch, with sweaty stockings and dirty underclothes.[18]

Textual analysis of activists' memoirs and diaries further reveals that the acceptance of defeat, revolution, and democratization were stigmatized as feminine, while resistance to these developments was seen as masculine behavior. The semiclandestine world of paramilitary movements in Central Europe thus provided an exclusively male counterculture to the allegedly feminine world of democratic emancipation.[19] If democratization and the rise of individualism were accused of causing moral degeneration, then the nation's pride could only be restored when masculinity had been reforged. This restoration of masculinity required the restoration of male domination over women's bodies.

Another important aspect for the explanation of violence against women after 1918 was the creation of subcultures in which the torture and killing of "rebellious" women was an acceptable form of behavior. Instead of focusing on "abnormal" psychological conditions, sadism, and the early childhood traumas of perpetrators (which may or may not be true), it is more important to focus on the group dynamics and moral framework of the perpetrator groups, whose attitude toward violence against women was distinctly different from the rest of society and indeed from the vast majority of soldiers who returned home after the war.

To understand the pattern of brutal violence against women after 1918, it is therefore necessary to look closely at the distinct subculture of the perpetrators—their perceptions of women and their radicalization process. The vast majority of perpetrators came from occupational backgrounds that were directly affected by the experience of defeat (i.e., the military) or the process of democratization and female emancipation (i.e., institutions of higher education). When we consider the social and educational backgrounds of those who actively participated in the militias of Central Europe after 1918, we encounter a relatively homogeneous group of activists, at least in terms of age and social background. The vast majority of activists were between twenty and thirty years old, some were under eighteen, but very few were over forty. Many activists were junior officers, particularly lieutenants and captains, who had fought for four years in the Austrian-Hungarian or German armies against the Allied Powers (Great Britain, the French Republic, and Russia). The brutality of the war had instilled in them a disregard for the value of life and had weakened past moral restraints.[20] The experience of defeat, revolution, and perceived national humiliation in the Treaties of Versailles, St. Germain, and Trianon seemingly invalidated their personal and collective sacrifices during the war. Very often, defeat and the perceived humiliation of the nation were associated with recollections of "politicized" women as one of the driving forces in the communist revolutions in Central Europe. Captain Hermann Ehrhardt, for example, described how his brigade encountered a large group of Communist women during their march into Braunschweig: "The advance was smooth, without any resistance; only at Gliesmarode there was a small incident. Here, the female workers of the local canning plant had positioned themselves. They . . . cursed and spat and screamed."[21]

The second largest group in the militias were officer cadets and nationalist students eager to prove themselves in battle. The militias provided them with the opportunity to make up for the missed opportunity of fighting in the Great War. Together, the former officers and the younger volunteers formed explosive subcultures of ultramilitant masculinity in which brutal violence was an acceptable form of political expression and the most common way to prove one's manliness. Their violence was channeled through German, Austrian, and Hungarian variants of the stab-in-the-back myth, which identified those responsible for weakening the home front, and causing military defeat and the revolutions of Central Europe—namely Jews, left-wing intellectuals and politicians, and "politicized" women.[22]

It would be wrong, however, to suggest that all militiamen shared the same motivations for getting involved in paramilitary fighting units and for resorting to violence against women. Catch phrases such as the *Freikorps* spirit" in Germany, the "Szeged Idea" in Hungary (Szeged being the headquarters of Horthy's counter-revolutionary National Army in 1919), or the ideas underpinning the "Korneuburger Oath" of the Austrian *Heimwehr* (Austrian Home Defense League) movement, are clearly suggesting a unity of political aims and motivations that never existed. They were retrospective constructions of unity that were intended to give meaning to violent actions that were usually carried out without a univocal political agenda. In fact, the counter-revolutionary movements of Central Europe were highly fragmented in that there were peasant movements in Carinthia and western Hungary, strong monarchist forces as well as protofascist activists who despised the monarchy nearly as much as they hated Communism. Yet, as long as the perceived threats of "international Bolshevism," "international

Jewry," and "international feminism," as well as a fear of national decay and territorial disintegration persisted, there was a clear common goal that temporarily seemed more important than disagreements about the future form of government. Still, in 1931 the German-born assassin of Rosa Luxemburg and subsequent military organizer of the Austrian *Heimwehr*, Waldemar Pabst, wrote a political program for a White International, his "favorite child of the future," in which he articulated a "minimal consensus" for counter-revolutionary movements across Europe[23]:

> The path towards a new Europe lies in the submission of men and women under the eternal laws that determine any positive life in a state or community. It lies in the replacement of the old Trinity of the French Revolution [*liberté, egalité, fraternité*] which has proven to be false, sterile, and destructive with a new Trinity: authority, order, justice. . . . Only on the basis of this spirit can a *new* Europe be built, a Europe that is currently torn up by class war and suffocated with hypocrisy.[24]

The restoration of "order" to which Pabst and others were aspiring included the brutal suppression of those women involved in (or associated with) Bolshevism. Given the "existential" nature of the struggle, the use of violence was acceptable if it served the purpose of "disciplining" the disorderly, of "teaching them a lesson" by humiliating or killing them "to set an example."

Despite all existing differences (as well as obvious dissimilarities in terms of individual personalities), the paramilitary activists all openly condemned the values of liberal society. They despised socialism and feminism while praising youth and masculinity. If we look at recruitment posters for paramilitary units in 1918, for example, it is evident that they were first and foremost promoting the values of male honor, strength, camaraderie, sacrifice, adventure, respect for ranks, and love for the fatherland. They praised the virile warrior who fights against both the external threat and a society "feminized" by democracy.[25]

Furthermore, the activists firmly believed in violence as a creative force. The Hungarian officer, Miklós Kozma, who had spent the war as a hussar under the command of the German General von Mackensen, fantasized about violent retribution when in early August 1919 he wrote:

> We shall see to it . . . that the flame of nationalism leaps high. . . . We shall also punish those who for months have committed heinous crimes must receive their punishment. It is predictable . . . that the compromisers and those with weak stomachs will moan and groan when we line up a few red rogues and terrorists against the wall. The false slogans of humanism and

other isms have helped to drive the country into ruin before. This second time they will wail in vain.[26]

Violent fantasies such as these often went hand in hand with an aesthetic glamorization of violence as a healthy "cleansing act" that would "cure" society from the ills of modernity—namely, internationalism, Bolshevism, and feminism. In a remarkable passage of Ernst von Salomon's autobiographical book *Die Geächteten* (*The Outlaws*), for example, the author describes the rituals of violence that dominated his *Freikorps* experience in the Baltic campaign of 1919–20, an account that could equally have been written during the German war of annihilation in Eastern Europe after 1941:

> We ran over fields of snow and stormed into the forests. We fired into surprised crowds and we raged, we shot and hunted. We chased the Latvians like rabbits over the fields, we burnt every house and destroyed every bridge and every telegraph mast. We flung the bodies into fountains and threw hand grenades on top. We slaughtered whoever fell into our hands; we burned whatever would catch fire. . . . There were no human feelings left in our hearts. . . . A giant smoke trail marked our path. We had set fire to the stake where we burnt . . . the bourgeois tablets, the laws and values of the civilized world.[27]

To be sure, Salomon's book was written in the late 1920s in a conscious attempt to shock "bourgeois society" with a possibly exaggerated account of the Baltic campaign, but there can be no doubt that he and other paramilitary activists adored violence. The glamorization of violence as a form of social protest against decadent bourgeois society was not, of course, confined to Central Europe, and its roots lay deeper than the Great War itself. Already in 1909 the Italian Futurist Filippo Marinetti had drawn on older anarchist ideas when he famously wrote in his manifesto: "We want to exalt movements of aggression . . . the blow with the fist. . . . We want to glorify war—the only cure for the world—and militarism, patriotism, the destructive gesture of the anarchists, the beautiful ideas which kill, and contempt for women. We want to demolish museums and libraries, fight morality, feminism, and all opportunist and utilitarian cowardice."[28]

The concrete experience of modern warfare and the subsequent revolutions certainly helped to radicalize such pre-war sentiments and to transform them into concrete action. For those militia activists who had participated in vicious fighting until 1918, the war remained "the great revelation" and induced a romanticized view of the masculine *Frontkämpfertum* (front fighting spirit), heroic bloodshed, and a distinct dislike of bourgeois civilian society.[29]

One striking parallel in the radicalization process of right-wing activists in Germany, Austria, and Hungary is the contempt for the politicized, effeminate crowds, which are generally contrasted with the orderly world of the disciplined soldier. Many of those who spent time in the *Freikorps*, the *Heimwehr*, or the Hungarian militias recounted the experience of returning from the front in 1918 to an entirely hostile world of Communist upheaval and collapsed political, military, and gender hierarchies. Several activists remembered being stripped of their military decorations by "effeminate crowds" as a particularly humiliating experience. The subsequent Austrian *Heimwehr* leader Ernst-Rüdiger Starhemberg, for example, described his first encounter with a revolutionary crowd as an experience that demanded retribution:

> On a grey November morning, I was allowed to leave [the barracks] for the first time. . . . When I came closer to the main streets of the city, I heard wild shouting. Soon I saw a larger crowd of people, among them several soldiers in combat uniform. . . . Some were wearing red armbands. Roughly twelve or fifteen of them were beating up two young officers . . . women were screaming "beat them to death, the damned officers!"[30]

Ernst von Salomon describes a similar experience. While walking through the streets of Berlin in his cadet uniform in November 1918, he was suddenly confronted with a crowd of revolutionaries:

> I felt how I turned pale, I pulled myself together and said to myself "stand to attention." . . . I sensed chaos and turmoil. A huge flag was carried in front of a long procession of people, and the flag was red. . . . I stood still and watched. Following the flag, tired crowds surged in a disorderly fashion. Women marched in front. They proceeded in their wide skirts, the grey skin of their sharp bony faces was wrinkled. . . . Covered in dark, ragged cloths they were singing a song which was out of tune with the hesitant heaviness of their march. . . . Here they were: the champions of the revolution. So this was the dark crowd from which the glowing flame [of revolution] was to emerge, the crowd set out to realize the dream of blood and barricades. It was impossible to capitulate to them. I sneered at their claims which knew no pride, no confidence in victory. . . . I stood straight and watched and thought "cowards" and "scum" and "mob" and I . . . watched these hollow, dissolute figures; they are just like rats, I thought, grey and with red-framed eyes, carrying the dust of the streets on their backs.[31]

This passage—true or not—reveals much about the activists' perception of the enemy they were fighting. What Salomon wanted the reader to encounter was the ugly face of revolution, a condensed image of everything that the Central European counter-revolution despised. The idea of the effeminate, faceless crowd was influenced by a vulgarized understanding of Gustave Le Bon's *Psychologie des foules* (1895), which stimulated much discussion in educated right-wing circles from the turn of the century.[32] Le Bon's contrast of the masses and the individual was also reflected in the way in which Salomon (and many others in Germany, Austria, and Hungary) described the return of the front soldiers. The soldier, who has fought an "honorable" war, returns home in an orderly fashion and can only feel disgust for the revolutionary crowd that betrays his sacrifice. "And when I saw these deadly determined faces . . . these eyes which looked away from the alien crowd, alien, disconnected, hostile . . . then I knew . . . these were men who did not belong to those who had gathered in the streets, who did not want to belong to them."[33]

The differentiation between the politicized "effeminate" crowd and the alienated "masculine" soldier served the purpose of emphasizing the legitimacy of armed resistance against revolution. The dehumanization of the "crowd" and the emphasis on "them" as "rats," spreading the "diseases" of Bolshevism, disorder, and gender equality, clearly marked important psychological steps toward the perceived "legitimacy" of their elimination, an act of "purification" through which society could be cured.

Many activists firmly believed that the participation of women in radical left-wing politics, and in the revolutions of 1918–19 in particular, offered proof of the dangerous relationship between female political participation and revolutionary politics, a theme that had been widely discussed in right-wing circles long before 1918. The prominent German counter-revolutionary, Max Bauer (a close aide of Erich Ludendorff), had been working continuously on a manuscript for a book entitled "Criticism of the Women's Movement" between 1900 and 1918, a period during which he collected hundreds of press clippings on the subject. The criticism that emerged in Bauer's (unpublished) manuscript centered upon two familiar arguments. The first was that the development of gender relations since the turn of the century had led to loose sexual morals among younger women, who had abandoned their traditional role as models of social virtues.[34] Second, he insisted that increasing female emancipation had led to a de-feminization of women's lives, which were becoming increasingly "male." This was expressed not only in the childlessness of university-educated women but also in the new role women played in the world of politics, "a job entirely unsuitable for women."[35]

From Bauer's perspective, events after 1918 seemed to confirm his view of feminism as major threat to political order. "Politicized women" such as Rosa Luxemburg had betrayed the home front and had executed a fatal "stab in the back" of the otherwise victorious Central European armies.[36] Although the image of "politicized women" leading revolutionary crowds into battle against the ancient régime was much older than the Great War, it was now explicitly linked to the notion of female *violence*, to which the militias claimed to respond in kind. The perpetrators of violence against women argued that their acts were legitimate because their victims had started the cycle of violence. In *Die Geächteten* Ernst von Salomon recalls a scene in which "politicized women" brutally abuse captured *Freikorps* men during the German Revolution of 1918–19—an image that can be found in many memoirs of militiamen written after the war: "The women," Salomon writes, were dressed in "ragged skirts, their wrinkly faces under windswept hair [were] red with anger, [and] they were beating us with sticks and stones, and hose-pipes and kitchenware. They spat . . . [and] screamed hysterically."[37]

An even more explicit account of female violence was provided by the militiaman Erich Balla. In his autobiographical book, *Landsknechte wurden wir* (*We Became Freebooters*), Balla describes the occupation of a Latvian village in which his men search a house occupied by two women. While searching the cellar they make a terrible discovery: "the corpses of five brutally mutilated German soldiers. Their eyes, noses, tongues and genitals have been cut off. Their faces and uniforms bear the marks of brutal kicks." Against this background, the *Freikorps* men's reaction is described as entirely "understandable." After finding their mutilated comrades, "two or three men, obsessed by the same thought, rush upstairs. One can hear the muffled sound of piston strokes, and the two women lie dead on the floor."[38]

Similar accounts of brutal violence used by "Bolshevik women" can be found for Hungary. The Hungarian lawyer Oscar Szóllósy, a councilor in the postrevolutionary Hungarian Ministry of Justice, for example, emphasized in a newspaper article on "The Criminals of the Dictatorship of the Proletariat" that women "were given a plentiful scope of activity by Bolshevism." He then described their "scope of activity" by pointing to incidents of torture and castration during the Red Terror, in which female doctors had actively participated.[39]

Descriptions of female violence went hand in hand with physical stereotypes of "politicized" Bolshevik women as short-haired, hysterical, and dressed in rags. The 1923 memoirs of Cecile Tormay, the founder and president of the arch-conservative National Association of Hungarian Women, for example, provide a photograph of a female medical doctor, Helen Peczkai, who allegedly "enjoyed" assisting in various executions during Kun's Red Terror, so that the reader could visualize the "typical" Bolshevik woman, who was presented as a legitimate target for the "forces of law and order."[40]

Conclusion

It has been argued in this chapter that the three major successor states of the collapsed Central European empires witnessed the simultaneous emergence of highly similar paramilitary movements, all of which resorted to brutal violence against "politicized women" as one of their key target groups. In the broader context of the White Terror, we have encountered mutilation and torture, rape, and murder as distinct but often overlapping forms of violence against women. To be sure, the violent acts against women described in this chapter can be found in many other war or civil war contexts. However, a thorough understanding of (sexual and nonsexual) violence against women in conflict zones requires a reconstruction of the specific motivations behind certain behavioral patterns. This chapter has therefore attempted to analyze the internal "logic" of paramilitary groups in a specific historical context rather than to explain violence against women through individual psychology. The violence described in this particular case study was primarily driven by the perpetrators' desire to subject "unruly women" to degradation so as to take revenge for their alleged crime of weakening the home front and to fulfill the general aim of "disciplining" a society that was apparently out of control. Violence against "politicized women" also served to compensate for military defeat and a corresponding crisis of masculine identity at a time that coincided with increasing female social and political emancipation. The victims of these violent acts—from rape to mutilation and murder—were portrayed as a threat to male domination and political order. The perpetrators suggested that "politicized women" were one of the main driving forces behind revolutionary unrest, against which the use of excessive violence was both a "just" act of "self-defense" and a form of social purification considered necessary for a national rebirth.

The "Big Rape": Sex and Sexual Violence, War, and Occupation in Post-World War II Memory and Imagination

Atina Grossmann

The defeated Reich that the victors encountered in the spring of 1945 wore a predominantly female face. German men had been killed, wounded, or taken prisoner, leaving women to clean the ruins, scrounge for material survival, and serve the occupiers, often as sexual partners and victims.[1] After years of remarkable inattention since the 1950s, and provoked in part by the sexual violence associated with the conflicts in former Yugoslavia in the early 1990s, Red Army rapes became the subject of vigorous scholarly and feminist debates on German women's role in the Third Reich. The sixtieth anniversary of war's end, with its new emphasis on recognizing, publicly and legitimately, German suffering as well as a growing popular awareness of rape as a war crime in civil and ethnic conflicts, brought renewed public attention—albeit in a less carefully contextualized manner—to the story of German women's victimization.[2] The numbers reported for these rapes vary wildly, from as few as 20,000 to almost one million, or even two million altogether as the Red Army pounded westward. A conservative estimate might be about 110,000 women raped, many more than once, of whom as many as 10,000 died in the aftermath; others suggest that perhaps one out of every three of about 1.5 million women in Berlin fell victim to Soviet rapes.[3]

Whatever the figures, it is unquestionably the case that mass rapes of civilian German women signaled the end of the war and the defeat of Nazi Germany.[4] Soviet rapes secured a particularly potent place in postwar memories of victimization, because they represented one instance in which Goebbels's spectacular anti-Bolshevik propaganda turned out to be substantially correct. Millions of Germans were trekking westward in flight from the Red Army, and millions of German soldiers were marched eastward as POWs, but as Berliners—primarily women, children, and elderly—emerged from their cellars during the piercingly beautiful spring of 1945, the Soviets did not kill everyone on sight, deport them to Siberia, or burn down the city. As the musician Karla Höcker reported with genuine surprise in one of the many diaries composed by women at war's end, "the Russians, who must hate and fear us, leave the majority of the German civilian population entirely alone—that they don't transport us off in droves!"[5]

In fact, the Soviet Military Administration (SMA) moved quickly and efficiently to organize municipal government, restore basic services, and nurture a lively political and cultural life. In regard to violence against women, however, the Nazi "horror stories" (*Greuelgeschichten*) were largely confirmed. Official Soviet policy, however, obstinately refused to acknowledge that soldiers who had sworn to be "honorable, brave, disciplined, and alert" and to defend the "motherland manfully, ably, with dignity and honor," would engage in atrocities on a greater scale than one of "isolated excesses."[6] Ilya Ehrenburg, having quickly assimilated Stalin's new more conciliatory line toward compliant Germans, insisted that "The Soviet soldier will not molest a German woman. . . . It is not for booty, not for loot, not for women that he has come to Germany."[7] "'Russian soldiers not rape! German swine rape!'" a Soviet interrogator bellowed at the actress Hildegard Knef when she was captured after having disguised herself as a soldier in an effort to escape the fate of the female in defeated Germany.[8] Clearly, however, that new message did not impress troops who had been engaged in a costly final battle and had been told that "every farm on the road to Berlin was the den of a fascist beast."[9] As exhausted, brutalized Red Army troops— "a raucous armada of men with their trousers down" as one officer described his men during their "hour of revenge"—finally crossed into the Reich, they entered not only the fascist lair but also a still-capitalist world of "butter, honey, jam, wine, and various kinds of brandy."[10] Shocked at the continuing affluence of the society they had so determinedly defeated, and the contrast to their own decimated country, Russian soldiers told their victims, "Russia my homeland, Germany my paradise."[11]

For German women in 1945, especially in Berlin and to its East, these Soviet rapes were experienced as a collective event in a situation of general crisis, part of the apocalyptic days of the fall of Berlin and of Nazism. "Rape had," many noted, "become routine"; the story of sexual violence was told as part of the narrative of survival in ruined Germany.[12] A certain matter-of-factness (*Sachlichkeit*), in some ways still reminiscent of the pre-Nazi Weimar New Woman, pervades many of these accounts. Margaret Boveri, a journalist who had continued working throughout the Nazi years, was laconic about the Soviet "liberators" in her Berlin "Survival Diary" for May 8, 1945: "The usual rapes—a neighbor who resisted was shot. . . . Mrs Krauss was not raped. She insists that Russians don't touch women who wear glasses. Like to know if that is true . . . the troops were pretty drunk but did distinguish between old and young which is already progress."[13] Others accepted their fate as an inevitable, expected consequence of defeat, almost like a natural disaster that could not be changed and must simply be survived: "In those days I endured the Russians as I would a thunderstorm."[14]

Surviving and Narrating Rape

In diaries composed at the time as well as in reworked diaries, memoirs, and oral histories recorded years later, women reported extremely diverse experiences of what they variously named as rape, coercion, violation, prostitution, or abuse. Indeed, the more one looks at the diaries, memoirs, and novels of the postwar years, rape stories are omnipresent, told matter of factly, told as tragedy, told with ironic humor and flourish. In a recurring trope, women are gathered at water pumps in bombed-out streets, exchanging "war stories" with a certain bravado. Sometimes women recounted stories of surprising escape or reprieve; often they resorted to generalities and passive voice (the awful scenes went on all night, we all had to submit) or referred specifically to the ghastly experiences of neighbors, mothers, and sisters that they they themselves had supposedly been spared. "But many fewer escaped than was later claimed," journalist Curt Riess asserted a few years later.[15]

In a compelling diary edited and published by a popular German writer in the 1950s, an anonymous "woman in Berlin" (recently identified as Marta Hillers, another young journalist who had continued to work in the Third Reich) recounted how, after a series of brutal rapes during the first chaotic weeks of April–May 1945, she decided, "It is perfectly clear. I need a wolf here who will keep the wolves away from me. An officer, as high as possible, Kommandant, General, whatever I can get."[16]

Such unsentimental directness in reporting and dealing with sexual assaults or efforts to elude them was quite typical. Curt Riess, a German Jew who had returned to Berlin, with deeply "mixed feelings," as a reporter with an American passport, was both horrified and cynical: "But it was strange, when the horrific had happened five or six times, it was no longer so horrific. That which one had thought one could not survive, was survived by many twenty or thirty times."[17] Another younger Berlin Jew, who had returned from Auschwitz, recorded with bittersweet amusement an exchange between two women in the familiar rough (and quite untranslatable) Berlin dialect that, almost despite himself, he was happy to hear again. Justifying her usurpation of a space on an overcrowded train, one loudly announced, "We Berliners had to let the bombs whip around our heads. I sat in a bunker for almost two weeks, was bombed out four times, and the Russians didn't exactly treat me with kid gloves either; in fact they raped me three times if you really want to know." This revelation provoked her equally loudmouthed competitor to an often-reported retort: "She actually seems to be proud that at her age the Russians would still take her."[18]

In a peculiar way, women's apparent sangfroid in the face of mass sexual assault became part of the story (and myth) of "Berlin *kommt wieder*," of the city's irrepressible irreverent spirit. Their self-preserving sexual cynicism can be attributed, at least in part, both to the modernist *Sachlichkeit* of Weimar culture and to the loosened mores of the Nazis' war, including women's experience of fraternization with foreign laborers recruited or forced into the war economy. Even more broadly, the fraying of bourgeois morality that had alarmed cultural conservatives at least since World War I and the Weimar Republic clearly continued into the Third Reich and the Second World War, albeit in complex and selective ways—a process recently delineated by Dagmar Herzog in her provocative study of sexuality during and "after fascism." The war had inevitably and paradoxically led to a loosening of domestic bonds and an eroticization "of public life," unevenly prosecuted, sometimes denounced and sometimes accepted by the populace. Indeed, as Annemarie Tröger already argued in an important 1986 essay, the dissociative endurance with which women survived rape as well as their instrumental fraternizing affairs bore an uncanny resemblance to the matter-of-fact, apparently detached encounters described in the Weimar "New Woman" novels of an Irmgard Keun or Marieluise Fleisser. German women, Tröger contended, had been trained into a sexual cynicism "freed *from* love," which served them well during the war and its aftermath.[19] In the autobiographical postwar novel, *Westend*, the main character narrates her rape with precisely the cool distant tone associated with New Woman writers: "he carried out the act which he perhaps saw as a kind of self-imposed duty coldly and without interest. She felt sorry for the man on top of her."[20]

The Russian, whose arrival had been so desperately anticipated by victims and opponents of Nazism and so dreaded by most Germans, became in Berlin an object not only of terror but of intense fascination and bewilderment. In keeping with the images provided by Nazi propaganda, he appeared as the drunken, primitive "Mongol" who descended on Germany like a vengeful "hungry locust" in an "orgy of revenge." These slanty-eyed ravagers from the Far Eastern steppes demanded watches, bicycles, and women; they had no clue that a flush toilet was not a sink or a refrigerator, and were astounded that the *Wurst* they had stored in the tank disappeared when a handle was pulled. They loaded expensive precision instruments, as if they were potato sacks, for transfer to the Soviet Union, only to have them rust on blocked roads or train tracks.[21]

The Soviets baffled the Germans with their strange behavior. As one woman remembered, "we never could quite make sense of the Russians, sometimes they were mild-mannered, sometimes sadistic."[22] They assaulted women but were tender and protective toward children and babies. They brazenly ripped a watch off someone's arm or grabbed a bicycle, and then offered a big bear hug, two kisses on the cheeks, and a friendly farewell. Women reported that their attackers could be distracted or even cowed, like a child or puppy, by firm commands. They seemed genuinely convinced that looting constituted proper restitution, and that rape too was merely part of their due. Both the Germans and the Allied victors were intrigued by the Soviets' capacity for drink, debauchery, and eye-popping portions of caviar. "We went to Berlin in 1945, thinking only of the Russians as big, jolly, balalaika-playing fellows, who drank prodigious quantities of vodka and liked to wrestle in the drawing room," U.S. Commander Frank Howley recalled. They had arrived not only with tanks and deafening cannons (the *Stalinorgel* that figures in so many memoirs) but with horse- and even camel-drawn vehicles; they quaffed gasoline and 4711 cologne in their endless search for alcohol. A Jewish youth remembered his first glimpses of his liberators, "They were dressed in olive-brown, high collar blouses and had rope belts around their waists. Their pants were stuffed into their boots. I had never seen anything like them. If they hadn't been so terrifying, they might have funny."[23] These contradictory impressions reflected the generally schizoid quality of the Soviet occupation: "By day they put the Germans, both men and women, to work in dismantling commandos, clearing up rubble, removing tank barricades; and by night they terrorized the city," even as some officers were moved to shoot offending soldiers on the spot.[24]

The rapacious *Ivan* was accompanied by the cultivated officer who spoke German, recited Dostoyevsky and Tolstoy, and deplored the excesses of his comrades, even as he used the threat of their assaults as a lure to attract "consensual" sex. Germans frequently counterposed these "cultivated" Soviets from European Russia to the equally if differently fascinating American occupiers who—rehearsing images of American POWs in Nazi newsreels—were categorized as vulgar, gum-chewing primitives. GI conquests, however, came primarily via nylons and chocolate, rather than rape. "The difference," Berliners quipped, "is that the Americans and the British ask the girls to dinner and then go to bed with them, while the Russians do it the other way round."[25] Yet the remarkably frank diary entries of one Ukrainian Jewish Red Army officer who professed himself horrified by the depredations of his comrades, differed little from the pleased descriptions of their "fraternization" experiences by American occupiers: German women in Berlin begged him, "I'm willing, just fuck me (*fick-fick*), I'll do anything you want, just rescue me from all these men."[26]

In the end perhaps, the many negative but also confused interpretations of the Soviets' behavior helped women to distance themselves from the horror of their own experience. The narrative of the Russian primitive or exotic curiously absolved him of guilt, as it also absolved women themselves. Such uncivilized, animal-like creatures could not be expected to control themselves, especially when tanked up with alcohol. Nor could women be expected to defend themselves against an elemental force, backed up, of course, in most cases by a rifle or revolver. As one woman remembered, after the initial panic about a fate worse than death, "It became clear to me that a rape, as awful as it might be, had nothing to do with loss of honor."[27]

More than a few women favorably compared Russian officers to contemptible, defeated German men, who either abetted women's humiliation or sought to punish them for it, sometimes to the point of killing them to preserve their honor. Pathetic parodies of the manly, SS-valorized Teutonic genus, preoccupied with saving their own skins, they were not above pressuring women to submit, to avoid endangering themselves; rape, after all, was a less horrific fate than Siberia or getting shot. The narrator of *A Woman in Berlin* wrote of the Soviet officer whom she finally cornered into her bed, hoping that he would fend off rivals: "On the other hand, I do like the Major, I like him the more as a person, the less he wants from me as a man. . . . Because among all male creatures of the last several days he is the most tolerable man and human being."[28]

In the 1951 potboiler, *The Big Rape*, American war correspondent James W. Burke's "composite" heroine Lilo describes her (temporary) protector Captain Pavel Ivanov in remarkably similar terms; he "was all that she had bargained for. He was kind, he was considerate, he was gallant. And he safeguarded her from wanton attack." Lilo in turn was determined not to have "painstakingly preserved her life thus far to foolishly lay it down at the altar of such a spurious and pretentious virtue."[29]

The turn of the millennium explosion of memory (and memory politics) about German suffering during and after the war relies in part on the nagging sense that this victimization was never adequately expressed or recognized, and always overshadowed in both West and East Germany by the demand for a recognition of collective guilt for Germany's crimes. This insistence on what historians have called "the silence that never was" certainly applies to popular perceptions that German women's massive and collective experience of sexual assault was quickly and profoundly silenced or made taboo. It is indeed the case that the ubiquitous stories of rape were downplayed or "normalized" by virtually everyone, including, in many ways, the victims themselves. Depending on who was talking, rapes were presented as the inevitable byproduct of a vicious war, or, in the "antifascist" narrative, as understandable retribution or exaggerated anti-Communist propaganda.[30] In no way, however, did these framings mean that rape stories were denied or silenced. On the contrary, in the direct aftermath of the war there was no lack of speech or documentation about rape. If anything, we find a plethora of talk in many different voices and venues, although it is indeed difficult to measure those expressions against our current expectations of treating and "working through" trauma.

Given the realities of mass rape, German communists and SMA authorities could not, particularly during the immediate postwar years 1945–47, impose a total silence around Red Army actions. They sought instead to find ways of containing both the massive incidence of rapes and the conversation about them. They denied, minimized, justified, and shifted responsibility. They freely admitted violations, excesses, abuses, and unfortunate incidents, and vowed to bring them under control (or to demand that the Soviet army do so). But they also trivialized rape, as an inevitable part of normal brutal warfare, as comparable to the violations of the Western Allies, and as understandable if not entirely excusable in view of the atrocities perpetrated on the Russians by the Germans. In a common pattern of simultaneous acknowledgment and denial, Communist Party memos and press reports referred frequently and openly to (purportedly unjustified) rumors of rape by Red Army soldiers, thereby reproducing and disseminating stories that, their coding as rumors or pernicious anti-Soviet propaganda notwithstanding, everyone presumably knew to be true. The *Berliner Zeitung*, which often resorted to cartoon characters speaking in Berlin dialect to explain unpopular positions (such as unwillingness to take responsibility for having profited from "aryanized" Jewish property), even ran a cartoon strip satirizing women's fears while encouraging their labor as *Trümmerfrauen*. Under the headline, "Mongols in Berlin, the latest rumor" (*Flüstergeschichte*, literally, "whispered stories"), the sensible Frau Piesepampel informs her hysterical neighbor Frau Schwabbel that she has "no time for such nonsense" and no intention of worrying about "Mongols" now that the war is finally over. There was cleanup work to be done, and she would not be distracted.[31] And while Soviet officers did sometimes exact summary punishment by shooting soldiers accused of rape, few worried as did the dissident Lev Kopolev in his memoirs of life as a political officer in the Red Army, "Why did so many of our soldiers turn out to be common bandits, raping women and girls one after another—on the side of the road, in the snow, in doorways? How did this all become possible?" His "bourgeois human[ist]" compunctions led to his arrest for being pro-German.[32]

All protestations notwithstanding, it was generally if not explicitly acknowledged that the communist-dominated Socialist Unity (SED) Party's embarrassing loss to the Social Democrats (SPD) in Berlin's first open elections in 1946 was due in no small part to a heavily female electorate remembering and responding to the actions of the Soviet "friends."[33] The Soviets had worked hard to present themselves as liberators, organizing city services, licensing newspapers and political parties, and promoting cultural revival, but in many ways their efforts came too late; the damage of the first few weeks could not be undone. In his report to the London paper *The Observer*, Issac Deutscher had predicted that "Next Sunday the women of Berlin will take their revenge against the humiliations that were forced upon them during the first weeks of occupation." The election results indicated that he was right.[34]

Rape continued to figure in German narratives of victimization for many years. Public conversation about the mass rapes was common during the immediate postwar period, despite all Communist and SMA efforts to block the discussion. Once conditions had somewhat normalized, however, such conversations were indeed curtailed in both the East and West. With the return of prisoners of war and the "remasculinization"[35] of German society, the topic was suppressed, deemed humiliating for German men and too risky for women who feared—with much justification given the reports of estrangement and even murder—the reactions of their menfolk. But rape stories continued to circulate and indeed were repeatedly invoked or alluded to by contemporary chroniclers, both German and occupier. In immediate reports and in later memoirs, women reported over and over that the cry "*Frau komm*" still rang in their ears.[36] Moreover, the importance of Berlin as the conquered capital and the millions of refugees from the East who poured into western Germany assured the centrality of rape stories in memories of defeat even in areas where there had never been a Red Army soldier.

Rape and American Conquerors

The continuing prominence of rape in German narratives of victimization in the period 1945–49 was not, as suggested by East German communists, due to propaganda by the Western allies. When Colonel Howley, who had served as the first U.S. commander in Berlin, published his virulently anticommunist memoirs in 1950, he wrote at length about the horrors of the Soviet regime of rape, murder, and looting.[37] In his earlier official military reports from Berlin, however, he had downplayed German anxieties about crime, disorder, and hunger. With a touch of sarcasm, he noted that the per capita crime rate in 1945–46 Berlin was lower than that of most cities in the United States, especially New York![38]

Even among the Americans, therefore, with whom such tales might have served as useful anticommunist propaganda, the discussion was restrained. In the early occupation years, U.S. officials were far from seizing on rape stories to discredit their Soviet allies and competitors, whom they viewed as "hard bargaining, hard playing, hard drinking, hard bodied, and hard headed."[39] Russians might be barbarian rapists but they were also tough fighters and exotic celebrators who could drink, eat, and copulate prodigiously—often to the admiring frustration of U.S. colleagues unable to match their levels of consumption. Nor were Americans necessarily unsympathetic to Soviet "excesses." Shortly before the war ended, a *Newsweek* reporter had no trouble explaining a rape "behind the barn" by a liberated Soviet POW who had been "badly treated, particularly by a farmer's daughter who was a Hitler Maiden and took delight in trying to prove the Russians were second-class human beings," as an act of "justice."[40] More than ten years later, in his lurid 1956 novel, *Fräulein*, the American writer James

McGovern sneered, "Poor Frau Graubach. When she had voted *ja*, she had not bargained for this."[41]

On September 6, 1945, military government officer John Maginnis noted, "We had another incident tonight. . . . The MPs were called in by the German police on an attempted rape by two Russians which ended in a shooting contest. Captain Bond went along the see the fun [sic] and almost got himself killed. The Russians were subdued but one of the MPs was shot in the thigh. I gave Captain Bond a good dressing down for getting mixed up in such a brawl; he should have known better."[42] This generally lighthearted tone of American reporting about Soviet abuses surely had something to do with the problems that the U.S. forces had, not only with fraternization and prostitution, but also with sexual violence.[43] When William Griffith took over as a denazification officer for the military government in Bavaria, where there were many more American troops than in divided Berlin, he discovered that an important task of the military police was "largely to parade weeping German rape victims past their suspected GI assailants for identification." Luckily for the GIs, "the poor girls, I regret to say, never identified any of our soldiers."[44] As American reporters Bud Hutton and Andy Rooney smirked about Soviet rapes, "The great novelty for the United States Army was, however, that for the first time in the history of living man someone was behaving worse than the American soldier."[45]

If German communists worried about the effects of Red Army behavior on support for the occupation and the Socialist Unity Party that they had established in April 1946, American officials and journalists certainly also debated the corrupting effects—on both occupier and occupied—of servicemen's looting, brawling, raping, and general "sexual antics."[46] Defeat and military occupation, with their enormous pressures to engage in instrumental sex, make it in many cases difficult to disentangle coercive, pragmatic, and what might be called genuinely consensual sex. Kay Boyle captured this ambiguous state well in one of her "Military Occupation Group" short stories, when an American occupier declares, "Let me tell you that Berlin's the territory for the man who's got a flair. They're still pretty hungry there, so they come to terms without too much of an argument."[47] Thomas Berger's fiercely comic (and presumably somewhat autobiographical) 1958 novel, *Crazy in Berlin*, begins with a GI shouting at a woman in a Berlin park, "Honey . . . *schlafen mit* me, oh won't you *schlafen mit* me!" and concludes with the lesson learned in occupied Germany: "Organize your sex life and all else followed, the phallus being the key to the general metropolis of manhood, which most of the grand old civilizations knew but we in America had forgotten."[48]

Certainly, the many American fictionalizations of postwar Berlin—a genre in itself, often written by men who served there—stressed the unique advantages of the GIs' sexual bonanza; what a historian of the U.S. occupation summarized as the "general willingness on the part of German women" and the American Jewish writer Meyer Levin, more bitterly, as "the lustful eagerness of the German girls to fulfill their roles as conquered women."[49] In McGovern's *Fräulein*, the jaded women survivors of the Battle of Berlin hopefully await the American conquerors: "The Americans had not suffered in the war. Their homes had not been bombed, their women raped, their industries razed. Their casualties in Europe had been smaller than those of the *Wehrmacht* at Stalingrad alone. They would be free from the spirit of revenge for which the French, British, and Russians could hardly be blamed." Cynically, the women repeat the dominant American view, "Rape? They don't have to rape. All those women who swarm outside their barracks would rape them for a carton of cigarettes or a chocolate bar." American privilege also assured a more benign general level of exploitation and looting: "The Russians steal power plants and cranes and whole factories, while the Amis are content to ship Meissen china, Zeiss cameras, and family heirloom jewels through their Army Post Office."[50]

Fraternization: Sexual, Political, and Racial Border Crossing

The putatively "other," but frequently difficult-to-disentangle side of the rape story, was sexual fraternization. The bans imposed with all serious intent by the Americans (and British) very quickly showed themselves to be utterly and hopelessly unenforceable, as "an immense and sordid joke." In one of the many apparently autobiographical novels published in the years right after the war, an officer marveling at the sudden bounty of "guns, wine, silver, paintings, women, and various combinations thereof" greeting the Americans, tells his men, "In this outfit we stand on Patton's unofficial ruling that it is not fraternization if you don't stay for breakfast. Sleep with 'em but don't shake hands."[51] With everyone agreeing that "surely it is necessary to go back to Prohibition to find a law so flagrantly violated and so rarely enforced," General Eisenhower eased the ban on July 7 just as the Americans were taking up their positions in Berlin, and then essentially lifted it by officially permitting public conversations between Germans and Americans on July 15, 1945.

Technicalities notwithstanding, any political fraternization suggested by a handshake was clearly not the major issue; as an American observer bluntly put it in 1946, "Fraternization is strictly a matter of sex. An American with a German woman is with her because she is a woman, not because she is a German."[52] The American Jewish intelligence officer Saul Padover noted the obvious when he wrote that "The dictionary" may have "define[d] fraternization as 'bringing into brotherly love,' but the relations between Americans and Germans did not belong in that category," and it quickly "came to have the exclusive signification of fornication," It was no accident that the ever-creative German joke makers nicknamed the military government "government by mistresses."[53]

Over and over again, using virtually identical phrases, reporters highlighted occupied Germany's ubiquitous *Fräuleinwunder.* "There is nothing like it this side of Tahiti," they marveled about the accessibility of young German women. When a young officer inquired about bringing his wife to his Berlin posting, he was greeted with incredulity, "Wife? You must be nuts!" said the general. "You're bringing a sandwich to a banquet."[54] Or as one decidedly not amused female American reporter sniffed about German women who treated "all American women with contempt and all American men as gods": "If there was any rape, it certainly wasn't necessary."[55] Particularly titillating was the picture of German women quickly shedding all the "baggage" of racial indoctrination, at least in matters sexual or romantic. Initial reports especially highlighted fraternization with both Jewish and African American soldiers as ironic racial transgressions: "the Negro troops are doing particularly well with the Fräuleins. . . . It is also true that Jewish boys are having a field-day."[56]

Field day or not, the politics of fraternization was particularly fraught for Jewish Allied soldiers. In a report on a "ride through Berlin," posted to the refugee weekly *Aufbau* in July 1945, a German-Jewish master sergeant reflected on how hard it was to resist the temptations of well-dressed, well-fed, and appealing *Fräuleins.* He described his own painful discipline of staring into their eyes and visualizing Buchenwald and Dachau.[57] For U.S. occupation official Moses Moskowitz, the fact that "German women have been known to be on intimate terms with Jewish men who only a year ago were behind concentration camp gates" was one of the most difficult and inexplicable aspects of the German "enigma of irresponsibility."[58] Kurt Hirsch, the Czech-Jewish American GI whom the actress Hildegard Knef married, was excruciatingly explicit about this clash of memories and identities. On their first date in bombed-out Berlin, he took her to the movies in the Russian sector to watch the Soviet newsreel about the liberation of Auschwitz. "'I lost sixteen relatives,'" he told her on the way home.[59]

The combustible mix of race and sex played out in different but—for occupation policy in a still-segregated military—even more tense ways for African American troops. William Gardner Smith, a reporter for the African American newspaper *Pittsburgh Courier*, echoed black GIs' own highly ambivalent feelings about fraternization in his semiautobiographical 1948 novel, *Last of the Conquerors*. Drinking with "sultry looking" German women, a GI remarks, "Two years ago I'd a shot the son of a bitch that said I'd ever be sittin' in a club drinking a toast with Hitler's children. . . . The same people we're sittin' with tonight is the ones that burned people in them camps and punched the Jews in the nose." One of the girls retorts angrily, "'How can you talk? What about the white Americans? In your country you may not walk down the street with a white woman.'" Musing on his initially carefree love affair with a "white girl" named Ilse, the narrator notes "bitter[ly]" how "odd, it seemed to me, that here, in the land of hate, I should find this one all-important phase of democracy." He remembered the pleasures of postwar Berlin, border crossing through the sectors, strolling along the Wannsee in the summer", or going to the opera in the East with his girlfriend, even as they "could still smell the bodies of the dead buried beneath the rubble as we walked." Not wanting to face the reality that Ilse's dream of marriage could never be fulfilled in Jim Crow America, he has no ready response to the buddy who blurts out, "I like this goddamn country, you know that. . . . It's the first place I was ever treated like a goddamn man. . . . You know what the hell I learned? That a nigger ain't no different from nobody else. . . . I hadda come over here and let the Nazis teach me that."[60]

Women had their own reasons for making themselves sexually available, as the sharp-eyed sociologist Hilde Thurnwald surmised in her report on family life in postwar Berlin. Aside from the bare necessities provided by American foodstuffs and supplies, the *Fräuleins* were perhaps lured less by sexual interest than by a general postwar "yearning for life's pleasures" (*Lebenshunger*). If soldiers' rations could ease "the hunger which had replaced the bombs in making life into hell," as Curt Riess put it, then Berlin's women were also seeking a bit of warmth, a bar of chocolate, an ice cream from the American club, some untroubled hours. The *Amis*, they said, in a reference to the Weimar enthusiasm for American rationalization, were "so streamlined." And indeed the crack Eighty-Second Airborne, which had marched into Berlin in July, was well fed, well groomed, and fragrant, as many recalled, with after-shave lotion; quite a contrast to the ragged German men returning from the front or POW camps (and in most cases the feared Russians).[61] Their entry into the destroyed capital was limned rather contradictorily in Burke's *The Big Rape*: "giants of men—tall, huge, powerful. . . . They were giants—all! In contrast to the Russians there was something immediately sharp and commanding about these troops. Their uniforms were neat, clean and trim. . . . Their faces were uniformly bright and clean. All seemed to be happy. There were no dark brooding faces. They were like a bunch of kids, away on a lark or outing."[62]

Yet, by July when the Americans entered Berlin, the experience of Red Army rapes shadowed the fraternization phenomenon that accompanied them. Indeed, the very experience of rape may have made embittered women less resistant to the casual prostitution that also characterized fraternization while simultaneously making them more open to the pleasures offered by the Eighty-Second Airborne. It was no secret in postwar Berlin that a politics of guilt, revenge, and punishment had been recently enacted on the bodies of German women. The "furlines" and Veronikas, as depicted in the politically and physically infected cartoon character Veronika Dankeschön (VD) in *Stars and Stripes*, as well as the stolid cleaner-uppers and self-sacrificing mothers designated as *Trümmerfrauen*, were both desirable and dangerous. They were freighted with the shame and horror of rape and the guilt of Nazism as well as emblematic of the victims that war produces. In James McGovern's 1956 novel, he professed to capture this mood: "The cook had lost one son at Orel, another at Kasserine pass, her husband and small apartment in a Liberator raid on Prenzlauer Berg, her modest life savings in the black market chaos, had narrowly escaped being raped by a Russian, and she stubbornly muttered that if she were going to feel guilty, or sorry for anybody, it would be for herself."[63]

Berlin's women appeared, however, not only as victims and villains but also as shameless sexually available *Fräuleins*—determined and unsentimental, willing to do whatever was necessary to survive. James Burke's fictional Lilo personified this tougher version: in July 1945, having made it through the initial Soviet occupation, she walked into the U.S. military government press office to offer her services. She had after all worked for the Nazi press; the Americans needed people with skills and experience; they could denazify her "later." Her motto was "Survival! Above all things she must survive. . . . She had survived the rape of Berlin. Surely she could manage from here on."[64] "One has long since lost the habit of pathos" (*Jedes Pathos hat man sich längst abgewöhnt*), the Berlin journalist Ursula von Kardorff, better known than Martha Hiller's *Anonyma*, who also continued to work in the Third Reich, noted in her journal on January 29, 1945.[65] It is indeed this lack of pathos, this insistently matter-of-fact tone, laconic, resigned, but determined to endure, sometimes laced with gallows humor— so evident in women's contemporary testimony—that challenges our understandings of both the victimization caused by, and inflicted on, German women as the Nazi empire collapsed.

War as History, Humanity in Violence: Women, Men, and Memories of 1971, East Pakistan/Bangladesh

Yasmin Saikia

"One of my brothers was politically involved in the liberation struggle. This enraged our Bengali and Bihari neighbors. One afternoon, five men stormed into our house. They were Montu, Jewel, and Ghyas Babu from our neighborhood, and two others from outside our colony.[1] Several Pakistani soldiers were also with them. They shot and killed my elderly grandfather and attacked my brothers. They also beat my sister and grandmother. My mother and I were together, but they dragged me away from her." With this vivid, though painful, opening statement, Khuku Rani began to recount her memory of rape and brutalization during the war of Bangladesh in 1971.[2] Khuku's experience is a shared story of suffering of many in East Pakistan (after 1971 known as Bangladesh).[3] Until the outbreak of civil unrest that was provoked by the military crackdown of Dhaka on March 25, 1971, Khuku's family, which consisted of her grandparents, parents, four brothers, and two sisters, lived in harmony in a neighborhood populated by Muslim and Hindu Bengalis and "Biharis."[4] As a result of the violence, neighbors became enemies and fought against each other, motivated by the explicit purpose to destroy the other.[5] The established boundaries of human respect broke down and women, in particular, were targeted for sexual attack. It was in this context that Khuku Rani was made to "pay" for her brother's political activities. She was forcibly taken from her home to a school compound where she was brutally raped, which she characterized as "torture." Recalling the "torture," she said, "I can't walk and my hand is paralyzed. I can't hold anything with it; they had broken my wrist with a rifle when I resisted the torture on my body. There were other girls in the room, but I was tortured the most."

Khuku's misery did not end with rape and torture of her body. After the liberation of Bangladesh, women like Khuku were neglected and forgotten by the state and society, transformed into a category called *birangonas*,[6] which in her admission is her "greatest sorrow." "In the last thirty years nobody asked me how I am doing and what do I want from my life. . . . I don't have a normal human life and cannot fulfill my most basic needs," she said emotionally and broke down into tears.

Khuku Rani's narrative unmasks several hidden stories and secrets of the war. We learn immediately from her testimony that there was no distinct and decipherable zone of conflict; violence was all around. The "normal" world made up of neighbors and friends disappeared, and multiple violent spaces controlled by enemies were established. At the heart of the horror was the combination of state-sanctioned violence and personal vendetta; men exploited the situation to abuse women. To this was added the established gender predispositions in a patriarchal society that played a catalyzing role in transforming social moods into actual behavioral manifestations. In the process, women's humanity was transgressed and destroyed, which Khuku Rani in her concluding statement makes poignantly clear to us.

Juxtaposed to the victim's narrative is a perpetrator's voice that interrogates the war and its purpose. Rahim Ali recalled that he was sent with eleven men to "clean out a rebel Bengali village." At the end of the day, Rahim saw that "the place was littered with decapitated bodies, dismembered arms and legs were strewn all over. Dogs and vultures were fighting over the body parts. When I looked at the dogs, I saw they had no hair on them. They were vicious, man-eating animals. They were eating human beings, like me." The similarity that he saw between himself and his victim made him "a prisoner [of his conscience]." But his lowly status as a soldier in the Pakistan Army combined with the sense of service for nation compelled Rahim Ali to continue to "obey orders" and perform "duty" without asking questions. Thus, despite a struggle with his conscience, Rahim fought and killed in the hope of "saving Pakistan."

Contrary to the expectation of men like Rahim Ali, at the end of nine months of violence Pakistan was dismembered. East Pakistan became a free country called Bangladesh on December 16, 1971. The surrendered Pakistani army soldiers were made prisoners of war (POWs) in India (the Indian Army had fought on behalf of the Bengalis).[7] In the POW camp Rahim and his cellmates gradually started talking about the violence they had committed during the war. These conversations and the recognition of his victims' humanity enabled Rahim to "find [his] *insāniyat* [humaneness/humanity]" and it made him "free, an *insān* [a human]." Upon returning to Pakistan after two and half years of captivity, Rahim resigned from the army because he said "[he] had found [his] *insāniyat.*"[8]

The term *insāniyat* to which Rahim Ali refers to requires a short explanation. *Insāniyat* is a concept and a term that is widely used in the Indian subcontinent. Its roots are in the Perso-Urdu culture of Sufi Islam that is popular in the region. With an esoteric Sufi explanation, *insāniyat* is 'love' within a human being that transcends ego, enabling one to recognize the shared human condition, which promotes a relationship to the Divine. Applied to the secular sphere, *insāniyat* has several possible explanations—humanity, humaneness, and humanism. In recent times, Islamic humanism or *insāniyat* has become a subject for understanding the Muslim world beyond the rhetoric of terror, militancy, and religious fundamentalism.[9] Although the term and concept of *insāniyat* is widely invoked in Pakistan, research shows that *insāniyat* is not a textbook lesson learned in school. The sources of *insāniyat* for common people are in lived experiences, and their interpretations are derived from an understanding of a shared condition that our interlocutor Rahim Ali so clearly articulates in his testimony.

The two testimonies recounted above expose, in the words of Veena Das, the "disturbing remains" of an unprocessed and unresolved history of violence that put into sharp focus the need for developing a new narrative based on *insāniyat* of survivors.[10] Nearly four decades later the memories of victims and perpetrators are not integrated into the national stories in South Asia, but hover outside public language in silence. Survivors' silence serves as a witnessing of people's trauma and becomes a form of testimony toward developing a human language of understanding.[11] To achieve this purpose, we must listen to both victims and perpetrators, and must probe the process of violence—in other words, the dehumanization of people during war.[12]

In this chapter, I examine the connections between nationalism, gender violence, and postcolonial nation building in South Asia, using the method of oral history. It is important to note at the outset that the method of oral history is not without problems; questions concerning believability and authenticity as well as use of memory to fit presenters' agendas are useful considerations to bear in mind. Methodologically, however, oral history is unique, because it provides a voice to the silenced and suppressed.[13] As well, it creates conditions for human interaction that permeate the research project,[14] requiring oral historians to contextualize the research method for answering larger questions that democratize history and memory.[15] The methodology of first-person narrative, I suggest, is a way to overcome the division between experience and analysis, and to gain "imaginative access"[16] to "catastrophic tales"[17] for bearing witness to a history that is suppressed and submerged within national history with the aim to forget.

The chapter is divided into four sections. In the first section I describe the events of 1971 and their violent history, paying particular attention to the identity-based politics of constructing Muslim and Hindu since the creation of India and Pakistan in 1947. Swimming against the tide of national "official" histories that blame "others" for violence, I engage in the next two sections the voices of survivors, both men and women, who tell their memories of the war. This leads to the final section on the possibility of writing a history after violence that focuses on humanity/*insāniyat* of survivors. This section engages the writings of Mevlana Jalauddin Rumi and Emmanuel Levinas, who suggest a search for a face-to-face encounter with "others" for humanizing history and privileging us with an epistemological tool to question received identities, such as nation, state, religion, and gender.

History and Markers: Inscribing Violence

The ethnic and religious violence that took place in East Pakistan in 1971 stems from previous episodes of violence aimed at destroying the "other." The history of "otherizing" in the subcontinent is long and convoluted.[18] Starting in the nineteenth century, the British rulers created caste, ethnic, and religious groups. They considered the "Hindu" and "Muslim" as two distinct communities, and divided and ruled them as separate subjects in British India. The British colonial categories of identity proved handy for generating divisive communitarian politics during the period of anticolonial nationalism of the twentieth century, which ultimately led to the partition and creation of India and Pakistan in 1947.

India was founded on the ethos of a secular republic but soon became mired in majoritarian Hindu politics expressed in communal/religious violence against the Muslims. Pakistan, on the other hand, was founded as a Muslim nation, yet its exclusive Muslim identity was downplayed immediately after its foundation. In his inaugural speech on August 11, 1947, Mohammad Ali Jinnah, the architect of Pakistan, announced, "You are free; you are free to go to your temples, you are free to go to your mosques or to any other place of worship . . . that has nothing to do with the business of the State."[19]

In addition to the confusion of Pakistan's identity, the multiple ethnic and linguistic communities of Punjabi, Bengali, Sindhi, Pathan, and Baluchi, along with the Urdu-speaking Mohajirs from Bihar and Uttar Pradesh (who went to Pakistan from India in 1947) that made up the Pakistani nation were divided physically, emotionally, politically, and culturally. Added to this mosaic of people, the newly created state was fractured into two wings, East and West Pakistan, with India in between.

The term "Hindu" was not at first used to signify the enemy of "Muslim." The initial policy of the state's indifference toward religion continued the colonial policy during the tenure of the military rulers Ayub Khan and Yahya Khan (1958–71). However, with national politics, during the early 1960s the term "Hindu" was invoked to mobilize Pakistan's struggle against India; later, after 1965, the categories India and Hindu were interchangeably used.[20] Zulfikar Ali Bhutto initiated an agenda of "Islamic Socialism" to reconstruct a Pakistani identity.

In India "the Muslim" emerged as a problematic figure in 1947. Although millions of Muslims migrated to Pakistan during partition, an equally large number continued to live in India.[21] Despite his proclaimed politics of secularism and socialism, Jawaharlal Nehru, India's first prime minister, could not translate his vision into reality, and frequent outbreaks of religious riots exacerbated tensions between the Hindus and Muslims.

In 1971, violence created mass panic on the subcontinent. The West Pakistani military were determined to destroy the Bengalis, who were deemed friends of India and the Hindus. The grievances of the Bengalis for equitable distribution of resources, greater political representation in Pakistan's national parliament, an end to economic exploitation, and the use of the Bangla language (also known as Bengali) in public were viewed as the result of Indian subversion.[22] The war of 1971 was triggered after the general election of 1970 and Sheikh Mujibur Rahman's victory. The ruling military junta, with the support of the West Pakistani politician Zulfikar Ali Bhutto, deployed the national army against the people of East Pakistan. For nine months, from March 25 until December 16, 1971, East Pakistan became the site of multiple wars.

One was a civil war and the other an international war. In the civil war, West Pakistani troops, along with local Urdu-speaking "Bihari" supporters, terrorized, raped, looted, and killed nationalist Bengalis, who were deemed "Hindu turncoats."[23] In turn, the Bengalis, with the active assistance of the Indian authorities, formed a guerrilla army, the *Mukti Bahini* (liberation force), and their soldiers wreaked havoc in non-Bengali communities.[24]

The international war fought between India and Pakistan, with the support of the Soviet Union and the United States, was part of a protracted series of Cold War battles in the Indian subcontinent region. Fueled by the memories of partition of 1947, India used the opportunity presented by the Bengalis to fight against Pakistan and break it up.[25] At the end of the war Pakistan was dismembered, and in the east a new nation-state of Bangladesh was created. The war of 1971 was the first successful overthrow of a military dictatorship by common people in twentieth century Asia; yet, alongside this heraldic feat was a terribly dark human story of loss and destruction. Ten million people became refugees, two hundred thousand women were raped, and several hundred thousand Biharis became "stateless."[26]

India and Bangladesh were victorious. Pakistan, on the other hand, adopted a policy of silence. The histories of 1971 that were subsequently produced reflected the official mood in the three countries, suppressing the dark stories of the war, particularly gender violence.

The national task in Bangladesh after the war was directed toward "domesticating" the women who had suffered sexual violence; they were viewed as "fallen" and an example of national shame. Rehabilitating the fallen women by teaching them domestic activities such as sewing, weaving, and midwifery became national enterprises. In the newly created domestic sphere of the nation there was no space to discuss gender violence. Furthermore, the identification of victims within a specific category called *birangona* or female hero, though initiated for the recovery and rehabilitation of survivors, created fresh problems. *Birangona* was reduced in men's speech to *barangona* or "penetrated" (prostitutes), and thus women were made guilty of rape and silenced.

Added to the social and collective loss of the memory of violence, the new government headed by Sheikh Mujibur Rahman inaugurated an abortion program to rid the nation of the "bastard Pakistanis." The cold count of victims as statistical numbers undermined women's humanity, and their pain was transformed into a battleground for continuing the wars of national self-interest. To this was added a lack of scholarly curiosity. Although the war of 1971 is considered to be one of the most intense brutalizations of women in twentieth-century conflict, it has been overlooked by scholars of gender studies internationally, with the rare exception of Susan Brownmiller's pioneering book, *Against Our Will: Men, Women, and Rape.*[27]

Within the culturally scripted practices of normative knowledge in South Asia, rape continues to be an uneasy topic of discussion. Cultural unease is expressed in the lack of an equivalent word for rape in Urdu, and the Bangla word *dharshan* is never used in women's testimony of war experiences. The problem of naming the violence compromises historical memory, but its failure does not mean an ethical language cannot develop to enable us to grasp the experiences of others and to have access to suffering for telling a history in women's words.[28] This task continues to be a formidable one in South Asia, where the religious cultures of Islam and Hinduism circumscribe the discussion of rape as a dishonorable matter. As well, the patriarchal community cultures have determined the limits of speech and have found ways to hide the embarrassing traces of women's experiences from public and social memory. Women's memories survive, it seems, in the private sphere and are dealt with as private matters by victims' families.

In the next section, I engage the survivors' memories of 1971. Even though the traumatic violence ruined their relationship to society, community, and even their sense of self, survivors' silence tells with certainty the pain that haunts them and seeks release in guarded speech.

State Silence, Women's Speech

No previous scholarly research laid pathways for me to reach survivors of sexual violence in Bangladesh. In hushed tones survivors whom I met through "underground" channels expressed fear that academic concern will not redress their condition. To this was added a cultural unease that discussion of sexual violence was a western fetish. Survivors' concerns urged a critical self-reflexivity, in Patricia Yaeger's term a "textual anxiety," raising questions on research ethics.[29] Given the dangers of commodification and risks of cultural hubris, I questioned my project.

Despite my anxiety, the memories of the "liberation war," Pakistani brutality and exploitation of women, the role of *rajakars* (collaborators), and the excavation of mass graves were strategically deployed for election campaigning in 2001. Each political party claimed to be the "original freedom fighters" and promised to try the war criminals if elected to power. The election campaign monopolized people's memories and stifled the women's question.

A search in the archives for a more nuanced history of the war proved fruitless. The issue of who controlled power for generating or forgetting the memories of 1971 and interrogating them, I realized, was essential to move beyond the rhetoric of blame and continued domination of women's voices. The challenge was to engage the cultural and institutional structures without reproducing a spectacle of violence.[30] Using the feminist approach of first-person narrative as the starting point to find and tell history, I traveled throughout Bangladesh to listen to women's accounts, viewing the different groups with the lens of "feminist humanism," that is, without discriminating on the grounds of ethnicity, class, religion, or language. My aim was to make available these women's stories so that we may "see" these people for who they are and engage their experiences for understanding the connection (or lack thereof) between the nation and its women, recognizing the different realities and the common conditions of the survivors.

Beauty, a "war-child," led me to an underground world of survivors in Bangladesh.[31] Beauty's mission is to trace her father who impregnated her mother during the war so that she can make sense of herself as a human person. Her poignant words were, "I look like a human being to you, but I don't have a human life." During my yearlong stay (2001–2) I interviewed more than two hundred survivors and collected fifty testimonies of sexual violence.

It is important to note here that the word 'rape' rarely surfaced in these conversations; instead, terms such as abduction, marriage, torture, or visit were used to convey the forced sexual interaction. Almost all women described the moment of rape as a state of unconsciousness and told me that it was not only the Pakistani soldiers, but also Bengali and Bihari politicians, strangers, neighbors, and even friends and family members who preyed on them during the war. Women also talked about sexual violence as a rampant phenomenon in the conflict zone. The victims were the rich and the poor, Bengali, Bihari, Jaiantia, Muslim, and Hindu women of East Pakistan.

The violent sexual experiences have led survivors to question the ethical dimension of nationalism and the cost of nation building. These women were bitter that no commemorative memorial has been dedicated to them despite the "double violence" they experienced—arrested and tortured for fighting for freedom and raped because of their gender. The long silences made initial discussion of rape very difficult. However, once women started talking they told multifold stories. Many admitted that sharing their traumatic memories was therapeutic. This shattered the myth that women did not want to talk. It became clear that it is not women, but structures and institutions beyond their control that restrict their speech and force them to forget what they endured.

Maimona Begum, a middle-class Bengali Muslim woman from northern Bangladesh, was thirty-six years old and a mother of seven children in

1971. She is now widowed and lives with two of her married sons in their family home. I went to visit Maimona to hear about her husband's work, who as a gynecologist had the opportunity to "help" many rape victims. Instead, during our meeting Maimona told me her story in these words:

> We were a large family; my in-laws also lived with us; there were thirty-two people in this house. At midnight I heard some voices outside our compound and I realized that the Pakistani soldiers were knocking on our door. They were demanding that my husband should come out. I also heard some of our neighbors. They told the soldiers, "we have shown you the house, now we are leaving. We cannot show our face to the doctor." . . . I pleaded with the soldiers not to take my husband; I knew that they would kill him. . . . The soldiers argued with me and tried to intimidate me. I kept moving backwards as they kept coming toward me. Suddenly, I was pushed into a corner room and the door was bolted shut. A large Pakistani soldier pinned me down and ripped off my sari; I became unconscious. When I regained my senses I realized what had happened. The soldier had raped me. I was lying on the floor and my husband was looking at me with tears in his eyes.[32]

Anyone who listens to Maimona's story has no trouble in understanding what happened to her on that fateful night when an ordinary solider with institutional power invested in him by the state and society had targeted a vulnerable woman. Maimona endured great pain and played the scripted gender role of protecting her family, but her role ended there. Henceforth she became a rape victim (*birangona*). How does one understand this violence? Even before I could pose the question, Maimona said:

> To understand the violence, you have to see the whole picture. The Bengalis were fighting the Pakistanis. It was a national war. But there were many internal wars that were fought simultaneously. . . . When neighbors fight against their neighbors, armies are immaterial. My neighbors led the soldiers to our house; how else would the Pakistanis have found us? That has hurt me the most. I have never felt whole again, although I still live in the same neighborhood. . . . I have lived with the pain of silence.

Maimona's suffering, no doubt, is personal, but her testimony reflects and embeds the context of the dispersed and generalized nature of violence. In her experience we encounter the face of horror that women saw in their own neighborhoods reflected in familiar faces that became those of strangers during the war. Violence took away Maimona's speech, and there was no more continuity between the past and present as her life became marked by silence. The irony is that no one, not even her own family, mustered the courage to take notice and ask her to tell her story.

Superficially, the life of Sajida Begum is very different from that of Maimona Begum. In Bangladesh she belongs to the teeming majority of the landless, laboring poor in Bangladesh, who are not considered actors in history. Sajida recalled:

> In 1971 I was a young woman. Many Bengalis and *rajakars* often came to our village and tortured the people. One afternoon, when I was washing utensils by the pond, they attacked me from behind. I shouted for help but even my mother ran away, everyone was running for their own lives. I fainted. When I regained my senses, I found I was in my house. I became ill for many days due to the loss of blood. My periods stopped for a few months and my mother took me to a doctor. They did a test and found that I was pregnant. I was so young, I did not understand anything. They did an abortion and my mother promised to take me home thereafter, but she did not come back to fetch me. I later heard that my father died of shock. Our country was independent by then. . . . But I never got anything I desired in my life. My children are ashamed of me. No one from my family has ever visited me. What was my crime?[33]

Sajida's testimony contains in its very core the unspeakable betrayal of family and community who punished her for her vulnerability. The human relationships and affection that she had hoped for were totally destroyed for her. Although Sajida tries to make a better life with her children, the haunting silence between them continues to disrupt a sense of togetherness.

Men raped women for many reasons: passion, anger, ideology, to establish power, to create terror, to humiliate and dishonor enemy men, or simply for the sake of it. Rape established a woman's vulnerability and a man's power. Yet men did more to terrorize women. The female body was an object of attack, and the fear of attack became dominant, so much so that it produced extreme anxiety in families. A young woman, whom I will refer to as Laila, recounted a poignant story of this uneasy relationship:

> From the terrace of our house we could see fire raging throughout the town. This was on April 14, 1971. My family told me to hide. . . . Next morning, when I returned home, I found out that my father was taken away in the night. My mother was waiting for me and she hurriedly moved us to another building where there were many people hiding, maybe ninety or so. . . . My father did not come back that night. Next morning it started to rain. We could smell rotten flesh outside the building. I looked out and saw that my father's body was there with several others. I wanted to go out

and bring his body inside. It felt so disrespectful to leave him in the street. But no one allowed me to go out. . . . Being a woman, my body was considered to be dangerous to myself and others, but I could not do anything because everyone was afraid. So we waited and hid inside the abandoned building all day. In the evening, some men came in a truck and picked up the dead bodies. I don't know who these men were, whether they were Bengali or Pakistani. They made a large shallow grave and put the dead bodies in it and left. I could see that my father's body was hardly covered with soil. But no one cared that he did not get a decent burial. I was helpless.[34]

Laila's world was sealed off, in the words of Primo Levi, by "monads," who by rejecting an association with vulnerable bodies, hers and her father's, were desperately struggling to stay alive, which they did but with a price that was paid by another.[35] Laila converted the lesson of her gender-based powerlessness during the war into a positive force by becoming involved in establishing primary health care for rural women, with which she is still actively involved.

In telling their multifold stories women created a space for interrogating community and nation from a human standpoint. The feminine that was attacked and destroyed in the war was not a simple biological category; rather, it was the domain of the interior, the location of emotion, and the place of home. According to women's evaluation, gender violence was the destruction of community and human trust simultaneously. For this reason many women have forced themselves to forget their memories so as to regain a normalized life within their community.

Occasionally when women spoke of their memories, they told complex stories of the war and urged us, their listeners, to go beyond the text of history and listen to a different narrative. An elderly Bihari refugee woman whom I will refer to as Sakeena related such an alternative narrative. After providing a graphic account of violence that she had witnessed, she ended her story with these words:

One evening, someone dumped a half-dead body of a child outside the mosque. . . . The child was bleeding profusely. She was in shock and could not speak. . . . I tried to save her, but she died three days later. I can never forget her. You ask me, who could have possibly done this to a child? Don't ask me, who killed whom, who raped whom, what was the religion, ethnic, or linguistic background of the people who died in the war. The victims in the war were the women of this country—mothers who lost children, sisters who lost their brothers, wives who lost their husbands, women who lost everything—their honor and dignity. In the war men victimized women. It was a year of anarchy. *Insāniyat* had died. Do I need to explain this?[36]

Women's testimonies and silences are acts of resistance and remembrance, calling into question the figure of the enemy, which they identified as the hypermasculinized state. This hypermasculinized state used its agents, men, to execute violence in the name of nationalism. Individual women who made up part of an integral whole were depersonalized, brutalized, and tormented. By making them anonymous after its brutal acts, the impersonal state and society freed itself of an obligation and relationship. To reclaim an autonomous memory, survivors demanded the foregrounding of women's *insāniyat* (humanity) and its destruction in sexual violence. To probe this, I turned to combatants, men, to reveal what they did in 1971 and have since hidden.

Questioning Humanity, Men's Talk

In Bangladesh, my first face-to-face encounter with a perpetrator took place one evening toward the end of my stay. After recounting the violence he committed against a young woman who "treated [him] like a brother," the veteran/perpetrator whom I will refer to as Kajol pondered, "in the eyes of the nation I am some kind of a hero, but do you think so? I had become a criminal, I understand it today."[37] Kajol's testimony challenged my assumption that perpetrators were cold, inhuman killers, or like animals. Rather, the perpetrator, like his victim, emerged against my power of intellectual capacity as an author of a different text and as a human endowed with a moral force who questioned the structures that controlled his life—nation, state, religion, and community. The awareness that at least some of the perpetrators also seem to suffer as a result of their violent actions compelled me to seek their memories for developing a new history of the war.

Because the states of Pakistan and India were involved in the war, my oral history project with combatants focused on these two locations. In Pakistan I conducted more than one hundred and fifty interviews with a sampling of army men, and in India I interviewed more than a dozen top-ranking army officials who were directly involved in the war.

Today many of them are reluctant to revisit their actions, and the majority used a common rhetoric of nationalism to justify their activities. Indian army men defended their armed infiltration into East Pakistan by claiming that "They [the people of East Pakistan] were all Indians in their heart."[38] While several recognized that rape was a big problem, a general told me, "One cannot count and give numbers. Remember all kinds of atrocities can be done to women by men. All armies are questionable in this matter," he added.[39]

The Pakistani army men also claimed the rhetoric of nationalism. They continue to believe that "initially, the Bengali people were not against us [Pakistanis]. Many of them continued to be pro-Pakistani to the end. But the Indians manipulated them. With the help of the Hindu intellectuals, who were Indian infiltrators, they engineered a civil war. . . . We were simultaneously fighting a variety of enemies there," they claim, which led them to use violence. They tried to sanitize the violence by explaining that "not too many people were killed in East Pakistan, no more than fifty or sixty thousand." The three million that Bangladesh claims were killed "is an exaggeration," according to them. Frequently, they talked about killing as "duty" and rarely addressed the issue of rape. Occasionally they admitted to having had "relationships," "affairs," and "girlfriends" in East Pakistan. One officer told me, "I had a girlfriend there. She was married, but it was mutual. Her husband did not stop us from meeting. Today, people like her scream and say, 'he raped me.' Then, it was not like that."[40] Even if we accept the rhetoric of "relationship," Pakistani men's reporting of these interactions without taking into account the hierarchies of power at work between a Pakistani officer and a Bengali housewife are truly disconcerting. A retired major in the Pakistan Army remarked, "It was like a picnic in Dhaka. We had no work to do during the day. In the evening we went to the Dhaka Club. After the surrender, the Indians behaved with us like friends. The war was over; there was no need to be uncivil."

The description of war as a state of picnic, the whitewashing of bloody murders as "duty" for nation, and the distancing of oneself from the reality of the use of force on women by calling it an "affair" are rationalizations. These explanations sanitize war and make it into an event for which no one is directly responsible. However, rationalizations fall short of addressing the more important and critical internal issues of the breakdown of human dignity and responsibility. In my discussions I probed the impact of violence on men. I will now examine two testimonies to provide a general sketch of the range of memories and scrutinize them to understand the moral frame of humanity that was destroyed.

As a trained doctor and a soldier, Major Adil remembered his experiences in East Pakistan with these words:

> When I arrived in Chittagong on April 4th, I saw dead bodies floating in the water. There were fifty or sixty dead bodies. . . . I saw a dead baby,

maybe six months old, without its neck or arms. . . . I wanted to get a sub-machine gun and kill any Bengali. . . . They had already killed so many non-Bengalis . . . they did not even spare women and children. . . . We were sent to Santahaar. . . . It was a railway colony and a railway junction. There were more than 30,000 people there, mostly Biharis, but there were some Hindu and Muslim Bengalis, too. When we entered the place we started firing. . . . Suddenly we saw some young children approaching us. They were crying. . . . They said, "They killed them all, our sisters, broth-ers, and our parents." They were all Urdu speakers. We started looking . . . thousands of dead bodies were there . . . this mess probably happened three [or] four days earlier. . . . The estimate was 22,000 killed, but it was not possible to count, we found some widows and they told us about hor-rible things that happened to them . . . we made several long graves and buried the dead bodies.[41]

This incident tremendously affected Major Adil, and he was in the mood for revenge. "I decided there had to be a bullet for a bullet." Yet when pro-vided with an opportunity to kill a wounded *Mukti Bahini* (rival Bengali) soldier, he could not do so. "I looked at the guy and said, 'I am a soldier and a doctor. I can kill my enemy as a soldier but not as a doctor.'" Instead, Major Adil treated him and sent him to the military hospital. The chapter of "1971 will always remain open," for Major Adil, he reminisced. In his mind it is an "unfinished memory" that leaves him "very dissatisfied." On probing his dissatisfaction, he revealed that his agony was much deeper and had its roots in the partition of 1947. He recalled:

In 1947, I was a young boy, about nine years old. We were given thirty minutes to leave our home. It was September 2nd. I still remember that day. There were thousands of refugees . . . we started walking. We cov-ered eleven miles. . . . I was very thirsty, but there was no water. I saw a lit-tle puddle of water and bent down like a dog to drink from it. My mother told me "don't do that, you will get jaundice," but I said, "I cannot live, I am dying of thirst." . . . That incident I will never forget, they [the Indi-ans] made us into dogs. . . . In 1971 it was like a flashback. We were fight-ing the Indians in our own home. They had planned it beautifully. First, they threw us out of our homes in the Punjab and, then, cut Pakistan into two. . . . But I could not take my revenge.

He reasoned that he could not kill in cold blood because he had been taught to respect human life, and his enemies demanded that he uphold this ethos during challenges to it. He did this with a mixed sense of pride and pain. Many in Pakistan expressed similar sentiments. The raw wound of 1947 and partition of their homeland, the ignominy of refugee life in West Pakistan, and the struggle to "make it" as first-generation émigrés were lessons many carried with them to the battlefields in East Pakistan, and they responded to that memory.

The story of the common soldier in the Pakistan Army, on the other hand, is quite different. He was not motivated by enmity with India, and he did not understand the intricacies of national politics. It was generally poverty that motivated these men to join the army. Given that the soldiers came from extremely impoverished conditions and were illiterate, it was not difficult to train them to be obedient, to follow orders of their superiors, and even to commit violence in the name of protecting religion and nation. A soldier whom I will refer to as Aziz recalled:

> Initially I did not know that we will be sent to Bengal. . . . I did not want to go there. But I could not defy orders. When we arrived there we heard that the Bengalis are killing the Biharis indiscriminately. We were told to teach them a lesson. Our leaders told us, "we don't care for people, we want land. In any case, most of the people here are from India." . . . We did violence in excess. We killed whoever we found, took their women and tortured them, burnt their fields and crop. . . . People fled their homes in fear. Sometimes, we would come across stray animals that were left behind, but entire villages were depopulated. . . . Once I caught a young man who was in the Mukti Bahini. My officer told me to throw him over the bridge and shoot him. I did so. I feel dreadful to tell you this. . . . One thing, however, I will tell you, keeping God as my witness, I did not commit sin. I did my duty as I was told.[42]

In Aziz's view, what he did in East Pakistan, even the cold-blooded murders and violence against civilians, was part of his "duty." For a soldier of his rank, at least in his explanation, it was not possible to question and disobey an order. However, when I probed the effects of violence on him, he explained it in a metaphorical language:

> My mother started having bad dreams. She was very perturbed and went to a local Sufi sheikh. He told her to sacrifice a goat in my name, which my mother did. When they cut the meat the muscles were still throbbing. My mother knew that I was in trouble. She did a lot of prayers and asked God to save and protect me from committing sins. . . . The Bengalis got their country because of the sacrifice of a few. The rest are enjoying it today. We are hiding in shame because we committed violence.

The recognition that men like him had committed violence has great consequences. Repentance, Aziz learned from his mother, was necessary for healing. Yet there is no political space in Pakistan for men like Aziz to discuss what they experienced and lost.

During another interview a soldier casually told me, "The war made me realize we have a long way to go before we become human beings." In this single sentence, told in a matter-of-fact manner, my interlocutor addressed poignantly the condition of men who were part of the war machinery. War had transformed them from human beings into caricatures following orders of others who held power over them. They could neither question nor disobey their superiors, but in executing the duty of killing they forgot the mutually subjective connection between human beings. Today, several decades later by remembering their violent acts and acknowledging the humanity of others, these men have started to reshape themselves and those they thought they had destroyed. A new human voice is slowly emerging at the margin of the national narrative and challenging the powerful official myth.

In Conclusion: Humanity of the "Other"

Based on their experiences, the male and female survivors of 1971 make a fervent appeal to reconsider the contingent nature of the public identities and, in turn, ask us to focus on *insāniyat* (humanity) that was disgraced in the war. They remind us that public identities are multiple, being constructed from nationalism, ethnicity, religion, gender, etc. Nevertheless, there is space to recognize the common humanity within the diversity of contingent identities. For survivors the ethics of *insāniyat* or shared humanity became clearer after violence, and they urge its recovery in writing a new history.

I draw, therefore, upon the discourses of Mevlana Jalaluddin Rumi and Emmanuel Levinas's on the subject of humanism and responsibility of self to other. Although Rumi and Levinas wrote in different times, locations, and philosophical and cultural traditions (Rumi was a twelfth-century mystical philosopher-poet of Konya, Turkey, and spoke about Islam and love, and Levinas is a twentieth-century Talmudic commentator who wrote after the Holocaust to address the mutually subjective relationship between the Germans and Jews in Europe), their messages of humanism resonate the common sentiments of a search for humanity. Like these thinkers, survivors urge us to create a common frame of humanity that reaches beyond nations and boundaries.

Levinas asks whether one can be liable for that which one has no personal responsibility? His penetrating inquiry is not a demand for knowing "facts" about the other, but is instead an appeal to acknowledge responsibility to the other. The appeal of ethical obligation is not intended to make common platforms for creating an instrumentalist agenda. Rather, the point is "the calling of consciousness into question,"[43] which does not reduce but exists within concern for the other and the other's call to justice that, for Levinas, represents the "trace" of the infinite, and to "transcendence," in which good surpasses "objective experience" and history.[44]

If we respond to Levinas's call to "feel" the moment of 1971, which survivors are asking of us, then we can perhaps begin to appreciate the limitations of the soldiers/perpetrators and the vulnerability of victims. We have to begin by accepting that the worlds of perpetrators and victims are separate. Hence the struggles of both perpetrators and victims for an enduring memory of their multiple experiences are also different. The inability to accept differences, as we know by now, formed the basis of the struggle between East and West Pakistan. Therefore, if we are to develop the ethic we need to understand the events of 1971, then our "first philosophy," to use Levanis's phrase, is to accept difference and not diminish the other to fit the classifications created by our own consciousness. The basis of this ethical humanism is the sheer fact of "otherness," which transforms us.

Several centuries before Levinas, Jalaluddin Rumi offered a new perspective on humanity. His poems and stories covered a wide field of knowledge concerning theological and spiritual matters. Within the vast range of Rumi's scholarship we find recurring references to love as a possibility of intrusion from outside—an encounter with another, a stranger, the Unknown—for interrupting the project of ego and forgetting the self. Rumi begins his famous book of poems, *The Mathnawi*, by reminding his listeners that in telling stories of others we begin to understand the secrets of our selves.[45] In Rumi's humanism, divisions between human beings are irrelevant, and the connotations of good and bad, east and west, self and other, disappear.

To exploit successfully Rumi's message of self-annihilation within a historical framework, we can begin to question the project of nationalism and the violence that accompanies the nation-building process for creating differences and the power of one group over others, which was the source of violence. The violent memories compel survivors to face the other and look at the image of their national selves, which is deformed and bloodied. This they want to reform and remedy now. They raise critical questions about the passive acceptance of nationalism and national identity, and provide us with a language of interrogation for developing agency. In turn, they enable us to create new vocabularies of knowing self and the other for remembering the fundamental ground of *insāniyat* (humanity).

The space of freedom to move beyond markers and inscriptions could offer a place for convening a new narrative of peace beyond the dominant national histories of hate in Pakistan, Bangladesh, and India, and enable people to share and understand their common human condition in South Asia. Telling a new history after the violence of 1971 in survivors' voices may be the way out of the bloodied mess of the past.

PART IV

Law and Civilization

Chapter 10
The Theory and Practice of Female Immunity in the Medieval West

Anne Curry

And if in war many evil things are done, they never come from the nature of war but from false usage, as when a man-at-arms takes a woman and does her shame and injury or sets fire to a church.

My opening quotation comes from *The Tree of Battles*, a treatise on warfare written by Honoré de Bonet around 1387.[1] Bonet begins his work with a fundamental question: what is war? "I answer . . . that war is nothing other than discord or conflict that has arisen on account of certain things displeasing to the human will, to the end that such conflict should be turned into agreement and reason." In other words, war was, to use a modern phrase, conflict resolution. Bonet then asks "where did war first exist and why?" "It was in heaven when our lord God drove out the angels," following Lucifer's attempt to usurp His position. "Hence it is no great marvel if in this world there arise wars and battles, since they existed first in Heaven." War was therefore seen as integral to human existence and to the Christian religion itself. Indeed, it is no coincidence that Bonet should write on the matter at the time he did, during the papal schism that had reinvigorated the Hundred Years' War because the English and French supported rival popes. We should not be surprised that one of Bonet's reasons for writing his *Tree of Battles*, as expressed in the dedicatory preface to Charles VI of France, read as follows: "I see all holy Christendom so burdened by wars and hatreds, robberies and dissensions that it is hard to name one little region, be it duchy or county, that enjoys good peace."

The problem of war had vexed the Christian Church from its earliest days. While it was an underground movement, it had been easy to pursue a belief in nonviolence.[2] Once it was the official faith of the Roman Empire and the barbarians were being converted, matters were less simple. While the waging of war against pagans, Muslims, or even Christian heretics was unproblematic because it was fought in the name of the faith, theologians had to justify war fought between Christians.[3] They therefore defined circumstances under which it was "legal," revolving largely around the notion that only properly constituted political authority could declare a "just war." This is commonly known as the *ius ad bellum*. What followed naturally from this was a definition of proper conduct in war itself—*ius in bello*. It was this to which Bonet was referring in the opening quotation. War was not in itself evil so long as "right usage" was maintained. But there needed to be limitations. In this passage Bonet tells us of sexual violence against women, and attacks on churches. The same juxtaposition is seen in the disciplinary ordinances for the English army issued two years previously for a campaign against the Scots. "Item that no one be so bold as to rob or pillage a church, nor to kill a man of holy church, nor a hermit, nor a woman, nor to take any prisoner unless they carry arms, nor to force a woman against her will."[4] The penalty for all of these offenses was death by hanging.

These quotations remind us of an important point when considering sexual violence in medieval warfare. Attempted limitations on soldiers' behavior did not derive from concern for women but from a broader concern for noncombatants in general. While Christian apologists could justify war between soldiers fighting on behalf of legitimate political authority, they considered that a just war between Christians should neither involve nor damage civilians. In reality, such a situation was difficult, if not impossible, to achieve. Medieval warfare was characterized not by pitched battles between soldiers but by sieges of towns, raids through rural areas that aimed at devastation of crops and buildings, burning and looting of villages, and attacks on or abductions of civilians. What we have before us, as in so many periods of history and geographical contexts, is a gap between theory and practice. Indeed, were that not the case, there would have been no need for pronouncements on the limitations of soldiers' behavior. To give a modern analogy, there would be no need for speed limits if no one ever speeded.

Although women were only one of several categories of noncombatants whom the theorists tried to protect, they had a special vulnerability. Not only could they be killed, wounded, or captured, but they could also be raped. This is clearly acknowledged in Bonet's text as also in the military ordinances of 1385. These references come from the later fourteenth century when warfare, at least in western Europe, was largely fought between legitimate political authorities, such as the war between England and France. What of earlier centuries when political authority was looser? Can we identify a particular concern then, too, about the possibility of sexual violence in warfare? And during the period as a whole, what conclusions can we reach about actual practice? Did medieval warfare include sexual violence?

Answering these questions is not easy. A perennial problem when attempting an overview of this kind is a reliance on snippets of surviving information from diverse periods and places. Although the Christian faith remained a force for homogeneity (even in times of papal schism, which were political rather than religious disputes), local cultures and traditions varied considerably across the medieval West, because it was geographically and ethnically diverse. We can never be certain that what was happening in one place at one time was necessarily representative. Furthermore, we cannot be sure that theoretical writings were known across the whole of the medieval West. For instance, Bonet's work was known in England and France but not in other areas of Europe. Another difficulty is the reliance on narrative accounts, such as annals or chronicles. These are not records of fact but of opinion, often written for a purpose. In this respect they have much in common with literary sources. Both genres are more useful for showing us what mattered to people at the time rather than what actually happened. And when I say people I mean elites, because literacy was severely limited. Chronicles and literary sources give examples of the use of sexual violence in warfare, but, as I will reiterate in my conclusion, it was something the opposition did, never the home side. This in itself is a clear indication that sexual violence was met with opprobrium; otherwise there would have been no advantage in using it as a means of denigrating the enemy.

In general, sources increase the further we get into the period. For instance, most of writings on which we rely for *ius in bello* derive from the eleventh century onward, inspired by the expansion of scholasticism and of canon law. This does not mean that the ideas they propounded were novel but that they were now being clarified, recorded, and disseminated more formally. Furthermore, the role of the secular state expanded, especially in terms of its legal capacity based on both Roman and common-law systems. Fundamentally, the Christian ethic of war remained constant, but it was reinterpreted and restated according to circumstances.

The same can be said of attitudes toward rape. Throughout the whole of medieval Christendom over the entire period, sexual attacks on women were forbidden. This applied equally to the context of peace as to war. Rape fell within the purview of the Church as a sexual offense and so required the performance of penance. Punishments can therefore be found in the handbooks produced by the church to lay down the appropriate punishments. These are known as the penitentials and are a particularly valuable source for the early medieval period. However, there was never a single system for the whole of Christendom. Even though we can know what penalties were meant to be, there is little evidence regarding actual implementation—another problem of theory as opposed to practice. The same problem applies in the secular context. Already in Roman law rape was a public offense, not a private wrong, and therefore punishable by the state.[5] As state authority diminished in the post-Roman period, the Church took a larger role in punishment of it, but as the power of secular rulers grew again, the prosecution of rape fell increasingly to them. In theory most imposed the death penalty, but, as many studies have shown, this was rarely implemented. The pursuit of alleged offenders was uneven, and many cases ended in acquittal.

The complex issue of consent loomed as large then as now. Moreover, in a society molded by Christian teachings on the evils of sex, a woman could find herself liable to penance for fornication even if an unwilling victim. According to Gratian, one of the key compilers of canon law in the twelfth century, the loss of virginity by whatever means prevented a woman from ever becoming a nun.[6] In Roman law, too, she was seen as an accomplice to the offense.[7] In both canon and civil law, the case hinged on the degree of force involved and the level of resistance that the woman had offered. It was only from the time of Pope Alexander III (1159–81) that a woman raped forcibly by someone other than her husband was not deemed guilty of adultery herself.[8] It is easy to see the treatment of rape—by a church, and by ecclesiastical and secular courts, all run by men—as yet another example of the denigration of women; yet, as James Brundage has shown, it can only be understood in the broader context of medieval views on sexual activity and social order. In this context again there is a gulf between theory and practice.

As I have already suggested, attempts to limit attacks on women stemmed from a more general concern for noncombatants as a whole. This was not simply inaugurated by the conversion to Christianity. The medieval West inherited much from the Greek and Roman past. Concepts of a just war date back at least to Aristotle. The Romans had some notion of it. In the words of Cicero, "not only must we show consideration for those we have conquered by force of arms, but we must also ensure protection for those who lay down their arms and throw themselves on the mercy of our generals."[9] Yet there was also the notion that a declaration of war abrogated any obligation to respect an enemy's rights and therefore allowed the capture of civilians.[10] Given that Roman military treatises were re-used in the Middle Ages, it is important to note what they said on the question of noncombatants and more especially women. The answer is, very little. Vegetius tells us that "those unfit for fighting by reason of age or sex were often shut out of the gates because of the need to conserve food;" this was not for their own benefit, but rather to save food for the male defenders.[11] Valerius Maximus praises Scipio for expelling 2,000 prostitutes from the army, because this purifies his army and enables its victory against the Numantinae. This notion of sexual activity weakening men is found in many medieval contexts. The disciplinary ordinances of the English army in the early fifteenth century not only retained the ban on rape seen in those of 1385 but also tried to exclude women from the camp and to control soldiers' access to sexual services.[12] In other words, a fighting force was expected to be clean living even if not wholly chaste. Although coming from different theoretical viewpoints from the ban on sexual violence, this attitude constituted another limitation on soldiers' behavior toward women. Another Roman treatise that became popular in later centuries was the *Strategemata* of Frontinus. He includes the story of Alexander who returned a beautiful virgin captive to her fiancé, the enemy leader. The implication is that he could have had her for his own pleasure, a reminder that in the classical period, captured women could be taken as wives or concubines. We shall return to the issue of sexual violence through capture later, because it is an important feature of both early medieval and crusading contexts. However, save for these references, Roman military treatises do not give attention to sexual or indeed any other attacks on women.

Nor do early Christian writers. Ambrose of Milan wrote that soldiers had a responsibility to the innocent. This word is in itself significant; the *innocentes* were those who were not "nocentes" (i.e., those who committed harm).[13] Other early writers, such as St. Augustine of Hippo and Isidore of Seville, implied civilian immunity but did not single out women. Certainly there is nothing to parallel the explicit comment in Bonet's *Tree of Battles* or in the military ordinances. This raises important questions. Is the explanation for the lack of emphasis on noncombatants that it was obvious that war would affect everyone, or that it was obvious that noncombatants should not be attacked, and/or that they were not? Does the complete lack of specific references to women as victims mean that they would be attacked and that because of their gender they would be subject to sexual as well as physical violence, or that it was so obvious that they were not to be attacked in either way? After all, the contemporary statements on rape were categorical. It was a capital offense. Yet arguments from silence are always problematic.

In this context a late seventh-century Irish text, the "Law of the Innocents" of Adomnán, abbot of Iona, is important. The text opens with the abbot's reminiscence of a visitation from an angel who struck him on the side with a lance saying, "Go forth into Ireland and make a law in it that women be not in any manner killed by men."[14] Whoever killed a woman was to be condemned to a twofold punishment: first, physical mutilation (the right hand and left foot cut off) followed by execution; and second, a compensatory payment of seven female slaves by the murderer's kin to the kin of his victim. The first punishment could be commuted by a fine, 14 years' penance, and an increase in the number of slaves to be handed over. This tendency to allow lesser penalties is common in the medieval context, as has been shown by the studies of rape in which the death penalty was rarely invoked yet never abandoned. It has to be said, of course, that there was a tension in Christian thought on execution in the same way as there was about warfare. While one death might justify another (that also being consistent with Celtic and Germanic traditions of vendetta), the imposition of the death penalty for rape was seen as disproportionate. The Church itself could not effect executions, because it could not kill, and therefore depended on the secular arm.

Because there was no fully effective secular authority at the time of Adomnán, it is not surprising that his suggested punishment for rape of a maiden is solely monetary. His attempt to encourage moral probity is revealed, however, by the smaller financial penalties he imposes for acts short of full penetration, which included placing a hand on her, putting a hand under her dress, tearing her clothes, or causing a blemish on her face or other parts of her body (these last references suggesting an expectation of resistance). There is no mention of gang rape, but in his section on murder we find:

> But if an army has done it (committed murder of a woman) every fifth man up to three hundred shall be condemned to the standard punishment. If fewer, they shall be divided into three parts. The first part shall be put to death by lots, hand and foot first cut off; the second part shall pay in full 14 female slaves; the third part shall be cast into exile beyond the sea, under the rule of hard regimen.

Yet Adomnán does not include any similar arrangement for rape. It is assumed that the offender will be known and can be prosecuted as an individual. This is also implied in a later section where compensations are payable "if a woman has been got with child by stealth, without contract, without full rights, without dowry, without betrothal," reminding us that one of the reasons for concern over rape was that it disrupted marriage practices, and indeed was sometimes used by young couples to effect a marriage against their parents' wishes. The offense was therefore against the family not simply the woman, which meant that compensation was commonly paid to them and not her. That Adomnán did not refer to sexual violence by the army could be taken as evidence that he did not consider such a practice likely, or that it could be handled within the standard arrangements for rape. It was certainly envisaged that the fighting classes might commit rape. Penitentials frequently include the requirement that they put their arms aside for the period of the penance, even though they do not specifically mention rape as an event associated with warfare.[15]

Adomnán also stipulates fines for inflicting wounds on women, clergy, and other innocents. This combination of groups is very similar to that of the ordinances of 1385, and, as we shall see, to the writings of the canon lawyers of the central Middle Ages. Other penitentials of the early medieval period give punishments for murder, but none single out women or mention rape in a context of war.[16] In the ninth-century Carolingian empire, however, we find some important statements. Most significant is the *Capitula judiciorum*, a compilation of penitential statements compiled in the second half of the century: "If anyone by force violates a woman either in the host (i.e. in the army) or in any place without her consent, she is not to pay penance for fornication."[17]

The basic problem of the moral culpability of the woman was not new. Byzantine sources show that it was a common dilemma in the minds of Church authorities. Yet what is significant here is the concession made in the military context, because it implies that rape might be expected in warfare. It is tempting to link the statement to the work of Hincmar, archbishop of Reims (d. 882), because he is known to have given a homily in the name of the emperor (Lothar) on the evils of rape ("de coercendo et exstirpando raptu viduarum, puellarum et sanctimonialium").[18] A further suggestion of Hincmar's influence may be revealed in the *Constitutio* (comparable with the later military ordinances) issued by Lothar when he launched an expedition to Benevento in 866: "And because the time of assembly is approaching Lent, during which time the precepts of God are to be observed, we order that anyone who breaks and enters a church of God, or commits adultery (*adulteria*) or arson, shall put their lives in jeopardy."[19]

The use of the word *adulteria* implies that troops were expected to indulge in sexual activity while on campaign. The ban may have been focused on camp followers as much as, or rather than, assaults on the women of the enemy, and was certainly linked to the moral salvation of the soldier rather than concern for noncombatant victims. Note, however, the linked contexts of sacrilege and sexual offenses, as in the late fourteenth-century context.

What we are probably seeing in these mid-ninth-century works is a precursor of the peace movement. This began at the turn of the century when the Frankish Church sought to limit the level of violence in the wars between the nobility that had broken out following the collapse of Carolingian royal authority. The Church tried to establish a code of nonviolence against noncombatants in war waged between Christians, first in the edict of the Peace of God in 898 and renewed in the Truce of God in 1027.[20] A good example of this is the oath made by the Capetian ruler of Western Frankia, Robert the Pious, between 996 and 1031:

> I will not infringe the church in any way. . . . I will not hurt a cleric or monk if unarmed. . . . I will not attack a villein or a female villein or servants or merchant for ransom. . . . I will not attack noble ladies travelling without their husbands nor their maids, nor widows or nuns unless it is their fault.[21]

Edicts were commonly pronounced at church councils, such as that at Narbonne of 1054, which banned attacks on clerics, monks, nuns, women, pilgrims, merchants, peasants, or visitors to churches and cemeteries, even giving details of the extent of the nonconflict zone around such areas.[22] In other words, the noncombatant was being defined, but in none of these sources is there reference to sexual violence against women. Because all attacks on women were banned, there seemed to be no need to provide an additional distinction. The same conclusion must apply to the Decretum of 1140. This was a compilation of canon law and other treatises made by Gratian at the University of Bologna, which contained a chapter on war, much of which was derived from Augustine of Hippo and Isidore of Seville. Thus far the edicts and penitentials we have discussed related only to the local context. The Decretum was widely disseminated, and with it we can start to speak of a Christendom-wide code of the immunity of the noncombatant. Gratian also exempted pilgrims, clerics, monks, women, and the unarmed poor from violence, imposing the penalty of excommunication.[23]

Furthermore, women were often omitted from subsequent writings of this kind. While Thomas Aquinas (d. 1274) debated the just war, he concentrated more on proper authority and the problem of clerical involvement.[24] He did, however, suggest that newly wedded men should be exempted from military service, because if they were killed their friends and relations would be demoralized.[25] Women were not included in the eight groups listed as having total security against the ravages of war in *De Treuga et Pace*, which was added to the corpus of canon law under Pope Gregory IX (1227–41). This omission is probably explained by the understanding that women already enjoyed what is called a negative immunity based on their inability to bear arms because of their sex. In other words, they could not fight, whereas groups like merchants and clerics were physically capable of bearing arms, but their office or function in society made it inappropriate for them to do so. Because the Decretalists believed that an unjust war should not be fought at all, there was no need to specify that there should not be attacks on noncombatants.[26] The omission of women is also, I think, related to the changing nature of armies. By the thirteenth century, armies were increasingly in the employ of the state and were therefore formally constituted to fight a war made legitimate by the proper authority. This was certainly the understanding of Aquinas.

Therefore, limitations on soldiers' treatment of women were left to the disciplinary ordinances issued for specific armies. This is well documented by the English evidence for the Hundred Years' War. Disciplinary ordinances were certainly issued by Edward III for his invasion of France in 1346.[27] Although no text survives, we can reconstruct them from chronicled evidence and be certain that they included a similar ban on rape as in the ordinances issued by Richard II in 1385. The same ban is also found in the ordinances issued by Henry V in his invasions of 1415 and 1417.[28] In his ordinances of 1419 they were expanded to include not only the killing and rape of a woman but also taking her prisoner.[29] Later in the fifteenth century (1487) they were made more expansive in the relevant clause on sexual violence: "nor yet to rob or spoil any manner man or woman upon pain of death . . . also that no manner of person nor persons whatsoever they be, ravish no religious man, nor man's wife, daughter maiden nor no man's nor woman's servant."[30] In 1419 Henry V added a further clause concerning the treatment of women, relating specifically to those in childbirth:

Also that nomaner man be so hardy to go in to no chambre, or loggyng where that eny woman lythe in geseme, her to robbe ne pile of no goodes, the whiche longeth unto her refressyng ne for to make none afray where thorough she and her childe might be in eny disease, or dispeyr.[31]

Why include this? Was it a result of a specific incident that had left its mark on the king? Or was it because Henry had read William of Tyre's account of Baldwin I, king of Jerusalem, who encountered the captive wife of a Bedouin chief during an expedition? She was in labor, so he left a bed, food, and women to care for her, even giving his own mantle to cover her and two camels for milk.[32] We know that Henry, as prince of Wales, had borrowed a chronicle of the crusades from his aunt, and we also know that medieval military education was based on *exempla* of the behavior of earlier commanders. The incident reminds us of how important personalities of commanders were in preventing or condoning violence against civilians, including women.

Why are we seeing more explicit references to limitations of soldiers' behavior toward women in late medieval English armies? One reason is undoubtedly the rise of a professional paid army, in which discipline and control were integral features. A second related element is the constant emphasis on the legitimacy of the English cause, in which as much attention was paid to *ius in bello* as well as *ius ad bellum*. This led to greater concern for good lordship toward civilians in war zones. This is particularly noticeable when the English occupied Normandy in the fifteenth century. Behind all of this was the contemporary notion that soldiers fighting a just war should be protectors rather than aggressors of the civilian population.[33]

What we are seeing, I think, is a secularization of the limitation of sexual violence. No longer is this limitation left to the Church's remit but rather placed under the control of the state, albeit under the strong influence of religious teachings. This is particularly noticeable in the implementation of the ordinances against rape under Henry V. For instance, on February 24, 1418, an order was issued to Henry Styng, Esquire. It had come to royal notice that certain malefactors in his company had raped a woman "against the form and effect of divers statutes, ordinances and appointments drawn up for the rule and government of the people of our army and against the form of divers proclamations made of late for the whole of our army."[34] Styng was ordered to find out who the culprits were so that they might be arrested and be brought before the king in person. It is significant that the order to Styng has the wording that those who committed the rape have failed to keep their eyes fixed on God or to be fearful of offending the king, and that it later describes their alleged crime as displeasing and offensive to God and hurtful to the royal majesty. In other words, the soldiers' breach of the ban on sexual violence was portrayed as a contestation of the power of the Almighty as much as of the king.

This secularization stems not only from the development of state authority during the period but also from the code of chivalry. The latter, a nebulous but nonetheless potent constraint on the warrior elite, was an influence not only during the Hundred Years' War but also in earlier conflicts in western Europe. It has even been suggested that women did not have to be specifically mentioned in the canon laws and other ecclesiastical writings on immunity, because they were protected by the traditional ideals of the knightly profession, which had as the driving force the threat of dishonor. Yet chivalric texts themselves tend to be socially selective. The order of the Golden Spur founded by Louis de Bourbon in 1364, for instance, obliged its members to honor "les dames et les demoiselles," while that of the White Lady of the Green Spur established by Marshal Boucicaut later in the century demanded the defense of "the right of all gentlewomen by their [i.e. the members of the order] power as it was requested of them." Chivalry is perhaps best understood as a code of the officer class rather than of soldiers more generally. How far it percolated down either the male or female social scale is dubious, however. Intriguingly too, the literature of chivalry is rather schizophrenic on its treatment of sexual violence in warfare. In the story of Merlin, for instance, Gawain observes two knights about to rape a young lady. He tells them that "they were already dead because they were assaulting a lady in King Arthur's land . . . for you know well that ladies are guaranteed their safety."[35] Yet romance literature is riddled with knights having their way with women, Arthur included.[36]

There is a further strain in military thinking that goes against the grain of noncombatant immunity, and that is the invocation of the Law of Deuteronomy, deriving from Mosaic pronouncements on how the Israelites should conduct themselves in warfare. It is likely that it was publicized by Thomas Aquinas through his biblical exegesis.[37] The relevant biblical text distinguished between cities that God had given to his people of Israel as their inheritance, where the direction was that "you shall save alive nothing that breathes," and cities that were "not cities of the nations here." If the latter offered resistance,

> you shall besiege it, and when the Lord your God gives it into your hand you shall put all its males to the sword but the women and the little ones, the cattle, and everything else in the city . . . you shall take as booty . . . and you shall enjoy the spoil of your enemies which the Lord your God has given you.

The first explicit reference to its invocation in an actual military context is Henry V's siege of Harfleur in 1415.[38] It may be that it was considered long before this date as standard justification for the sacking of towns that refused to surrender peaceably. As Keen puts it:

> In a city taken by storm almost any licence was condoned by the law. . . . Women could be raped, and men killed out of hand. The prospect of this free run of his lusts for blood, spoil and women was a major incentive to a soldier to persevere in the rigours which were likely to attend a protracted siege.[39]

A problem is knowing whether it was implemented all that often in medieval warfare. Harfleur surrendered and did not face a storming. This scenario was common, because the vast majority of places surrendered by composition. Even when they did suffer assault, such as at Caen in 1346, there is suggestion that there were attempts to curb the incidence of sexual violence. Froissart tells us that Godfrey de Harcourt rode through the streets ordering on behalf of King Edward III that no man should commit arson, murder, or rape.[40] On another occasion Froissart credits Sir John Chandos with saving the daughters of the count of Poix from some archers who would otherwise have raped them.[41] There is clearly a class element here. In the tradition of chivalric writing, sexual violence was only committed by those outside the knightly "caste."

The taking of cities was highly ritualized. Commanders exploited the opportunity to show their power by having the citizens at their mercy and yet showing magnanimity. Chronicles tell us that once Harfleur was in Henry's hands, he allowed the women of the town to leave. He had them escorted through his army under armed guard "lest they be molested on the way by the thieves among us who are more given to pillage than to pity and who care nothing for the tears of the innocent as long as they can lay their hands on plunder."[42] In other words, Henry V reminded his soldiers of the disciplinary ordinances. A French chronicle mentions that Henry V had it proclaimed that no one should do anything to the women, adding that it was their own countrymen who attacked them once they were well away from the town.[43] What we have here, then, is an example of politicization of sexual violence, a point to which I shall return.

A later passage in Deuteronomy explained the conqueror's rights more fully:

> When you . . . see among the captives a beautiful woman, and you have a desire for her and would take her for yourself as a wife, then you shall

bring her home to your house and she shall shave her head and pare her nails. And she shall put off her captive's garb and shall remain in your house . . . a full month. After that you may go into her and be her husband and she shall be your wife.[44]

By the later Middle Ages it was no longer customary to carry women away. Both the military ordinances and the chivalric code forbade taking women prisoner, or putting them to ransom. In earlier centuries, however, women were taken away by their captors. The expectation was that they would be forced into having sexual relations. The Romans had, after all, taken the Sabine women by force because they needed wives. Subsequently, Roman law had, as Laiou puts it, "contended with the problem of married women who slept with their captors in the context of war."[45] This was looked at procedurally from the position of what it meant for their marital status. Because captivity deprived the woman of free status, her marriage was arguably dissolved once she was carried off and renewed when she was returned. Legists claimed that her husband could at that point bring charges of adultery, but that if she had been *forced* to sleep with her captor no action would then be taken against her—what Diana C. Moses calls "a wartime force exception."[46] The impact of Christianity is apparent when we look at how the Byzantine canonists reinterpreted the problem of the sexual relations in terms of penance rather than of marital status. According to St. Gregory of Neo-Caesarea (d. ca. 275), if the woman was previously of good repute it would be automatically assumed that she had acted under duress. If not, then it would be assumed that she had been a willing victim. For Zonaras (d. after 1159), however, war captives were enslaved and had no free will. Therefore, they could not sin and could not be punished. St. Basil (d. 379) had followed the same line of reasoning in his forty-ninth canon: "seductions carried out by force carry no guilt." Balsaman (d. after 1195), on the other hand, suggested a variety of punishments according to the seriousness of the offense, arguing that women who slept with barbarians should suffer an ecclesiastical punishment but one that was light. The issue found its way into the penitentials of western Europe, reminding us that women ran the risk of violation through capture. The issue here was how long a husband would have to wait until he married again. For Theodore, archbishop of Canterbury at the end of the seventh century,

> If an enemy carries away any man's wife and he cannot get her again, he may take another. To do this is better than fornication. If after this his former wife comes again to him she ought not to be received by him if he has

another, but she may take to herself another husband if she has had only one before.[47]

The problem resurfaced during the early crusades. Both sides took women captive rather than killing them. As Friedman puts it, "the sexual abuse of female captives was more or less taken for granted."[48] The Muslim law of war permitted it, because it was no more than an extension of a booty-winning polygamous society. Indeed, it was assumed that Muslim women who were captured would suffer a similar fate. The Tabari Kitab al-Jihad spoke of how they were to behave if taken by the Christians: "if the prisoner is a woman who is subjected to physical hardship, she must at first endure persecution, but if she fears death, she is permitted to submit to enemy demands unwillingly,"[49] a line that is very similar to the Roman legal assumption. Not surprisingly, Christian chroniclers are silent on whether the crusaders violated their captives. Muslim writers did not see any difficulty in dealing with the matter; witness the fulsome account of Saladin's secretary, Imad ad-Din Al-Isfahani, on the fate of the crusaders' families captured at the fall of Jerusalem.[50]

> The women and children together came to 8,000 and were quickly divided up among us . . . how many well guarded women were profaned . . . miserly women forced to yield themselves, women who had been kept hidden stripped of their modesty . . . virgins dishonored and proud women deflowered . . . how many noblemen took them as concubines.

There is poetic hyperbole at play here, meant to reinforce the scale of victory against the Christian enemy. As for Christian women taken prisoner by the Muslims, the same issues of female culpability prevailed as in Roman and Byzantine law. William of Tyre tells us of a man whose French wife was taken prisoner at Banyas in 1132, who then repudiated her on the grounds that "her conduct while with the enemy had not been altogether discreet. She had not satisfactorily preserved the sanctity of the marriage couch as a noble matron should."[51] This situation was not common. Indeed, that is why the chronicler chooses to mention it. Most captured women were accepted back by their present and future husbands, although there are known cases of unmarried women who chose instead to enter a nunnery on their return. There again, Albert of Aachen tells us of a nun in Trier who had been forced into what he calls "a vile and detestable union with a Turk." When she was restored to Christian control, she was granted forgiveness but told what form her repentance should take. The chronicler tells us that she decided instead to return to her former captor the next day, because she was afraid of the harsh penance imposed on her.[52]

A good story, and a useful reminder of how problematic the evidence of sexual violence in medieval warfare is. In the later Middle Ages we have court records that show prosecutions of soldiers for rape. These are of individuals. I have not come across any examples of groups of men being prosecuted, nor in fact of any cases linked to specific military actions. That does not mean to say that sexual violence was not seen as a weapon of war. The nature of the offense and the speed with which many armies passed through areas mean that it would have been impossible to detect and prosecute. The only circumstances that made it feasible were in the context of an occupation, such as that sustained in the fifteenth century by the English in northern France, where garrison soldiers were discouraged from keeping concubines. Much reliance was placed on the commanders as a controlling force and also on the religious education that soldiers, along with the rest of the population, would have had. Both secular and religious contexts used the language of threat. Indeed, medieval Christian culture was very much based on this. A central part of the Catholic faith was judgment after death for deeds on earth.

It would be unreasonable to suppose that secular and religious threats were enough to keep soldiers under control. But this leads to a further problem in assessing the question. Women were used as an emblem of suffering in the contexts of war and occupation.[53] There was a strong sense that women could not, and indeed should not, participate in warfare and therefore should be protected and cherished by men. The treatment of women was very much a test of civilization, and nowhere more so than in the context of military conflict.

This contributes to the major problem that a medieval historian faces when investigating the subject of sexual violence in conflict zones. Mentions of it, especially in narrative sources, tend to occur in distinctive contexts as a means of denigrating the enemy. This is very noticeable when the enemy is not Christian. In addition to examples from the Crusades, we can also note the retrospective portrayal of the Vikings in English chronicles of the twelfth and thirteenth centuries. The focus is on "the demonic evil of the invaders, graphically evinced in images of the violation of women." The story is heightened by the use of direct speech. Abbess Ebba of Collingham is made to say:

> There have come lately into these parts most wicked pagans, destitute of
> all humanity, who roam through every place, sparing neither the female

sex nor infantine age, destroying churches and clergy, ravishing holy women and consuming every thing in their way.[54]

Her alleged response, to save herself from rape, was to take a razor and cut off her nose and her upper lip, "presenting herself a horrible spectacle to those who stood by," prompting several of her nuns to do the same. The truth of this incident is dubious. The juxtaposition of attacks on the Church and on women is a common ploy in the denigration of even a Christian enemy. For instance, the parliament of 1461, celebrating the triumph of the King Edward IV of York over his rival, Henry VI of Lancaster, condemned the latter's queen (Margaret of Anjou) and her supporters for leading their army from the north,

> destroying and despoiling the realm on their way, not sparing God's church or refraining from its violation and that of its ministers: ravishing and seducing nuns, maidens, widows and men's wives; shedding innocent blood like tyrants, intending the final and utter destruction and over-throw of your realm as their cruel violence proves.[55]

The aim was to show how the Lancastrians had offended God. The French chronicler noted earlier, who blamed his own people rather than the English for attacks on women after the surrender of Harfleur, had a similar aim in explaining why God had turned away from the French. It was not uncommon for rape to be included in a mantralike list of offenses, along with arson, assault, and pillage, to show the collapse of social order and the failure of a government to act. Take, for example, the letter that Edward III wrote to Hugh Calverley and other English soldiers serving as mercenaries for Charles of Navarre in 1364, and whom he accused of "seizing, robbing and ransoming the people, burning and destroying buildings, violating and ravishing widows, virgins and other women, and taking, occupying and detaining fortresses."[56] Or the fact that there was a deliberate inclusion in the articles of deposition against Richard II in 1399 that his bodyguard of Cheshire archers had committed rape, murder, and robbery.

Attacks on women were therefore conceptually and philosophically significant in the medieval Christian context. This does not make it easy for us to assess the level of sexual violence in warfare, because so much of medieval writing was for effect and for a didactic purpose, rather than for record. It is not "evidence" in the modern sense of the word. We cannot know the scale or incidence of sexual violence in medieval warfare. All we can say is that it existed but was condemned.

Chapter 11

Law, War, and Women in Seventeenth-Century England

Barbara Donagan

In modern accounts of dismaying actions, whether in war, civil unrest, or mere everyday violence, we are familiar with a standard trope that is intended to heighten both the horror of the actions and our sense that those who commit them are outside the ranks of decent and humane people. It is so familiar and routine that it has probably lost much of its power. We read almost daily of offenses against "women, children, and even the elderly."

Here I shall confine my discussion to women in the western tradition and the early modern world, and my examples of early modern theory and practice will largely be drawn from Britain, primarily England. There, the situation was further defined by the fact that the experience was that of *civil* war between fellow countrymen. English theory and practice, however, were not insular but part of a continental culture of war. The business of war, in fact, offers an example of early modern globalization.

The obligation to extend special protections to certain categories of persons and things has a long history, going back at least to the "Truce of God" movement of the early Middle Ages. These early attempts to limit violence extended their protections from holy places and persons to the weak and harmless—specifically women, children, and the old—and eventually to a wide range of persons and occasions, from merchants to fairs to long weekends. The movement had no teeth beyond excommunication and was an expression of good intentions rather than an effective regulator of conduct.[1] The duty to refrain from harming the harmless remained, however, even as the movement withered. It was recognized as one of the unwritten laws of war that derived from natural law, Christian morality, and, implicitly, self-interest.

The absence in succeeding centuries of formal written codes governing relations between enemies did not mean the absence of conventions or
"rules" of conduct. Before the emergence of international treaties regulating
conduct in war, of the kind familiar to us through the Geneva and Hague
Conventions, many aspects of the relations between enemies were governed
by the *un*written laws of war. These addressed, for example, the treatment
of prisoners, including their exchange and ransom, and the differing permissible fates of captured towns, depending on whether they surrendered
on agreed conditions or were taken by storm. In *Henry V* Shakespeare had
made clear the awkward tension between norms of protection and permitted violence (such as that allowed after a successful storm), as well as the
impossibility of enforcing either written or unwritten rules when troops
were "enraged" in hot blood. In his speech before the gates of besieged Harfleur Henry V warned of the consequences for women:

> I will not leave the half-achieved Harfleur
> Till in her ashes she lie buried.
> The gates of mercy shall be all shut up
> And the fleshed soldier, rough and hard of heart,
> In liberty of bloody hand shall range
> With conscience wide as hell, mowing like grass
> Your fresh fair virgins and your flowering infants . . .
> What is't to me, when you yourselves are cause,
> If your pure maidens fall into the hand
> Of hot and forcing violation?
> What rein can hold licentious wickedness
> When down the hill he holds his fierce career?
> We may as bootless spend our vain command
> Upon th'enraged soldiers in their spoil
> As send precepts to the Leviathan
> To come ashore.[2]

In the 1630s the prolific narratives of Germany's sufferings in the Thirty
Years' War that appeared in England only confirmed Shakespeare's vision of
the vulnerability of women to the horrors that could accompany war.[3]

Regulation of military violence was nevertheless not only a matter of
adherence to unwritten norms of war. From the late medieval period at least,
armies issued formal "articles of war" or codified army regulations, intended
primarily to discipline their own troops but also to address some inter-army
matters (such as treatment of prisoners) and some aspects of treatment of
civilians. The earliest extensive English articles that I know of date from the

reign of Richard II.[4] These articles were expanded in the reigns of Henry V and Henry VI; they were not an exotic form of knowledge but part of soldiers' professional formation. Over the years there were additions and rearrangements, but the disciplinary code issued for Henry VIII's army in 1544 was still materially that of Henry V from the early fifteenth century. Among the constants of these codes were such military standbys as prohibition of desertion, for obvious reasons, and protections for women and children.

Taken together, the unwritten and the written codes reveal a double attitude towards women in war. On the one hand they should be protected; on the other, if they did not conform to accepted standards of "harmlessness" they lost their right to protection. When bad things happened they might be excused by the classic "blame the victim" argument—"you yourselves are cause." In Henry V's words: the victims had invited their fate by their failure to confine themselves to conduct that was recognized as acceptable or, for example, by having the misfortune to live in a town that refused to surrender.

Before turning to the question of what actually happened and how distinctions between "harmless" and "harmful" were negotiated, it will be helpful to say something about military legislation. It was, as I have indicated, both protective and punitive. The second article of Henry V's code (the first dealt with the basic duty of obedience to king and commanders) was headed "For Holy Church." It linked sacrilege—killing a priest, touching the sacrament, or pillaging church property—to a prohibition of "sley[ing] or enforce[ing] any woman"; both crimes were punishable by death. So was the crime of "taking a religious p[er]son [of either sex] prisoner."[5] A subsequent article protected "eny woeman ly[ing] in gesom [childbed]" from robbery, pillage, or endangerment of herself or her child; an offender was to lose his goods and his life.[6] The first of these articles gives a specifically religious turn to protection of women against death or rape; the second, protecting women in childbed, suggests a rather different tradition of "holiness." Taken together the two articles echo ancient taboos and linkages of purity and danger.

By the beginning of Henry VIII's reign the protection of women had taken on a more secular cast. Killing or taking prisoner a religious person, male or female, still merited death, but the provision had been separated from the sacrilege of touching the sacrament or pyx. Rape—"ravishing of women"—now joined robbing merchants en route to market and murder in general as capital crimes.[7] Women in childbed and their children were still protected, and the penalty remained loss of life or goods.[8] Other regulations, however, were designed to punish rather than protect women. Among a group designed to promote "good rule" in the army, which included prohibition of such disruptive actions as "dicing" and murderous affrays, was one "For bordel keeping in the hosts." It specified that men who took women across the sea—Henry VIII was about to embark for France— or kept women in their lodgings were liable to imprisonment and loss of goods or wages. "Common" women were prohibited from coming within three miles of the army: the penalty for a first offense was to be burned on the right cheek; a second offense earned imprisonment and further punishment at discretion. These penalties at least mark some progress from provisions that had appeared in Henry V's later articles, presumably in response to practical problems encountered in the field, for they appeared alongside regulations covering burial of waste—"carren and bowels"—and the making of "good sufficient" ladders. They also increased the earlier penalty for women discovered in camp: all the woman's money was to be confiscated, and the discoverer was "to take a staff and dryve her out of the hoste and breake her arme." Her male partner merely lost a month's wages.[9]

By 1544, when Henry VIII was again preparing an expedition to France, the protection of religious persons had disappeared, not altogether surprisingly, although the penalties for sacrilege retained their savagery.[10] There appears to be no specific prohibition of rape, but the protections of women in childbed and the penalties for women found in the army remained the same as those of 1513. These articles, however, marked the end of an era in English military regulation and in the organization of war.

Records for the later sixteenth and early seventeenth centuries are thin—for England the early seventeenth century was, on the whole, a relatively pacific period—but by the end of the 1630s the country was again fully engaged in wars. These were domestic—first against Scotland (largely fought in the north of England), then in Ireland (where both English and Irish civilians were massacred), and finally on home ground. From 1639 to 1651 the country was either at war or, for brief periods, in a state of uneasy peace. The plentiful articles of war for the period are very different from those of Henry VIII and reflect, among other things, change in the nature of war and of the state, notably the transition from entrepreneurial war, in which ransom and division of the spoils were crucial to the formation and maintenance of an army (and hence extensively regulated in the articles of war), to armies that were nationally organized and paid.[11]

In the 1640s both parties to the English civil war continued to legislate morally, prohibiting blasphemy and drunkenness and mandating attendance at church services. They also prohibited rape and unnatural abuses—in par-liament's articles these came under the heading "Of Duties Morall"—and in both armies they earned a mandatory death penalty.[12] Parliament, under the same head, added a blanket prohibition of "Adulterie, fornication, and other dissolute lasciviousnesse," which earned discretionary punishment. The roy-alists, more specifically, said in their expanded articles of 1643, "No Whore shall be suffered in the Leaguer," but allowed soldiers' wives to accompany them if they had the general's permission.[13]

Aside from these provisions specifically directed at women, both par-ties attempted to restrict actions that injured women as much as men, such as plunder or indiscriminate burning of houses or barns, destruction of crops and fruit trees, and beating of the unfortunate civilians on whom sol-diers might be quartered. In these cases, too, punishments were discretion-ary. The protections for civilians and their property, however, came with a significant reservation: if actions were committed on orders from a com-mander, they were not crimes.[14]

Two things are already clear. The first is that women were seen as both victims and offenders: crimes against them should be punished, but women by their own actions could also merit just punishment. The second is that armies and women could not be separated. The compilers of articles of war assumed that women would be present in the army, either illicitly or use-fully—as wives and also in certain crucial capacities such as nurses and laundresses. Furthermore, they were part of the general population amidst which the army operated, and whose houses, goods, cattle, crops, stores of food, and other necessities of life were at risk. There was no such thing as a "home front" distinct from a "war front," for the war's battles, sieges and marching armies ranged widely across the kingdom. Even areas that had a relatively quiet war shared in a phenomenal increase in tax burdens that reached to the humblest levels, while they were vulnerable to seizures, often of dubious legality, for the benefit of armies. The ensuing burden of domes-tic intrusions and bullying with nominal official sanction fell on women as well as men, and highly colored accounts of the depredations of undis-ciplined soldiers emphasized the sexual charge behind much of the casual violence offered to women and the pleasure taken in humiliation at loss of dignity and modesty. When parliamentarian soldiers entered Dean Bar-grave's house late one night in 1642, claimed a royalist writer, they

> forc[ed] Mistris *Bargrave*, a virtuous good Gentlewoman (whom their hasty Summons had permitted to cast only her Night-gowne about her)

to wait upon them from roome to roome, not suffering her to turn aside (though for Modesty sake [she] requested that favour at their hands) to draw on her Stockings, unless they might stand by and see it done.[15]

The same writer, Mercurius Rusticus, reported maid-servants' claims that soldiers "*threatn[ed] to plunder all under the petty-coat*, and other uncivill immodest words, not fit for them to speak, or me to write." Soldiers left another woman "a Lamentable spectacle of their cruelty" in the roadway after flogging her and dragging her over "the Stony rough wayes." They abused "a Great-bellied Gentlewoman" and forced another to give birth in the street, and addressed a cavalier's wife "in beastly, immodest scurrilous language, which I shall omit to relate as offensive to Christian eares." To increase the disgust and humiliation aroused by such offenses, they were committed by officers and men alike, including the "greazy Common Souldier" who had insulted Lady Butler and trashed the medicines she kept for the poor.[16] Sexual insult was joined to the overturning of class distinction and to physical revulsion at exposure to the great unwashed.

Mercurius Rusticus was hardly an unbiased reporter, and such affronts as these formed only a part of his polemic, but he exemplified the links between generalized violence and sexual cruelty and humiliation that formed the picture, exploited by both sides, of the horrors of war as conducted by the enemy, Moreover, he knowingly reminded English readers that such horrors were not confined to continental Europe. In a civil war such as England's these evils had particular intimacy. Enemies and civilians spoke the same language; allegiance crossed lines of kinship and neighborhood, and protagonists of both sides claimed adherence to an existing set of national and civilian laws that shaped ideas of crime, proper punishment and justice.

English men and women had begun their war fully aware of the cruelties of contemporary warfare in Germany, the Netherlands and Ireland. Circumstantial accounts and lurid illustrations had familiarized them with the "miseries" of the Thirty Years' War, in which formerly prosperous regions were devastated by fire, massacre, mutilation, rape, hunger, and the ruin of a once-productive country. They feared that England might become like the Germany of their imaginations. The news pamphlets that flooded the English market following the Irish rebellion of 1641 exploited to the full the stories of massacres of English inhabitants and of sexual brutalities against women. These prewar accounts evoked horror, pity and fear, but those relating to the sufferings of women had a powerful element of titillation as well.

The combination recurred in civil war reports. Like Mercurius Rusticus, writers were touching a known nerve and played on traditional responses to, for example, sacrilege and defilement, as in the story of the women raped and killed, some at the foot of the market cross, in Uttoxeter:

> They [the royalists] have ravished divers women, and some of them to death. . . . Widow *Dives* at *Uttoxature* was shot by them in her owne house that she died suddenly. Mistresse *Wood* of the same place had like to have dyed of a Fright. Divers women (as we have heard) were ravished there, and some at the very market Crosse, an horrible thing to be spoken.[17]

It is clear from these examples that the nature of the reporting of war and its consequences for women raises problems when we try to evaluate what actually happened, for the combination of formulaic atrocities and partisan and selective narration means that the stories must always be treated with a strong dose of skepticism. A further consideration when trying to evaluate what the civil war meant to women is the need to be aware of a broader context than that relating to sexual violence. To some women, at least, the war brought benefits and respect. So before turning to sexual offenses, I will briefly note a few of the elements that made up the background to the violence recorded here. First, as civilian victims of war, their lot was in major ways the same as men's. Both suffered from starvation in long-lasting sieges, as at Colchester in 1648. Both endured the sicknesses that accompanied war: Lady Cholmley never fully recovered from "a tuch of the scurvie then riffe" during the siege of Scarborough castle, and both Rachel Pitt and her husband Edward died of prison-bred disease.[18] Men and women were equally likely to be killed by stray bullets or terror bombardments, like the young man killed by a musket shot when his curiosity led him to look over the town wall or the girl killed by a random cannonball. Both sexes experienced the plunder and vandalism of rampant soldiers and the ensuing material losses, whether a stool, an iron pot, or a cow, or rich tapestries and cherished plate, the latter both a capital asset and a symbol of status. Such takings represented more than economic loss and, for the poor, a threat to livelihood; they asserted the breakdown of a known and ordered society and the insecurity of persons and property.

Second, women were not just passive victims. They were notable protesters whose efforts harassed politicians and commanders and sometimes forced them to change course, as in the case of the vocal women who so wore down Sir Thomas Fairfax that he engaged (successfully) in a "hazardous . . . Attempt" to acquire enemy prisoners with whom to negotiate for the release of their husbands. In the siege of Colchester in 1648 the men left it to the women of the town to demonstrate against the embattled royalist governor.[19] In such cases there was often a conscious exploitation of the women's putatively "protected" status. Some women were actively and skillfully engaged in military operations, like Lady Bankes who defended Corfe castle, or Lady Harley who defended Brampton Bryan while also playing the card of the poor weak woman whose neighbours should be ashamed of besieging her. Some women worked on town defenses or acted as messengers and spies, and male and female spies were subject to the same penalties if they were caught. Furthermore, women were paid for their labor, which brings us to a third point: for some, the war brought new opportunities for cash income, most notably for their services as laundresses and nurses. These were thriving wartime occupations, and were often organized in remarkably large-scale and entrepreneurial ways.

When we turn to the specifically sexual manifestations of violence against women, they prove to be of three kinds: first, those in which intrinsically "normal" phenomena of war became infused with a strong sexual element; second, crimes *against* women, as legally defined in the articles of war; and third, crimes committed *by* women, less specifically defined but prosecuted under military law and in military courts.

Phenomena of the first kind, that is, "normal" military actions, usually occurred in military or civilian mob situations, and tended to be viewed as deplorable but nonetheless understandable events, committed in hot blood and therefore less heinous than offenses committed in cold blood. In a notorious case early in the war, an Essex mob pillaged the house of Countess Rivers (a suspected Catholic) and hounded her with sexual threats.[20] In 1648, in another example of rampaging violence with a strong sexual element, parliamentary soldiers in Essex seized the house of the royalist Lord Lucas and, in their "brutall rage" at the absence of plunder, took their revenge on the bodies in the family vault, including those of the mother and sister of the present owner who were so recently buried that "their sinues and haire were unconsumed." They scattered the bones, cut off the hair and wore it in their hats, all accompanied by "profane jests."[21] Defiance of ancient taboos against mistreatment of the bodies of the dead, of prohibitions of sacrilege, and of norms of respect for women combined to enhance disgust at the offense.

Perhaps the most famous, or infamous, case of a "normal" military event turning feral, in which the victims were women, occurred after the parliamentary victory at Naseby in 1645. In the pursuit after the battle many of the fleeing royalists were killed. Women were among the victims, but both their number and their nature remain uncertain. Estimates ranged from more than one hundred to three or four hundred killed among whom, the Earl of Clarendon noted disapprovingly, were the "Wives of Officers of Quality."[22] To kill the defeated who attempted to surrender was in itself an offense against the laws of war, although the guilt was mitigated in the eyes of some by the fact that it occurred in the hot blood of overwhelming victory. Nevertheless, the killing of women was less excusable, and the handling of the event by parliamentary reporters revealed both discomfort and attempts to justify it by recalling, for instance, recent and comparable ferocity on the part of royalist troops when they stormed Leicester, or by transferring guilt to the victims. Some accounts of the battle preferred to ignore the event. Others merely noted "Many Ladies" among the prisoners and three or four hundred women killed "in the pursuit," or "Abundance of women (some conceived to be Ladies and Gentlewomen of quality) taken, and above a Hundred slain." Other reporters, however, went on the attack, arguing that the victims had, morally speaking, deserved their fate: "100 of your Harlots with golden Tresses killed upon the place," said one.[23] According to another they were knife-carrying and inhuman Irish whores who had intended to cut the throats of parliamentarian prisoners and had disqualified themselves from protection by being armed (it was a common accusation that Irish women carried long "Skeans" and they were in any case, as barbarian and Catholic Irish, outside the law).[24] Many of the women who escaped alive were mutilated: "Most of the whores and Camp-sluts that attended that wicked [royalist] Army, were marked in their faces and noses with slashes and cuts, and some cut off: just rewards for such wicked strumpets."[25] The conjunction of sex, race, moralism and sadism is striking in these accounts. The emphasis on the sinfulness of the victims indicates a desire on the part of some reporters to validate killings that could still shock, but for others triumphalist vengeance—on female deviance and Irish barbarity—predominated. This was not the only occasion of brutal killing of Irish women, but no other incident elicited apologia that conflated ethnicity and depravity comparable to those following Naseby. It is curious that royalist propagandists did not make more of these killings, although it may partly be explained by royalist demoralization after Naseby.

Ironically, when we turn to legally designated crime and the paradigmatic offense against women victims, namely rape, much less is known. We have already noted the problem of authenticity in dealing with partisan and formulaic atrocity stories, but other kinds of evidence of rape are scarce. As a military offense meriting a mandatory death sentence, rape was triable before military courts martial, but unfortunately only two runs of court martial records are—as yet—known. Beyond them, we have only the odd, serendipitous reference, such as a report that a parliamentary officer was to be court martialed for rape. Of the two sets of records (both parliamentarian), one dates from 1644 and covers an army on active service. It includes crimes by soldiers against civilians (such as highway robbery) but primarily deals with strictly military offenses; there are no reports of rape or other offenses against women.[26] The second set of records comes from the parliamentary army of occupation in Dundee in 1651.[27] Like the first, it reveals the conscientiousness of the members of the court in reaching decisions and their careful attention to legal processes and to the nature of the charges on which the accused were to be tried (e.g., whether they were to come under the rubric of felony or misdemeanour and of capital or lesser crime). It also reveals the care with which punishments were chosen. They were intended to be deterrent, exemplary and *in terrorem*, and, as such, to be public and shaming.

Soldiers in Dundee in 1651 were idle, cold, and often drunk. There were, it seems, ample opportunities for sexual sins, but only one rape case is recorded. It reveals, however, both the procedural care with which a court martial acted, its nice distinctions over the seriousness of charges, and the range of possible punishments in such a case, which here ran from flogging to hanging. James Grahame had come to a house at midnight, forced an entrance, "pulled off his clothes" and, when Elizabeth Michelson rebuffed him, had beaten her and her child black and blue. He then turned on Margaret Patterson, beat her, and threatened to send in the moss troopers and burn her house. The evidence was clear and convincing, and the court had no trouble in convicting him; although the sentence was harsh, however, it was not capital. Presumably, as the rape was unconsummated, the case fell into the category of "dissolute lasciviousnesse" and thus merited a discretionary sentence rather than the mandatory death penalty specified for rape. The members of the court, following the normal practice, offered in turn their verdicts along with proposed punishments, beginning with the most junior officer present. He proposed that Grahame be whipped from Bonnett Hill to Westgate with sixty lashes, ducked, and afterward imprisoned at the general's pleasure. With only two exceptions, the rest of the court concurred, although they dropped the ducking from the final sentence. One of the dissenters had favored hanging, the other suggested forty lashes.[28]

One case of hard evidence of crime, with the attendant evidence of the seriousness with which a military court dealt with even an attempted rape, is thin material from which to draw conclusions about either incidence or punishment. It seems probable that at least some of the more lurid and propagandist cases discussed earlier actually happened. It is also clear that rape remained a crime regarded with horror and was never a "legitimizable" offense. Even when a stronghold was taken by storm rather than surrender, which meant that plunder and killing of soldiers and civilians became permissible according to the laws of war (even though excessive cruelty was normally deplored), rape remained a crime. It seems, in fact, even allowing for the usual under-reporting, that it was a relatively rare offense in the English civil war—an impression, and it cannot be more, that is shared by other historians of the period.

When we turn to the third category, that of sexual offenses by women (as legislated in articles of war), Dundee again offers evidence of the system in action, although admittedly the opportunities for sin were better for an occupying army resident among civilians than for one in camp or on the move, as in 1644. The record offers no suggestion that the women involved were forced, other than by the usual economic pressures, to be partners in crime. Instead the cases reveal the interlocking disciplinary interests of the army command and civilian society, and an evenhanded application of penalties to both parties to the offense. Such crimes, it will be remembered, were covered by the blanket provision in the parliamentary articles that prohibited "Adultery, Fornication, and other dissolute lasciviousnesse," on pain of punishment "according to the quality of the Offense."[29]

In the case of Marian Gurdon, this meant a severe sentence. She had, testified Isabel Alexander who shared a room with her, "since the army's first entrance into this town entertained into her naked bed" a series of "distinct men for the most part & most of them English men." Isabel Rankin, who occupied the room above Marian Gurdon, testified that she saw her lie "in naked bed" with Thomas Peacock, an Englishman, whereupon she informed the gentleman at arms at Peacock's quarters. He sent a guard to apprehend them and their accomplice Agnes Askin, who "held the candle for them." Gurdon and Peacock were sentenced to sixty stripes each at the cart's tail as they were whipped from Westgate to Eastgate; Agnes Askin was led through the town with them, and all three were ducked from the quay. Finally the women were to be boated over into Fife.[30] In this and other cases the publicity, pain, and humiliation of the offenders served as a call to moral reformation as much as to obedience to military law, although the final expulsion of the women presumably only served to move sin elsewhere.

In conclusion, I would argue that the English civil war offers an example of control of sexual violence toward women and of sexual offenses by women through a system that combined written and triable military law with unwritten codes of conduct. It was premodern in the scope allowed to discretion and in reliance on public, exemplary, deterrent punishment, and its success was imperfect, but it succeeded in preventing a breakdown of social and moral norms of the kind that many had feared when the war began. In part this was due to a utilitarian sense of common interest between enemies: both sides were aware of the dangers of a war that spiraled down into a conflict governed by reprisal. It also owed something to shared professional, moral, and religious values that, despite failures, were not abandoned, and also—a benefit of civil war—to shared social and economic interests that crossed party lines. It was possible to achieve consensus both on the moralistic grounds for condemning Marian Gurdon and on the professional and religious duty to—mostly—treat women with a modicum of restraint, if not respect. Examples of generous conduct by soldiers to "enemy" women that reveal the survival of a sense of shared social links and moral values can be set against the more enthusiastically reported lapses into cruelty. Furthermore, women were themselves capable of unappealing actions. As in Dundee, women informed on other women, and the women of Lyme in Dorset were said to have torn Irish women to pieces.

Accounts of the civil war reveal a society in which women retained a degree of autonomy greater than studies of law or of normative conduct books suggest, and one in which women cannot merely be seen as victims of male oppression. The ethical stance of *A Dialogue Betwixt a Horse of Warre, and a Mill-Horse* (1643) may be deplorable, but it is not an account of rape or even forced acquiescence; its village maidens may have been deluded, but they were—at least as represented—partners rather than victims. Compared with all too many modern examples, the fate of women in civil war England was benign. The most visible large-scale crime against women in the 1640s was in fact only indirectly linked to the war: at least a hundred people, most of them women, were executed in the East Anglian witchhunts of 1645. It has been plausibly argued that the success of the pogrom and the popular support it temporarily enjoyed can be traced to social, religious, and sexual strains nurtured by civil war.[31] It was, however, a civilian phenomenon in which both agents and victims were civilians, and it was played out in a nasty by-way of civilian law.

In the relations between civilians and soldiers there was no large-scale breakdown of army discipline, although there were scattered mob incidents, sometimes of horrifying cruelty and sometimes with a strong sexual component. There were also individual cases of cruelty, often exacerbated by sexual—and class—humiliation. Yet in general the protections of military, moral and national law were not abandoned. The temptation to relegate enemies to the condition of traitors and their women to that of legitimate victims was resisted by both sides. Both parties continued, despite some notable lapses, to acknowledge and enforce the claims of English and military law and of morality, but also, most importantly, to recognize the power of threats of reciprocity and reprisal to restrain extreme conduct. The calculations were utilitarian as well as legal and ethical. The enforcement of army discipline safeguarded society as a whole from the threat of violence that would endanger men and women alike, from the moral and material disasters that English men and women believed had accompanied the Thirty Years' War in continental Europe, and from the wholesale maiming, killing, and rape featured in reports of the Irish rebellion.

Although the underlying bonds of English society were strained by this intimate civil war, most participants drew back from the danger of breaking them irreparably. Irish women could be relegated to the status of "others" to whom laws need not apply. English women suffered hardships, from starvation to the seizure and vandalism of their goods, and from abuse and ridicule to sexual attack, but they were not outside the law. Their voices were heard—if sometimes unwillingly, as in demands for peace or surrender— and the protections nominally due to them remained norms of conduct, albeit imperfectly observed. The English civil war demonstrated on the one hand the vulnerability of women to physical violence, from rape to battle wounds, sexual insult and material loss, and on the other the fragile survival of the moral and military norms mandating their protection in war and of the restraints imposed by those norms.

Chapter 12
"Unlawfully and Against Her Consent": Sexual Violence and the Military During the American Civil War

E. Susan Barber and Charles F. Ritter

Sexual violence has been a ubiquitous part of warfare since the beginning of recorded time. From ancient myths and wars to modern conflicts, the dehumanization and punishment of a conquered people have included sexual violence against the enemy's women, and sometimes its men. Until recently, the American Civil War has been considered an anomaly to this pattern of sexual violence in conflict zones. Our research, however, demonstrates that nearly four hundred soldiers were prosecuted for crimes of sexual violence in U.S. army courts-martial and military commissions. A handful of these assaults took place in the North; the majority were perpetrated on Southern women by soldiers of the invading Union army. The story that emerges from these trials is complex. It dispels the currently held idea that the American Civil War was exceptional with regard to sexual violence. Furthermore, it opens a window on the opportunities that women in a conflict zone employed to obtain sexual justice. The army's response to these accusations was driven primarily by the need to preserve order and discipline within the ranks. In prosecuting these cases, however, Union military tribunals also attempted to address the suffering of some of the war's female victims. It is also clear that gender and race informed these deliberations that took place when women brought charges of sexual violence before the military justice system. Sometimes courts-martial decisions reinforced gender and racial stereotypes about the inviolability of white women and the lasciviousness of black women and men. At other times, the courts challenged notions of gender and sexuality by admitting the testimony of black witnesses and by delivering a measure of sexual justice to black women and girls.

Unlike recent cases of modern warfare, when Union and Confederate armies went to war in 1861, military commanders never deliberately intended to use the assault of women as an instrument of war. Many rank-and-file soldiers, however, seem to have taken a different view. Apparently some considered women part of the "spoils of war" to which the victors were entitled. Indeed, the language of ravishment and domination sometimes permeated the language of the war itself. Thus, military occupation of the South exposed sexual tensions between the occupiers and the female civilian population that made sexual justice a necessity. Margaret Brooks's experience illustrates this point.

Brooks, a young, white, married mother of two, set out with a supply wagon and a carriage for nearby Memphis, Tennessee, on March 12, 1864, to purchase supplies for her family. Brooks's travail began on the way home, when her little caravan crossed Nonconnah Creek. There, the supply wagon's trace chain broke, leaving it stalled midstream. Brooks's wagon driver, George Bradshaw, unhitched one of the mules and rode it in the direction of the Brooks farm to fetch Margaret's husband, John, to help repair the broken wagon. Margaret Brooks, meanwhile, remained in the buggy with her driver, Mr. Moore, to await her husband's arrival. Within minutes, Brooks and Moore were set upon by three white Union soldiers from the Second New Jersey Cavalry, who, according to Brooks, "hooted and hollowed" as they untied the other mule, searched the wagon, and demanded that Brooks hand over the "greenbacks" they believed she had in her possession.

When Brooks repeatedly refused to hand over the cash, the soldiers shifted their attention to the twenty-four-year-old woman herself. Before the military commission that later heard Brooks's testimony, she recounted how one of the men, eighteen-year-old John Callahan, told her the men didn't want goods. "He then came towards me" she related, "and Said, 'we want a little Fucking and we intend to have it right here and the Stiller you are about it the better it is for you.'" It was at this point that Brooks's ordeal began in earnest. The young mother screamed and shouted for help, claiming that she would "die right here before I will submit to any such thing." Mr. Moore, Margaret Brooks's erstwhile buggy driver, apparently chose this opportunity to make a quick escape; his whereabouts were still unknown when the trial commenced eight days later. Callahan then drew a revolver, pulled back the hammer, and pointed it at Brooks's head. "We will shoot you dead," he replied, "and we won't ask you any more. We will do it any how." Then he handed the revolver to Jacob Snover, one of his accomplices, and climbed into the buggy. Brooks screamed and struggled with Callahan who tore her clothes and choked her mouth and throat until she was "trembling and helpless." Then the other two men, Jacob Snover and Thomas Johnson, held her legs against the buggy's dashboard while Callahan sexually assaulted her. When he was through, Snover and Johnson raped her as well. "Then the first one got in again," Brooks later testified, "and Said, 'By God, you would not let me get through, and I intend to have it over again' and went through the Same motions." Then the trio robbed Brooks of the $250 she had hidden in her bosom, plus an additional $60 or more secreted in her "companion."[1]

Brooks's experience was one shared by at least several hundred white and black women and girls who were sexually assaulted by Union and Confederate soldiers during the American Civil War. Until now their stories have been inadequately studied by Civil War scholars, who have focused more on battlefield victories and defeats than on the war's effects on the civilian population. Some contemporary historians have conceded that rapes occurred during the war, but they claim that the evidence is primarily anecdotal or that the records necessary for a thorough analysis have not survived. Others suggest that the evidence is too disparate or that most cases either went unreported or were settled outside a court of law. Others note that sexual assaults were only perpetrated on working-class white women or slave and free women of color, thus introducing a class and racial perspective on the topic.[2] This chapter, and the larger research project of which it is a part, restores the voices of Brooks and other women like her to the historical narrative of the war and accounts for the ways in which the Union and Confederate armies dealt with this most intimate crime.

The Sexual Justice in the American Civil War Project[3] is the first comprehensive study of the instances of the sexual violence against women and girls by soldiers and civilians associated with the Union army (1861–65). It begins a previously unwritten chapter of the American Civil War that exists at the nexus of the military and civilian arenas, where social history interfaces with military and legal history. It illuminates the attitudes of the military command toward the civilian population. It examines the dialogue between the state legislatures' definitions of rape and the punishments meted out, and the military's interpretation of those laws and the verdicts they rendered. This dialogue took place against the background of nineteenth-century attitudes toward gender and sexuality. It brings forth the voices of women and men, both black and white, who were caught in the turmoil and brutality of war, and who turned to the military justice system seeking redress. It alerts scholars to be mindful of the ubiquity of sexual violence against women and girls throughout history, especially, though not exclusively, in combat zones, even to this day. In this way, the Sexual Justice in the American Civil War Project breaks fertile ground by advancing our understanding of the impact of the war on civilians, especially women, and by focusing on the ways in which military and civilian authorities addressed the problem of soldiers committing civilian crimes, especially those of a sexual nature. Indeed, the Union army's treatment of these charges represents the first full-scale modern application of a battlefield justice system that dealt with sexual and other civilian crimes.

The Union military prosecuted more than 80,000 cases during the war, most of which were infractions of the Articles of War, such as desertion, drunkenness, and sleeping while on duty. In addition to these military crimes, Union court-martial records, housed in Record Group 153, the Records of the United States Judge Advocate General's Office, at the National Archives and Records Administration in Washington, D.C., document the prosecution of an array of civil crimes, among them sexual violence against women and girls. Sexual crimes were not a part of the Articles of War when the war began. The U.S. Congress militarized sexual crimes and other civilian crimes such as murder, robbery, theft, and assault in March 1863.[4] During the war the military prosecuted over 1,100 cases concerning these newly militarized crimes. More than one-third of these involved sexual violence. Furthermore, Union courts-martial heard approximately one hundred cases of crimes against women that appear to be related to gender. These cases involve indecent exposure, the use of lewd and obscene language, and behavior that constituted crimes of humiliation. While these crimes may not be properly considered rape or attempted rape, they certainly constitute sexual crimes.

What is distinctive about the American Civil War is the decision to prosecute soldiers for committing civilian and, in particular, sexual crimes—a decision that, according to Rhonda Copelon, armies seldom make.[5] In the United States this prosecution of civilian crimes by military courts has a history that can be traced at least to the early nineteenth century. Historically, the Articles of War provided that soldiers who committed such crimes be turned over to civilian authorities.[6] During the Mexican-American War, however, General Winfield Scott established military commissions to try soldiers who committed civilian crimes, such as arson, assault and battery, murder, rape, and attempted rape in Mexican territory.[7] When the Civil War began in April 1861, General Henry Halleck, while commanding the Department of Missouri, continued the practice of using military commissions to try soldiers for civilian offenses. Other commanders followed suit.[8] Congress specified the civilian crimes subject to military prosecution in section 30 of the Enrollment Act of 1863, and thereafter the prosecution of civilian crimes became a standard feature of military justice.[9]

At the same time that the U.S. Congress passed the Enrollment Act, the War Department issued General Orders 100.[10] This monumental document resulted from the collaboration of Henry Halleck and Francis Lieber, a distinguished professor of political science at Columbia College. General Orders 100 was intended to govern the behavior of the U.S. Army in the field and treated such subjects as martial law and the treatment of prisoners. It was particularly noteworthy for its rules governing the treatment of the civilian population, particularly women. Article 44 of this order stated that

> All wanton violence committed against persons in the invaded country, all destruction of property not commanded by the authorized officer, all robbery, all pillage or sacking, even after taking a place by main force, all rape, wounding, maiming, or killing of such inhabitants, are prohibited under the penalty of death, or such severe punishment as may seem adequate for the gravity of the offense.[11]

As a result of section 30 of the Enrollment Act and General Orders 100, white and black female plaintiffs brought charges of sexual violence against Union soldiers throughout the war.

Union provost marshals and judge advocates, military officials charged with administering justice, took accusations of sexual violence seriously. Commanders and judges moved with alacrity to arrest and try accused soldiers, and punish the convicted. Their motives apparently reflected a determination to ensure discipline in the ranks as well as a desire to maintain order in the community. In the process of accomplishing these two goals, military courts also meted out sexual justice to female plaintiffs. Indeed, these military courts began to articulate a concept of sexual justice in combat zones by creating a venue for women to confront their attackers. This was especially true of African Americans, individuals often deemed by Southern legislatures to be unfit to testify in a court of law. This practice was made explicit by Judge Advocate General Joseph Holt. "Negroes," he opined, "may testify before a military court, notwithstanding any disqualifying statute or custom in the State where the court is held."[12]

Any general officer commanding a Union army or field officer commanding a department or brigade could convene general courts-martial. Typically the courts were convened within a month, and sometimes a few days, of an accusation. Trials proceeded quickly, usually in one or two days, although complex cases could go on for months. The courts consisted of seven to thirteen officers and a judge advocate who was both a member of the court and the prosecuting attorney. The judge advocate also represented the accused if he did not have counsel, which—given the lack of resources available to most enlisted men—describes the situation of most of the cases in our study. Trials proceeded with direct testimony and cross-examination, both conducted by the judge advocate. Decisions of the court were reviewed by the superior officer who originated the court-martial, and severe punishments were reviewed by the secretary of war, the president, and the judge advocate general in Washington, D.C. The president had to approve death sentences until Congress relieved him of that duty in 1863. There were anomalies in the system peculiar to military justice, however. For instance, the judge advocate, who prosecuted the case and often represented the defendant, was a member of the court and deliberated on defense objections, though not on guilt or innocence. Also, defendants who wished to appeal the court's decision could do so only through letter-writing campaigns.

Women entering any court of law in the nineteenth century entered a relatively alien world dominated by men. All of the judges were male, as were the attorneys trying the cases and the juries who deliberated. Although some women occasionally appeared in court to settle estates, dispute claims by creditors, or answer misdemeanor and felony accusations, many women lived their entire lives without testifying in a court of law. For Southern women bringing claims against Union soldiers, this search for sexual justice was made even more complex by the enemy status of the men they faced. For white Southern women, the Union army bore multiple and conflicting identities. At the very basic level, it represented the enemy and the source of their travail. Yet the military command system also signified an attempt to impose order in a community made chaotic from the days and weeks of battle, including the plunder and pillage by both soldiers and civilians. In areas where civil law had been suspended, Union courts-martial represented the only avenue for seeking legal redress, including sexual justice. For black Southern women, the presence of the Union army, at least by 1862, additionally represented freedom from slavery but freedom that sometimes came at a heavy physical price. Nearly 40 percent of the women in our study were African Americans who claimed they were sexually assaulted by Union personnel.

In the aftermath of an assault, some women appeared to know the procedures necessary to bring an accusation forward, while others were at a loss about how to proceed. Many made a charge, either in person or through a surrogate, to a commanding officer within a day or two of the assault. Kate Bayliss, for example, went to the camp of the Sixteenth U.S. Colored Troops (U.S.C.T.) on the morning of December 27, 1863, and identified Richard Mitchelson as the soldier who had assaulted and attempted to rape her at her home the previous evening.[13] Elizabeth McDougal's brother, William Gardener, reported her assault to a commander in the camp of the Fourth U.S. Colored Heavy Artillery on the day following her October 10, 1864, attack. Later that day, two officers visited McDougal and arranged for her to appear in camp the following morning, October 12, where she picked her assailant, Henry Duncan, out of a lineup.[14] Some would-be assaulters got more than they bargained for. After Sarrah Beuford, a married free woman of color, foiled Private John Lewis's attempted assault, she began following him back to the camp of the Sixteenth U.S.C.T. threatening to report him. Lewis tried to stop her by shooting at her, but Beuford persisted until she tired and abandoned her pursuit. The next day she appeared in camp and reported Lewis to Lieutenant John Scott, commander of Company C.[15] Mary Kirskey, on the other hand, was unfamiliar with the process of bringing a charge against a soldier and sought advice from several soldiers before pressing her claim of a violent assault and rape perpetrated on her by Charles Hunter on the morning of May 18, 1864.[16]

Some women also sought immediate medical attention, which often became the basis of useful information when cases came to trial. Margaret Brooks, for example, was examined by Dr. F. T. Payne on Sunday, March 13, 1863, the morning after the attacks on her took place. At trial, Payne testified that Brooks's "face and eyes were swollen and her eyes suffused with tears. The surface of [her] neck had the appearance of being chapped with slight abrasions under the eye." When asked to offer his professional opinion as to the cause of her condition, Payne replied that it was due to "physical abuse . . . and rough handling."[17] Shortly after being examined by Dr. Payne, Brooks reported the attack at the headquarters of the Second New Jersey Cavalry at White Station, eight miles from Memphis, and identified her assailants in the office of a detective who was probably a civilian employed by the military.[18] America Pearman was examined by a military surgeon shortly after her father, Henry, filed a complaint at the headquarters of the First New York Engineers, stationed at Fort Harrison, Virginia, on April 25, 1865. At the trial the doctor testified that the ten-year-old's hymen had recently been ruptured by a sexual assault. As a result of his and young America's testimony, Thomas Mitchell was convicted of rape and sentenced to serve three years of hard labor at the Norfolk Penitentiary.[19]

Because the accused and the victims were both white and black, elite and poor, and young and old, these cases offer tantalizing insights into the ways that gender, race, class, and age informed or complicated the trials' outcomes. As the military tribunals rendered their verdicts, they confirmed and occasionally challenged existing stereotypes about womanhood. For instance, Southern rape statutes often held that white women were more virginal than black women and thus more inviolate. Black women were thought to be licentious and therefore could not be considered victims of a sexual assault. By bringing these cases to trial, Union courts-martial challenged these Southern stereotypes about the "rapeability" of women of color. By admitting testimony by African American witnesses, the courts overturned Southern notions about the appropriateness and reliability of testimony by black witnesses. Furthermore, these cases reveal the origins of practices that until recently were common in contemporary courts hearing accusations of sexual crimes—questioning the character and sexual history of the plaintiff and requiring evidence that she did not consent to the act.

Nineteenth-century stereotypes typically characterized men as strong and women as weak. Yet, these stereotypes were often reversed in cases involving sexual assault. Most rape laws required women to demonstrate that they had resisted with all their might, usually with a showing of bruises and other marks of violence, to avoid a judgment of complicity in the assault. Men, on the other hand, often pleaded the "alcohol defense" by claiming that the evil spirits had weakened their ability to resist their baser instincts. Thirty-two-year-old Thomas Dawson, for example, claimed that he was so drunk that he had no recollection of the night he raped Frances West, a white widow living in Morrisville, Virginia. The court-martial rejected Dawson's argument, found him guilty, and sentenced him to death by hanging. Following military procedure, Dawson's case was forwarded to President Lincoln along with a note from Judge Advocate General Joseph Holt, noting that, although the condemned man had been drinking, "he was not so drunk that he did not know the enormity of the crime he had committed, for when arrested, he remarked to the guard that he (the prisoner) ought to be ashamed of himself, an old soldier to be caught in such a scrape." Lincoln approved the sentence, and Dawson was executed before the entire Nineteenth Massachusetts Infantry on April 25, 1864.[20]

These cases also contribute to an historical understanding of rape statutes in the United States in the mid-nineteenth century. Because rape was not a military crime until 1863 and there was no federal law concerning rape, courts-martial relied on the definition of rape in English common law and on the laws of states where the crime occurred. Rape was legally understood as a heterosexual crime requiring genital contact that resulted in sexual penetration.[21] Jurist William Blackstone defined rape as "carnal knowledge of a woman forcibly and against her will," a definition that many states adopted.[22] The charge of attempted rape encompassed a broader array of behaviors that included fondling, kissing, and what were often referred to as "lewd" or "indecent suggestions." With only a few exceptions, no Civil War cases involved other types of vaginal penetration or homosexual assaults.[23]

Union military tribunals were required by federal law to follow state law for the minimum punishments they meted out, although they could, and frequently did, exceed those minimums.[24] Those laws varied widely in their clarity and precision. In Louisiana, for example, there was no statutory definition of either rape or attempted rape in the 1856 code. The law merely provided the death penalty for those who committed rape. Louisiana's Black Code provided that a slave or free black person who raped a white woman would also be subject to the death penalty.[25] Georgia employed the Blackstone definition of rape, criminalized assault with intent to rape, and defined assault. The penalty for rape was "imprisonment at labor" for from two to twenty years, and for an attempted rape, imprisonment for one to five years.[26] Curiously, Tennessee's general statutes did not refer to females by race and seemed to intend the law to be applied to all women. The Tennessee slave statutes, however, made it clear that black and mulatto men, whether slave or free, could only be accused of raping or assaulting white women. In 1833 the Tennessee legislature provided that any black or mulatto man who "shall make an assault upon any white woman, with intent to commit a rape" would, upon conviction, die by hanging.[27] In 1842 the legislature defined the term "white woman" in the 1833 statute to mean "all and every white female."[28]

Women who brought assault charges to Union officials came with the expectation that their accusations would be heard. Trials provided women with the opportunity to confront their assailants and testify against them. While Union courts-martial provided receptive venues for women to air their charges, female plaintiffs still had to establish their credibility regarding their reputation, their age, and their ability to testify, as was the case in civilian courts. The burden of proof was on the female plaintiff who had to prove she was sexually violated and that she neither encouraged nor acquiesced to the assault. Almost routinely poor white women and women of color could expect to have their reputations and integrity questioned. For example, Martha Tabor, a free woman of color who worked as an itinerant domestic in North Carolina, was identified in testimony as "a drunken dissipated woman" who kept a "a bad [and "disorderly"] house."[29] The court found the defendant in this case, Private James E. Lee, innocent of raping Tabor. Similarly, Martha Hall and her sisters, the daughters of William Hall, a poor white Tennessee farmer who moved his family to Camp Nelson, Kentucky, where the girls worked as laundresses and cooks for the Union army, were accused of being prostitutes. Defending Captain Samuel Fitch from charges of invading the Hall home and threatening to "fuck some of you before I leave," defense attorney J. B. Houston argued that, even though Fitch knew the house was not a house of ill fame, it was "undeniable that it had that reputation and was so esteemed by the accused. . . . This is sufficient," Houston concluded, "for this defense." In this case, the court convicted this defendant and his accomplice, Captain Jacob Schuck, and dismissed them from the service.[30] Even girls as young as ten-year-old Alice McDonnagh and twelve-year-old Nancy Short could expect to have their chastity called into question when soldiers stood accused of rape or sexual assault.[31] These burdens, however, did not deter some women, many of whom had little or no education, from bringing complaints before the court. This suggests that, despite the exigencies of war and the high standards of accountability, some women expected to receive, at the very least, a hearing of their complaints.

In addition to having their reputations challenged, young plaintiffs were often required to provide proof of their age, a requirement more easily satisfied by white girls than by African American girls whose accurate age was often unknown. Amelia Brown's parents, for example, submitted for Amelia and her mother an 1856 bill of sale as proof of their daughter's youth.[32] Age of consent varied among the states, but in the mid-nineteenth century South it was sometimes quite low. In Louisiana, Mississippi, and Kentucky, for example, the age of consent was ten. The Tennessee slave statutes set the age of consent for the rape of a white child by a black man at ten years, and, of course, established the death penalty for a conviction of the crime.[33] As was typical of the rest of the country at this time, other Southern states set the age of consent at twelve.[34]

The age-of-consent issue was critical. If the plaintiff was younger than the age of consent, the defendant could not claim that the plaintiff acquiesced in the alleged assault. Also, typically the law provided that these defendants, if convicted, receive the harshest penalties, although these penalties were occasionally mitigated on legal technicalities, often involving irregularities in court procedure.

Women of color occasionally faced the added burden of having to prove their right to testify. For example, the attorneys representing Private James E. Lee constructed an elaborate objection to claim that Martha Tabor, a mulatto, was incompetent to offer evidence, "because she is a free person of color, within the fourth degree," meaning that she "has one sixteenth negro blood. To this extent the Negro race is excluded," they argued. "Such," they said, "is the rule of evidence in North Carolina, and has been for many years before the rebellion of 1861." The court rejected Lee's objection.[35] Indeed, although defendants often challenged their competency, the military courts accepted the testimony of African Americans, usually without hesitation. Thus, several white soldiers, including officers, were tried and found guilty on the testimony of slaves or free people of color, primarily in cases involving black victims. For example, Private William Hilton, of the Sixteenth Indiana Infantry, was convicted of the rape and murder of Julia, a slave girl, on the testimony of Felix Jackson and Nancy Simpson, two other slaves on the Louisiana plantation where the crime occurred.[36] In March of 1865, Dudley O. Bravard, a second lieutenant in Company K of the Fifty-fourth Kentucky Volunteer Infantry, was sentenced to dismissal from military service and five years of hard labor at the Kentucky State Penitentiary for the rape of eleven-year-old Biddy Lewis, on the testimony of her parents, Beverly and Sarah Lewis. The Lewises were all people of color living in Greensburg, Kentucky.[37] And in June of 1865, Adolph Bork, a private in Company H, of the 183rd Ohio Volunteers, was sentenced to be shot for the rape of Susan, a twenty-four-year-old pregnant woman of color, living on a plantation near Salisbury, North Carolina.[38]

Even though Union courts-martial were progressive in admitting testimony by African Americans, they were seldom able to rise above conventional stereotypes that viewed black men as sexual predators. More than 80 percent of these Union courts-martial cases involved crimes committed by soldiers. The remaining 19 percent involved civilian assailants—usually men under contract to the Union army as drivers, surgeons, or other hospital workers—who were tried by military commissions. Of the soldiers tried for sexual crimes, 82 percent were white and 18 percent were African Americans. Yet of the twenty-four soldiers executed for sexual crimes, 61 percent of these executed men were black. All the executed black soldiers were convicted of raping or attempting to rape white women. Clearly then, African American men were being executed for sexual crimes at a rate that was inconsistent with the same crimes committed by whites, especially when the alleged victim was a white female. Men who committed crimes against black

women and girls received lighter sentences that were more frequently mitigated upon review.

The Confederacy, too, was concerned about the treatment of the civilian population, particularly women. Logic, therefore, would suggest a study
of comparable crimes in the Confederate military justice system, which
resembled the Union system, with a few exceptions. In addition to a regular
court-martial system, the Confederate Congress created a system of standing military courts that were attached to Southern armies.[39] These courts
all functioned procedurally in much the same way as courts-martial and in
1862 were also granted jurisdiction over civilian crimes. However, the existing evidence suggests that these standing military courts seldom, if ever,
prosecuted crimes of sexual violence.[40] Furthermore, most Confederate
courts-martial transcripts were destroyed at the war's end, and those that
have survived contain only scattered evidence detailing prosecutions for a
handful of sexual offenses.[41]

What accounts for this paucity of evidence for sexual violence committed by Confederate soldiers? One explanation may be that the Confederate
military command implemented preventive measures that limited the interactions between soldiers and civilians and thus reduced the possibility of
depredations of any kind by Confederate soldiers on the civilian population.
Indeed, Confederate records contain many general orders aimed at controlling the behavior of Confederate troops. For example, as early as August
of 1861, Brigadier General John Bankhead Magruder noted that "depredations committed on private property by the troops of this command as so
base and cowardly . . . as to throw discredit on all officers, non-commis-
sioned officers, and men who compose it." In response, Magruder ordered
the placement of "sentinels over the houses, premises, and fields of all citizens in the vicinity of their camps, and to send out patrols to take up all
offenders [to] be punished . . . by their commanding officers in a most severe
and summary manner."[42] Some commanders warned of the consequences
of this behavior. For example, a general field order from John Bell Hood's
command reminded its men that "this unbridled spirit of plunder recently
caused the defeat of our army in the Valley of Virginia after they had driven
the enemy from the field."[43]

Other general orders restricted the movements of Confederate soldiers by requiring them to remain in camp and to drill continuously, or
by restricting the number of passes issued to soldiers for visits to nearby
towns. Brigadier General John Floyd, for example, ordered his regimental
commanders to "see that men remain in Camp, and not be prowling about

over the Country."[44] Similarly, John Bell Hood ordered his commanders to have "the arms constantly kept stacked on the color lines and Company roll called frequently during the day to ascertain the absentees from camp."[45] Brigadier General Wise, commander of the Fifth to Seventh Military Districts, ordered double sentries placed on the lines of camp and forbade anyone to leave without a pass.[46]

Another explanation may involve differences between the behavior of an invading and a defending army. As the defending army, it was incumbent upon Confederate soldiers to protect the civilian population, especially defenseless women and children, and to do them no harm. Such a policy would retain their loyalty. As the invading army, however, the Union had no such objective and, indeed, the goal of dominating and subduing the Southern military may have extended, in at least some Union soldiers' minds, to include the sexual domination of Southern women by Northern men. Whatever the explanation, the question of sexual justice for crimes committed by Confederate soldiers remains shrouded by the past.

*   *   *

In the twentieth and twenty-first centuries, women's bodies have increasingly become the terrain on which war is waged. From the women in East Congo to the widespread rape of women in Darfur to the thousands of Muslim women in refugee camps, these atrocities attest to the prevalence of sexual violence in conflict zones. Unlike contemporary examples, Union army courts-martial trials during the American Civil War represent a time in which, however brief, a military court system attempted to provide female victims with sexual justice. From the pages of these trials, women and men speak to us about unspeakable crimes. Sometimes these courts rose above the conventions of the day to render sexual justice; sometimes they did not. Their presence, however, indicates a pioneering attempt to mediate against the ravages of war on innocent women and girls and to render justice for sexual violence in conflict zones.

PART V

Toward an International Human Rights Framework

Chapter 13
Legal Responses to World War II
Sexual Violence: The Japanese Experience

Yuma Totani

Since the establishment of international criminal tribunals in the 1990s, legal scholars, human rights experts, and policy makers have debated the significance of international prosecution not only in meting out punishment to grave human rights violators but also in achieving "restorative justice." Certain researchers such as Mark Osiel have explored the educational potential of war crimes prosecution, pointing out that trials can help victims and perpetrators of mass atrocity find common grounds to establish facts about large-scale violence and begin restoring the fabric of the torn community. Other scholars have expressed less sanguine views. Lawrence Douglas cautions that the ability of the court to offer a history lesson could be limiting because, among other reasons, laws applied at criminal trials tend to constrict the construction of charges and narrow the court's ability to tell the story of mass atrocity. This, in fact, was the case with the handling of evidence pertaining to the Holocaust at the Nuremberg trials. Furthermore, a recent study by Eric Stover of court witnesses at the Hague tribunal shows that the oft-assumed therapeutic effect of witness testimony may not be empirically substantiated.[1]

This chapter turns to a historical example from the mid-twentieth century—the Allied war crimes program in the Pacific region (1945–52)[2]—to explore how the Allied trials addressed a range of issues on postconflict justice. This chapter will provide a focused discussion of the International Military Tribunal for the Far East (commonly known as the Tokyo trial of 1946–48), pertaining to the prosecution of rape, organized sexual slavery, and other forms of sexual violence that commonly accompanied the Japanese conduct of war and occupation during World War II. A segment of present-day reparation lawsuits concerning "comfort women" (organized sexual slavery by the Imperial Japanese Army and Navy) will also come under consideration. By comparing the two contrasting legal proceedings in the postwar period, this chapter will consider what lessons there are to be learned from the Japanese experiences.

This chapter's basic position is generally to support the cautionary views of the critics about the "restorative" effect of international prosecution. It is true that in the wake of war the Allies undertook a fact finding mission on an unprecedented scale and that they succeeded in extensively documenting Japanese-perpetrated war crimes and determining the locus of responsibility. However, the Tokyo trial suffered various structural limitations that severely compromised its educational significance. Ultimately, it stopped short of having a positive impact on the postwar reconciliation processes for the peoples and communities concerned. By contrast, noncriminal civil lawsuits being pursued in Japan today seem to be having a measure of success. Although most reparation lawsuits have so far ended in dismissals, these litigations have at least offered an opportunity for the Japanese citizens and survivors of wartime atrocity to start afresh dialogues about war memory, war guilt, and issues of responsibility. One might argue that the Japanese courts, in this regard, are fulfilling a "restorative function" of a sort, however limited it may be.

Japanese Military Sexual Violence: An Overview

It is indisputable that during World War II, large numbers of the Japanese armed forces committed sexual violence against women of diverse age, race, and ethnicity on a vast scale. This, however, does not necessarily mean that the highest ranking commanders and staff officers approved it. On the contrary, during the late Meiji period (1868–1912) the Imperial Japanese Army and Navy adopted criminal laws stipulating that rape and looting constituted criminal offense, and that those who committed these acts could face punishment, ranging from a seven-year term to life imprisonment. The same laws further stipulated that capital punishment would be applied if the criminal conduct resulted in the death of the victim.[3] Despite these strict rules, however, murder, rape, looting, and other forms of brutality figured prominently in Japanese military actions in various theaters of war.

Realizing early that their troops had disciplinary problems, the Japanese military authorities attempted to rectify the situation by court-martialing offenders. According to statistical information that the defense counsel prepared for the Tokyo trial, 522 Japanese servicemen in China were prosecuted on charges of rape during the four years (1938–41) following the Marco Polo Bridge Incident. A separate Japanese source further indicates that during the Pacific War an additional 319 were court-martialed on grounds of rape.[4] These data, collected by the Japanese military authorities themselves, show that a very large number of rape cases were reported, that many disciplinary actions were taken, but that despite repeated prosecutions, Japanese military justice proved ineffective to combat widespread rape.

To explain these violations of the conduct of war, several circumstances should be considered. The Japanese troops, for instance, were susceptible to the dehumanizing circumstances of the war, the culture of insubordination that plagued the Imperial Japanese Army, the breakdown of the military chain of command in certain combat situations, and the lack of soldiers' training concerning their international obligations under the Hague and Geneva Conventions. Yet with the extent and frequency of sexual violence, these explanations seem insufficient. Recent research, in fact, points to the existence also of policies ranging from field commanders' tacit approval to government-level authorizations.

As an example, consider the behavior of those Japanese troops who fought Chiang Kai-shek's armed forces from the coastal areas of Shanghai and Hangzhou to Nanjing (then the seat of Chiang Kai-shek's national government) during the latter half of 1937. According to Japanese researchers, sexual crimes in this theater stemmed in part from the task force commanders' orders to "requisition" supplies from local Chinese. The requisition policy was in effect an authorization to forage. This reckless policy had the benefit of sustaining the assault forces' momentum in their pursuit of Chiang's army and expediting the Japanese capture of Nanjing. However, it also had serious repercussions on troop morale and behavior, in that the requisition orders were interpreted by the Japanese soldiers as permission to attack Chinese villages with impunity. This, in turn, created within the army an environment that tolerated rape, looting, arson, and the like.[5]

In different combat areas, the Japanese armed forces committed sexual violence against women apparently as a subset of a scorched-earth policy. Many brutal sexual crimes were committed, for instance, during the battles against the Chinese Red Army in Shanxi and Hebei provinces. In 1941, the Japanese North China Area Army formally launched a three-year policy of systematically decimating those villages that were suspected of providing military intelligence and logistical support to the Eighth Route

Army, a communist army that was then rapidly expanding its control of the countryside. The ultimate goal of the scorched-earth policy was to break the resistance of the Chinese Communist power; the Japanese soldiers offered no humanitarian protection to the civilian population in the targeted villages. The Chinese people referred to this particular military campaign by the enemy forces as "Three-All Policy," because of the Japanese thoroughness to "kill all, burn all, and loot all." In implementing this policy, Japanese soldiers openly committed abduction, rape, sexual slavery, and various other grave sexual crimes against the targeted civilian population.[6]

Finally, the establishment of "comfort stations" (Japanese military brothels) is another policy dimension that requires consideration when explaining the frequency and extent of Japanese military sexual violence. The wartime Japanese government authorized recruitment, detention, and sexual enslavement of the female civilian population as a means to cope with widespread military disciplinary problems. However, implementing a policy that sanctioned institutionalized rape and sexual slavery was counterproductive, because it failed to abate widespread sexual violence or address the problem of military discipline. It fostered instead a pervasive attitude among the Japanese servicemen that life, dignity, and well-being of the female civilian populations in combat zones amounted to little or nothing.[7]

The Allied Prosecutorial Effort

Among the first Allied war crimes trials at which Japanese-perpetrated sexual violence became prominent was that of General Yamashita Tomoyuki. Known as the "Tiger of Malaya," Yamashita had gained fame at the beginning of the Pacific War because of his successful invasion of British Malaya. Three and a half years later, he found himself posted in the Philippines with a near-impossible task of defending the Japanese-occupied island nation from coordinated attacks by the U.S. Army and Navy. His forces engaged in delaying tactics for several months, but Yamashita surrendered in September 1945 after Tokyo accepted the Allies' Potsdam terms.[8] At the first U.S. military trial in Manila (Oct.–Dec. 1945), Yamashita was accused of allowing his troops to commit large-scale massacre, rape, arson, and other forms of atrocity against the city residents in early 1945, just before the U.S. invasion. (This instance of mass atrocity is still remembered as the "rape of Manila.") After hearing numerous firsthand testimonies from eyewitnesses

and survivors of atrocity, the judge panel concluded that Yamashita was der-
elict in his duty to take control of his subordinate troops and sentenced him
to death. He was hanged the following year.[9]

After this highly publicized trial, sexual violence continued to figure
prominently in the Allied prosecutorial effort. The Tokyo trial in particular followed the Yamashita precedent in two important respects. First, the
prosecuting agency brought to court a selection of other highest ranking
military and political leaders of the wartime Japanese government so as to
establish their individual responsibility for mass atrocity. Second, as was
the case at the Yamashita trial, war crime charges at Tokyo were built primarily on the theory of criminal negligence rather than criminal orders or
authorizations. Prosecutors at Tokyo needed to rely on the theory of criminal negligence, because they were faced with the Japanese government's
obstructionism and a dearth of Japanese military documents resulting from
it. In the weeks before the formal Allied occupation of Japan began, the
Imperial Japanese government had ordered the destruction of records relating to the war that it feared were potentially incriminating. The Japanese
armed forces had days and weeks to carry out the government's orders. As
of August 14, 1945, when Japan accepted the terms of the Potsdam Declaration, the Allies were far from ready to assume control of the vast territories
of the Japanese empire. By the time the Allied troops actually took control, they could do little to recover the government's records. The director
of the Japanese Defense Agency's archives estimated in 2003 that "as much
as 70 percent of the army's wartime records" were destroyed during the last
weeks of the war.[10] To overcome the challenges created by the government-
orchestrated destruction of documents, it thus became necessary for the
prosecution at Tokyo to seek proof of guilt in criminal negligence rather
than criminal orders. The prosecution's major task in court, therefore,
would not consist so much of documenting individual defendants' direct
authorization of war crimes, but would be to show instead that war crimes
were either widespread or systematic; that the accused knew or had reason
to know that their subordinate troops were committing atrocities; and that
the accused had the duty to stop the crimes and yet did nothing effective to
fulfill the duty.[11]

This method of substantiation was ultimately successful. The judgment of the Tokyo Tribunal read that "torture, murder, rape and other cruelties of the most inhumane and barbarous character were freely practiced
by the Japanese Army and Navy." It continued: "The Tribunal heard evidence . . . from witnesses who testified in detail to atrocities committed in

all theaters of war *on a scale so vast, yet following so common a pattern in all theaters, that only one conclusion is possible that atrocities were either secretly ordered or willfully permitted by the Japanese Government or individual members thereof and by the leaders of the armed forces.*"[12] With this ruling the Tokyo Tribunal upheld the prosecution's basic contention that Japanese-perpetrated war crimes, including rape, were widespread; that members of the Japanese government and military at the highest level must have had knowledge of it; and that despite this knowledge, they tolerated the continued atrocity by way of inaction if not outright authorization. In the same judgment the tribunal further took note of the evidence of "enforced prostitution" that had been presented in court by the prosecution.[13] In the absence of proof of criminal orders, however, the tribunal stopped short of giving any conclusive ruling regarding the Japanese government's *institutional* responsibility for this type of offense.

With respect to individual verdicts, the tribunal found ten out of twenty-five defendants guilty of war crimes, and three among the ten guilty ones were linked to instances of mass rape. One was General Matsui Iwane, commander-in-chief of the Central China Area Army that invaded Nanjing. Matsui was aware of widespread war crimes according to the tribunal's finding, and had the power, duty, and authority to stop his subordinates from committing them, but had done nothing effective to prevent them. Hirota Kōki, foreign minister at the time of the mass atrocity in Nanjing, was also found guilty. The tribunal's finding was that Hirota, as a minister of state, had the duty to ensure his government's observance of international obligations, which included the duty to protect the civilian populations in the Japanese-occupied territories. Despite voluminous evidence, however, Hirota did not take necessary measures to fulfill his duty. A staff officer of Matsui's army, Lieutenant General Mutō Akira, was acquitted of the charge associated with the atrocity in Nanjing for the reason that he was not in the position to discipline the soldiers. However, the tribunal found him guilty in connection with the rape of Manila, during which he served as chief of staff to Yamashita's army.[14]

These findings by the Tokyo Tribunal are arguably of historical importance, but their educational impact on the Japanese people seems to have been minimal. The reason is partly structural. Although the prosecuting agency did present evidence on sexual violence, the same agency attached far greater importance to substantiating charges of "crimes against peace," that is, the planning, preparation, initiation, and waging of aggressive war, or participation in a common plan to carry out such acts. Crimes against peace, or the "crime of aggression" as it is currently called in the Rome Statute of the International Criminal Court, had, in fact, been the centerpiece of the prosecutorial effort at both Nuremberg and Tokyo. It was as a result of the joint policy decision of the Allies that a clear legal precedent on individual criminal liability for aggression should be established at this historical juncture, thereby strengthening the international peace mechanism in combating future aggressors in the post–World War II era. This policy of attaching primary importance to crimes against peace was introduced first at Nuremberg, and then seconded at Tokyo. The Charter of the Tokyo Tribunal actually required that crimes against peace be the principal charges to be made against prospective defendants, while deeming war crimes and crimes against humanity optional. Consequently, most of the court battles revolved around substantiating charges concerning aggression. The disproportionate emphasis that the Allied policy makers placed on crimes against peace had far-reaching consequences, in that the court sessions on crimes against peace shaped the Japanese memory of the Tokyo trial, whereas the references to wartime atrocity did not inspire much public debate for many years to follow.

The educational potential of the Tokyo trial was further compromised by the general skepticism among the Japanese people about the purpose of the Allied war crimes program. Although there were certain individuals who regarded the Tokyo trial as a beacon of a new Japan, the public tended to assume that the Tokyo trial was no more than a venue for victor nations to take revenge on the vanquished nation. General Douglas MacArthur, the supreme commander for the Allied Powers (SCAP) and the chief of the Allied occupation of Japan, was also not helpful in improving the public image of the Tokyo trial, because he had little faith in the international criminal justice system. He regarded it as slow and inefficient and rather preferred the U.S. Army's military tribunals. Enjoying little personal attention from the SCAP, the Tokyo trial eventually lost its prominence in the postwar occupation reform agenda and became vulnerable to criticisms of victors' justice.[15]

Reparation Lawsuits

Since 1972 more than seventy war-related reparation lawsuits have been initiated in Japan. The plaintiffs consist of war veterans, war orphans, atomic bomb victims, and survivors of Japanese wartime atrocities.[16] Ten cases among these lawsuits focused on comfort women, the first one starting in 1991. The plaintiffs comprised women from China, Korea, the Netherlands, the Philippines, and Taiwan, who had been victims in the comfort women system. Their shared goal is to establish facts pertaining to the Japanese military's organized sexual slavery and have the Japanese government recognize its responsibility for damages. Nine cases have already gone up to the Supreme Court and have been dismissed. At this writing, the decision for one last case is pending at the appeals court. (See the appendix to this chapter for a summary of cases and outcomes.)

Japanese human rights lawyers who have been assisting the reparation lawsuits generally agree that trial court judges are generally sympathetic to the plaintiffs' cause. It has in fact become fairly common for the trial court judges to evaluate evidence carefully, document circumstances of sexual enslavement, and declare its criminality. Consider, for instance, the lawsuit filed by ten victims of sexual slavery from Shanxi Province with the Tokyo District Court in October 1998. In its decision (Apr. 24, 2003) the court condemned the sexual savagery that the Japanese armed forces had committed and urged that the Japanese government initiate dialogues to resolve disputed reparation issues. Lawyers representing the plaintiffs welcomed the judgment, because it showed that despite the conservative nature of the Japanese justice system, the plaintiffs' personal tragedies as told in court could awaken the conscience of individual judges and compel them to take a stern position vis-à-vis the government. That said, the very same court stopped short of establishing the Japanese government's *legal* responsibility to compensate the victims; it recommended only that the Japanese side initiate intergovernmental talks. Their original goal in the lawsuit thus unfulfilled, the plaintiffs promptly appealed. The High Court, however, ruled against them, and in November 2005 the Supreme Court confirmed the dismissal of the case.[17]

Let us consider another lawsuit, filed with the Yamaguchi District Court (Dec. 25, 1992). In its decision (Apr. 27, 1998), this court, too, criticized the comfort women system, denouncing it as a "manifestation of thoroughgoing sexist and racist thought" (*tetteishita josei sabetsu, minzoku sabetsu shisō no araware*).[18] The court went on to rule that both wartime and postwar governments had the legal obligation to implement restitution measures. The court then ordered that the present government of Japan pay damages to the three plaintiffs—even though compensation amounted to a pittance of 300,000 yen (approximately U.S. $3,000) each. The court determined the $3,000 figure on the basis of the following findings: (1) that the Japanese government made public admission in 1993 of the wartime state-sponsored sexual slavery; (2) that upon the admission, the government assumed legal responsibility to institute an adequate reparation program within three years; and (3) that the government, however, had procrastinated and failed to fulfill this obligation. The postponement of governmental action beyond the three-year window, according to the court's calculation, translated into a $3,000 award per plaintiff. Admittedly, $3,000 hardly compensated for the six decades of the plaintiffs' personal tragedies and sufferings. The plaintiffs' lawyers nonetheless welcomed the judgment by reasoning that the court *did* establish, in this case, the Japanese government's responsibility to compensate the plaintiffs. This fact alone, in their opinion, sufficed to make it a landmark judgment. Quite predictably, however, the trial court decision was overturned at the appeals level. In March 2003, the Supreme Court confirmed the dismissal of the case.[19]

Lawyers on reparation trials agree that the major obstacle to winning their lawsuits, which are not limited to the comfort women cases, is the readiness of the Japanese courts to accept conservative interpretations of the law as advanced by the government. As an example, defense lawyers representing the government commonly argue that the Hague Conventions of 1907, on which many reparation lawsuits are based, do not accord any right to individual victims of atrocity to sue the Japanese government for war-related damages. Any transactions associated with reparation, so the argument goes, can only take place between the *states*. Second, it is asserted that the Constitution of the Empire of Japan (1889), or the Meiji Constitution as it is known, protected the government from lawsuits by individuals. There was therefore no legal recourse for the victims of wartime atrocity to seek damages. Third, the statute of limitations on war-related claims, the government argues, has already run out under the postwar Japanese civil law. Even if not, plaintiffs' own countries of origin have renounced such right either by signing the San Francisco Peace Treaty (1951) or by concluding separate bilateral treaties. The government's position is that for these reasons, too, reparation lawsuits have no valid legal grounds.[20] The Japanese courts have shown time and again their willingness to uphold one or more of these interpretations of the law. Mark Levin's analysis of the 2007 Supreme Court decisions on Chinese forced labor and comfort women cases confirms this trend.[21]

Conservatism of the Japanese courts has been a huge disappointment for the plaintiffs as well as their supporters. Lawyers try to see the positive side of legal defeat, as the two preceding case studies have just shown. However, a series of dismissals have been deeply upsetting for the plaintiffs. That a single lawsuit can last for a decade or more before it reaches the Supreme Court, and then have the predictable result of dismissal, has added to the frustration. During these years of waiting, the aging plaintiffs are fighting hard, physically and emotionally, hoping to see justice achieved before their own time expires.

The establishment of the International Women's War Crimes Tribunal (Dec. 8–12, 2000), commonly known as the Women's Tribunal, carries special significance when read against the general trend of reparation trials in Japan. Modeled on the Russell-Sartre Tribunal of the Vietnam War era, the Women's Tribunal was a nonbinding public hearing organized by grassroots activists and citizens groups. In Tokyo for four days, the Women's Tribunal received testimony from some sixty survivors of the comfort women system and then handed out a copy of its judgment to each. The judgment of the Women's Tribunal concluded, among other things, that the comfort women system constituted a war crime as well as a crime against humanity and that the Japanese emperor, Hirohito (1901–89), along with other highest ranking political and military leaders of wartime Japan, was personally responsible for the crime. This judgment was largely symbolic and had no legal effect. Nonetheless, Matsui Yayori, the lead organizer, maintains that the Women's Tribunal was able to provide a venue where judicial authorities would stand by the victims of Japanese military sexual violence and help restore their rights and human dignity, which the Japanese courts had repeatedly failed to offer.[22]

Meanwhile, legal battles in the Japanese courts continue, including the last comfort women lawsuit. At the center of the current reparation trials is the Japan Democratic Lawyers' Association, a nationwide association of Japanese human rights lawyers. This group has decades of experience in civil litigations related to labor rights and environmental pollution. Some lawyers have also been part of the famous Textbook Trials (1965–97), in which they assisted an outspoken education professor, Ienaga Saburō, and citizen groups in challenging the Ministry of Education's screening of high school history textbooks.[23] In the early 1990s the members of the Japan Democratic Lawyers' Association began providing legal assistance to Chinese victims of wartime Japanese violence on the grounds that not being a signatory of the 1951 San Francisco Peace Treaty, the Chinese victims of war had a good chance of winning reparation trials. For the same reason, the lawyers also decided to use these trials for raising public awareness on reparation issues and galvanizing citizens' activism in support of the Japanese government's reform legislation. Clarifying the association's basic position, the lead lawyer, Onodera Toshitaka, once wrote the following.

> The goal of our Chinese postwar reparation trials is to secure victory for each of what we designate as the representative lawsuits, use the victories [of the representative cases] as weapons with which to force the government into altering its erroneous policy of denying postwar reparation; and realize genuine "historical reconciliation" with the victims of war crimes.[24]

This statement points to both humanist and instrumentalist approaches that the Lawyers' Association has adopted in its assistance of Chinese reparation lawsuits. On the one hand, the lawyers are committed to helping individual plaintiffs in preparing lawsuits and winning cases. On the other hand, they also engage in publicity to pressure their government into joining the decades-long citizens' effort to achieve reconciliation between Japan and its former victim nations.

The fact still remains, however, that none of the key reparation lawsuits of the Chinese war crimes cases, including the comfort women cases, has yet achieved conclusive victory in court. Given the general pattern of the court rulings, it indeed appears unlikely that the result of the last comfort women case would be any different. In this respect, the "historical reconciliation" that Onodera speaks of may be more a distant hope than an imminent reality. Whether or not this view will hold true remains to be seen, while the courtroom battles continue.

Update

On March 2, 2010, the Supreme Court rejected the appeal of the last comfort women case (involving nine plaintiffs from Hainan Island). Lawyers representing the plaintiffs promptly released a statement that expressed their disappointment with the outcome and their determination to continue fighting on behalf of the plaintiffs.[25]

Historical Lessons

This chapter has shed light on two types of postwar judicial response to World War II Japanese military sexual violence. It has shown that at one level, all trials, whether international or national, criminal or civil, can provide a venue for documenting wartime violence, establishing the locus of individual and institutional responsibilities, and facilitating victim rehabilitation and social reconstruction. This was partly true at Tokyo, where there was an earnest effort by the prosecution, the defense, and the tribunal to set the record straight about the Japanese conduct of war, military occupation, and war crimes. With respect specifically to sexual violence, Allied prosecutors presented evidence of rape and other forms of women-targeted atrocity by the Japanese armed forces and also established the guilt of some defendants. That said, certain constraints—the limited mandate of the tribunal, skepticism of the Japanese public about the Allies' impartiality, and the SCAP's relative lack of interest in promoting a positive image of the trial, among other things—resulted in diminishing the educational potential of the Tokyo trial.

Current reparation trials also have their own limitations, but they appear to have had some success with regard to restorative justice. One notable difference between Tokyo and reparation trials may be that the latter have been a much more "inclusive" process. By this I mean that reparation trials are focused on victims rather than perpetrators, allowing survivors of sexual violence to have a far greater degree of control over the trial process. A few notable features are that it is these individuals who initiate the lawsuits, act as the key witnesses for their own cases, and command broad grassroots support from human rights lawyers and citizens' groups within and outside Japan. In turn, certain of the Japanese trial court judges have made a personal commitment to recognizing the criminality of the comfort women system and urging the Japanese government to consider restitution. These modest successes in the present-day reparation movement do not necessarily negate the historical significance of the Tokyo trial. However, international prosecution cannot be effective if justice (both retributive and restorative) is not achieved on behalf of all peoples and communities concerned, and if this justice does not eventually become their common heritage. The Japanese historical example shows that a combination of international criminal proceedings, civil litigations, educational outreach efforts, and other processes at both governmental and grassroots levels is crucial. The validity of this conclusion will be debated, tested, and scrutinized for many years to come as the world continues to face challenges of war, mass violence, and calls for justice in the twenty-first century.

Appendix: "Comfort Women" Reparation Lawsuits, 1991–2010

This appendix was prepared on the basis of information provided at the following websites: VAWW-Net Japan, http://www1.jca.apc.org/vaww-net-japan/english/, accessed May 6, 2008; Shimonoseki hanketsu o ikasukai (Group in Support of the Shimonoseki Decision), http://www.geocities.jp/ikasukai98, accessed Apr. 1, 2006; Hayo tsukurō! "ianfu" mondai kaiketsuhō, netto Fukuoka (Let's Make It! Fukuoka Network for the Expeditious Legislation of the "Comfort Women" Resolution), http://homepage3.nifty.com/net_fukuoka/index.htm, accessed Apr. 1, 2006; Hainan netto (Hainan Net), http://hainannet.org/02-saiban/01-passage.html, accessed May 8, 2008; Chūgokujin sensō higaisha no yōkyū o sasaeru Miyagi no kai (Miyagi Association in Support of the Victims of War in China), http://www.suopei.jp, accessed May 8, 2008, Apr. 25, 2010; and Homepage Harada, http://www.zephyr.dti.ne.jp/~kj8899/contents.html, accessed Dec. 1, 2006.

1. Korean Victims of the Asia-Pacific War (fifty plaintiffs including eight former comfort women)

   Dec. 6, 1991. Filed with the Tokyo District Court.

   Mar. 26, 2001. Claims dismissed. Appealed to the Tokyo High Court.

   July 22, 2003. Appeal dismissed. Appealed to the Supreme Court.

   Nov. 29, 2004. Appeal dismissed.

2. Pusan "Comfort Women" and Women Labor Corps members (ten plaintiffs including three former comfort women)

   Dec. 25, 1992. Filed with the Yamaguchi District Court.

   Apr. 27, 1998. Claims partially upheld.[26] Appealed to the Hiroshima High Court by the government.

   Mar. 29, 2001. Lower court decision overturned. Appealed to the Supreme Court by the plaintiffs.

   Mar. 25, 2003. Appeal dismissed.

3. Filipino "Comfort Women" (forty-six plaintiffs)

   Apr. 2, 1993. Filed with the Tokyo District Court.

   Oct. 9, 1998. Claims dismissed. Appealed to the Tokyo High Court.

   Dec. 6, 2000. Appeal dismissed. Appealed to the Supreme Court.

   Dec. 25, 2003. Appeal dismissed.

4. Song Shin-do (one plaintiff)

   Apr. 5, 1993. Filed with the Tokyo District Court.

   Oct. 1, 1999. Claims dismissed. Appealed to the Tokyo High Court.

Nov. 30, 2000. Appeal dismissed. Appealed to the Supreme Court. Apr. 28, 2003. Appeal dismissed.

5. Dutch Prisoners of War and Civilian Internees (multiple plaintiffs including one former comfort woman)

Jan. 24, 1994. Filed with the Tokyo District Court.

Nov. 30, 1998. Claims dismissed. Appealed to the Tokyo High Court.

Oct. 11, 2001. Appeal dismissed. Appealed to the Supreme Court.

Mar. 30, 2004. Appeal dismissed.

6. Chinese "Comfort Women," First Group (four plaintiffs)

Aug 7, 1995. Filed with the Tokyo District Court.

May 30, 2001. Claims dismissed. Appealed to the Tokyo High Court.

Dec. 15, 2004. Appeal dismissed. Appealed to the Supreme Court.

Apr. 27, 2007. Appeal dismissed.

7. Chinese "Comfort Women," Second Group (two plaintiffs)

Feb. 23, 1996. Filed with the Tokyo District Court.

Mar. 29, 2002. Claims dismissed.[27] Appealed to the Tokyo High Court.

Mar. 18, 2005. Appeal dismissed. Appealed to the Supreme Court.

Apr. 27, 2007. Appeal dismissed.

8. Victims of Sexual Violence in Shanxi Province, China (ten plaintiffs)

Oct. 30, 1998. Filed with the Tokyo District Court.

Apr. 24, 2003. Claims dismissed.[28] Appealed to the Tokyo High Court.

Mar. 31, 2005. Appeal dismissed. Appealed to the Supreme Court.

Nov. 18, 2005. Appeal dismissed.

9. Taiwanese "Comfort Women" (nine plaintiffs)

July 14, 1999. Filed with the Tokyo District Court.

Oct. 15, 2002. Claims dismissed. Appealed to the Tokyo High Court.

Feb. 9, 2004. Appeal dismissed. Appealed to the Supreme Court.

Dec. 15, 2005. Appeal dismissed.

10. Hainan Island "Comfort Women" (nine plaintiffs)

    July 16, 2001. Filed with the Tokyo District Court.

    Aug. 30, 2006. Claims dismissed. Appealed to the Tokyo High Court.

    Mar. 2, 2010. Appeal dismissed.

Chapter 14
Toward Accountability for Violence Against Women in War: Progress and Challenges

Rhonda Copelon

Since the 1990s, sexualized violence has drawn international attention as particularly gruesome, atrocious, widespread, and systematic in many conflicts. This includes the former Yugoslavia, Rwanda, Sierra Leone, Haiti, Liberia, Peru, Guatemala, and more recently the Democratic Republic of Congo, the Central African Republic, and Uganda. Although rape has been, at least since the late nineteenth century, condemned either implicitly or explicitly under international law, it has also largely been accepted as inevitable. When wartime rape did become an issue, it was usually not out of concern for victimized women but, instead, to advance the political interests of a warring party or world power. Likewise, although some national military systems have at various times prosecuted rape vigorously, the perpetrators of rape and sexualized violence have generally enjoyed impunity under both international and national law. There have been few conflicts where rape and sexualized violence have been absent or effectively sanctioned. Thus, while rape need not be a concomitant of war, it largely is.

Today, nearly two decades after the revelations of large-scale rape in Bosnia and Rwanda, sexualized violence is still epidemic in war and conflict. While men and boys may be victims, this violence overwhelmingly targets women and girls. In some situations women are the booty of war. In others, sexualized violence is a core tactic of war and/or genocide designed to destroy women physically and mentally, undermining their role in sustaining communities. It also functions to expel, stigmatize, and marginalize women as accepted members of their familial, social, and cultural circles. It can be opportunistic misogyny or an act committed to humiliate the male population. Survivors and international feminist and human rights activists have pushed the global community to end impunity for this crime and to address survivors' needs for justice and reparations, seeking women's full and equal participation in peace making and building. At the same time, activists have fought for effective protection from gender violence both during and after conflicts.

As the search for justice commenced, scholars, feminist human rights activists, victim advocates, nongovernmental organizations (NGOs), and judicial delegates debated—and continue to debate—key political questions concerning gender violence in conflict.[1] Would rape be recognized as a result of the sexualized violence in Bosnia by virtue of exceptionalism, because this was a European conflict involving "white" women?[2] Would rape be recognized only when considered to be "genocidal" or "ethnic" as opposed to "normal" rape?[3] Would the emphasis on numbers render rape significant only when called "mass" or "systematic"?[4] Would rape attract scrutiny only when characterized as "a weapon of war," a war crime only when it was conscious military strategy?"[5] Would wartime rape be recognized while women raped in everyday life—in prisons, streets, and homes—remain suspect and excluded from the international system? Would the acknowledgment of gender violence be confined to rape or include all forms of sexual violence? Would the emphasis on rape and sexualized violence play to protectionist or voyeuristic instincts, threatening to obscure other forms of gender violence that, under patriarchal systems and structures, victimize women in both war and so-called times of peace?

These issues continue to influence cultural attitudes and therefore impact the drafting of human rights documents. However, broad women's human rights initiatives have successfully ensured that sexual violence would not be limited to formal recognition only when occurring in the most extreme circumstances, such as genocide, crimes against humanity, or war crimes. Since the 1990s, as a result of coordinated and multipronged international feminist mobilizations, both human rights and international criminal law norms have been re-envisioned to incorporate a wide spectrum of gender-based violence.[6] Theoretically, rape and various forms of sexualized violence are now war crimes, torture, acts of genocide, and acts of crimes against humanity as well as human rights violations when perpetrated or tolerated by the state. This has paved the way to hold accountable, through various mechanisms, states and individuals who commit or are complicit in gender violence. These initiatives energized efforts to expand the positive human rights of women, including rights to equality, to reproductive and sexual health, and to participate in all spheres, including reconstruction, peace, and development.[7]

Despite these encouraging though imperfect developments, the effective prosecution of sexualized and gender violence requires intensive mobilization and often risk by women's groups on the ground and in international forums. Additionally, inconsistent implementation and the failure to seek, let alone heed, the advice of women's groups or to prioritize women's needs feeds both the perpetrators' sense of impunity and the survivors' frustration and despair with the lack of justice. In addition, widespread foot-dragging on the elimination of violence against women in daily life perpetuates women's inequality and subordination. This, in turn, propagates the culture of violence that is exacerbated in conflict. In short, while women have achieved significant legal building blocks, they continue to face many obstacles.

After a brief review of the legal history of rape and sexualized violence in international humanitarian and human rights law, this article surveys the developments in addressing sexual violence in conflict zones, contextualizing them in the initiatives and mobilizations of survivors' groups and women's human rights advocates. My goal is not to be comprehensive, as I draw largely on projects in which I have been engaged. Instead, it is to signal the key role of women's movements and NGOs in the multifaceted transformation of law. Like most progress in human rights, this transformation finds its source in the perspectives and labor of survivors and international women's activists. Together these groups constitute a loosely defined global women's human rights movement. I will discuss the progress made with respect to sexualized violence in war and conflict through engagement in three key foci: a series of United Nations (UN) Conferences in the 1990s, which enabled the genesis of the global campaign for women's human rights; the ad hoc Tribunals for the former Yugoslavia and Rwanda, which generated breakthrough jurisprudence; and the negotiations of the Statute of Rome that created the first permanent International Criminal Court (ICC), which in large measure produced the recent legal and policy changes that recognize sexualized violence as among the gravest international crimes. These developments also helped to press the Security Council to recognize that gender issues play a critical role in fulfilling the Council's responsibility to maintain peace and security. Finally, I conclude with a partial list of ongoing legal and social justice challenges that all women and girls face during the postconflict process.

Legal History of Rape in International Humanitarian Law

Historically, as an international legal matter, rape may have been prohibited but was rarely prosecuted.[8] Although there is evidence of prohibitions against rape by soldiers, legal exceptions permitted all kinds of attacks on civilian populations. The failure to limit these attacks meant that rape was endemic in armed conflict. The 1863 Lieber Code, developed during the U.S. Civil War and often cited as a precursor to the codification of the international laws and customs of war, prohibited rape and treated it as a capital offense.[9] Two Hague Peace Conferences in 1899 and 1907 (the first major international attempts to codify the laws of war) departed from the Lieber Code approach and prohibited rape and sexualized violence implicitly rather than explicitly. The 1907 Hague Convention IV Respecting the Laws and Customs of War on Land referenced sexualized attacks on women by providing that "Family honour and rights . . . must be respected."[10] As such, Hague treated women as carriers of male honor and did not clearly criminalize sexual violence.[11] The subsequent Geneva Convention of 1929, providing for women prisoners of war, indicated that they "shall be treated with all consideration due to their sex."[12] Thus, the early conventions addressed rape in terms of honor and gender-based propriety, not as acts of violence against women.

The next significant development of international law with respect to war crimes involved the post-World War II Tribunals, which had jurisdiction over the laws and customs of war as well as the newly codified "crimes against humanity."[13] The Tribunal Charters did not name rape and sexual violence as crimes. Rape and sexual violence were, however, prosecutable under such violations as "ill-treatment . . . of civilian population" (war crimes) or "other inhumane acts" (crimes against humanity). Although prosecutors charged no one with rape at Nuremberg, several submitted evidence of rape and, since the Tribunal Judgement does not identify all the individual crimes, rape can be considered subsumed in the Judgement.[14] Scholars have attributed the failure to prosecute rape officially, at least in part, to a reluctance to confront acts that some of the Allied troops had also committed.[15] Allied Control Council Law No. 10 subsequently authorized additional trials of Nazi war criminals and did list rape as a violation under crimes against humanity. However, authorities prosecuted no one.[16] While the naming of rape was historic, the absence of prosecution perpetuated impunity.

By contrast, sexualized violence, including rape, played a significant role in the prosecution of the Japanese civilian and military leadership.[17] Given the international outcry at the attacks on civilians during the Japanese military's conquest of China, symbolized by the "rape of Nanking," the International Military Tribunal for the Far East in Tokyo could hardly ignore sexualized violence.[18] At the same time, the Tribunal, run by the U.S. Military Command, did ignore the extensive system of military sexual slavery.[19] At least 200,000 women and girls from occupied countries were bought, abducted, or deceived and made "comfort women" to provide female bodies for the soldiers and to reduce the danger of both sexually transmitted diseases and local resistance.[20] The brutal coercive nature of the "comfort stations" was no secret given documented awareness of the virtually constant rape inflicted on these women.[21] It is not entirely clear why prosecutors excluded this massive slavery system. However, the fact that U.S. memos referred to the comfort stations as "brothels," thus branding it as a form of prostitution, and the revelations that the United States shares a similar guilt might help to explain this lacuna.[22]

The next major international codification of the "laws and customs of war" and humanitarian law—the Fourth Geneva Convention of 1949 (Geneva IV)—only weakly prohibited rape. Geneva IV, under the guidelines for *international* armed conflict, required *protection* of women from "any attack on their honour, in particular against rape, enforced prostitution, or any form of indecent assault."[23] However, rape was not listed as a *crime* under the category of "grave breaches," which named the most serious crimes and carried a universal obligation to prosecute. Geneva IV thereby treated rape and sexualized violence as a matter of domestic discretion rather than international concern.[24] Although the "honour" at stake appears to be, at least in part, the woman's, the convention still did not identify rape as violence against the person.[25] As to the rules for *noninternational* armed conflict, Article 3, common to all four Geneva Conventions, prohibited discrimination based, *inter alia*, on sex.[26] It absolutely prohibited "violence to life and person, in particular murder . . . mutilation, cruel treatment and torture," as well as "outrages upon personal dignity, in particular humiliating and degrading treatment."[27] Rape thus remained an implicit prohibition generally assigned to the latter category.

The 1977 Protocols, amending and expanding the Geneva Conventions, enlarged the prohibitions of sexualized violence but again did not explicitly recognize it as a "grave breach." For *international* armed conflict, Protocol I treated "enforced prostitution and any form of indecent assault" as among the "fundamental guarantees," adding this onto the category "outrages against personal dignity."[28] Protocol I designated these acts as "prohibited at any time and in any place" whatsoever and thus clearly considered them to be nonderogable crimes—not simply protections.[29] Still, the Protocol did not explicitly identify rape and sexualized violence as a grave breach or international war crime.[30] Protocol II, which pertained to *noninternational* armed conflict, likewise expanded common Article 3, adding "rape, enforced prostitution, and indecent assault" to the crime of "outrages upon personal dignity."[31] Thus, neither Protocol explicitly recognized rape and sexualized violence as clear crimes of violence.

The treatment of rape and sexualized violence under humanitarian law appears to have mirrored domestic treatment. Like wartime rape, domestic law technically prohibited everyday rape, but it also rarely made prosecution a priority.[32] Civil law countries widely treated rape as "an offense against morals" and thus distinct from a crime of violence against the person.[33] Under the Anglo-American legal tradition, prosecutors often met rape accusations with disbelief in the veracity of the allegation and with challenges to women's morality.[34] This made domestic prosecution virtually impossible except where other factors, such as virulent racism in the United States, overcame the reluctance to prosecute.[35] Therefore, local laws rarely provided an avenue of justice for individual victims, which, in turn, enabled international jurists to trivialize rape and sexual violence in conflict zones.

Legal History of Sexualized Violence in Human Rights Law

Until the 1990s, human rights law, which focuses on violations by the state, lagged even farther behind than international humanitarian law. Neither the 1948 Universal Declaration of Human Rights nor the 1966 International Covenant on Civil and Political Rights mentions gender violence.[36] While gender violence might have been addressed by combining discrimination based on sex with the state's failure to respect and protect life, liberty, and security of person or to prohibit torture and cruel, inhumane, or degrading treatment, it was not.[37] Even the 1979 Convention on the Elimination of All

Forms of Discrimination Against Women did not mention gender or sexualized violence.[38] Indeed, before the advent of the global women's human
rights movement in the early 1990s, mainstream human rights groups pursued an androcentric vision of human rights.[39]

Thus, for example, a woman prisoner could be a victim of torture if
she were *beaten*, but not if she were *raped*. If reported, officials dismissed
rape under the suspicion that the act was consensual. Or, they dismissed it
as an "unofficial" or a "private" matter.[40] It was a Chilean feminist scholar
who documented and analyzed the rape of women in the prisons of Pino-
chet and Southern Cone dictatorships—not human rights organizations.[41]
By contrast, officials stolidly condemned male rape in prison (also under-
reported) when it came to light, classifying the electric prod on the penis
unquestionably as torture. In 1986 the Special Rapporteur on Torture first
identified prison rape of women as torture.[42] Only in 1995, however, did
the first human rights treaty body—the Inter-American Commission on
Human Rights—rule that the rape of women could be classified as a tool of
political intimidation and gender discrimination, which then qualified it as
torture.[43] Exemplifying traditional attitudes, during the Commission's discussion, one member objected to identifying rape as torture with words to
the effect: "You put it in; you take it out; what's the big deal?" Another member over-rode the objection, recalling that the picana on the penis is considered torture.[44]

Despite rape's widespread character and pertinent international precedent, before the 1990s there was no mainstream NGO recognition that privately inflicted violence against women merited a human rights concern
even where the state failed to respond.[45] When feminist activists demanded
international attention, opponents argued that such violence was a "private"
matter in the sense that the state was not the batterer, erroneously claiming that a violation of human rights depended on direct state perpetration.[46]
Some human rights advocates argued, and still believe, that to include privately inflicted violence against women would "dilute" the human rights
framework.

The global women's human rights movement nonetheless finally overcame the public-private divide. Activists made visible the breadth and horrendous nature of violence against women worldwide as well as the official
impunity and cultural acceptance that protects and encourages it. At the
outset of the women's human rights campaign, examples of specific misog-
ynistic cultural practices that did not implicate Western culture, such as

female genital cutting, genital mutilation, and dowry deaths, drew extensive media attention and became signature women's human rights issues. This ignored the "cultural practice" of everyday gender violence, feeding a sense of Western cultural superiority and distorting popular understandings of the meaning of women's human rights.

At the same time, feminist activists everywhere pressed for recognition of a wider range of privately inflicted gender violence. In 1989, for example, the UN Center for Social Development and Humanitarian Affairs published a landmark study on family violence against women, which emphasized the frequency and character of such violence across virtually all cultures.[47] In 1992, initiated by NGOs and official experts, the Committee to End Discrimination Against Women (CEDAW Committee), which monitors compliance with the Convention on the Elimination of All Forms of Discrimination Against Women (CEDAW Convention), published its historic General Recommendation No. 19: "Violence Against Women." This corrected the Convention's previous omission of gender violence. It recognized gender violence as a per se form of discrimination, setting out a broad program for addressing both official and private violence.[48] General Recommendation No. 19 is today seen as an integral part of the CEDAW Convention; it has also encouraged a broader acceptance of gender violence as a form of discrimination within the human rights system.[49] At the same time, the concept that the state has an obligation to prevent private gender violence through the exercise of due diligence finally took hold.[50]

The growing movement impacted the 1993 World Conference on Human Rights. As a result, sexual and gender violence in both conflict and everyday life have gained recognition as priority human rights issues. Because women's advocacy to recognize gender violence proceeded on many different tracks, it foreclosed the early concern that international law would address only states of exception instead of the egregious in everyday life.

Survivors, Advocates, and World Conferences: The Global Campaign for Women's Human Rights

A series of UN World Conferences in the 1990s enabled women's rights activists to come together from many parts of the globe to organize collectively, advancing women's issues as human rights issues. The 1985 Third World Conference on Women, held in Nairobi, Kenya, identified violence against women (and other harms we now identify as women's human rights) as a serious obstacle to women's equality, but it placed neither violence nor gender equality within the larger human rights framework.[51] However, the Nairobi Conference, and the UN Decade for Women that preceded it, inspired and made possible women's challenges in the 1990s to the male-defined boundaries of the human rights system.

The emerging global women's human rights movement used the networking and negotiating opportunities of the 1990s UN World Conferences to expand the movement and advance the systematic integration of gender into human rights mechanisms. Women did so by sharing problems, visions, and strategies, by conducting Women's Tribunals—through which women's testimonies underscored the scope of relevant violations—and by organizing women's NGOs and activists' participation in the official negotiations of the regional, preparatory, and final Conference documents. This work ultimately shaped the integration of gender into international law and treaty interpretations.[52]

The first major interrelated initiative by activists and survivors took place at the 1993 Second World Conference on Human Rights in Vienna, Austria—a watershed for the establishment of women's human rights internationally. Global meetings of feminist leaders convened by the Center for Women's Global Leadership at Rutgers University (New Brunswick, N.J.) and regional NGO meetings each hammered out programs of demands that became incorporated into a set of vetted conference objectives. NGOs participated in official regional negotiations, international strategy sessions, and the United Nations' preparatory meetings. As a result, women went to Vienna well organized and with a mandate for women's human rights, including political, civil, social, and economic rights.[53] Because state violence had traditionally assumed a privileged position within the international human rights system, the global campaign, which became the Women's NGO Caucus at the conference, stressed the severity and universality of violence against women, drawing attention to its ubiquity in official, conflict, and private settings and occurring in times of both war and peace.[54]

Before Vienna, two massive violations against women in war surfaced and became the subject of major action. In 1991 Kim Hak Soon, a South Korean survivor of the "comfort woman" system, was the first to speak out about the atrocities committed against her. Many survivors in Korea, the Philippines, and other formerly occupied countries followed Kim Hak Soon's lead.[55] Naming the "comfort system" as sexual slavery, activists and survivors began building a campaign using international human rights mechanisms and continuing local litigation to seek recognition and redress in the form of apology and compensation from the Japanese government.[56]

Additionally, after months of silence, the media reported the widespread rape of Bosnian and Croatian women in the wars of former Yugoslavia, just two hundred miles away from Vienna. Bosnian survivors had a major and militant presence at the Vienna Conference, demanding recognition and condemnation.[57] The Women's NGO Caucus in association with the Global Tribunal on Violations of Women's Human Rights presented testimonies linking all forms of violence with the subordinate status of women. It also organized a broad program, including plenary discussions and resolutions, opportunities for networking and media, and a negotiating committee that concentrated on influencing the official UN negotiations.

Thanks to the convergence of survivors and feminist activists in Vienna and the work of the Caucus, the World Conference on Human Rights adopted, by consensus, the long-overdue but historic *Vienna Declaration and Programme of Action*. Vienna recognized that "The human rights of women and of the girl-child are an inalienable, integral and indivisible part of universal human rights." Additionally, "The full and equal participation of women in political, civil, economic, social and cultural life, at the national, regional and international levels, and the eradication of all forms of discrimination on grounds of sex are priority objectives of the international community."[58] The *Vienna Declaration* identifies all forms of gender-based violence, public and private, as violations. It also insists that the "systematic rape of women in war situations . . . be punished and . . . immediately stopped." The Programme section urged the integration of women's equality and their human rights into the mainstream of the United Nations. This included "the elimination of gender bias in the administration of justice and the eradication of any conflicts . . . between the rights of women and harmful effects of certain traditional or customary practices, cultural prejudices and religious extremism." Finally, the *Vienna Declaration* stated that "violations of women's rights in situations of armed conflict, including in particular murder, systematic rape, sexual slavery and forced pregnancy, require a particularly effective response." However, the *Vienna Declaration* did not suggest an international mechanism for such a response.[59]

After Vienna, violence against women became a major subject of international concern. The UN General Assembly, acting on Vienna, approved the Declaration on the Elimination of Violence Against Women, and the

Human Rights Commission appointed and subsequently renewed the Special Rapporteur on Violence Against Women, Its Causes and Consequences. The Rapporteur's thematic and mission reports have created a rich repository of legal precedents and policy approaches to violence against women in many contexts.[60] The Vienna consensus and the continuing and ever-expanding mobilization of women from different sectors of feminist organizing formed the basis of an expanded vision of women's human rights. This vision has grown in subsequent UN conferences and has initiated the integration of gender perspectives and the prohibition of gender violence into human rights bodies and the larger UN system.[61] While activists saw integration or "mainstreaming" of gender as a critical step, unfortunately, it has also become an excuse for eliminating or defunding gender-specific mechanisms and autonomous feminist organizations, which are critical to ensuring that effective integration takes place.[62]

The Ad Hoc International Criminal Tribunals for the Former Yugoslavia and Rwanda

Women's rights activists' demands for international justice contributed to the UN Security Council's establishment of the first two ad hoc International Criminal Tribunals for the former Yugoslavia (ICTY) in 1993 and for Rwanda (ICTR) in 1994.[63] Intensive advocacy was necessary at every stage to ensure recognition and prosecution of sexualized violence as among the gravest crimes in international law.

The drafting of the ICTY Statute was the first challenge.[64] Adopted in May 1993 by the Security Council, the ICTY Statute followed the post-World War II Local Council Law No. 10 by identifying rape as conduct constituting crimes against humanity.[65] However, the Statute did not name gender or sexual violence in respect to either war crimes or genocide. While this was problematic, the omission created both the necessity and an opportunity for a gender-inclusive judicial interpretation of rape and sexual violence.[66]

The ICTR Statute, approved by the Security Council in November 1994, was a modest improvement. It retained rape as a crime against humanity and added rape, enforced prostitution, and any form of indecent assault (the Geneva language) as war crimes.[67] However, the Statute still listed these crimes as "outrages against personal dignity" instead of the more forceful "violence to life, health and physical or mental well-being of persons."[68] Moreover, like the ICTY, the ICTR Statute adopted the 1948 Genocide Convention's definition unchanged.[69] Even though the Convention includes, as acts of genocide, "causing serious bodily or mental harm," the drafters limited genocide to killing.

Both Tribunals' Rules of Evidence required that provision be made for the protection of victims and witnesses.[70] Several feminist organizations made submissions to the ICTY in an effort to shape the Rules of Evidence and Procedure, emphasizing the need to support and protect victims and witnesses as well as to eliminate the traditional sexism that plagues the prosecution of sexual violence.[71] The Rules established a Victims and Witnesses Unit, protected the confidentiality of witnesses, and precluded both the requirement of testimony corroboration and the introduction of prior sexual conduct evidence. It also severely limited consent defenses in sexualized violence cases.[72] The Rules adopted by the ICTR tracked the ICTY Rules in this regard.[73]

Shaping the composition of the Court was also crucial. First, to create an environment welcoming to sexual violence victims and witnesses, activists supported the candidacy of two women jurists with feminist credentials for the ICTY.[74] Their presence was essential to the development of gender-sensitive rules and methods as well as the advance of gender-inclusive jurisprudence. Second, because the Court generally is limited to deliberating on charges presented by the Prosecutor, the personnel in the Office of the Prosecutor were also critical. The ICTY's first Chief Prosecutor, Richard Goldstone, had courageously defended human rights in apartheid South Africa and recognized the importance of facilitating the prosecution of gender crimes and the development of jurisprudence. Responding to demands of the movement, he created the post of Gender Legal Advisor, to which he appointed Patricia Viseur Sellers. She brought expertise and vision to the job, keeping the lines of communication open to both NGOs and gender experts. As a result, the integration of gender in international law began in earnest.

The situation was less salutary at the ICTR. Of the six Judges, the United Nations elected only one woman, a strong feminist, to the bench. Until 2003, the Office of the Prosecutor in The Hague also acted as the Chief Prosecutor for the ICTR. However, the ICTR lacked the close oversight provided by an on-site high-level gender legal advisor. This arrangement did not advance the prosecution of sexualized violence in Rwanda. The absence of a coherent strategy and the poor selection, training, and coordination of investigators aggravated the inattention to sexual violence in the Prosecutor's office. From 1999 to 2003, the Chief Prosecutor, Carla del Ponte took positions that actively undermined the prosecution of gender crimes.[75] Despite these many obstacles, monitoring by international feminist groups and advocates helped lead to several early path-breaking Judgements: *Akayesu* in the ICTR and *Kunarac* in the ICTY. These Judgements grounded the jurisprudence that established accountability for crimes of gender and sexualized violence.[76]

ICTR: The Akayesu Judgement

The ICTR established that the rape of women constituted acts of genocide. This stemmed from the courageous, spontaneous testimony by two women witnesses, the initiatives of two Judges, and close monitoring and intervention by NGOs.[77] Despite available documentation of misogynist propaganda as well as open, notorious, and ubiquitous sexualized violence against Tutsi women, the first ICTR indictment against Jean Paul Akayesu failed to include rape or sexual violence.[78] The Prosecutors limited their interpretation of genocide to killing even though the Genocide Convention contains a more expansive definition.[79] Prosecutors' lack of will and legal imagination as well as investigators' dismissive, insensitive, and sometimes dangerous methods papered over the crimes by claiming that women would not testify to sexual violence.[80] Yet, in the course of the trial, when questioned by two of the Judges, two female witnesses surprised the Prosecutor by testifying about rape and the involvement of the accused. The Judges pursued their testimony, establishing not only the fact of sexual violence but also the responsibility of the defendant.[81]

When the Coalition for Women's Human Rights in Conflict Situations, which had been monitoring the Tribunal, learned that the Prosecutor had done nothing to follow up on these revelations, it joined with Rwandan women's organizations to file an *amicus curiae* brief.[82] The *amicus* brief called upon the court to exercise its statutory authority to request that the Prosecutor consider amending the indictment to include charges of rape and sexual violence. Several weeks later, minimizing the role of the *amicus* brief, the Prosecutor moved to amend the indictment to include charges of sexual violence as crimes against humanity, war crimes, and implicitly as genocide.[83] The Trial Chamber accepted the amendment, adjourning for three months to enable both sides to prepare. During this time, women in Rwanda organized the first women's march for justice. When the trial reconvened, five additional witnesses gave explicit testimony about their rape and sexual violence and/or that of other women and girls. Critical testimony also demonstrated Akayesu's knowledge, encouragement, and authorization of rape, including his notorious statement: "Never ask me again what a Tutsi woman tastes like."[84]

The historic *Akayesu* Judgement has greatly influenced international law. It was the first international Judgement on the crime of genocide and the first to recognize rape and sexual violence as crimes of genocide. The Judgement made clear that the gender violence inflicted upon women was not marginal to but instead a critical part of genocide.[85] Legally, the crime of genocide is properly not limited to killing, although rape in Rwanda was often a prelude to and an instrument of death. Having found the requisite genocidal intent to destroy the Tutsi population and relying partly on the propaganda that used "sexualized representation of ethnic identity," the Trial Chamber recognized that perpetrators targeted women because they were Tutsi.[86] The Judgement held that rape was an act of genocide and "one of the worst ways of inflicting harm on the victim as he or she suffers both bodily and mental harm."[87] *Akayesu* also found that "Sexual violence was a step in the process of destruction of the Tutsi group—destruction of the spirit, of the will to live, and of life itself."[88] Beyond these fact-specific findings, sexualized violence can constitute proof of all the general acts of genocide delineated by the Convention.[89]

The *Akayesu* Judgement is also notable for providing a groundbreaking conceptual definition of rape and sexualized violence.[90] It defined rape as "a physical invasion of a sexual nature."[91] This definition dispensed with the traditional penile/vaginal focus, incorporating "the insertion of objects and/or the use of bodily orifices not considered intrinsically sexual."[92] The *Akayesu* Judgement defined noninvasive sexualized violence—forced public nakedness, naked parading, and gymnastics—as "any act of a sexual nature."[93] For both crimes, the element of coercive *circumstances* replaced requirements that emphasized force, coercion, and the victim's nonconsent.[94] With regard to Akayesu's criminal responsibility for these acts, it was sufficient that he was aware of, and aided and abetted, giving official tolerance to rape and sexualized violence.[95] Thus, the Judgement broadened the definition, limited the potential for sexist defense arguments, and sought to foreclose the need for detailed testimony from the victim. However, due to the failure of prosecutors to consistently and effectively prosecute sexualized violence, many subsequent ICTR cases did not follow *Akayesu*'s lead.

The *Akayesu* Judgement has, though, influenced the ICC negotiations on both genocide and the definition of rape.[96]

ICTY: The Kunarac Judgement

In contrast to the ICTR, the ICTY, guided by an on-site gender expert and supported by the first Prosecutor, undertook a number of cases involving sexual violence that deeply influenced jurisprudence. The very first case, the *Tadic* Judgement, involved the forced castration of a male detainee by two other detainees.[97] Three cases followed *Tadic* that recognized rape and sexualized violence against women as war crimes and crimes against humanity.[98] As a result of feminist interventions and the work of the Gender Legal Advisor, these cases also acknowledged rape and sexualized violence as among the gravest international crimes, such as torture, enslavement, or inhumane treatment. The most significant is the Appeals Judgement in *Prosecutor v. Kunarac*.[99]

Indeed, one goal of feminist advocacy in this period was to ensure that prosecutors treated rape as among the gravest forms of violence.[100] This made it harder to trivialize or ignore. Because the ICTY Statute did not explicitly name rape or sexualized violence as a war crime, the Prosecutor's legal advisors debated whether to consider rape as torture or as "willfully causing great suffering or serious injury to body or health."[101] Fortunately, the Chief Prosecutor opted to view rape as torture, giving rise to a line of Judgements to this effect.[102] The *Kunarac Appeal* Judgement held that rape always satisfies the first element of torture—the infliction of severe physical or mental suffering.[103] As to the element of torture that requires impermissible purpose, it found that rape was a tool of ethnic discrimination. However, the Judgement did not specifically mention gender.[104]

The *Kunarac* Judgements are also significant for applying the modern approach to slavery as sexualized violence. This is in contrast to the earlier view of slavery as the exchange of a person as chattel. The new definition of enslavement provides a flexible approach, recognizing that detention involving repeated rape, forced domestic labor, and other possessory actions constitutes enslavement. At the same time, the Judgements note that absolute detention or prolonged duration is not required.[105] Finally, like the ICTR, the *Kunarac Appeal* also recognized that various forms of sexual violence, such as forced nakedness and sexualized entertainment, constituted inhumane treatment.[106]

Kunarac also clarified how sexual violence qualifies as war crimes and crimes against humanity. For example, so long as the perpetrator is aware of the armed conflict in which he or she operates, one act of rape (like any other named crime) can be a war crime. Additionally, it need not be shown to be a "weapon of war." Similarly, rape need not be massive or systematic in and of itself to be a crime against humanity; instead, rape can be one of many crimes constituting a widespread or systematic attack on a civilian population.[107] This understanding was critical to establishing rape on an equal footing with other crimes.

The *Kunarac Appeal* Judgement did not, however, accept Akayesu's conceptual approach to defining rape. While it broadened the definition of rape considerably, it did so by detailing the elements of invasion, penetration, and coercive circumstances.[108] In addition, Kunarac's discussion of rape and enslavement muddied the waters surrounding the role of consent. While recognizing that full and voluntary consent is impossible in the context of force, threat of force, or coercive circumstances, the Judgement nonetheless accepted that nonconsent is a defining element of rape. Therefore, the Prosecutor must demonstrate nonconsent.[109] While in my view the complexity of human experience does not permit ruling out consent in situations of conflict, this issue is purely theoretical. The courts should presume nonconsent when the victim is subject to coercive circumstances and should hold perpetrators strictly liable under conditions of detention or other forms of control. Acquiescence to rape or forced marriage to save or feed oneself or one's children, for example, cannot be consent. Indeed, given the potential for discrimination and traumatization of victim-witnesses, it is reasonable to argue that evidence of consent should be prohibited altogether. If permitted, it should be under the narrowest of circumstances and with the strictest safeguards against harassment.

The International Criminal Court

These jurisprudential developments and both the positive and negative experience of women in the ad hoc Tribunals underpinned the fourth and most significant gender development in international criminal law: the Rome Statute of the International Criminal Court (ICC; Rome Statute). The Rome Statute, which created the ICC, provides extensive structural, procedural, and evidentiary provisions designed to ensure gender-inclusive justice. The Statute codifies the prohibition against sexualized and reproductive violence as well as gender-based persecution. Though imperfect, it is a watershed.[110] It is the first permanent international criminal tribunal dedicated to ending impunity for war crimes, crimes against humanity, genocide, and, eventually, aggression.[111] Again, feminist NGOs played a key role. There was scant attention—even to rape as a crime—before the interventions of the Women's Caucus for Gender Justice in the ICC.[112] From 1997 to 2002 the Women's Caucus led the work, despite opposition, to forge a consensus on the inclusion of gender concerns throughout the Rome Statute, its Rules of Procedure and Evidence, and the Annexes (on Elements of Crimes and Rules of Procedure and Evidence), which are intended to guide but not bind the Court.[113] Although highly contested, mostly by the Vatican and religiously conservative delegations, the ICC documents are largely progressive in a feminist sense.[114]

The ICC Statute erases any doubt as to whether rape and most sexualized violence rank among the gravest international crimes.[115] For an act of sexual violence to qualify within the ICC jurisdiction, it must, however, meet threshold or "chapeau" requirements that define genocide, crimes against humanity, and war crimes.[116] Opposition to the prosecution of gender crimes affected some of these debates, producing constructively ambiguous provisions that will ultimately depend upon the Court's interpretations.

Debates over gender played a role in the establishment of the genocide and war crimes thresholds. Although the definition of genocide was not open to question, a footnote, inspired by the *Akayesu* Judgement, recognizes that infliction of severe mental or physical suffering includes acts of "torture, rape, sexual violence or inhuman and degrading treatment."[117] The Statute also contains a significant, nonexclusive list of criminal acts, including "rape, sexual slavery, enforced prostitution, forced pregnancy, enforced sterilization and other sexual violence." These constitute war crimes if they occur "in the context of and . . . associated with" either an international armed conflict [including occupation] or noninternational conflict.[118] Thus, for example, the abuse of one's military status off the battlefield can transform a common crime into a war crime. Importantly, the chapeau for war crimes preserves the possibility of punishing one criminal act as a war crime but suggests that the ICC will prioritize situations of extensive violations.[119]

The chapeau for "crimes against humanity" raised numerous gender issues. Sexualized violence constitutes crimes against humanity "when committed as part of a widespread or systematic attack directed against any civilian population, with [the perpetrator having] knowledge of the attack."[120] This clarifies that neither connection to war nor state involvement is required.[121] It also makes clear that constituent acts such as rape need not be "mass," widespread, or systematic, but need only to occur in the context of a larger attack.[122] However, in an effort to limit its applicability to tolerated, traditional, and/or endemic gender or other violence, the Statute requires both "multiple acts" *and* a "State or organizational policy to commit the attack."[123] This requirement undermines the insistence in *Kunarac*, that *either* widespread conduct *or* a policy is sufficient.[124] Because it is clear that rape and sexualized violence do not require a policy, this is problematic. A policy of sexualized violence should be inferred from either the widespread perpetration of the constituent crimes or the failure to punish and/or train troops not to engage in sexual violence.

The negotiations on the Elements Annex also provided an opportunity to confront gender-based persecution. Because "crimes against humanity" do not require a connection to war, nor a State or official perpetrator, they can occur in everyday life. Thus, these crimes should encompass gender crimes, including in the family, when they are either encouraged or, as matters of custom, tolerated by a State or organizing entity. Eleven Islamic states issued a proposal to exclude all matters of family law from crimes against humanity. This included rape, sexual slavery, and other sexual violence when related to religion, culture, and family. The proposed exclusion specifically targeted relations between husbands and wives and/or parents and children.[125] This shocking proposal, which admitted that various cultural norms and common practices could be crimes against humanity, was overwhelmingly rejected in a plenary discussion. However, it morphed into an effort (as the introducers intended) to exclude a prohibition on the toleration of crimes against humanity. As a result, the Introduction to the Elements Annex indicates that a State must "actively encourage or promote the attack." Further, it argues that "the existence of a policy cannot be inferred solely from the absence of governmental or organizational action."[126] Fortunately, the Elements Annex is not binding on the Court. However, if accepted, the Annex position would significantly gut the protection of the Statute, opening wide the door to impunity through plausible deniability in a broad range of circumstances.[127]

Additionally, the sexualized violence that constitutes war crimes or crimes against humanity is no longer confined to the category of "outrages against personal dignity" or "humiliating or degrading treatment." Rather, it is identified as among the gravest violence.[128] Reflecting the *Kunarac* jurisprudence, sexualized violence can also be prosecuted as constituting other grave crimes such as torture, enslavement, or genocide.[129] Both enslavement and sexual slavery, included as crimes against humanity, encompass "trafficking in persons, in particular women and children."[130] There were, however, significant debates, mostly at the Elements stage, over the definitions of these crimes, which resulted in nonbinding limitations. This was especially the case regarding rape, sexual slavery, and the Statute's definition of forced pregnancy, which drafters forged in an attempt to exclude an impact on abortion.[131]

The Rome Statute's addition of gender-based persecution under "crimes against humanity" also reflects a very significant, though highly contested, advance over previous humanitarian law.[132] Conservative and religiously driven delegations attempted to exclude sexual orientation, transgender identities, and otherwise transgressive women in two ways: by limiting the grounds of persecution to those "universally recognized as impermissible" and by confining "gender" to a biologically and socially essentialist male-female dichotomy. By contrast, the majority of delegations sought language that would include the social construction of gender and thereby apply to sexual orientation and transgender identities. The conflict resulted in an opaque definition of gender, which contains both sex-based essentialism and social constructionist language. The definition's ambiguity enables the Court to interpret the term "gender" broadly.[133] Because persecution on the basis of gender, like religion or political opinion, targets both those who obey the prevailing orthodoxy and those who resist it, and because persecution is never permissible, the effort to confine the statute to hetero-normative obedience is unlikely to succeed.

The ICC Statute and the Rules of Procedure and Evidence Annex also contain many important provisions designed for the safety and privacy of victims and witnesses, and to ensure that sexualized violence is properly prosecuted. The Women's Caucus pressed these provisions based on both positive and the negative experience of sexual violence victims in domestic and international contexts. These crucial provisions include criteria relating to the composition of judges, requiring both a "fair representation of female and male judges" and the presence of expertise on sexual and gender violence. The provisions also require the hiring of such experts by the Prosecutor and the Registry.[134] The Court must establish a Victims and Witnesses Unit in the Registry of the Court and must recognize the right of victims to participate in the proceedings generally through legal representatives.[135]

The most contested rules concerned activists' efforts to exclude prior sexual conduct of victim-witness and to limit evidence of consent. Their intent was to exclude irrelevant and discriminatory evidence, encourage women's participation in justice, and strike an appropriate balance between the rights of the accused and a fair and impartial trial. Initially, some Latin American and other civil law delegates opposed the use of exclusionary mechanisms, because they were not part of their traditional practice. However, this contingent came to accept advance protection as appropriate and necessary to obtain the testimony of a sexual violence witness. The persistent opposition was visibly led by a Swiss delegate who insisted on the potential relevance of a prior sexual relationship between the victim and accused. Thus, the preclusion of prior (and subsequent) consent, which was absolutely barred as irrelevant in the ICTY Rules, is not quite absolute in the ICC Rules. Instead, prior relationships are subject to consideration of their probative value and prejudicial impact.[136] Similarly, defense evidence of consent is not barred absolutely but narrowly cabined by an excellent set of principles outlining the circumstances under which it is impermissible to infer consent. Additionally, the principle calls for an *in camera* procedure to test the evidence before the court can subject the witness to cross-examination.[137]

The Statute also contains a critical overarching provision, requiring that the interpretation and application of the Statute be consistent with human rights law. It also prohibits any form of discrimination, including that which is gender based.[138] Thus, the Statute bars the Court from adopting a discriminatory interpretation of crimes or rules. It also enables the Court to prevent discrimination that may emanate from the institution's other branches. Even though these provisions were one of the last and most hotly contested, they may turn out to be the most important safeguards of gender-inclusive justice.

Finally, it must be emphasized that the ICC Statute has potential significance well beyond the Court itself. It comprises a set of universally agreed-upon norms and processes that should be incorporated into domestic laws and used to shape informal justice mechanisms, such as Truth and Reconciliation Commissions.[139] While the ICC Statute does not require ratifying states to reform their laws, it encourages this through the principle of complementarity, which allows the Court to exercise jurisdiction only where the responsible State is unable or unwilling to prosecute. Thus, if a State lacks adequate provisions in domestic law recognizing ICC crimes, has inadequate or nonexistent procedures to prevent harassment of victims or witnesses, or if a prosecution is carried out domestically in bad faith, the ICC can exercise jurisdiction.[140] For these reasons it is wise for ratifying States to adopt the ICC provisions as a minimum standard, although States are free to provide more expansive gender-protective laws so long as they are not inconsistent with international law. Thus far, the domestication of ICC gender provisions is inconsistent.[141]

Security Council Resolutions 1325 and 1820: Women, Peace, and Security

The Security Council has long been hostile to, or at least wary of, integrating violence against women into its work. Pressed by survivors of sexualized violence and women's human rights and peace activists, Security Council Resolutions 1325 (2000) and 1820 (2008) address gender issues in conflict and peace building. They acknowledge that both the protection and the participation of women in conflict situations are within its responsibility to "maintain or restore international peace and security."[142] Though watershed developments, these resolutions remain more rhetorical than real in their achievements.

Women face enormous problems of marginalization, violence, displacement, and destitution during and after conflict. Violence against women and girls in communities and in their homes after conflict may exceed levels before conflict. Trafficking and prostitution are often coerced, implicating peacekeepers and humanitarian workers in a gross abuse of power.[143] Eighty percent of refugees are women and children, living in purportedly temporary quarters and subject to violence from many sources. These phenomena are also a consequence of the lack of options for women and girls, including the absence of educational opportunities and development initiatives designed to provide survivors of sexualized violence with meaningful and sustainable livelihoods. The repatriation of girl soldiers is unequal to that provided boys and also fails to meet their social and economic needs.[144] Trafficking and sex work are thus, for many, the means of survival.

In terms of legal structure, Security Council Resolution 1325 is the "mother" document. Its power lies in the combined recognition of the need to prevent women's victimization during and after conflict and to ensure women's participation in decision making at all levels of peace making and building. Resolution 1325 calls for holding perpetrators accountable, incorporating gender-sensitive training and methods in peacekeeping and other field operations, adopting a gender perspective in all negotiations so as to recognize women's needs, supporting local women's initiatives, and protecting women's human rights in relation to the legal aspects of social reconstruction.[145]

Unfortunately, Resolution 1325 has produced little change.[146] As requested by the Resolution, the Secretary-General reports annually to the Security Council regarding "progress on gender mainstreaming throughout peacekeeping missions and all other aspects relating to women and girls."[147] These reports have not been particularly sanguine, and instead of proposing implementation mechanisms, they have simply called for the Security Council to intensify its monitoring.[148] In a lethargic response to these reports, the Security Council has held a formal day of discussion on women, peace, and security, and an occasional side meeting.

In addition, despite the encouragement of women's participation in peace making and peace building in Resolution 1325, we have seen little commitment on the international level to engaging women in that process. Although women and their organizations often play a significant role in bringing about peace, they are generally forgotten or relegated to a minor place in postconflict diplomacy; they are rarely provided a seat at the negotiating table or a significant voice in the peace-building process.[149]

In 2008, with the virulence of the rape in Congo drawing attention, the Security Council took up the issue of sexual violence, which resulted in Resolution 1820. While the Resolution should lead to moving beyond rhetorical condemnation into effective implementation, results are far from clear. Consider, for example, the critical yet highly qualified provision that "expresses [the Security Council's] . . . readiness . . . to, where necessary, adopt appropriate measures to address widespread or systematic sexual violence."[150] On the issue of peacekeeper abuses, Resolution 1820 essentially reiterates 1325, calling upon the Secretary-General to develop training for peacekeepers and humanitarian personnel and to increase implementation of the no-tolerance policy. However, Resolution 1820 contains no mention of meeting the economic and social needs of women and girls. The clear obligation to prosecute sexual violence under international law and the potential role of the ICC are referred to obliquely as "other actions to ensure full accountability."[151]

In an equally troubling move, Resolution 1820 sidelines the critical provisions of Resolution 1325 that call for the participation of women in all aspects of decision making. It does so in favor of attention to sexual violence.[152] Women are thus popular as victims but avoided as agents. However, Resolution 1820 does open by reaffirming Resolution 1325 and thus must be understood as addressing only one aspect of the more comprehensive resolution, not as replacing it. At the same time, it will require increased vigilance and mobilization at all levels to ensure that Resolution 1820 becomes a vehicle for meaningful protection and that the participation goals of Resolution 1325 do not become a dead letter.

The Challenges

Although I have concentrated on recent developments in the law recognizing sexualized violence as war crimes, crimes against humanity, and genocide, legal texts, and protections are but a starting point. They guarantee neither enforcement nor deterrence. In the hope that current and future work will shed light on these issues, let me end by identifying some of the problems that continue to face women as they seek justice and labor to reconstruct their lives and societies. In this crucial transitional period during which gender violence seems only to increase, these are issues as to which historical antecedents and the historian's craft can play an important role.

First, we need to foster conditions under which justice may have a deterrent effect on sexualized violence. Thus far, it does not appear that the codification of law has caused it to abate; justice, whether formal or informal, remains largely a remedy after the fact. To create deterrence we need consistency of prosecution so that potential perpetrators fear accountability. The ICC Statute does not eliminate cultures of sexism, ignorance, subtle resistance, disregard, or outright backlash. This is true even of those charged with enforcing the law. The full integration of gender experts and training as well as persistent monitoring and interventions by women's advocates will be required. For example, the ICC Prosecutor has yet to appoint a permanent high-level gender legal advisor, and his early indictments indicate a lack of commitment to and understanding of gender justice.[153] If justice can act as a deterrent, we must end impunity for sexualized violence by using and improving upon the available enforcement mechanisms.

Second, both formal and informal justice must promote the empowerment and voice of women. Testimony has the potential to be a vehicle of such empowerment, but it may also instrumentalize women by further traumatizing the speaker or by focusing solely on sexualized violence at the expense of other traumatic violations. For those who bravely participate and are properly supported, involvement in the justice process may be part of recovery and can also provide support to others who cannot speak. Thus, there must be private and confidential contexts for bearing witness. Furthermore, particularly where sexualized violence is concerned, there is a time for forgetting, a time for reconstituting one's life, a time for remembering, a time for speaking, and a time for silence. Justice should not be cabined by unrealistically short timetables. The relationship between victimization and agency in women's experience of conflict and postconflict situations must be addressed. This will foster women's empowerment and their growing resistance to traditional stereotypes of helplessness.[154]

Third, the prevention of gender violence in conflict must be taken seriously. Although the Security Council resolutions address the protection of women in war from sexual violence, there has been inadequate attention to broader methods of prevention. Examples culled from history, where the military has taken suppression of such violence seriously and where ideology has supported such action, can provide important guides.

Fourth, the gross sexual violence visited on women in conflict situations often continues in the aftermath. This is ultimately a product of an endemic system of socially based gender violence and discrimination. Thus, it is critical to overcome "conflict exceptionalism." Recognition of rape in conflict does not necessarily break down the dichotomy between the innocent war victim and the supposedly "willing" victim in everyday life. Focusing on sexual violence in conflict zones does not necessarily challenge the equation of masculinity with dominance and aggression, nor does it interrogate the dehumanization ideologies that underlie gender violence and stereotypes of female passivity.

Additionally, sexualized violence against men remains largely hidden, especially when it takes the form of rape, which shames men through feminization. For similar reasons, gay, bisexual, transgender, and other transgressive identities draw sexualized violence. The revelations of sexualized abuse and torture by U.S. soldiers and agents at Abu Ghraib have opened an important window on violence that ought not to be ignored by feminists. To do so allows it to function as an engine of building and reinforcing violent masculine identities.

Fifth, women are defining the issue of individual and collective reparations from a gender perspective. This is reflected in the recent Nairobi Declaration on Women's and Girls' Right to a Remedy and Reparation.[155] Reparations include compensation, restitution for past wrongs, and rehabilitation or reintegration to enable people to reconstruct their lives. More broadly, reparations also include guarantees of nonrepetition, legal reform, cultural and educational initiatives, research, and public memorials. For women, nonrepetition requires societal transformation. The recent Nairobi

Declaration states: "Reparation[s] must go above and beyond the immediate reasons and consequences of the crimes and violations; they must aim to address the political and structural inequalities that negatively shape women's and girls lives."[156] The most powerful guarantee of nonrepetition, as well as healing, may be in women's opportunity to participate in rebuilding their societies. Women's groups have organized in amazing ways to support survivors and families victimized by conflict, to obtain resources, and to influence policies.

Finally, global economic processes, which should be harnessed to assist women, are contributing to their further impoverishment and marginalization. Although, for example, the United Nations has a policy of "no tolerance" regarding sexual activity between peacekeepers and local women, it is not combined with a policy of providing development options to women who are often rendered desperate by the conflict, or by the impact of global policies.[157] It is also clear that multinational corporations and individual entrepreneurs play a major role in fueling conflict as well as impoverishment. The larger effect of complicit global actors and policies in destroying livelihoods and communities obstructs reconstruction. Additionally, it also feeds insecurity and despair, which is easily manipulated into religious extremism, hatred of difference, and violence against women in homes and communities.

Sexualized violence in war and conflict is thus inseparable from violence, abuse, gender inequality, racisms, and poverty—all of which contribute to the oppression of women in daily life and form a matrix that can exacerbate violence in war. Transformation requires providing women with the means to strengthen themselves, their networks, their creativity, and their resistances. Ending impunity and responding to the urgent needs of women for effective protection and participation are critical aspects. The broader task is building equality in a peaceful and human-centered world. Scholars of sexual and gender violence in conflict must shed light on how women have historically engaged in healing and peace building. We need to reveal the obstacles that women faced and demonstrate how the potential of women's initiatives can build hope and a better world out of the ashes of ineffable loss.

Notes

Introduction: The History of Sexual Violence in Conflict Zones

1. Valerie Oosterveld, "The Special Court for Sierra Leone's Consideration of Gender-based Violence: Contributing to Transitional Justice?" *Human Rights Review* 10 (2009): 73–98; Laura Flanders, "Rwanda's Living Women Speak: Human Rights Watch—Rwanda's Living Casualties," in *War's Dirty Secret: Rape, Prostitution, and Other Crimes Against Women*, ed. Anne Llewellyn Barstow (Cleveland: Pilgrim Press, 2000), 95–100; Chunghee Sarah Soh, "Human Rights and the 'Comfort Women'," *Peace Journal* 12 (2000): 123–29; Alexandra Stiglmayer, ed., *Mass Rape: The War Against Women in Bosnia-Herzegovina* (Lincoln: University of Nebraska Press, 1994). On varying figures for Germany, see Grossmann, this volume.

2. International feminist organizing was key to ensuring visibility; see Charlotte Bunch and Niamh Reilly, *Demanding Accountability: The Global Campaign and Vienna Tribunal for Women's Human Rights* (New Brunswick, N.J.: Rutgers University, Center for Women's Global Leadership, 1994); Indai Lourdes Sajor and Asian Center for Women's Human Rights, *Common Grounds: Violence Against Women in War and Armed Conflict Situations* (Quezon City, Philippines: Asian Center for Women's Human Rights, 1998); Human Rights Watch, *The Human Rights Watch Global Report on Women's Human Rights* (New York: HRW, 1998); Amnesty International, *It's in Our Hands: Stop Violence Against Women*, (New York: Amnesty International, 2004). On the project of bringing a gendered lens to human rights work more generally: Charlotte Bunch, "Transforming Human Rights from a Feminist Perspective," in *Women's Rights, Human Rights: International Feminist Perspectives*, ed. Julie Stone Peters and Andrea Wolper (New York: Routledge, 1995), 11–18; Kenneth Cmiel, "The Recent History of Human Rights," *American Historical Review* 109 (2004): 117–35; Rebecca Cook, ed., *Human Rights of Women: National and International Perspectives* (Philadelphia: University of Pennsylvania Press).

3. Michelle J. Jarvis, *Sexual Violence and Armed Conflict: United Nations Response* (New York: United Nations Division for the Advancement of Women, Department of Social and Economic Affairs, 1998).

4. Urvashi Butalia, "Muslims and Hindus, Men and Women: Communal Stereotypes and the Partition of India," in *Women and Right Wing Movements: Indian Experiences*, ed. Tanika Sarkar and Urvashi Butalia (London: Zed Books, 1995), 58–81.

5. Joshua S. Goldstein, *War and Gender: How Gender Shapes the War System and Vice Versa* (Cambridge: Cambridge University Press, 2001), 3.

6. Ximena Bunster, "Surviving Beyond Fear: Women and Torture in Latin America," in *Surviving Beyond Fear: Women, Children and Human Rights in Latin America*, ed. Marjorie Agosín and Monica Bruno (Fredonia, N.Y.: White Pine Press, 1993), 98–125; Hannah Rosen, "'Not That Sort of Woman': Race, Gender, and Sexual Violence During the Memphis Riot of 1866," in *Sex, Love, Race: Crossing Boundaries in North American History*, ed. Martha Hodes (New York: NYU Press, 1999), 267–93; Akram Mirhosseini, "After the Revolution: Violations of Women's Human Rights in Iran," in *Women's Rights, Human Rights*, eds. Peters and Wolper, 72–77; Jacky Hardy, "Everything Old Is New Again: The Use of Gender-Based Terrorism Against Women," *Minerva* 19 (2001): 3–38.

7. Cynthia Enloe, *Maneuvers: The International Politics of Militarizing Women's Lives* (Berkeley: University of California Press, 2000); Madeline Morris, "In War and Peace: Rape, War, and Military Culture," in *War's Dirty Secret*, ed. Barstow, 167–203; George Hicks, *The Comfort Women: Japan's Brutal Regime of Enforced Prostitution in the Second World War* (New York: Norton, 1997); Paul Higate, *Military Masculinities: Identity and the State* (Westport, Conn.: Praeger, 2003).

8. Susan Brownmiller, *Against Our Will: Men, Women, and Rape* (New York: Simon & Schuster, 1975); Kathleen Barry, *Female Sexual Slavery* (Englewood Cliffs, N.J.: Prentice-Hall, 1979).

9. Rhonda Copelon, "Surfacing Gender: Reconceptualizing Crimes Against Women in Time of War," in Stiglmayer, ed., *Mass Rape*, 197–218.

10. Frances Hasso, "Modernity and Gender in Arab Accounts of the 1948 and 1967 Defeats," *International Journal of Middle East Studies* 32 (2000): 491–510; Shahrzad Mojab, "No 'Safe Haven': Violence Against Women in Iraqi Kurdistan," in *Sites of Violence: Gender and Conflict Zones*, ed. Wenona Giles and Jennifer Hyndman (Berkeley: University of California Press, 2004): 134–51.

11. Maureen Healy, "Civilizing the Soldier in Postwar Austria," in *Gender and War in Twentieth-Century Eastern Europe*, ed. Nancy M. Wingfield and Maria Bucur (Bloomington: Indiana University Press, 2006), 47–69; Elizabeth Nelson, "Victims of War: The First World War, Returned Soldiers, and Understandings of Domestic Violence in Australia," *Journal of Women's History* 19 (2007): 83–106.

12. Saundra Pollock Sturdevant and Brenda Stoltzfus, *Let the Good Times Roll: Prostitution and the U.S. Military in Asia* (New York: New Press, 1993); Katharine H. S. Moon, *Sex Among Allies: Military Prostitution in U.S.-Korea Relations* (New York: Columbia University Press, 1997); Patricia H. Hynes, "On the Battlefield of Women's Bodies: An Overview of the Harm of War to Women," *Women's Studies International Forum* 27 (2004): 431–45.

13. Kelly Dawn Askin, *War Crimes Against Women: Prosecution in International War Crimes Tribunals* (The Hague: Kluwerl, 1997); Copelon, this volume.

14. Reports not specific to a single conflict include Jarvis, *Sexual Violence and Armed Conflict*; Jeanne Ward, *If Not Now, When? Addressing Gender-Based Violence in Refugee, Internally Displaced, and Post-Conflict Settings: A Global Overview* (New York: Reproductive Health for Refugees Consortium, 2002); Amnesty Inter-

national, *Broken Bodies, Shattered Minds: Torture and Ill-Treatment of Women* (New York: Amnesty International, 2001); UN Office for the Coordination of Humanitarian Affairs, *Our Bodies—Their Battleground: Gender-Based Violence in Conflict Zones* (IRIN: UN Office for the Coordination of Humanitarian Affairs, 2004); Elizabeth Rehn and Ellen Johnson Sirleaf and UN Development Fund for Women, eds., *Women, War & Peace: The Independent Experts' Assessment on the Impact of Armed Conflict on Women and Women's Role in Peace Building* (New York: UNIFEM, 2002).

15. Brownmiller, *Against Our Will*; Barry, *Female Sexual Slavery*.

16. Ron Dudai, "'Can You Describe This?' Human Rights Reports and What They Tell Us About the Human Rights Movement," in *Humanitarianism and Suffering: The Mobilization of Empathy*, ed. Richard Ashby Wilson (Cambridge: Cambridge University Press, 2009), 245–64.

17. Catharine A. MacKinnon, "Rape, Genocide, and Women's Human Rights," in Stiglmayer, ed., *Mass Rape*, 183–96.

18. Yoshiaki Yoshimi, *Comfort Women: Sexual Slavery in the Japanese Military During World War II*, trans. Suzanne O'Brien (New York: Columbia University Press, 2000); Margaret D. Stetz and Bonnie B. C. Oh, *Legacies of the Comfort Women of World War II* (Armonk, N.Y.: Sharpe, 2001).

19. Norman M. Naimark, *The Russians in Germany: A History of the Soviet Zone of Occupation, 1945–1949* (Cambridge, Mass.: Belknap Press of Harvard University Press, 1995); Catherine Merridale, *Ivan's War: The Red Army 1941–45* (London: Faber, 2005); Atina Grossmann, "A Question of Silence: The Rape of German Women by Occupation Soldiers," *October* (April 1995): 43–63.

20. Louise Taylor, *We'll Kill You If You Cry: Sexual Violence in the Sierra Leone Conflict* (Washington, D.C.: Human Rights Watch, 2003); Physicians for Human Rights, *War-Related Sexual Violence in Sierra Leone: A Population-Based Assessment* (Washington, D.C. Physicians for Human Rights, 2002); Tara Gingerich and Jennifer Leaning, *The Use of Rape as a Weapon of War in the Conflict in Darfur, Sudan* (Boston: U.S. Agency for International Development/OTI, 2004).

21. Meredeth Turshen and Clotilde Twagiramariya, "'Favours' to Give and 'Consenting' Victims: The Sexual Politics of Survival in Rwanda," in *What Women Do in Wartime: Gender and Conflict in Africa*, ed. Meredeth Turshen and Clotilde Twagiramariya (London: Zed Books, 1998), 101–17, 105.

22. Ruth Seifert, "War and Rape: A Preliminary Analysis," in Stiglmayer, ed., *Mass Rape*, 54–72; Goldstein, *War and Gender*; Inger Skjelsbaek, "Sexual Violence and War: Mapping out a Complex Relationship," *European Journal of International Relations* 7 (2001): 211–37; Jonathan Gottschall, "Explaining Wartime Rape," *Journal of Sex Research* 41 (2004): 129–36.

23. Elisabeth Jean Wood, "Variation in Sexual Violence During War," *Politics and Society* 34 (Sept. 2006): 307–41.

24. Richard C. Trexler, *Sex and Conquest: Gendered Violence, Political Order, and the European Conquest of the Americas* (Ithaca, N.Y.: Cornell University Press, 1995), 64. Trexler relies on the interpretation of Gerda Lerner, *The Creation of Patriarchy* (New York: Oxford University Press, 1986).

25. Trexler, *Sex and Conquest*.

26. Dagmar Herzon, ed., *Brutality and Desire: War and Sexuality in Europe's Twentieth Century* (New York: Palgrave Macmillan, 2009).

27. Marianne Kamp, *The New Woman in Uzbekistan: Islam, Modernity and Unveiling Under Communism* (Seattle: University of Washington Press, 2006).

28. Hasso, "Modernity and Gender in Arab Accounts"; Mojab, "No 'Safe Haven.'"

29. Aaronette M. White, "All the Men Are Fighting for Freedom, All the Women Are Mourning Their Men, But Some of Us Carried Guns: A Raced-Gendered Analysis of Fanon's Psychological Perspectives on War," *Signs* 32 (2007): 857–84; Meg Samuelson, "The Disfigured Body of the Female Guerrilla: (De)Militarization, Sexual Violence, and Reeducation in Zoe Wicomb's *David's Story*," *Signs* 32 (2007): 833–56.

30. Samuelson, "The Disfigured Body."

31. Meredeth Turshen, "The Political Economy of Rape," in *Victims, Perpetrators or Actors? Gender, Armed Conflict and Political Violence*, ed. Caroline N. O. Moser and Fiona Clark (London: Zed Books, 2001), 55–68; Debra Blumenthal, *Enemies and Familiars: Slavery and Mastery in Fifteenth-Century Valencia* (Ithaca, N.Y.: Cornell University Press, 2009).

32. White, "All the Men Are Fighting for Freedom"; Samuelson, "The Disfigured Body"; Oosterveld, "Special Court for Sierra Leone's Consideration of Gender-Based Violence."

33. For a differing interpretation see Patricia A. Weitsman, "The Politics of Identity and Sexual Violence: A Review of Bosnia and Rwanda," *Human Rights Quarterly* 30 (2008): 561–78.

34. Atina Grossmann, *Reforming Sex: The German Movement for Birth Control and Abortion Reform, 1920–1950* (New York: Oxford University Press, 1995); Pascale R. Bos, "Feminists Interpreting the Politics of Wartime Rape: Berlin 1945; Yugoslavia, 1992–1993," *Signs* 31 (2006): 995–1025.

35. Blumenthal, *Enemies and Familiars*.

36. Katherine Derderian, "Common Fate, Different Experience: Gender-Specific Aspects of the Armenian Genocide, 1915–1917," *Holocaust and Genocide Studies* 19 (2005): 1–25; Ara Sarafian, "The Absorption of Armenian Women and Children into Muslim Households as a Structural Component of the Armenian Genocide," in *In God's Name: Genocide and Religion in the Twentieth Century*, ed. Omer Bartov and Phyllis Mack (New York: Berghahn, 2001), 209–21; Urvashi Butalia, *The Other Side of Silence: Voices from the Partition of India* (New Delhi: Viking Penguin India, 1998); Ritu Menon and Kamla Bhasin, *Borders and Boundaries: Women in India's Partition* (New Delhi: Kali for Women, 1998); Veena Das, "National Honour and Practical Kinship: Of Unwanted Women and Children," in *Critical Events: An Anthropological Perspective on Contemporary India*, ed. Veena Das (Delhi: Oxford University Press, 1995), 55–83.

37. *Prosecutor v. Alex Tamba Brima, Brima Bazzy Kamara and Santigie Borbor Kanu*, SCSL-04-16-T, Judgment (20 June 2007) (Special Court for Sierra Leone, Trial Chamber II) ¶45, quoted in Oosterveld, "Special Court for Sierra Leone's Consideration of Gender-Based Violence," 85.

38. Leslie Dwyer, "The Intimacy of Terror: Gender and the Violence of 1965–66 in Bali," *Intersections* (Aug. 2004): 1–19.

39. This thesis is expressed in Robert Hayden, "Rape and Rape Avoidance in Ethno-National Conflicts: Sexual Violence in Liminalized States," *American Anthropologist* 102 (Mar. 2002): 27–41.

40. Katherine R. Jolluck, "The Nation's Pain and Women's Shame: Polish Women and Wartime Violence," in Wingfield and Bucur, eds., *Gender and War in Twentieth-Century Eastern Europe*, 193–219.

41. Elizabeth D. Heineman, "The Hour of the Woman: Memories of Germany's 'Crisis Years' and West German National Identity," *American Historical Review* 101 (1996): 354–95.

42. Human Rights Watch Africa, *Shattered Lives: Sexual Violence During the Rwandan Genocide and Its Aftermath* (New York: Human Rights Watch, 1996).

43. Kirsten Campbell, "Legal Memories: Sexual Assault, Memory, and International Humanitarian Law," *Signs* 28 (2002): 149–78; Kay Schaffer and Sidonie Smith, *Human Rights and Narrated Lives: The Ethics of Recognition* (New York: Palgrave, 2004).

44. Yuma Totami, *The Tokyo War Crimes Trial: The Pursuit of Justice in the Wake of World War II* (Cambridge, Mass.: Harvard University Press, 2008).

45. Compare, for example, UN International Commission of Inquiry on Darfur, *Report of the International Commission of Inquiry on Darfur to the United Nations Security-General* (Geneva: United Nations, 2004), 61ff., 87ff., 102ff.

46. Bos, "Feminists Interpreting the Politics of Wartime Rape"; Grossmann, "A Question of Silence."

47. Nayanika Mookherjee, "Ethical Issues Concerning Representation of Narratives of Sexual Violence" (2003 cited); available from http://www.drishtipat.org/1971.

48. Shani D'Cruze and Anupama Rao, "Introduction," in *Violence, Vulnerability and Embodiment: Gender and History*, ed. Shani D'Cruze and Anupama Rao (Malden, Mass.: Blackwell, 2005), 9.

49. Susan Sontag, "Regarding the Torture of Others," *New York Times Magazine*, May 23, 2004.

50. Sybil Milton, "The Camera as Weapon: Documentary Photography and the Holocaust," *Simon Wiesenthal Center Annual* 1 (1984): 45–68; Marianne Hirsch, "Surviving Images: Holocaust Photographs and the Work of Postmemory," in *Visual Culture and the Holocaust*, ed. Barbie Zelizer (New Brunswick, N.J.: Rutgers University Press, 2001); James Allen, *Without Sanctuary: Lynching Photography in America* (Santa Fe, N.M.: Twin Palms, 2000).

51. Karen Strassler, "Gendered Visibilities and the Dream of Transparency: The Chinese-Indonesian Rape Debate in Post-Suharto Indonesia," in D'Cruze and Rao, eds., *Violence, Vulnerability and Embodiment*, 196–232.

52. Eliza Ablovatski, "Between Red Army and White Guard: Women in Budapest, 1919," in Wingfield and Bucur, eds., *Gender and War in Twentieth-Century Eastern Europe*, 70–92.

53. Correspondence with Karen Hagemann; see the program for the 2007 conference, "Gender, War, and Politics: The Wars of Revolution and Liberation: Trans-

atlantic Comparisons, 1775–1820," http://history.unc.edu/fields/womengenderhistory/brochure.pdf. Accessed May 1, 2010.

54. See also Astrid Aafjes, *Gender Violence: The Hidden War Crime* (Washington, D.C.: Women Law & Development, 1998), 2.

55. Liz Philipose, "The Politics of Pain and the Uses of Torture," *Signs* 32 (2007): 1047–71.

56. Siobhan K. Fisher, "Occupation of the Womb: Forced Impregnation as Genocide," *Duke Law Journal* 46 (October 1996): 91–133.

57. Mirjana Morokvasic-Müller, "From Pillars of Yugoslavism to Targets of Violence: Interethnic Marriages in the Former Yugoslavia and Thereafter," in Giles and Hyndman, eds., *Sites of Violence*, 134–51.

58. Jasbir K. Puar, "Abu Ghraib: Arguing Against Exceptionalism," *Feminist Studies* 30 (2004): 522–34.

59. Lynn Hunt, *Inventing Human Rights: A History* (New York: Norton, 2007).

Chapter 1. Rape in the American Revolution:
Process, Reaction, and Public Re-Creation

Thanks to Danielle Vigneaux for outstanding assistance with this chapter.

1. Since Susan Brownmiller's foundational study, *Against Our Will: Men, Women, and Rape* (New York: Simon & Schuster, 1975), more recent analyses, often coming out of human rights efforts, such as Amnesty International, *Lives Blown Apart: Crimes Against Women in Times of Conflict, Stop Violence Against Women* (London: Amnesty International, International Secretariat, 2004); Alexandra Stiglmayer, ed., *Mass Rape: The War Against Women in Bosnia-Herzegovina* (Lincoln: University of Nebraska Press, 1994) focus largely on twentieth-century wars.

2. For an expanded analysis of the marginalization of women from public discourses of rape, see Sharon Block, "Rape Without Women: Print Culture and the Politicization of Rape, 1765–1815," *Journal of American History* 89, no. 3 (2002): 849–68.

3. For a complete list of sources, see Sharon Block, *Rape and Sexual Power in Early America* (Chapel Hill: University of North Carolina Press, 2006), 250–64. Military sources included seventeen volumes of British War Office Court Martial records as well as an array of personal diaries, letters, and other official military records.

4. In addition to works in note 1, on the multiplicity of twentieth-century women's experiences of sexual violence in conflict zones, see Marlene Epp, "The Memory of Violence: Soviet and East European Mennonite Refugees and Rape in the Second World War, *Journal of Women's History* 9, no. 1 (1997): 58–87; Atina Grossman, "A Question of Silence: The Rape of German Women by Occupation Soldiers," in *West Germany Under Construction: Politics, Society, and Culture in the Adenauer Era*, ed. Robert G. Moeller (Ann Arbor: University of Michigan Press, 1997), 33–52.

5. "Trial of Robert Brown and John Dillon, Jan 1778," WO 71/149, 9–18, National Archives of the UK: Public Record Office, London (hereafter TNA:PRO); "Trial of Thomas Gorman, Aug 1778," WO 71/86, 170–74, TNA:PRO; "Trial of Serjeant Boswell, June 7, 1779," WO 71/88, 524–28, TNA:PRO.

6. Papers of the Continental Congress, 35, 33, 29. For some of the few uses of guns during a peacetime sexual assault in eighteenth-century America, see the kidnapping and rape in "Notes of Evidence, Respublica v. Timothy Cockly, et al., May 10, 1786 for a rape," Yeates Legal Papers 9, May–June 1786), fol. 4, Historical Society of Pennsylvania, Philadelphia; *Carlisle (Pennsylvania) Gazette*, Nov. 19, 1788.

7. "Trial of John Dunn and John Lusty, Sept. 7, 1776," WO 71/82, 419–20, TNA:PRO; Papers of the Continental Congress, 37, 39.

8. "Trial of Brown and Dillon," 9–18; "Trial of Gorman," 170–74; "Trial of Dunn and Lusty," 405–6, 412–25; "Trial of Bartholomew McDonough, Aug. 7, 1778," WO 71/86, 200–7, TNA:PRO.

9. See, for instance, *The Conductor Generalis* (New York, 1788), 302.

10. Papers of the Continental Congress, Reel 66, Item 53, 236–38; *Orderly Book of the Three Battalions of Loyalists Commanded by Brigadier-General Oliver De Lancy, 1776–1778* (Repr. Baltimore: Genealogical Publishing Co., 1972), 86, 93–94; "Trial of Brown and Dillon," 9–18.

11. "Trial of Dunn and Lusty,". 405–6, 412–25; "Trial of Serjeant Boswell," 524–28; Edward Field, ed., *Diary of Colonel Israel Angell, 1778–1781* (Providence, R.I.: Preston and Rounds, 1899), 26–27.

12. "Trial of Dunn and Lusty," 405–6, 412–25; Papers of the Continental Congress, 29; "Trial of McDonough," 200–207; Trial of William Green, 1779?, WO71-150b, TNA:PRO.

13. On the "seemingly unshakeable association of rape with physically violent misconduct," see Stephen J. Schulhofer, "Taking Sexual Autonomy Seriously: Rape Law and Beyond," *Law and Philosophy: Philosophical Issues in Rape Law* 11, no. 1–2 (1992): 35.

14. On the process from incident to legal involvement, see Block, *Rape and Sexual Power*, 88–125. At least 10 percent of eventually prosecuted incidents took more than three months to involve the criminal justice system.

15. "Trial of Brown and Dillon," 9–18; "Trial of Dunn and Lusty," 405–6, 412–25.

16. "Trial of Serjeant Boswell, 524–28; "Trial of McDonough," 200–7; "Trial of Brown and Dillon," 9–18.

17. One exceptional military trial, in Quebec in 1761, involved several witnesses who swore that the victim, who had been drinking at the time of the sexual assault, was "an irregular disorderly" and "very bad Woman." "Trial of McClear, Hunter and Lyons, Sept 1761," WO 71/71, 5–8, TNA:PRO.

18. For a notable exception in a military trial, see "Trial of Gorman," 170–74. On men's defenses to rape in civilian courts, see Block, *Rape and Sexual Power*, 180–86.

19. "Trial of Serjeant Boswell," 524–28; "Trial of John Fisher, Feb. 24, 1778," WO 71/149 bundle 8, pp. 7–19, TNA:PRO; "Trial of John Barron, Jan. 27, 1763," WO

71/73, 101–108, TNA:PRO; "Trial of William Sanders, Aug. 7, 1779," WO 71/150a bundle 14, 26, pp. 7–13, TNA:PRO.

20. Block, *Rape and Sexual Power*, 192. Enslaved men, largely tried at separate courts without the legal protections provided by British Common Law, had much higher conviction rates.

21. On criminal court sentencing shifts for rape, see Block, *Rape and Sexual Power*, 143–44, 195–96.

22. Field, ed., *Diary of Colonel Israel Angell*, 26–27; "Trial of Timothy Spillman, 26 Dec 1775," WO 71/82, 250–56, TNA: PRO; "Trial of Brown and Dillon," 9–18; "Trial of Thomas Higgins, 17 July 1760," WO 71/46, 306–8, TNA: PRO.

23. On the rhetorical power of rape in conflict zones, see Nicoletta F. Gullace, "Sexual Violence and Family Honor: British Propaganda and International Law During the First World War," *American Historical Review* 102 (1997): 714–47; Ruth Harris, "The 'Child of the Barbarian': Rape, Race and Nationalism in France During the First World War," *Past & Present* 141 (1993): 170–206.

24. Mercy Otis Warren, *History of the Rise, Progress and Termination of the American Revolution Interspersed with Biographical, Political and Moral Observations*, ed. Lester H. Cohen (1805; Indianapolis: Liberty Classics, 1988), 191; emphasis original.

25. *Pennsylvania Evening Post*, Dec. 28, 1776; *Pennsylvania Gazette*, Sept. 10, 1777; Phillips Payson, "A Sermon, Boston, 1778," in *American Political Writing During the Founding Era, 1760–1805*, ed. Charles S. Hyneman and Donald S. Lutz, 2 vols. (Indianapolis: Liberty Press, 1983), I:535; *Norwich Packet and the Connecticut, Massachusetts, New-Hampshire, and Rhode-Island Weekly Advertiser*, Nov. 10–17, 1777; "General Orders, Jan. 1, 1777," in *The Writings of George Washington from the Original Manuscript Sources, 1745–1799*, ed. John C. Fitzpatrick (Washington, D.C.: United States Government Printing Office, 1937), 6: 466; *Pennsylvania Packet*, Jan. 4, 1777, Aug. 4, 1778.

26. Letter from Adam Stephen to Thomas Jefferson, Dec. 20, 1776, in *The Papers of Thomas Jefferson*, ed. Julian P. Boyd (Princeton, N.J.: Princeton University Press, 1950), 1: 659; *Pennsylvania Gazette*, Feb. 22, 1775; *Pennsylvania Evening Post*, April 24, 1777, in *Diary of the American Revolution, 1775–1781*, comp. Frank Moore (New York: Washington Square Press, 1967), 217–18.

27. "Trial of Gorman," 170–74; "Trial of McDonough," 200–7; Papers of the Continental Congress, 236–37.

28. *Pennsylvania Evening Post*, Dec. 28, 1776; *Broadside published in Bucks County, Dec. 14, 1776*; *Pennsylvania Evening Post*, April 26, 1777, in Larry Gerlach, ed., *New Jersey in the American Revolution 1763–1783: A Documentary History* (Trenton, N.J.: New Jersey Historical Commission, 1975), 233; Warren, *History of the Rise, Progress and Termination of the American Revolution*, 191.

29. Governor and Council. Pardon Papers, 1788. Box 4, fldr. 47. Maryland State Archives, Annapolis; "Dom Rex. v. James Brown, Aug. 1722," Chester County Quarter Sessions Indictments, Chester County Archives, West Chester, Pennsylvania.

30. Susan Estrich, *Real Rape: How the Legal System Victimizes Women Who Say No* (Cambridge, Mass.: Harvard University Press, 1987).

Chapter 2. Sexual Violence in the Politics and Policies of Conquest:
Amerindian Women and the Spanish Conquest of Alta California

1. Fray Junipero Serra to Antonio María de Bucareli y Ursua, Mexico City, May 21, 1773, in *Writings of Junipero Serra*, ed. Antonine Tibesar, O.F.M., 4 vols. (Washington, D.C.: Academy of Franciscan History, 1955), 1:363.

2. Serra to Father Rafaél Verger, Monterey, Aug. 8, 1772, in *Writings*, 1:257.

3. Serra to Bucareli, Mexico City, May 21, 1773, in *Writings*, 1:361.

4. Serra to Bucareli, Mexico City, May 21, 1773, in *Writings*, 1:363.

5. Serra to Father Guardian [Francisco Pangua], Monterey, July 19, 1774, in *Writings*, 2:121.

6. Serra to Verger, Monterey, Aug. 8, 1772, in *Writings*, 1:259, 261.

7. Serra to Father Francisco Pangua or his Successor, Monterey, June 6, 1777, in *Writings*, 3:159.

8. José Francisco Ortega, Diligencias Practicadas por Sargento Francisco de Aguilar, 1777, Julio 11, San Diego, *Archives of California*, 55:279, Bancroft Library, University of California, Berkeley.

9. Sherburne F. Cook, *Conflict Between the California Indian and White Civilization* (1943; Berkeley: University of California Press, 1976), 24.

10. Serra to Father Juan Figuer, Monterey, Mar. 30, 1779, in *Writings*, 3:305.

11. Robert F. Heizer and Albert B. Elsasser, *The Natural World of the California Indians* (Berkeley: University of California Press, 1980), 25.

12. Hugo Reid, "Letters on the Los Angeles County Indians," in *A Scotch Paisano: Hugo Reid's Life in California, 1832–1852*, ed. Susana Dakin (Berkeley: University of California Press, 1939), App. B, 215–16, 240; Heizer and Elsasser, *Natural World of the California Indians*, 52–53.

13. Reid, "Letters on the Los Angeles County Indians," 262.

14. Reid, "Letters on the Los Angeles County Indians"; see also Herbert Howe Bancroft, *History of California*, 7 vols. (San Francisco: Bancroft, 1984–85), 1:180 and n. 29 (same page).

15. Pedro Font, *Font's Complete Diary: A Chronicle of the Founding of San Francisco*, trans. and ed. Herbert Eugene Bolton (Berkeley: University of California Press, 1931), 256.

16. Font, *Font's Complete Diary*, 247.

17. Font, *Font's Complete Diary*, 251–52.

18. Charles E. Chapman, *A History of California: The Spanish Period* (New York: Macmillan, 1930), 246–47.

19. Cook, *Conflict*, 24.

20. Cook, *Conflict*, 25–30, 101–34.

21. Edwin A. Beilharz, *Felipe de Neve: First Governor of California* (San Francisco: California Historical Society, 1971), 72–73.

22. This argument is based on my analysis of the documents.

23. Reverend Heribert Jone, *Moral Theology, Englished and Adapted to the Law and Customs of the United States of America by Reverend Urban Adelman* (Westminster, Md.: Newman Press, 1960), 145–61.

24. The conflict between church and state in California, which Irving Richman calls the conflict between State Secular and State Sacerdotal, is extensively discussed in general histories of Spanish California. See Bancroft, *History of California*, vol. 1; Irving Berdine Richman, *California Under Spain and Mexico, 1535–1847* (Boston: Houghton Mifflin, 1911), 142–58.

25. Serra to Father Fermín Francisco de Lasuén, Monterey, Jan. 8, 1781, in *Writings*, 4:63; Beilharz, *Felipe de Neve*, 77; Richman, *California Under Spain and Mexico*, 116–337.

26. Serra to Bucareli, Mexico City, Mar. 12, 1773, in *Writings*, 1:295–329; see also Bernard E. Bobb, *The Viceregency of Antonio María Bucareli in New Spain, 1771–1779* (Austin: University of Texas Press, 1962), 163.

27. Serra to Bucareli, Mexico City, Mar. 13, 1773, in *Writings*, 1:299, 301, 305, 307; Serra to Teodoro de Croix, Santa Barbara, Apr. 28, 1782, in *Writings*, 4:129.

28. Magnus Morner, in *Race Mixture in the History of Latin America* (Boston: Little, Brown, 1967), 35–37, discusses interracial marriage in the early colonial period as part of the early social experiments of the sixteenth century. I discuss the promotion of intermarriage more specifically as an instrument of conquest in Chapter 5 of "Presidarias y Pobladoras: Spanish-Mexican Women in Frontier Monterey, California, 1770–1821" (Ph.D. dissertation, Stanford University, 1990).

29. Serra to Bucareli, Mexico City, Mar. 13, 1773, in *Writings*, 1:325.

30. Serra to Bucareli, Mar. 13, 1773.

31. Serra to Bucareli, Monterey, Aug. 24, 1775, in *Writings*, 2:149, 151, 153.

32. This is my interpretation of the documents.

33. Serra to Bucareli, Mexico City, Apr. 22, 1773, in *Writings*, 1:341.

34. Bancroft, *History of California*, 1:206–19; Bobb, *Viceregency of Bucareli*, 162–63; Chapman, *History of California: The Spanish Period*, 289–91.

35. As quoted in Beilharz, *Felipe de Neve*, 77.

36. Serra to Lasuén, Monterey, Jan. 8, 1781, in *Writings*, 4:63.

37. Bancroft, *History of California*, 1:546–49; George Harwood Phillips, *Chiefs and Challengers: Indian Resistance and Cooperation in Southern California* (Berkeley: University of California Press, 1975), 23.

38. Fages al Comandante General, 7 de noviembre de 1785, Monterey; 30 de diciembre de 1785, San Gabriel; 5 de enero de 1786, San Gabriel—all in *Archives of California*, 22:348–49. For the interrogation of Toypurina and her fellow leaders of the rebellion at Mission San Gabriel, see *Diligencias que del órden del Gobernador practica el Sargento Joseph Francisco Olivera . . . , Archivos general de la nación: Provincias Internas*, vol. 120, microfilm, Bancroft Library, University of California, Berkeley. For a popular account of Toypurina's leadership role in the rebellion, see Thomas Workman Temple II, "Toypurina the Witch and the Indian Uprising at San Gabriel," *Masterkey* 32 (Sept.-Oct. 1958):136–52. For a discussion of Amerindian rebellions in California, see Bancroft, *History of California*, 1:249–56; Cook, *Conflict*, 65–90; Phillips, *Chiefs and Challengers*, 1–6, 71–94.

39. As quoted in Beilharz, *Felipe de Neve*, 83.

40. Bobb, *Viceregency of Bucareli*; Alfred Barnaby Thomas, *Teodoro de Croix and the Northern Frontier of New Spain, 1776–1783* (Norman: University of Oklahoma Press, 1941).

41. Thomas, *Teodoro de Croix*, 16–57, 230–46; Max L. Moorhead, *The Presidio: Bastion of the Spanish Borderlands* (Norman: University of Oklahoma Press, 1975), 27–160; Sidney B. Brinckerhoff and Odie B. Faulk, *Lancers for the King: A Study of the Frontier Military System of Northern New Spain, with a Translation of the Royal Regulations of 1772* (Phoenix: Arizona Historical Foundation, 1965), 7.

42. Representación de Don Pedro Fages sobre el estupro violento que cometerion los tres soldados que espresa, año de 1774, Californias, *Archivos general de la nación: Californias*, vol. 2, part 1, microfilm. The five-year chonology of this case is from Beilharz, *Felipe de Neve*, 27–30.

43. Beilharz, *Felipe de Neve*, 29.

44. Bobb, *Viceregency of Bucareli*, 128–171; Thomas, *Teodoro de Croix*, 17–57, 230–46; Beilharz, *Felipe de Neve*, 29.

45. Beilharz, *Felipe de Neve*, 29–30.

46. Beilharz, *Felipe de Neve*, 29–30.

47. Ortega, Diligencias, 1777, Julio 11, San Diego, *Archives of California*, 55:258–79; Cook, *Conflict*, 106–107.

48. Beilharz, *Felipe de Neve*, 67–84, 160–62.

49. Pedro Fages to Diego González, Monterey, July 1, 1785, *Archives of California*, 54:175; Cook, *Conflict*, 106.

50. As quoted in Beilharz, *Felipe de Neve*, 73; see also Neve's instructions to Fages, his successor, in Appendices, same source, 161–62.

51. Fages to Gonzalez, July 1, 1785, *Archives of California*, 54:175.

52. Branciforte al Gobernador de California, "Sobre escoltas a los religiosos . . . ," 5 de octubre de 1785, México, *Archives of California*, 7:256; Gobernador a Comandantes de Presidios, "Excesos de la tropa con las indias, su corrección . . . ," 11 de abril de 1796, Monterey, *Archives of California*, 23:421–22.

53. Bancroft, *History of California*, 1:601.

54. Serra to Bucareli, Mexico City, June 11, 1773; Serra to Pangua, Monterey, June 6, 1777, in *Writings*, 1:383, 3:159.

55. Oakah L. Jones, Jr., *Los Paisanos: Spanish Settlers on the Northern Frontier of New Spain* (Norman: University of Oklahoma Press, 1979); Brinckerhoff and Faulk, *Lancers for the King*; Max L. Moorhead, "The Soldado de Cuera: Stalwart of the Spanish Borderlands," and Leon G. Campbell, "The First Californios: Presidial Society in Spanish California, 1760–1822," in *The Spanish Borderlands: A First Reader*, ed. Oakah L. Jones, Jr. (Los Angeles: Lorrin L. Morrison, 1794), 87–105 and 106–18, respectively. Moorhead's essay was originally published in the *Journal of the West* in January 1969, and Campbell's first appeared in the *Journal of the West* in October 1972.

56. Moorhead, "The Soldado de Cuera," 91.

57. Jones, *Los Paisanos*, 252–53.

58. Juan de Solórzano y Pereyra, *Política indiana*, 5 vols. (Buenos Aires: Compañía Ibero-Americana de Publicaciones, 1972); José María Ots y Capdequi, *Instituciones* (Barcelona: Salvat Editores, S.A., 1959), and *Historia del derecho español en América y del derecho indiano* (Madrid: Ediciones S.A. de Aguilar, 1967).

59. The discussion about rape and other forms of sexual violence against women is based on the following sources: Gerda Lerner, *The Creation of Patriarchy*

(New York: Oxford University Press, 1986); Susan Brownmiller, *Against Our Will: Men, Women and Rape* (New York: Bantam Books, 1976); Christine Ward Gailey, "Evolutionary Perspectives on Gender Hierarchy," and Carole J. Sheffield, "Sexual Terrorism: The Social Control of Women," in *Analyzing Gender: A Handbook of Social Science Research*, ed. Beth B. Hess and Myra Marx Ferree (Newbury Park, Calif.: Sage, 1987), 32–67 and 171–89, respectively; Jalna Hammer and Mary Maynard, "Introduction: Violence and Gender Stratification," in *Women, Violence and Social Control*, ed. Jalna Hammer and Mary Maynard (Atlantic Highlands, N.J.: Humanities Press International, 1987), 1–12; Anne Edwards, "Male Violence in Feminist Theory: An Analysis of the Changing Conceptions of Sex/Gender Violence and Male Dominance," and David H.J. Morgan, "Masculinity and Violence," in *Women, Violence and Social Control*, ed. Hammer and Maynard, 13–29 and 180–92, respectively.

60. Lerner, *Creation of Patriarchy*, 80.

61. Lerner, *Creation of Patriarchy*, 80; Brownmiller, *Against Our Will*, 23–24; Edwards, "Male Violence in Feminist Theory," 19; Ramón Arturo Gutiérrez, "Marriage, Sex, and the Family: Social Change in Colonial New Mexico, 1690–1846" (Ph.D. dissertation, University of Wisconsin-Madison, 1980), 15.

62. Lerner, *Creation of Patriarchy*, 96; Brownmiller, *Against Our Will*, 18–20; Sheffield, "Sexual Terrorism," 173–74.

63. Tzvetan Todorov, *The Conquest of America: The Question of the Other*, trans. Richard Howard (New York: Harper and Row, 1982).

64. Lewis Hanke, *The Spanish Struggle for Justice in the Conquest of America* (Philadelphia: University of Philadelphia Press, 1949), 111–32; Verena Martínez-Alier, *Marriage, Class, and Color in Nineteenth-Century Cuba: A Study of Racial Attitudes and Sexual Values in a Slave Society* (Cambridge: Cambridge University Press, 1974), 76; Morner, *Race Mixture*, 3–5, 36; Health Dillard, "Women in Reconquest Castile: The Fueros of Sepulveda and Cuenca," in *Women in Medieval Society*, ed. Susan Mosher Stuard (Philadelphia: University of Pennsylvania Press, 1976), 86.

65. Martínez-Alier, *Marriage, Class, and Color in Nineteenth-Century Cuba*, 76.

66. Edwards, "Male Violence in Feminist Theory," 28, n. 4. Although some feminist scholars prefer not to make an analytical distinction between sex (biological) and gender (sociocultural) categories, I believe the distinction is important because of the oppositions within which each category places women. The biological distinction of sex places women in opposition and in a subordinate position relative to men; the sociocultural distinction of gender places women in opposition and in inferior position to other women. This sociocultural distinction is based on concepts of sexual morality and conduct that are informed by political and economic values. With few exceptions, however, the sociocultural construction of gender has not accounted for the political and economic dimensions that historically related (if not defined) a woman's sexual morality and gender value to her sociopolitical (religion, race, class) status—and vice versa.

67. Lerner, *Creation of Patriarchy*, 80–88; Sylvia Marina Arrom, *The Women of Mexico City, 1790–1850* (Stanford, Calif.: Stanford University Press, 1985), 71; Health Dillard, *Daughters of the Reconquest: Women in Castilian Town Society,*

1100–1300 (Cambridge: Cambridge University Press, 1984), 12–35, esp. 30–32, and "Women in Reconquest Castile," 86, 91.

68. For the concept of women's honor and dishonor drawn from codes of sexual conduct and used as a basis for devaluation of women in medieval Spain, see Dillard, *Daughters of the Reconquest*, 168–212; for the concept of family honor and the political issues inherent in the devaluation of women on the basis of class and race, see Martínez-Alier, *Marriage, Class, and Color in Nineteenth-Century Cuba*, 11–41, 71–81; for these issues in the northern frontier of colonial New Spain, see Ramón A. Gutiérrez, "From Honor to Love: Transformations of the Meaning of Sexuality in Colonial New Mexico," in *Kinship Ideology and Practice in Latin America*, ed. Raymond T. Smith (Chapel Hill: University of North Carolina Press, 1984), 237–63; see also Gutiérrez, "Marriage, Sex, and the Family."

69. Hanke, *The Spanish Struggle for Justice*, 133–46.

70. Moorhead, "The Soldado de Cuera," 102.

71. For discussion of sexual violence in the national history of Spain, first during the reconquest and then during the conquest of Mexico, see Dillard, *Daughters of the Reconquest*, 206–7, and "Women in Reconquest Castile," 85–89; Todorov, *Conquest of America*, 48–49, 59, 139, 175.

72. Refutation of Charges, Mission of San Carlos of Monterey, June 19, 1801, in *Writings of Fermín Francisco de Lasuén*, 2 vols., trans. and ed. Finbar Kenneally, O.F.M. (Washington, D.C.: Academy of American Franciscan History, 1965), 2:194–234; quotes 220.

73. *Writings of Fermín Francisco de Lasuén*, 2:217.

74. Sheffield, "Sexual Terrorism," 171–89.

Chapter 3. Femicide as Terrorism: The Case of Uzbekistan's Unveiling Murders

This chapter is based on Marianne Kamp, *The New Woman in Uzbekistan: Islam, Modernity, and Unveiling Under Communism* (Seattle: University of Washington Press, 2006). Another version appears in *Belief and Bloodshed: Religion and Violence Across Time and Tradition*, ed. James K. Wellman, Jr. (Lanham, Md.: Rowman and Littlefield, 2007).

1. Dilarom Alimova, *Zhenskii vopros v srednei azii: istoriia izucheniia i sovremeniie problemy* (Tashkent: Fan, 1991), 25, 76; M. Jo'raev et al., eds., *Ozbekistonning yangi tarikhi* (Tashkent: Sharq, 2000), 2:379–84; Shoshana Keller, *To Moscow, Not Mecca: The Soviet Campaign Against Islam in Central Asia, 1917–1941* (Westport, Conn.: Praeger, 2001). Douglas Northrop discusses murders as "crimes of everyday life" in *Veiled Empire: Gender and Power in Stalinist Central Asia* (Ithaca, N.Y.: Cornell University Press, 2004).

2. Shirin Akiner, "Contemporary Central Asian Women," in *Post-Soviet Women: From the Baltic to Central Asia*, ed. Mary Buckley (Cambridge: Cambridge University Press, 1997), 271.

3. Islamic "clergy" include imams, mullahs, and leaders of Sufi orders. On femicide, Jill Radford and Diana E. H. Russell, eds., *Femicide: The Politics of Women Killing* (Buckingham: Open University Press, 1992), 3; Rod Skilbeck, "The Shroud

over Algeria: Femicide, Islamism, and the Hijab," *Journal of Arabic, Islamic, and Middle Eastern Studies* 2 (1995): 43–54; Diana Russell and Roberta Harmes, eds., *Femicide in Global Perspective* (New York: Teachers College Press, 2001).

4. Meredith Turshen, "Algerian Women in the Liberation Struggle and Civil War: From Active Participants to Passive Victims?" *Social Research* 69 (2002): 880–911; Karima Bennoune, "SOS Algeria: Women's Human Rights Under Seige," in *Faith and Freedom: Women's Human Rights in the Muslim World*, ed. Mehnaz Afkami (Syracuse, N.Y.: Syracuse University Press, 1995); and François Burgat, *Face to Face with Political Islam* (London: Tauris, 2003). Burgat explained these murders as intimate violence (102–16). Shahrzad Mojab, "No Safe Haven: Violence Against Women in Iraqi Kurdistan," and Asha Hans, "Escaping Conflict: Afghan Women in Transit," in *Sites of Violence: Gender and Conflict Zones*, ed. Wenona Giles and Jennifer Hyndman (Berkeley: University of California Press, 2004), 108–33 and 213–31, respectively.

5. Cheryl Benard, "Rape as Terror: The Case of Bosnia," *Terrorism and Political Violence* 6 (1994): 43.

6. W. Fitzhugh Brundage, "Introduction," in *Under Sentence of Death: Lynching in the South*, ed. W. Fitzhugh Brundage (Chapel Hill: University of North Carolina Press, 1997), 11.

7. Sources do not reflect incitement to rape but instead incitement to "punish" or to "kill."

8. Keller, *To Moscow, Not Mecca*, 141–74.

9. Rustambek Shamsutdinov, *O'zbekistonda sovetlarning quloqlashtirish siyosati va uning fojeali oqibatlari* (Tashkent: Sharq, 2001), 30–35.

10. *Russian State Archive of Socio-Political History*, Moscow (*RGASPI*) f. 62, d. 1691, 3–4.

11. Kamp, *New Woman*, chap. 6.

12. The OGPU (later KGB) reports give few details on the clergy whose words they recorded. The party associated antiveiling with "obscurantist" clergy, but they also distrusted the "red" clergy who supported unveiling.

13. *RGASPI* f. 62, d. 1503, ll. 47–48.

14. *RGASPI* f. 62, d. 1691, ll. 7–10.

15. *RGASPI* f. 62, d. 1503, p. 49.

16. *RGASPI* f. 62, d. 883, ll. 52–53. "Sharixonda yana bir yavvoiliq," *Qizil O'zbekiston*, Mar. 22, 1927, 2. G'oibjon-qizi's husband was also murdered, as were some other male activists for unveiling. Northrop attributes party members' reveiling of their wives in Shahrixon to their "primarily loyalty" to "Uzbek Muslim culture." *Veiled Empire*, 224.

17. *RGASPI* f. 62, d. 1691, ll. 75–85, 6–8. Jan. to Aug. 1928.

18. Oral History interviews: Mafrat-hon M. (b. Kokand, 1914) Apr. 1993; Rahbar-oi Olimova (b. Tashkent, 1908) May 1993; Aziza I. (b. Marg'ilon, 1910) May 2003.

19. *RGASPI* f. 62, d. 1691, ll. 5–13, 68–93.

20. *RGASPI* f. 62, d. 1691, l. 109.

21. *RGASPI* f. 62, d. 1691, l. 50.

22. Fatima Iuldashbaeva, *Moia Sud'ba* (Tashkent: Yosh Gvardiia, 1972), 66–68.

23. *RGASPI* f. 62, d. 1503, ll. 49–50.

24. *RGASPI* f. 62, d. 883, ll. 52–53.

25. *RGASPI* f. 62, d. 1391, ll. 9–10. Reports from Feb. to Oct. 1928. Northrop's *Veiled Empire* includes a translation of one such collective report (359–63).

26. *RGASPI* f. 62, d. 1691, ll. 5–15; f. 62, d. 883, ll. 39–40.

27. The Communist Party in Uzbekistan in 1923: 1,700 members and candidates; in 1924, 7,538 members and candidates; by 1925, 14,623 members including 6,254 Uzbeks. In 1928, members were 31,133 with 14,285 Uzbeks, 379 of whom were women. *Kommunisticheskaia Partiia Uzbekistana v tsifrakh: sbornik statisticheskikh materilov, 1924–1977 gg.* (Tashkent: Uzbekistan, 1979), tables 2, 3, 13, 21, 26, 37, 42.

28. On the party's removal of members for opposing the *Hujum*, see Douglas Northrop, "Languages of Loyalty: Gender, Politics, and Party Supervision in Uzbekistan, 1927–1941," *Russian Review* 59, no. 2 (2000): 179–200.

29. *RGASPI* f. 62, op. 2, d. 1691, l. 93.

30. Kamp, *New Woman*, 205–12.

31. "Xotinqizlarni himoya qilish yo'lida," *Qizil O'zbekiston*, Apr. 3, 1929, 1, *Uzbekistan State Archive* f. R-86, d. 4450, l. 14.

32. Rosa Karryeva, *Ot bespraviia k ravenstvu* (Tashkent: Uzbekistan, 1989), 126; this triggered the use of Article 8 of the criminal code and demanded the death penalty.

33. Carroll Smith-Rosenberg, *Disorderly Conduct: Visions of Gender in Victorian America* (New York: Knopf, 1985), 48–49.

34. *RGASPI* f. 62, op. 2, d. 2103, l. 5; f. 62, op. 2, d. 2136, l. 213.

35. Oliver C. Cox, "Lynching and the Status Quo," *Journal of Negro Education* 14, no. 4 (1945): 576, 578, n. 5. Cox, an African American scholar and activist, was one of the participants in a debate over the use of the term "lynching." See Christopher Waldrep, "War of Words: The Controversy over the Definition of Lynching, 1899–1940," *Journal of Southern History* 66 (2000): 75–100. The term itself has been used in numerous ways, and one of its uses, "popular justice," muddies the significance of its use in the history of America's race relations. As Cox points out, lynching victims were sometimes accused of a crime; in many cases it seemed that "the destruction of almost any Negro will serve the purpose."

36. De la Roche differentiates terrorism from lynching in terms of "system of liability" and "degree of organization." Roberta Senechal de la Roche, "Collective Violence as Social Control," *Sociological Forum* 11, no. 1 (1996): 97–128; and "Toward a Scientific Theory of Terrorism," *Sociological Theory* 22 (2004): 1–4.

37. Zulhomor Solieva, "Saodatli zamonda yashaimiz," *Saodat* (Toshkent) 11 (1988): 20–22.

38. See, for example, Amnesty International, "Culture, Community, and Violence," http://asiapacific.amnesty.org/actforwomen/scandal-5-eng, accessed Oct. 1, 2010.

39. Lynn Welchman and Sara Hossain, "'Honour,' Rights and Wrongs," in *"Honour": Crimes, Paradigms, and Violence Against Women*, ed. Lynn Welchman and Sara Hossain (London: Zed, 2005), 7.

40. Purna Sen, "'Crimes of Honour,' Value and Meaning," in *"Honour,"* eds. Welchman and Hossain, 50.

41. In the Middle Eastern, South Asian, and Balkan context, these incidents are called "honor killing" or "crimes of honor." In the Mediterranean, European, Latin American, and North American context, the term "crime of passion" is used in similar cases. Purna Sen explores the commonalities and differences between these two modes of violence against women, in "Crimes of Honour." Amira Sonbol's work shows that during colonial rule in the Middle East, European administrators who codified Islamic law in Middle Eastern colonies drew on the European crime of passion understanding to validate local practices. Sonbol, "Adults and Minors in Ottoman Shari'a Courts and Modern Law," in *Women, the Family, and Divorce Laws in Islamic History*, ed. Amira Sonbol (Syracuse, N.Y.: Syracuse University Press, 1996); Sonbol, *Women of Jordan: Islam, Labor and the Law* (Syracuse, N.Y.: Syracuse University Press, 2003). In recent times, murders of women for "crimes of honor" may be more prevalent among Muslims than in other societies and have certainly received more media coverage.

42. The argument that culture, not Islam, sanctions honor killing is based in an understanding of religion as a set of ideas and not the real-world practices of its followers; if murderers justify their acts religiously, their justification is dismissed as wrong understanding. However, following Bruce Lincoln's definition of religion, which includes discourses and practices, I argue that when Muslim religious leaders defend a practice using religious reasoning, we must assume that their audience also associates that practice with Islam. Bruce Lincoln, *Holy Terrors: Rethinking Religion After September 11* (Chicago: University of Chicago Press, 2003), 5–7. Fadia Faqir emphasizes that honor killing does not conform to Quranic dictates, and yet she also notes that Islamic religious authorities argued that changing Jordanian law that permits honor killing would violate Shari'a: "Intrafamily Femicide in Defence of Honour: The Case of Jordan," *Third World Quarterly* 22, no. 1 (2001): 65–82. Interpretations within Islam vary. However, *hadd* laws, based in Shari'a, condemn women to harsher punishments for nonmarital sexual activity than men, including death. Objection often arises to extralegal punishments (i.e., honor killing), rather than to death sentences for sexual misconduct itself. Recent challenges to sentences of stoning for women in Iran, for example, hinge on court cases mishandled rather than on a conceptual rejection of death or corporal sentences for sexual misconduct. In international human rights contexts, activists have struggled to deal with the link that is often made between Islam and "honor killings," noting that the problem is not exclusive to Islamic societies and that many Muslim leaders strongly condemn such interpretations of Islam. See chapters in Welchman and Hossain, eds., *"Honour."*

43. The Nalivkins, nineteenth-century ethnographers, noted that girls who lost their virginity might be forced into an undesired marriage. Anecdotally, this is still the way some Uzbek families deal with the dishonor of female inchastity. V. P. Nalivkin, and M. Nalivkina, *Ocherk byta zhenshchiny osedlago tuzemnago naseleniia Fergany* (Kazan': Tipografiia Imperatorskago Universiteta, 1886).

44. Sonbol, ed., *Women, the Family, and Divorce Laws in Islamic History*, notes this feature of colonial law in Jordan; Sen also attributes this aspect of interpretation of "crimes of honor" to colonial law. The Russian Empire's legal system in Central Asia from 1865 to 1917 operated on a dual basis: immigrants were subject

to Imperial law, while sedentary natives were subject to Shari'a. Only an Imperial court could levy a death sentence, so any Shari'a-based death penalties disappeared in Turkestan, though not in Bukhara or Xorazm. In 1927 the Soviets abolished the remaining Islamic courts. Neither Imperial nor Soviet law regarded "passion" or "honor" as mitigating murder.

45. Mentions of clergy incitement appear in archival files, referred to above, and in published accounts, including Keller, *To Moscow, Not Mecca*, 116, 126; Northrop, *Veiled Empire*, 92, 202.

46. Nadera Shaloub-Kevorkian, "Reexamining Femicide: Breaking the Silence and Crossing 'Scientific' Borders," *Signs: Journal of Women in Culture and Society*, 28 (2002): 581–608. Shaloub-Kevorkian's complex discussion of femicide/honor killing among Palestinians under Israeli domination draws connections between femicide and another political factor, colonialism. Although colonialism presents itself as another possible factor in the Uzbek wave of unveiling murders, and indeed Douglas Northrop (*Veiled Empire*) views colonialism as a primary cause of Uzbek antiunveiling actions, I do not find this a compelling explanation. The violence in these cases of honor killing involves Palestinian men and Palestinian women, and in the Uzbek case, Uzbek men killing Uzbek women. Honor killings take place in other Middle Eastern countries that have not experienced colonialism; while colonialism certainly exacerbates community tensions, it seems more an excuse than an explanation for brutal murders of women by men of their own families and communities.

47. Here I disagree strongly with Northrop's assertion (*Veiled Empire*, 322–29) that veiling increased in the 1930s; neither prior accounts nor most archival materials nor my own rural research supports this. See Kamp, *New Woman*, chap. 9.

48. Shahrzad Mojab, "Honor Killing: Culture, Politics, and Theory," *MEWS Review* 17, no. 2 (2002): 7.

Chapter 4. Girls, Women and the Significance of Sexual Violence in Ancient Warfare

1. Ruth Seifert, "War and Rape: A Preliminary Analysis," in *Mass Rape: The War Against Women in Bosnia-Herzegovina*, ed. Alexandra Stiglmayer, trans. Stiglmayer and Marion Faber (Lincoln: University of Nebraska Press, 1994), 62; Ruth Seifert, "The Second Front: The Logic of Sexual Violence in Wars," *Women's Studies International Forum* 19 (1996): 39; Claudia Card, "Rape as a Weapon of War," *Hypatia* 11 (1996): 5–6. See too Milan Markovic, "Vessels of Reproduction: Forced Pregnancy and the ICC," *Michigan State Journal of International Law* 16 (2007): 439–58; Kelly D. Askin, "Prosecuting Wartime Rape and Other Gender-Related Crimes Under International Law: Extraordinary Advances, Enduring Obstacles," *Berkeley Journal of International Law* 21 (2003): 288–349; Elisabeth Jean Wood, "Variation in Sexual Violence During War," *Politics and Society* 34 (2006): 307–41; *Sex Trafficking: A Global Perspective*, ed. Kimberly A. McCabe and Sabita Manian (Lanham, Md.: Lexington Books, 2010), 11.

2. Susan Brownmiller, *Against Our Will: Men, Women, and Rape* (New York: Simon & Schuster, 1975), 38; Andrea Dworkin, *Our Blood: Prophecies and Discourses on Sexual Politics* (New York: Harper, 1976), 32.

3. Kelly Dawn Askin, *War Crimes Against Women* (The Hague: Nijhoff, 1997), 21; Catherine Niarchos, "Women, War, and Rape: Challenges Facing the International Tribunal for the Former Yugoslavia," *Human Rights Quarterly* 17, no. 4 (1995): 649, n. 2; Kathryn Farr, *Sex Trafficking: The Global Market in Women and Children* (New York: Worth, 2005), 170–73, esp. n. 27.

4. "Women, War, and Rape," 658.

5. *War Crimes Against Women*, 19.

6. See, for example, Stiglmayer's chapter "Rapes in Bosnia-Herzegovinia" in Stiglmayer, ed., *Mass Rape* (1994).

7. Polybius 2.56.1–10, and see also W. K. Pritchett, *The Greek State at War* (Berkeley: University of California Press, 1992), 5: 152–53. References to ancient Greek and Roman sources generally follow the list of source abbreviations in the *Oxford Classical Dictionary*, 3rd rev. ed. (New York: Oxford University Press, 2003). All translations are my own, unless otherwise indicated.

8. Pritchett, *Greek State at War*, 239; Pierre Ducrey, *Le traitement des prisonniers de guerre dans la Grèce antique* (Paris: De Boccard, 1999), 113; William V. Harris, *War and Imperialism in Republican Rome* (New York: Oxford University Press, 1979), 52–53; David Schaps, "Women of Greece in Wartime," *Classical Philology* 77 (1983), 203–4. For the anonymity of female suffering in warfare, see Angelos Chaniotis, *War in the Hellenistic World* (Oxford: Blackwell, 2005), 111–14. Hans Volkmann with Gerhard Horsmann, in *Die Massenversklavungen der Einwohner eroberte Städte in der hellenistisch-römischen Zeit* (Stuttgart: Steiner, 1990), 10, acknowledge that the wartime assault on "women and children" served on the scene of the attack as an immediate "tool of terror in the arsenal of ancient war methods," but go no further in their analysis. The one notable exception to this rule of cursory treatment is Paul Bentley Kern, *Ancient Siege Warfare* (Bloomington: Indiana University Press, 1999), 22–25, 62–85, 135–62, 227–36, 323–51, but he mistakenly treats this aspect of warfare as though it were largely restricted to sieges in which the aggressors prevail, 5, 25.

9. Angeliki Laiou, ed., *Consent and Coercion to Sex and Marriage in Ancient and Medieval Societies* (Washington, D.C.: Dumbarton Oaks, 1993); Susan Deacy and Karen F. Pierce, eds., *Rape in Antiquity* (London: Duckworth, 1997), 1–41, 97–141, 163–84, 231–66; and Sylvana Tomaselli and Roy Porter, eds., *Rape: An Historical and Social Enquiry* (Oxford: Blackwell, 1986), 216–36.

10. Bernard Brodie, as cited by Michael Howard, *Clausewitz* (Oxford: Oxford University Press, 1983), 1.

11. My focus in this chapter is on the sexual subjugation of captive women and girls through ancient warfare, for the preponderance of evidence points toward the targeting of girls and women in the main for capture and sexual subjugation, partly with a view to exploiting their reproductive capacity and other talents and labor, Kathy L. Gaca, "Ancient Warfare and the Mass Rape of Girls, Virgins, and Women," manuscript under review for publication.

12. See especially Pritchett, *Greek State at War*, 170–73, 223–45.

13. Harry Sidebottom, *Ancient Warfare* (New York: Oxford University Press, 2004), 69.

14. K. L. Gaca, "The Andrapodizing of War Captives in Greek Historical Memory," *Transactions of the American Philological Association* 140 (2010): 117–61.

15. "It is a law established for all time among all people that when a city is taken in war, the persons and property of the inhabitants thereof belong to the captors," Xenophon, *Cyr.* 7.5.73.

16. As Agamemnon states, if he had his way, Chryseis for the rest of her life would have been "far from her fatherland, going up and down the loom and into my bed" (*Il.* 1.29–31). In the modern day, too, female war captives "are frequently forced into domestic slavery by day and sexual slavery by night," Askin, *War Crimes Against Women*, xvi. In other words, they are "raped every day," by armed captors and their cronies, "and then have to work for them on top of that!" as stated by a young Bosnian mother named Azra who survived such captivity at the hands of Serbian paramilitaries (Stiglmayer, *Mass Rape*), 110. For Homeric epic on the sexual exploitation, see *Il.* 8.287–91 and 9.663–68, and for the "day shift" labor, see *Il.* 6.450–61, 9.658–61, 11.624–41, 14.5–8, 23.263, 23.704–5, 24.643–48, and *Od.* 20.105–10.

17. *Pol.* 1255b37–40. Plato similarly likens second-phase predatory warfare to an animal hunt, *Laws* 823b1–7, 823e2–4.

18. The phrase *agra hetoimê* comes from the Byzantine historian George Pachymeres (1242–ca. 1310), *Andron. Palaeolog.* 5.21 (287D, p. 414, ed. Bekker). See also Kathy L. Gaca, "Reinterpreting the Homeric Simile of *Iliad* 16.7–11: The Girl and Her Mother in Ancient Greek Warfare," *American Journal of Philology* 129 (2008): 145–71.

19. Orlando Patterson, *Slavery and Social Death* (Cambridge, Mass.: Harvard University Press, 1982), 7–8.

20. See also *Il.* 8.164–66, 8.287–91, 19.291–300, 24.723–45; *Od.* 9.39–42.

21. For my argument that the andrapodized and sold Hykkarans were predominantly children and women, see Gaca, "Andrapodizing War Captives," 124.

22. The nations near at hand are to be annihilated altogether, at least as a matter of the war policy of the ban prescribed by Israelite priests and prophets, Deut. 20:16–18.

23. Emily Vermeule, *Greece in the Bronze Age* (Chicago: University of Chicago Press, 1964), 109, 337, n. 8.

24. On the connections between ancient piracy and predatory warfare, see Philip de Souza, "Piracy," in *The Greek World*, ed. Anton Powell (New York: Routledge, 1995), 179–98.

25. "The Greeks considered taking . . . by force . . . to be a normal and legitimate mode of acquisition; the toil of the spear was a valid mode of production," Tracey Rihll, "War, Slavery, and Settlement in Early Greece," in *War and Society in the Greek World*, ed. John Rich and Graham Shipley (New York: Routledge, 1993), 79.

26. Hdt. 1.146.2. This fact tends to be muted by scholars who tend to assume that Greek colonization was generally a matter of friendly interethnic cooperation, such as J. N. Coldstream, "Mixed Marriages at the Frontiers of the Early

Greek World," *Oxford Journal of Archaeology* 12 (1993): 89–107; Jean Rouge, "La colonisation grecque et les femmes," *Cahiers d'histoire* 15 (1970): 307–17; René van Compernolle, "Femmes indigènes et colonisateurs," in *Forme di contatto e processi di trasformazione nella società antiche* (Rome: Collection de l'École française de Rome, 1981), 1033–49. For a recent skeptical assessment, see Walter Scheidel, "Sex and Empire," in *The Dynamics of Ancient Empires*, ed. Ian Morris and Walter Scheidel (New York: Oxford University Press, 2009), 288.

27. M. M. Austin, "Hellenistic Kings, War, and the Economy," *Classical Quarterly* 36 (1986): 454–55. See A. B. Bosworth, *Alexander and the East: The Tragedy of Triumph* (Oxford: Clarendon Press, 1996), for an important study comparing the conquests of Alexander with those of conquistadors in the Americas.

28. See, for example, Gaca, "Andrapodizing War Captives," 120, n. 7, the Roman evidence included in 130, n. 29, and the especially memorable instance of Aemilius Paullus in Epirus in 167 B.C.E., Polyb. 30.15, Livy 45.33.7–34.10.

29. The oath simply refers to children (*tekeôn*), but sons are meant, as Agamemnon makes clear later to Menelaus, *Il.* 6.55–60.

30. This passage in Thucydides exemplifies the frequent disparity between ancient historical narratives about retributive brutality against males as opposed to females among the enemy. In Corcyra, men of the democratic faction locked the captured men of the oligarchical faction in a large building, and then brought the prisoners out in groups of twenty, bound together, and sent them between two lines of armed citizens to be beaten and stabbed by their personal enemies while the prisoners were whipped along from behind to make them keep going. When the remaining oligarchs trapped in the building realized that they were not being transferred, most of them tried to kill themselves before being killed, and some of them succeeded, either by plunging arrows into their throats that were shot at them from the pierced roof or by hanging themselves with cords and strips of clothing. The rest were hit from above by their enemies. When day came, the men of the democratic faction cast the corpses of the oligarchs on wagons crosswise like lumber and led them from the city. As for the still-living female relations of the slaughtered oligarchs, by contrast, Thucydides permits but the one verb "andrapodize" alone to convey what the men in the democratic faction then proceeded to do to them: "They andrapodized (*êndrapodisanto*) all the women they captured," 4.47.3–48.5.

31. On the reasonableness of this fear, Aristotle, *Nic. Ethics* 1115a12–23.

Chapter 5. The Victimization of Women in Late Precolonial and Early Colonial Warfare in Tanzania

1. Yvonne Adhiambo Owuor, "Weight of Whispers," in *Kwani?* 01 (Nairobi: Kwani Trust, 2003): 8–37 (quote from p. 29).

2. John Iliffe, *A Modern History of Tanganyika* (Cambridge: Cambridge University Press, 1979), 131–32.

3. Marcia Wright, *Strategies of Slaves and Women: Life-Stories from East/Central Africa* (New York: Barber, 1993).

4. Heinrich Fonck, "Im Aufstandsgebiet Uhehe-Ubena-Pangani-Mikindani," in "Aus dem Krieg und Frieden in Deutsch Ostafrika: Lose Blätter aus dem Tagebuch eines alten Afrikanere," A77, Nachlass Fonck, Hamburgisches Museum für Volkerkunde und Vorgeschichte (typescript), is full of references to female slaves, for example, 192, 195, 207, 209.

5. Fonck, "Im Aufstandsgebiet," 240.

6. Fonck, "Im Aufstandsgebiet," 203.

7. Tom von Prince, "Bericht des Hauptmanns Prince über den Abschluss der Wahehe-Expedition," *Deutsches Kolonialblatt*, 8; *Mitteilungen aus den deutschen Schutzgebieten*, 10 (1897): 262; on Sangu attacks on Ubena, see Wilhelm Arning, "Aus dem deutsch-ostafrikanischen Schutzgebiete: die Wahehe," *Mitteilungen aus den deutschen Schutzgebieten*, 10 (1897): 49.

8. "Nachrichten aus Uhehe," *Missionsblätter der St. Benedictus-Genossenschaft zu St. Ottilien, Post Gelendorf, Oberbayern* (1898): 37.

9. Brief mention of slave raiding is found in Edward Mwenda, "Historia na Maendeleo ya Ubena," *Swahili: Journal of the East African Swahili Committee* 33, no. 2 (1963): 108, 110–11, and Seth Ismael Nyagava, "A History of the Bena" (Ph.D. dissertation, University of Dar es Salaam, 1988), 141–42, 184. On slave trading by the Hehe and ivory trading by Mkwawa, see Hans Glauning, "Uhehe," Deutsche Kolonial-Gesellschaft, Abteilung Berlin Charlottenburg, *Proceedings 1897–8*, no. 2: 60, 63. On Hehe slave and ivory trading, Kompagnieführer von Elpons, "Uhehe," *Mitteilungen aus den deutschen Schutzgebieten* 9 (1896): 77.

10. Fonck, "Im Aufstandsgebiet," 217.

11. Fonck, "Im Aufstandsgebiet," 195, 198, 204, 206, 210, 241, 243, 248.

12. "Deutsch-Ostafrika," *Berliner Missionsberichte* (1906): 457.

13. "The Maji Maji Rising in Kidugala," Maji Maji Research Project, University of Dar es Salaam, 1968 (hereafter MMRP), 4/68/4/1. See also Likangavi Nywagi, MMRP 3/68/3/3, and Boniface Makombe, MMRP 3/78/3/3/4.

14. Quoted in "The Maji Maji Rising in Kidugala," MMRP 4/68/4/1.

15. Mzee Lupyana Msangilwa, MMRP 4/68/3/3/2.

16. Ndikwege, MMRP 5/68/1/1. Interviewers also learned that both Maji Maji forces and Hehe allies of the Germans seized many captives during Maji Maji: Mhongole, MMRP 3/68/1/1, Mzee Kwadanalamu Mwachula, MMRP 3/68/1/3/9, Mwalimu Msola, MMRP 3/68/1/3/10, Mzee Tapigila Chungu, MMRP 3/68/1/3/12, and Tembibala Mwitula, MMRP 3/68/2/3/11.

17. Ramadhani Mjengwa, MMRP 5/68/1/5/7.

18. Mlaya Mhavanginonya Merere, MMRP 5/68/1/5/8.

19. Bibi Mbilinyi, MMRP 5/68/1/3/9.

20. Quoted in Ndikwege, MMRP 5/68/1/1.

21. Mhongole, MMRP 3/68/1/1. See also Mzee Soliyambingu Mwachonya, MMRP 3/68/1/3/13, and Friedrich Fülleborn, *Beiträge zur Physischen Anthropologie der Nord-Nyassaländer* (Berlin: Dietrich Reimer, 1902), 10.

22. Maynard Pangamahuti, Utengule, Nov. 15, 1997.

23. James Giblin, "Passages in a Struggle Over the Past: Stories of Majimaji in Njombe, Tanzania," in *Sources and Methods in African History: Spoken, Written,*

Unearthed, ed. Toyin Falola and Christian Jennings (Rochester: University of Rochester Press, 2003), 295–311.

24. Tanzania National Archives (hereafter TNA) G9/11, excerpt from Missionary Gröschel's Report for third quarter 1900 in "Auszüge von Stellen aus den amtlichen Tagebüchern unserer Missionare in Deutsch-Ostafrika."

25. TNA G9/11, letter of Paul Gröschel to the Government, Dar es Salaam (Mpangile, May 6, 1900), fol. 14.

26. TNA G9/11, excerpt from Missionary Gröschel, "Weiter zu derselben Zeit des Jahres 1901," in "Auszüge von Stellen aus den amtlichen Tagebüchern unserer Missionare in Deutsch-Ostafrika."

27. TNA G9/11, excerpt from account by Missionary Klamroth of Oct. 6, 1901 in "Auszüge von Stellen aus den amtlichen Tagebüchern unserer Missionare in Deutsch-Ostafrika."

28. Mama Kapwani, Makambako, May 18, 1992.

29. For a report of the victimization of women by local chiefs in southern Ubena at this time see "Der Bezirk Songea," *Deutsches Kolonialblatt* 16 (1905).

30. TNA G9/11, excerpt from Missionary Gröschel's Report for third quarter 1900 (see note 24 above).

Chapter 6. War Crimes or Atrocity Stories? Anglo-American Narratives of Truth and Deception in the Aftermath of World War I

1. Arthur Ponsonby, *Falsehood in War-Time: Containing an Assortment of Lies Circulated Throughout the Nations During the Great War* (London: Allen & Unwin, 1928), 132.

2. Harold D. Laswell, *Propaganda Technique in the World War* (New York: Knopf, 1927) and H. C. Peterson, *Propaganda for War: The Campaign Against American Neutrality, 1914–1917* (Norman: University of Oklahoma Press, 1939).

3. John Horne and Alan Kramer, *German Atrocities, 1914: A History of Denial* (New Haven, Conn.: Yale University Press, 2001), 419; Ruth Harris, "'The Child of the Barbarian' Rape, Race, and Nationalism in France During the First World War," *Past & Present* (November 1993): 170–206; Lawrence Zuckerman, *The Rape of Belgium* (New York: NYU Press, 2004).

4. M. L. Sanders and Philip M. Taylor, *British Propaganda During the First World War, 1914–1918* (London: Macmillan, 1982), 169.

5. Nicoletta F. Gullace, "Sexual Violence and Family Honor: British Propaganda and International Law during the First World War," *American Historical Review* 102 (June 1997): 714–47.

6. Peterson, *Propaganda for War*, 243.

7. Nicoletta F. Gullace, *"Blood of Our Sons": Men, Women and the Renegotiation of British Citizenship During the Great War* (New York: Palgrave, 2002), chap. 1.

8. Theodore A. Cook, *The Crimes of Germany* (London: Field and Queen, 1917), 5–7.

9. Cook, *Crimes*, 11; and Committee on Alleged German Outrages, *Appendix to the Report of the Committee on Alleged German Outrages, Evidence and Documents* (London: H. M. Stationery Office, 1915), 14.

10. Susan Kingsley Kent, *Making Peace: The Reconstruction of Gender in Interwar Britain* (Princeton, N.J.: Princeton University Press, 1993), chaps. 1, 2.

11. Cook, *Crimes*, 7.

12. James Morgan Read, *Atrocity Propaganda, 1914–1919* (1941; New York: Arno Press, 1972), 207.

13. David Lloyd George, *Memoirs of the Peace Conference* (New Haven, Conn.: Yale University Press, 1939), 55.

14. Lord Birkenhead, quoted in Lloyd George, *Memoirs*, 59.

15. *United States v. Herberger*, no. 167: District Court, W.D. Washington, ND. 272 F 278; 1921 U.S. Dist. LEXUS 1340, April 2, 1921, 3.

16. Nicoletta F. Gullace, "Barbaric Anti-Modernism: Representations of the 'Hun' in Britain, North America, Australia, and Beyond," in *Picture This: World War I Posters and Visual Culture*, ed. Pearl James (Lincoln: University of Nebraska Press, 2009), 61–78.

17. Peter Buitenhuis, *The Great War of Words: British, American, and Canadian Propaganda and Fiction, 1914–1933* (Vancouver: University of British Columbia Press, 1987), 11–12; and Committee on Alleged German Outrages, *Report of the Committee on Alleged German Outrages* (London: H. M. Stationery Office, 1915).

18. Charles Masterman to James Bryce, June 7, 1915, Oxford, Bodleian, Modern Manuscripts, UB 57 Bryce.

19. Max Muller to Bryce, January 29, 1917, Oxford, Bodleian, Modern Manuscripts, UB 57 Bryce.

20. Bernard J. Snell to Bryce, June 25, 1919, Oxford, Bodleian, Modern Manuscripts, UB 57 Bryce.

21. Quoted in Ponsonby, *Falsehood in War-Time*, 19, 81.

22. Laswell, *Propaganda Technique*, 81.

23. Laswell, *Propaganda Technique*, 87.

24. Laswell, *Propaganda Technique*, 82.

25. Peterson, *Propaganda for War*, 55.

26. Peterson, *Propaganda for War*, 58.

27. Horne and Kramer, *German Atrocities*, 2.

28. George Sylvester Viereck, *Spreading Germs of Hate* (London: Duckworth, 1931).

29. Sir Campbell Stuart, *The Secrets of Crewe House* (London: Hodder & Stoughton, 1920); George Creel, *How We Advertised America* (New York: Harper & Brothers, 1920).

30. Trevor Wilson, "Lord Bryce's Investigation into Alleged German Atrocities in Belgium, 1914–1915," *Journal of Contemporary History* (July 1979): 369–83.

31. Edward L. Bernays, *Propaganda* (New York: Horace Liveright, 1928), 9.

32. Gullace,"*Blood of Our Sons*," 188.

33. John Maynard Keynes regarded Belgium's suffering as less than Australia's and did much to discredit Belgian victimization as grounds for the harsh peace.

Larry Zuckerman, *The Rape of Belgium: The Untold Story of World War I* (New York: NYU Press, 2004), 259–60.

34. Jay Winter, *Sites of Memory, Sites of Mourning: The Great War in European Cultural History* (Cambridge: Cambridge University Press, 1995); Robert Graves, *Goodbye to All That* (1929; New York: Doubleday, 1985), 67.

35. See Rosa Maria Bracco, *Merchants of Hope: British Middlebrow Writers and the First World War 1919–1939* (Oxford: Berg, 1993), chap. 124.

36. Janet Watson, *Fighting Different Wars: Experience, Memory, and the First World War in Britain* (Cambridge: Cambridge University Press, 2004), chaps. 5, 6.

37. Graves, *Goodbye to All That*, 183.

38. Graves, *Goodbye to All That*, 318.

39. Graves, *Goodbye to All That*, 228.

40. Colonel R. P. Dickerson, Commander in Chief of the National Loyalty League to William of Hohenzollern. Clipping in Northcliffe collection London, British Library, Manuscripts, Add 62163 fol. 131–33.

41. *United States v. Herberger*, 3.

42. Cook, *Crimes*, 8.

43. Creel, *How We Advertised America*, 30–33.

44. Creel, *How We Advertised America*, 4.

45. Mark Wollaeger, *Modernism, Media, and Propaganda: British Narrative from 1900 to 1945* (Princeton, N.J.: Princeton University Press, 2006), xvii.

Chapter 7. Sexual and Nonsexual Violence Against "Politicized Women" in Central Europe After the Great War

I am grateful to the Harry Frank Guggenheim Foundation (New York), the Irish Research Council for the Humanities and Social Sciences, and the European Research Council for providing generous funds that enabled me to undertake the necessary research for this chapter.

Epigraph: Marguerite Yourcenar, *Coup de grâce*, trans. Grace Frick (London: Farrar, 1984), 111–12.

1. Vejas Gabriel Liulevicius, *War Land on the Eastern Front: Culture, National Identity and German Occupation in World War I* (Cambridge: Cambridge University Press, 2000). One of the few good accounts of the *Freikorps*' Baltic campaign remains Bernhard Sauer, "Vom 'Mythos des ewigen Soldatentums': Der Feldzug deutscher Freikorps im Baltikum im Jahre 1919," *Zeitschrift für Geschichtswissenschaft* 10 (1995): 869–902.

2. Emil J. Gumbel, *Vier Jahre politischer Mord* (Berlin: Neue Gesellschaft, 1922); Manfred von Killinger, *Ernstes und Heiteres aus dem Putschleben* (Berlin: Vormarsch, 1927), 52–53. See, too, the glorified account of the *Freikorps* campaigns of the Nazi period: *Darstellungen aus den Nachkriegskämpfen deutscher Truppen und Freikorps*, vol. 4, *Die Niederwerfung der Räteherrschaft in Bayern 1919* (Berlin: Mittler, 1939).

3. Max Zeller, as quoted in Nigel H. Jones, *Hitler's Heralds: The Story of the Freikorps 1918–1923* (London: John Murray, 1987), 182.

4. British Joint Labor Delegation to Hungary, *The White Terror in Hungary: Report of the British Joint Labour Delegation to Hungary* (London, 1920).

5. It is impossible to give exact figures of the number of deaths inflicted by post-war paramilitary violence. According to official (non-gender-specific) police and military accounts, 557 people lost their lives during the fighting in Munich in 1919 (only 38 of these were *Freikorps* soldiers and government troops). See Heinrich Hillmayer, *Roter und Weißer Terror in Bayern nach 1918: Ursachen, Erscheinungsformen und Folgen der Gewalttätigkeiten im Verlauf der revolutionären Ereignisse nach dem Ende des Ersten Weltkrieges* (Munich: Nusser, 1974), 150. The White Terror in Hungary lasted much longer than in Germany. Oszkár Jászi, the bourgeois radical and member of the 1918 Károlyi government, estimated that the White counter-revolution had claimed at least 4000 victims, although this figure remains highly disputed. Oszkár Jászi, *Revolution and Counter-Revolution in Hungary* (London: King, 1924), 120. For Austria, Gerhard Botz has established the relatively low figure of 859 deaths in violent clashes during the first Austrian Republic, that is, between November 12, 1918 and February 11, 1934. See Gerhard Botz, *Gewalt in der Politik. Attentate, Zusammenstöße, Putschversuche, Unruhen in Österreich 1918 bis 1938*, 2nd ed. (Munich: Fink, 1983). Much more difficult to establish, however, is the figure for casualties inflicted by paramilitary units in the borderlands of Lithuania, upper Silesia, western Hungary, and Carthingia, where thousands of people "disappeared" without a trace.

6. On Germany, see Robert G. L. Waite, *The Vanguard of Nazism: The Free Corps Movement in Post-War Germany 1918–1923* (1952; New York: Norton, 1970); James M. Diehl, *Paramilitary Politics in the Weimar Republic* (Bloomington: Indiana University Press, 1977); Hagen Schulze, *Freikorps und Republik 1918–20* (Boppard: Boldt, 1968, 1973); Dieter Fricke et al., eds., *Lexikon zur Parteiengeschichte 1789–1945: Die bürgerlichen und kleinbürgerlichen Parteien und Verbände in Deutschland*, vol. 2 (Leipzig: Bibliographisches Institut, 1984), 669–681 and 674–677; David Clay Large, *The Politics of Law and Order: A History of the Bavarian Einwohnerwehr, 1918–1921* (Philadelphia: American Philosophical Society, 1980). On Austria: Botz, *Gewalt*. See, too, Francis L. Carsten, *Revolution in Central Europe, 1918–19* (Berkeley: University of California Press, 1972). On Hungary, see Béla Bodo, "Paramilitary Violence in Hungary After the First World War," *East European Quarterly* 38 (2004): 129–72.

7. Klaus Theweleit, *Male Fantasies*, 2 vols. (several editions, subsequently quoted from the Polity Press edition of 1987).

8. See, for example, Richard J. Evans, "Geschichte, Psychologie und die Geschlechterbeziehungen," *Geschichte und Gesellschaft* 7 (1981): 597–606.

9. See Bodo, "Paramilitary Violence" and Eliza Johnson Ablovatski, "Cleansing the Red Nest: Counterrevolution and Terror in Munich and Budapest, 1919" (Ph.D. dissertation, Columbia University, 2004).

10. Edwin Erwin Dwinger, *Die letzten Reiter* (Jena: Diederichs, 1935), 141–44.

11. John Horne and Alan Kramer, *German Atrocities, 1914: A History of Denial* (New Haven: Yale University Press, 2001) and, for Austria-Hungary and atrocities in Serbia, John Reed, *The War in Eastern Europe* (New York: Scribner, 1916).

12. Friedrich Freksa, ed., *Kapitän Ehrhardt: Abenteuer und Schicksale* (Berlin: Scherl, 1924), 45.

13. British Joint Labour Delegation, *White Terror in Hungary*, 8–10. Other incidents of torture and murder of female victims are reported in Desző Nemes, ed., *Az ellenforradalom hatalomrajutása és rémuralma Magyarországon, 1919–1920* (Budapest: Szirka, 1953), 266–70; and József Pogány, "Az egri fehérterrorról," in *Magyar Pokol: A magyarországi fehérterror betiltott és üldözött kiadványok tükrében*, ed. Györgyi Markovits (Budapest: Szirka, 1964), 254–60.

14. Another young Hungarian woman who testified to the British Joint Labour Delegation reported that she was arrested in Budapest in October 1919 and taken to the Harsfa police station where she was questioned about being a Communist, deprived of food, and repeatedly raped in her cell before she managed to escape to Vienna. British Joint Labour Delegation, *White Terror in Hungary*, 16–17.

15. John Horne, "Masculinity in Politics and War in the Age of Nation-States and World Wars, 1850–1950," in *Masculinities in Politics and War. Gendering Modern History*, ed. Stefan Dudink, Karen Hagemann, and John Tosh (Manchester: Manchester University Press, 2004), 22–40. See too George L. Mosse, *The Image of Man: the Creation of Modern Masculinity* (Oxford: Oxford University Press, 1996).

16. For Germany: George L. Mosse, *Fallen Soldiers: Reshaping the Memory of the World Wars* (New York: Oxford University Press, 1990). For Austria: Ernst Hanisch, *Männlichkeiten: Eine andere Geschichte des 20. Jahrhunderts* (Vienna: Böhlau, 2005), 52–54.

17. On the widespread perception of a "world turned upside down" after 1918, see Martin H. Geyer, *Verkehrte Welt: Revolution, Inflation und Moderne, München 1914–1924* (Göttingen: Vandenhoek & Ruprecht, 1998), 19.

18. Joseph Roth, *The Spider's Web* (Woodstock, N.Y.: Overlook Press, 2003), 8–9.

19. See Sven Reichardt, *Faschistische Kampfbünde: Gewalt und Gemeinschaft im italienischen Squadrismus und in der deutschen SA* (Cologne: Böhlau, 2002), 667.

20. István I. Mócsy, *The Effects of World War I: The Uprooted: Hungarian Refugees and Their Impact on Hungary's Domestic Politics, 1918–1921* (New York: Columbia University Press, 1983).

21. Freksa, *Kapitän Ehrhardt*, 45.

22. On Germany: Boris Barth, *Dolchstoßlegenden und politische Desintegration: Das Trauma der deutschen Niederlage im ersten Weltkrieg 1914–1933* (Düsseldorf: Droste, 2003). On Austria: Alois Götsch, *Die Vorarlberger Heimwehr: Zwischen Bolschewistenfurcht und NS-Terror* (Feldkirch: Schriftenreihe der Rheticus-Gesellschaft, 1993), 24. On the Hungarian "stab-in-the-back," see Paul Lendvai, *Die Ungarn: Ein Jahrtausend Sieger in Niederlagen*, 4th ed. (Munich: Bertelsmann, 1999), 423.

23. Pabst to Kapitän von Pflugk-Harttung in Stockholm (4 November 1931), Pabst Papers, BA (Berlin), NY4035/6 (Weisse Internationale), 1.

24. Pabst Papers, BA (Berlin), NY4035/6, 37–39.

25. An interesting parallel here is France after 1940. See Joan Tumblety, "Revenge of the fascist knights: masculine identities in *Je suis partout*, 1940–1944," *Modern and Contemporary France* 7/1 (1999): 11–20. See, too, Luc Capdevila, "The Quest for Masculinity in a Defeated France, 1940–1945," *Contemporary European History* 10 (2001): 423–45.

26. Miklós Kozma, *Az összeomlás 1918–1919* (Budapest, 1935), 380.

27. Ernst von Salomon, *Die Geächteten*, 3rd ed. (Berlin: Rowohlt, 1933), 144–45.

28. Marinetti, as quoted in Ian Kershaw, "War and Political Violence in Twentieth-Century Europe," *Contemporary European History* 14 (2005): 107–23.

29. Quotation from Hans Albin Rauter, NIOD (Amsterdam), Doc. I-1380, map H (interview), 15. See, too: Robert Wohl, *The Generation of 1914* (Cambridge, Mass.: Harvard University Press, 1979), 51.

30. Ernst Rüdiger Starhemberg, *Memoiren* (Vienna: Amalthea, 1971), 37–38.

31. Salomon, *Die Geächteten*, 10–11.

32. Gustave Le Bon's *Psychologie des foules* (Paris: E. Flammarion, 1895). On the continued interest after 1918 see, too, Wilhelm Schwalenberg, *Gustave le Bon und seine psychologie des foules* (Bonn: Wurm, 1919).

33. Salomon, *Die Geächteten*, 30–31.

34. «Kritik der Frauenbewegung,» unpublished manuscript, in Bauer papers, Bundesarchiv Koblenz, N 1022 / 1c / 199 b. On this theme, see, too, Cornelie Usborne, «The New Women and Generation Conflict: Perceptions of Young Women's Sexual Mores in the Weimar Republic,» in *Generations in Conflict: Youth Revolt and Generation Formation in Germany 1770–1968*, ed. Mark Roseman (Cambridge: Cambridge University Press, 1995), 137–63. For Austria, see, too, Franz Schweinitzhaupt, "Die Frauenarbeit," in Franz Schweinitzhaupt Papers, Universitätsbibliothek Innsbruck, 137–38.

35. "Kritik der Frauenbewegung," Bauer papers, N 1022 / 1c / 198–99.

36. See, too, the famous case of Marie Sandmayr, who was hanged by *Freikorps* men for reporting a secret hideout for illegal arms to the police. Gumbel, *Vier Jahre politischer Mord*.

37. Salomon *Die Geächteten*, 184.

38. Erich Balla, *"Landsknechte wurden wir..."*: *Abenteuer aus dem Baltikum* (Berlin: Kolk, 1932), 111–12.

39. Oscar Szóllósy, "The Criminals of the Dictatorship of the Proletariat," as printed in Cecile Tormay, *An Outlaw's Diary*, 2 vols. (London: Philip Allan, 1923), 2: 226–27.

40. Tormay, *Outlaw's Diary*, vol. 1 (not paginated).

Chapter 8. The "Big Rape": Sex and Sexual Violence, War, and Occupation in Post-World War II Memory and Imagination

Parts of this article are based on Chapter 2, "Gendered Defeat," of my book *Jews, Germans, and Allies: Close Encounters in Occupied Germany* (Princeton, N.J.: Princeton University Press, 2007).

1. One Berlin district counted 1,873 women to 1,000 men in August 1945, and the city ratio was 169 to 100. In August the total population was counted at 2,784,112 (1,035,463 male, 1,748,649 female) versus 4,332,000 in 1939. The male population had been halved, female population reduced by a quarter. The 100 men, 169 women figure compared to 100 to 119 in 1939. *Berliner Volks, Berufs und Arbeitstättenzählung*, Aug. 12, 1945, in *Berliner Zeitung* 1, 91 (Aug. 29, 1945): 1. On the meaning of

the female "surplus" at war's end, see Elizabeth D. Heineman, *What Difference Does a Husband Make? Women and Marital Status in Nazi and Postwar Germany* (Berkeley: University of California Press, 1999), 10.

2. See the well-received and publicized but controversial publication in Germany, Britain, and the United States of a revised and retranslated text about mass rapes in Berlin, *Anonyma, Eine Frau in Berlin: Tagebuchaufzeichnungen vom 20 April bis zum 22 Juni 1945* (Frankfurt am Main: Eichborn, 2003); in English, *A Woman in Berlin: Eight Weeks in the Conquered City,* by Anonymous, trans. Philip Boehm, with foreword by Antony Beevor (New York: Metropolitan, 2005). This interest was preceded by the positive response to Beevor's discussion of rape in *The Fall of Berlin 1945* (New York: Viking, 2002). Research published in the 1990s includes Norman Naimark, *The Russians in Germany: A History of the Soviet Zone of Occupation, 1945–1949* (Cambridge, Mass.: Harvard University Press, 1995); *Heimatmuseum Charlottenburg Ausstellung: Worüber kaum gesprochen wurde: Frauen und allierte Soldaten. 3 September bis 15 Oktober 1995* (Berlin: Bezirksamt Charlottenburg, Abt. Volksbildung, 1995); and the text accompanying Sander's film on the topic, Helke Sander and Barbara Johr, eds., *BeFreier und Befreite. Krieg, Vergewaltigungen, Kinder* (Munich: Antje Kunstmann, 1992). For earlier feminist analyses, see Ingrid Schmidt-Harzbach, "Eine Woche im April. Berlin 1945. Vergewaltigung als Massenschicksal," *Feministische Studien* 5 (1984): 51–62; Erika M. Hoerning, "Frauen als Kriegsbeute. Der Zwei-Fronten Krieg. Beispiele aus Berlin," in *"Wir kriegen jetzt andere Zeiten": Auf der Suche nach der Erfahrung des Volkes in antifaschistischen Ländern. Lebensgeschichte und Sozialkultur im Ruhrgebiet 1930 bis 1960,* vol. 3, ed. Lutz Niethammer and Alexander von Plato (Berlin: J. H. W. Dietz, 1985), 327–46; and Annemarie Tröger, "Between Rape and Prostitution: Survival Strategies and Chances of Emancipation for Berlin Women After World II," in *Women in Culture and Politics: A Century of Change,* ed. Judith Friedlander, et al. (Bloomington: University of Indiana Press, 1986), 97–117. For an even earlier feminist consideration of sexual violence in World War II, including attacks by Soviet liberators on German women, see Susan Brownmiller, *Against Our Will: Men, Women, and Rape* (New York: Simon & Schuster, 1975), 48–79. On the thorny problems of historicizing rape at war's end and the controversy about Sander's film, see Atina Grossmann, "A Question of Silence: The Rape of German Women by Occupation Soldiers," *October* 72 (Spring 1995), 43–63; reprinted in Robert G. Moeller, ed., *West Germany Under Construction: Politics, Society, and Culture in the Adenauer Era* (Ann Arbor: University of Michigan Press, 1997), 33–52.

3. Barbara Johr, "Die Ereignisse in Zahlen," in Sander and Johr, eds., *BeFreier und Befreite,* 48, 54–55, 59. See also Erich Kuby, *Die Russen in Berlin 1945* (Bern/Munich: Scherz, 1965), 312–13, and especially Naimark, *Russians in Germany,* 69–90.

4. Naimark, *Russians in Germany,* 132–33, 79–80, 106–7, 86. Beevor's *Fall of Berlin* presents much of the same material.

5. Karla Höcker, *Beschreibung eines Jahres. Berliner Notizen 1945* (Berlin: Arani Verlag, 1984), 42.

6. Harold J. Berman and Miroslav Kerner, *Soviet Military Law and Administration* (Cambridge, Mass.: Harvard University Press, 1955), 48.

7. Ilya Ehrenburg, *The War: 1941–1945*, vol. 5, *Of Men, Years-Life* (Cleveland: World, 1964), 175. See also Hoerning, "Frauen als Kriegsbeute," 327–46.

8. Hildegard Knef, *The Gift Horse: Report on a Life* (New York: McGraw-Hill, 1971), 95.

9. *The Economist*, Oct. 27, 1945, in Issac Deutscher, *Reportagen aus Nachkriegsdeutschland* (Hamburg: Junius Verlag, 1980), 130.

10. For a careful and sensitive discussion of the rage and frustration as well as sheer exhaustion, brutalization, and alcohol that fueled Red Army rapes, see Catherine Merridale, *Ivan's War: Life and Death in the Red Army, 1939–1945* (New York: Henry Holt Metropolitan, 2006), 299–335, 302, 309, 307.

11. Landesarchiv Berlin, Acc. 2421. Gabrielle Vallentin, "Die Einnahme von Berlin Durch die Rote Armee vor Zehn Jahren. Wie ich Sie Selbst Erlebt Habe," 1955, 37.

12. Michael Wieck, *Zeugnis vom Untergang Königsbergs. Ein "Geltungsjude" berichtet* (Heidelberg: Heidelberger Verlagsanstalt und Druckerei, 1990), 261

13. Margaret Boveri, *Tage des Überlebens. Berlin 1945* (first published 1968; Munich: Piper, 1985), 121–23.

14. Interview with G. C., conducted in early 1990s, quoted in Heimatmuseum Charlottenburg, "Worüber nicht gesprochen wurde," 22.

15. Curt Riess, *Berlin Berlin 1945–1953* (first published ca. 1953; reprint, ed. Steffen Damm, Berlin: Bostelmann & Siebenhaar, 2002), 19.

16. My translation from Anonymous, *Eine Frau in Berlin*, 78. See the republished version, *Anonyma* (2003), and subsequent debates about the legitimacy of "outing" Anonyma's name and identity as the journalist Marta Hillers, a kind of Nazi "New Woman," who had written minor texts for Goebbels' propaganda ministry before the war (*Kleinpropagandistin*), which played out on the *Feuilleton* pages of major newspapers among male scholars and journalists. See especially Jens Bisky, *Süddeutsche Zeitung*, Sept. 24, 2003. See also the enthusiastically received 2005 American edition, *A Woman in Berlin*, and the 2009 film version. On the controversy about the German republication, see Elizabeth Heineman, "Gender, Sexuality, and Coming to Terms with the Nazi Past," *Central European History* 38, no. 1 (2005): 41–74, esp. 53–56.

17. Riess, *Berlin Berlin 1945–1953*, 23, 26, 19.

18. Hans Winterfeldt memoir, Leo Baeck Institute archives, ms. 690, 438.

19. Tröger, "Between Rape and Prostitution," 113. As Heineman observes, a "regime obsessed with racial purity had become the catalyst of an unprecedented number of relationships between Germans and foreigners." Heineman, *What Difference*, 58. See also Dagmar Herzog, *Sex After Fascism: Memory and Morality in Twentieth Century Germany* (Princeton, N.J.: Princeton University Press, 2005).

20. Annemarie Weber, *Westend* (Munich: Desch, 1966), 104.

21. Issac Deutscher, *The Observer* Oct. 7, 1945; *The Economist* Oct. 27, 1945, in *Reportagen*, 122–24, 129–30.

22. Margarete Dörr, *"Wer die Zeit nicht miterlebt hat . . ." Frauenerfahrung im Zweiten Weltkrieg und in den Jahren danach* (Frankfurt: Campus Verlag, 1998), 408.

23. Bert Lewyn and Bev Saltzman Lewyn, *On the Run in Nazi Berlin* (Bloomington, Ind.: Xlibris, 2001), 277.

24. Eugene Davidson, *The Death and Life of Germany. An Account of the American Occupation* (New York: Knopf, 1959), 74.

25. Anne-Marie Durand-Wever, *Proceedings of the International Congress on Population and World Resources in Relation to the Family. August 1948* (London: H. K. Lewis and Co, n.d.), 103.

26. Wladimir Gelfand, *Deutschland Tagebuch 1945–1946: Aufzeichnungen eines Rotarmisten* (Berlin: Aufbau, 2005), 78–79.

27. Gudrun Pausewang, in Heinrich Böll, ed. *NiemandsLand. Kindheitser-innerungen an die Jahre 1945 bis 1949* (Bronheim-Merten: Lamuv Verlag, 1985), 62.

28. Anonymous, *Eine Frau in Berlin*, 138.

29. James Wakefield Burke, *The Big Rape* (Frankfurt am Main: Friedrich Rudl Verleger Union, 1951), 145, 197. The similarities between Lilo and the Anonyma of *A Woman in Berlin*, first published three years later, are striking and worth further study.

30. Consider the contentious discussions surrounding Helke Sander's film *BeFreier und Befreite*, which explicitly claimed to "break the silence" around Soviet rapes of German women. On the 1990s debates, see the special issue of *October* 72 (Spring 1995) on "Berlin 1945: War and Rape, 'Liberators Take Liberties,'" particularly Grossmann, "A Question of Silence," 43–63.

31. *Berliner Zeitung* 1:10 (May 30, 1945): 2.

32. Lew Kopelow, *Aufbewahren für alle Zeit*,with Afterword by Heinrich Böll (Munich: DTV, 1979, first published in Russian, 1975), 19, 51, 137.

33. According to the West Berlin women's magazine *sie*: 45 (Oct. 13, 1946): 3, women outnumbered male voters 16 to 10.

34. Deutscher, *The Observer*, Oct. 13, 1946, in *Reportagen*, 187. The communist Socialist Unity Party (SED) received only 19.8%.of the vote. See Donna Harsch, "Approach/Avoidance: Communists and Women in East Germany, 1945–9," *Social History* 25:2 (May 2000): 156–82, and in general, among many sources, Naimark, *Russians in Germany*, 119–21.

35. I borrow the term "remasculinization" from Robert Moeller; he refers to Susan Jeffords, *The Remasculinization of America: Gender and the Vietnam War* (Bloomington: University of Indiana Press, 1989).

36. See, for example, LAB Rep 2651/2/184/1, report by Erna Kadzloch.

37. Frank Howley, *Berlin Command* (New York: Putnam, 1950), 65–66.

38. *Six Month Report*, Jan. 4–July 3, 1946 (U.S. Army Military Government, Report to the Commanding General U.S. Headquarters Berlin District), 8.

39. *Six Month Report*, 8. By 1950, with the Cold War in full swing, Frank Howley, who had been the American commander in Berlin, had changed his relatively benign bemused view of the "jolly" Soviets, asserting that, "we know now—or should know—that we were hopelessly naive." Howley, *Berlin Command*, 11.

40. Bill Downs, CBS and *Newsweek* correspondent, *Newsweek* Apr. 16, 1945, 62.

41. James McGovern, *Fräulein* (New York: Crown, 1956), 79. Here, too, similarities to *The Big Rape* and Anonyma's *Woman in Berlin* are worth investigating. See also the 1958 film, directed by Henry Koster for 20th Century Fox, starring Dana Wynter and Mel Ferrer.

42. John J. Maginnis, *Military Government Journal: Normandy to Berlin*, ed. Robert A. Hart (Amherst: University of Massachusetts Press, 1971), Sept. 6, 1945, 294.

43. See, for example, William L. Shirer, *End of a Berlin Diary* (New York: Knopf, 1947), 148.

44. William E. Griffith, "Denazification Revisited," in *America and the Shaping of German Society 1945–1955*, ed. Michael Ermarth (Providence. R.I.: Berg, 1993), 155. On American sexual violence in Bavaria, see Heide Fehrenbach, *Race After Hitler: Black Occupation Children in Postwar Germany and America* (Princeton, N.J.: Princeton University Press), 54–55.

45. Bud Hutton and Andy Rooney, *Conquerors' Peace. A Report to the American Stockholders* (Garden City, N.Y.: Doubleday, 1947), 67.

46. Harold Zink, *The United States in Germany, 1944–1955* (Princeton, N.J.: Van Nostrand, 1957), 138. Among numerous contemporary sources, see also Julian Bach, Jr., *America's Germany. An Account of the Occupation* (New York: Random House, 1946), especially "GIs Between the Sheets," 71–83.

47. Kay Boyle, "Summer Evening," in *Fifty Short Stories*, ed. Kay Boyle (New York: New Directions, 1992), 405–6 (first published in *New Yorker*, June 25, 1949).

48. Thomas Berger, *Crazy in Berlin* (New York: Ballantine, 1958), 6, 236, 405.

49. Harold Zink, *American Military Government in Germany* (New York: Macmillan, 1947) 173; Meyer Levin, *In Search: An Autobiography* (New York: Horizon, 1950), 179. For a recent fictionalization, see Joseph Kanon, *The Good German: A Novel* (New York: Henry Holt, 2001).

50. McGovern, *Fräulein*, 118.

51. David Davidson, *The Steeper Cliff* (New York: Random House, 1947), 63, 33.

52. Bach, *America's Germany*, 71–72, 75.

53. Saul K. Padover, "Why Americans Like German Women," *The American Mercury* 63:273 (Sept. 1946): 354–357.

54. Drew Middleton, *Where Has Last July Gone? Memoirs* (New York: Quadrangle, 1973), 148.

55. Judy Barden, "Candy-Bar Romance—Women of Germany," in *This Is Germany*, ed. Arthur Settel (New York: William Sloane, 1950), 164–65.

56. See Cedric Belfrage, *Seeds of Destruction: The Truth About the US Occupation of Germany* (New York: Cameron & Kahn, 1954), 67–68.

57. "Fahrt durch Berlin. Aus einem Brief von Master Sgt Charles Gregor, *Aufbau* (Aug. 17, 1945): 32.

58. Moses Moskowitz, "The Germans and the Jews: Postwar Report: The Enigma of German Irresponsibility," *Commentary* 2 (1946): 7.

59. Knef, *Gift Horse*, 120–23. The marriage did not last.

60. William Gardner Smith, *Last of the Conquerors* (New York: Farrar, Straus & Co., 1948), 35, 44, 57, 67–68. On Smith, see also Fehrenbach, *Race After Hitler*, 35–39, and Petra Goedde, *GIs and Germans: Culture, Gender, and Foreign Relations 1945–1949* (New Haven, Conn.: Yale University Press, 2003), 109–12.

61. Riess, *Berlin Berlin*, 60, 59. See also Hilde Thurnwald, *Gegenwartsprobleme Berliner Familien: Eine soziologische Untersuchung an 498 Familien* (Berlin: Weidman, 1948), 146.

62. Burke, *Big Rape*, 258.
63. McGovern, *Fräulein*, 129.
64. Burke, *Big Rape*, 10, 259.
65. Ursula von Kardorff, *Berliner Aufzeichnungen aus den Jahren 1942 bis 1945*, rev. ed. (Munich: Bilderstein, 1962), 240.

Chapter 9. War as History, Humanity in Violence: Women, Men, and Memories of 1971, East Pakistan/Bangladesh

1. All names in this chapter are pseudonyms to protect interview subjects' identity.
2. My discussions with Khuku spanned the period from February to October 2001.
3. The estimated number of rape victims varies. Bangladesh claims two hundred thousand women were raped, while Pakistan says this is an exaggeration. The real problem I am concerned with is not the question of numbers or who raped whom but that the state had sanctioned violence in the war. The subject of sexual violence in 1971 continues to haunt feminist scholars in South Asia, but no thorough investigation has yet been undertaken. The archive of the Red Cross International in Geneva is a rich source, but the 1971 papers have not yet been declassified.
4. The term *Bihari* is used in Bangladesh to refer to a variety of Urdu-speaking people who emigrated from India to East Pakistan in 1947.
5. Biharis and Bengalis started attacking each other on March 3 in Mymensingh, in central East Pakistan, and Chittagong, in the southeast. Visual and documentary evidences of the ethnic massacres are available in the International Committee of the Red Cross (ICRC) library in Geneva. The Mymensingh and Chittagong massacres, however, are rarely spoken about in present-day Bangladesh.
6. In a later section in the chapter I discuss the making and neglect of *birangonas* in Bangladesh.
7. Of the 92,000 taken as prisoners to India, 52,000 were soldiers and the remaining 40,000 were civilians, including 3,600 women and children. These numbers are recorded by the International Review of the ICRC, 1972, Geneva.
8. Lahore, Pakistan, Dec. 14, 2004.
9. There is a growing scholarly interest toward understanding Muslim views on ethics, rights, and morality. See Lenn Goodman, *Islamic Humanism* (New York: Oxford University Press, 2003); Abdullahi Ahmed An-Na'im, "A Kinder, Gentler Islam," *Transition* 52 (1991): 4–16; Robert C. Joansen, "Radical Islam and Nonviolence: A Case Study of Religious Empowerment and Constraint among Pakhtuns," *Journal of Peace Research* 34 (1997): 53–71; Irene Oh, *The Rights of God: Islam, Human Rights, and Comparative Ethics* (Washington, D.C.: Georgetown University Press, 2007); Tony Davies, *Humanism: The New Critical Idiom*, 2nd ed. (London: Routledge, 2008).
10. Veena Das argues that although the circumstances and conditions of violence may become known, the trauma remains unanalyzed. See Das, *Critical Events: An Anthropological Perspective on Contemporary India* (Delhi: Oxford University

Press, 1995), and "The Act of Witnessing: Violence, Poisonous Knowledge and Subjectivity," in *Violence and Subjectivity*, ed. Veena Das, Arthur Kleinman, Mamphela Ramphale, and Pamela Reynolds (Berkeley: University of California Press, 2000), 205–25.

11. Cathy Caruth has looked closely at the gaps between traumatic experience and speech to understand the inability of speech of Holocaust victims who create their silent narratives. See Caruth, *Unclaimed Experiences: Trauma, Narrative, and History* (Baltimore: Johns Hopkins University Press, 1996).

12. Ashis Nandy, "History's Forgotten Doubles," *History and Theory* 34 (1995): 44–66, argues that the limited method of writing history that historians of South Asia follow in keeping with the western model is a totalizing discourse disenfranchising and oppressing people who do not organize the memory of the past in those terms. He has called on South Asian historians to search for alternative ways of telling people's experiences on their terms.

13. For some excellent reading on the challenges and potential of an oral history of violence, see Jean Herzfeld, *Machete Season: The Killers of Rwanda Speak* (New York: Farrar, Straus and Giroux, 2005); Mahmood Mamdani, *When Victims Become Killers: Colonialism, Nativism, and Genocide in Rwanda* (Princeton, N.J.: Princeton University Press, 2001); Alistair Thomson, "Fifty Years: An International Perspective on Oral History," *American Historical Review* 85 (1998): 581–95.

14. Gitta Sereny, *Into That Darkness: An Examination of Conscience* (New York: Vintage Books, 1983); Ritu Menon and Kamla Bhasin, *Borders and Boundaries: Women in India's Partition* (New Brunswick, N.J.: Rutgers University Press, 1998); Urvashi Butalia, *The Other Side of Silence: Voices from the Partition of India* (originally published in 1998; Durham, N.C.: Duke University Press, 2000); Simon Redlich, *Together and Apart in Brzenzany: Poles, Jews and Ukrainians, 1919–1945* (Bloomington: Indiana University Press, 2002).

15. See essays in Daphne Patai and Sherna Gluck, eds., *Women's Words: Feminist Practice of Doing History* (New York: Routledge, 1991). Also, for an ethnography of the interaction and impact of fieldwork on research method and outcome see Ruth Behar, *Translated Women: Crossing the Border with Esperanza's Story* (Boston: Beacon Press, 1993); Lila Abu-Lughod, *Writing Women's World: Bedouin Stories* (Berkeley: University of California Press, 1993).

16. Susan Brison, *Aftermath: Violence and the Remaking of Self* (Princeton, N.J.: Princeton University Press, 2002).

17. Igna Clandinnen, *Reading the Holocaust* (Cambridge: Cambridge University Press, 1999).

18. For a history of "otherizing" leading to the partition of 1947 see Gyan Pandey, "The Prose of Otherness," in *Subaltern Studies VIII: Essays in Honour of Ranajit Guha*, ed. David Arnold and David Hardiman (Delhi: Oxford University Press, 1994), 188–221.

19. Jinnah's speech has been reproduced in many sites. I have consulted Stephen Hays, *Sources of Indian Tradition*, vol. 2, *Modern India and Pakistan*, 2nd ed. (New York: Columbia University Press, 1988).

20. For an extended reading of the changes that took place within the army leading to the Islamization of its image, see Husain Haqqani, *Pakistan: Between*

Mosque and Military (Washington, D.C.: Carnegie Endowment for International Peace, 2005). For a reading of the ambivalent search for a narrative to construct an official history of Muslim Pakistan to fit evolving state agendas and politics, see Ayesha Jalal, "Conjuring Pakistan: History as Official Imagining," *International Journal of Middle East Studies* 8 (1974): 73–89; David Gilmartin, "Partition, Pakistan, and South Asian History: In Search of a Narrative," *Journal of Asian Studies* 57 (1998): 1068–95.

21. In present-day India, nearly 15 percent of the population are Muslims. India has one of the largest Muslim populations in the world, over 170 million.

22. See *National Assembly of Pakistan Debates*, National Archive, Islamabad, Pakistan.

23. Anthony Mascarenhas, *The Rape of Bangladesh* (New Delhi: Vikas, 1972); Richard Sisson and Leo E. Rose, *War and Secession: Pakistan, India and the Creation of Bangladesh* (Berkeley: University of California Press, 1990).

24. Ben Withaker, Ian Guest, and Rt. Hon David Ennals, *The Biharis in Bangladesh*, Minority Rights Group Report 10 (London: Amnesty International, 1975).

25. Conversations with Ashok Mitra, economic advisor to Mrs. Gandhi in 1971, Calcutta, 2005; General Lakshman Singh Lehl, who was the brigade commander in 1971 and also in the postwar reconstruction process, Delhi, 2005; and General Jacobs, who was second in command of the army operations in 1971, Delhi, 2005.

26. These numbers are provided by the Indian and Bangladeshi sources. The Pakistani sources question these numbers and say they are exaggerated.

27. Susan Brownmiller, *Against Our Will: Men, Women, and Rape* (New York: Simon and Schuster, 1975).

28. Emmanuel Levinas's discussion on the subject of ethical humanism engages the issue of responsibility to the other. See Emmanuel Levinas, *Humanism of the Other*, trans. Nidra Poller (Urbana: University of Illinois Press, 1972); Emmanuel Levinas, *Otherwise Than Being or Beyond Essence*, trans. Alphonso Lingis (The Hague: Nihhoff, 1981).

29. Patricia Yaeger, "Consuming Trauma, or, The Pleasure of Merely Circulating," *Journal X* 1.2 (1997): 226–51.

30. There is substantial literature in Bangladesh that has capitalized on the women's question.

31. See Bina D'Costa, "Coming to Terms with the Past in Bangladesh: Forming Feminist Alliance Across Borders," in *Women, Power and Justice: Global Feminist Perspectives*, vol. 1, *Politics and Activism: Ensuring the Protection of Women's Fundamental Human Rights*, ed. Luciana Ricciutelli, Angela Miles, and Margaret McFadden (London: Zed, 2005), 227–47, on war children.

32. Conversation in northern Bangladesh on Feb. 17, 2001.

33. Conversation in her village home at the border of India and Bangladesh on Feb. 22, 2001.

34. Conversation in Dhaka, Bangladesh, Oct. 2001.

35. Laila's story forcefully reminded me of a parallel narrative in Primo Levi's *The Drowned and the Saved*, trans. Raymond Rosenthal (New York: Vintage, 1989), 38.

36. My conversation with Sakeena was in the public space of a refugee camp in northern Bangladesh. Sakeena whispered her narrative in my ears. It was one of the most important conversations I had in Bangladesh and had a deep impact in shaping my research questions.

37. Conversation in Chittagong, Bangladesh on Nov. 14, 2001.

38. This sentiment likewise was expressed by the Pakistani army.

39. General Lakshmann Singh Lehl in Delhi, 2005.

40. Conversation with a general in Rawalpindi, Pakistan, 2004.

41. Conversation in Lahore, Pakistan, July 2004.

42. Conversation in Lahore, Pakistan, Dec. 2004.

43. Levinas, *Humanism of the Other*, xxix.

44. See Emmanuel Levinas, *Totality and Infinity*, trans. Alphonso Lingis (Pittsburgh: Duquesne University Press, 1969); and *Otherwise Than Being*.

45. For this chapter, I consulted Book One, trans. Jawid Mojaddedi (New York: Oxford University Press, 2004).

Chapter 10. The Theory and Practice of Female Immunity in the Medieval West

1. *The Tree of Battles of Honoré Bonet*, ed. and trans. G. W. Coupland (Liverpool: Liverpool University Press, 1949).

2. R. H. Bainton, *Christian Attitudes Toward War and Peace* (Nashville, Tenn.: Abingdon Press, 1960), 81.

3. Frederick H. Russell, *The Just War in the Middle Ages* (Cambridge: Cambridge University Press, 1975), 2.

4. *The Black Book of the Admiralty*, ed. T. W. Twiss, 1, Rolls Series (London: Longman, 1871), 453.

5. James A. Brundage, *Law, Sex and Christian Society in Medieval Europe* (Chicago: University of Chicago Press, 1987), 107.

6. Brundage, *Law, Sex and Christian Society*, 250.

7. Brundage, *Law, Sex and Christian Society*, 107.

8. Brundage, *Law, Sex and Christian Society*, 397

9. *De officiis*, I/XI, cited in Paul Christopher, *The Ethics of War and Peace: An Introduction to Legal and Moral Issues*, 2nd ed. (Englewood Cliffs, N.J.: Prentice Hall International, 1999), 14.

10. Russell, *Just War*, 7.

11. *Vegetius: Epitome of Military Science*, ed. and trans. N. P. Milner (Liverpool: Liverpool University Press, 1993).

12. Valerius Maximus, "Valerii Maximi Dictorum et Factorum Memorabilium," in *Collection des auteurs latins*, ed. D. Nisard (Paris: Dubochet, 1851), 603; Anne Curry, "Sex and the Soldier in Lancastrian Normandy, 1415–1450," *Reading Medieval Studies* 14 (1988): 20–21.

13. John Finnis, "The Ethics of War and Peace in the Catholic Natural Law Tradition," in *The Ethics of War and Peace: Religious and Secular Perspectives*, ed. Terry Nardin (Princeton, N.J.: Princeton University Press, 1996), 27.

14. John T. McNeill and Helena M. Garner, eds., *Medieval Handbooks of Penance* (New York: Columbia University Press, 1938), 135–39; T. M. Charles-Edwards, *Early Christian Ireland* (Cambridge: Cambridge University Press, 2000), 70, 281, 566–69.

15. Penitential of Cummean ca. 650: if a man deflowers a vowed virgin and causes her to have a child; or if a layman turns to fornication and the shedding of blood, he must pay three years penance without arms (McNeill and Garner, eds., *Medieval Handbooks*, 104–5).

16. See, for instance, those ascribed to Bede (McNeill and Garner, eds., *Medieval Handbooks*, 224).

17. Hermann J. Schmitz, *Die Bussbücher und das Kanonische Bussverfahren nach handschriftlichen* (Dusseldorf, 1898), 225.

18. J-P. Migne, ed., *Patrologiae*, 1, 1018–20.

19. *Monumenta Germaniae Historica. Legum Sectio II. Capitula Regum Francorum*, vol. 2 (Hannover, 1890), 94.

20. Thomas Head and Richard Landes, eds., *The Peace of God: Social Violence and Religious Response in France Around the Year 1000* (Ithaca, N.Y.: Cornell University Press, 1992).

21. Ludwig Huberti, *Studien zur Rechtsgeschichte der Gottesfrieden und Landfrieden*, I (Ausbach, 1892), 314–15.

22. Bainton, *Christian Attitudes*, 110.

23. Russell, *Just War*, 70.

24. Thomas Aquinas, *St. Thomas Aquinas: Political Writings*, ed. R. W. Dyson (Cambridge: Cambridge University Press, 2002), 239–47.

25. Russell, *Just War*, 275.

26. Russell, *Just War*, 187.

27. H. J. Hewitt, *The Organization of War Under Edward III* (Manchester: Manchester University Press, 1966), 97, 123.

28. F. Taylor and J. S. Roskell, eds., *Gesta Henrici Quinti* (Oxford: Clarendon Press, 1975); T. Hearne, ed., T. Livii Foro-Juliensis, *Vita Henrici Quinti* (Oxford, 1716), 33.

29. *Black Book*, 1, 282, 460.

30. P. L. Hughes, ed., *Tudor Royal Proclamations*, vol. 1 (New Haven: Yale University Press, 1964), 14.

31. *Black Book*, 1, 468.

32. Cited in Yvonne Friedman, *Encounter Between Enemies. Captivity and Ransom in the Latin Kingdom of Jerusalem* (Leiden: Brill, 2002), 174.

33. Philippe Contamine, "The Soldier in Late Medieval Urban Society," *French History* 8 (1994): 1–13.

34. T. D. Hardy, ed., *Rotuli Normanniae* (London: Record Commission, 1835), 366.

35. Cited in Richard Kaeuper, *Chivalry and Violence in Medieval Europe* (Oxford: Oxford University Press, 1999), 226.

36. Cited in Kaeuper, *Chivalry and Violence in Medieval Europe*, 228–29.

37. Russell, *Just War*, 9, 284. Deuteronomy 20:10, 12–15.

38. Matthew Strickland, *War and Chivalry. The Conduct and Perception of War in England and Normandy 1066–1217* (Cambridge: Cambridge University Press, 1996), 35, 222.

39. Maurice H. Keen, *The Laws of War in the Late Middle Ages* (London: Routledge and Kegan Paul, 1965), 121–22.

40. Peter F. Ainsworth and George T. Diller, eds., *Froissart, Chroniques, Livres 1 et II* (Paris: Le Livre de Poche, 2001), 551–52.

41. John Barnie, *War in Medieval Society* (London: Weidenfield and Nicholson, 1974), 71, n. 43.

42. Taylor and Roskell, eds., *Gesta*, 55.

43. G. Bacquet, *Azincourt* (Bellegrade: Les Presses de la Scop-Sadag, 1977), 91–92.

44. Deuteronomy 21:10–14.

45. Angeliki E. Laiou, "Sex, Consent and Coercion in Byzantium," in *Consent and Coercion to Sex and Marriage in Ancient and Medieval Societies*, ed. Angeliki E. Laiou (Washington, D.C.: Dumbarton Oaks Research Library, 1993), 187.

46. Diana C. Moses, "Lucretia and the Validity of Coerced Consent," in Laiou ed., *Consent and Coercion*, 57. In the Jewish tradition it was stipulated that, in capture, the woman's freedom took precedence over that of the male: Friedman, *Encounter*, 178.

47. McNeill and Garner, eds., *Medieval Handbooks*, 210.

48. Friedman, *Encounter*, 168.

49. Friedman, *Encounter*, 170.

50. Francesco Gabrieli, *Arab Historians of the Crusades* (London: Routledge and Kegan Paul, 1969), 163.

51. Friedman, *Encounter*, 181.

52. Friedman, *Encounter*, 182.

53. Corinne Saunders, "Women and Warfare in Medieval English Writing," in *Writing War: Medieval Literary Responses to Warfare*, ed. Corinne Saunders, Françoise Le Saux, and Neil Thomas (Cambridge: D. S. Brewer, 2004), 187–212.

54. Cited in Saunders, "Women and Warfare," 194.

55. Rosemary Horrox, *Parliament Rolls of Medieval England XIII* (Woodbridge, UK: Boydell & Brewer, 2005), 12.

56. Cited in Michael Prestwich, *Armies and Warfare in the Middle Ages: The English Experience* (New Haven: Yale University Press, 1996), 156.

Chapter 11. Law, War, and Women in Seventeenth-Century England

1. See Julius Goebel, *Felony and Misdemeanour. A Study in the History of Criminal Law* (Philadelphia: University of Pennsylvania Press, 1976), passim. This is a reprint of *Felony and Misdemeanour. A Study in the History of English Criminal Procedure*, vol. 1 (New York: 1937).

2. William Shakespeare, *Henry V*, III.4, 8–27.

3. B. Donagan, "Halcyon Days and the Literature of War: England's military education before 1642," *Past and Present* 147 (1995): 74–78.

4. An earlier, embryonic set of articles survives. Issued by Richard I in 1189 for troops going by sea to Jerusalem, it was brief and brutal. A soldier who killed a man at sea, for example, was to be "bound to the dead man, and thrown into the sea"; a thief was to have his head shaved, boiling pitch poured on it, and "down and feathers shaken over it," after which he was to be set ashore at the next landfall. J. H. L., "Articles of War," *Journal of the Society for Army Historical Research* 5 (1926): 202–3.

5. "Ordinances for Warre," in Francis Grose, *The Antiquities of England and Wales*, 8 vols. (London: [1787]–97), 1.33, "For Holy Church."

6. Grose, *Antiquities*, 1.42–43; the article included a provision for pardon.

7. *Hereafter Ensue certayne Statutes* (London: 1513), A3, no. [I]; B1, no. [XI]. A set of articles from 1493 appears to be very similar to those of 1513, "Huth fragment," Henry E. Huntington Library.

8. *Hereafter Ensue*, C3, no. [XXXVI]; the provision for pardon remains.

9. *Hereafter Ensue*, B3, no. [XVI]; Grose, *Antiquities*, 1.48, 50–51.

10. It will be remembered that in *Henry V* Bardolph is hanged for stealing a pyx—"Exeter hath given the doom of death / For pax of little price," III.6 and IV.7.

11. The importance of ransom and spoils had led to extremely detailed and complex rules for their division that took up a large portion of the articles of war. By 1640 this had become a very minor component of English articles.

12. The royalists's earliest articles omitted both sexual crimes and murder, but they were shortly reinstated as capital crimes.

13. *Lawes and Ordinances of Warre Established for the Better Conduct of the Army by . . . the Earle of Essex* (London: 1642), B2–[B2v.]; *Military Orders and Articles Established by His Maiesty, for the Better Ordering and Government of His Maiesties Army* (Oxford: 1643), 18.

14. *Lawes and Ordinances . . . Essex*, 20, "Burning and Wasting."

15. *Mercurius Rusticus* (n.p. 1646), 69.

16. *Mercurius Rusticus*, 9–10, 66–67, 75, 145, 159, 163, 165–66.

17. *Parliaments Post*, no. 6 (London: June 10–17, 1645), 4.

18. Jack Binns, ed., *The Memoirs and Memorials of Sir Hugh Cholmley of Whitby 1600–1657*, Yorkshire Archaeological Society, Record Series, 153 (1997–98), 117; B. Donagan, "Family and Misfortune in the English Civil War: The Sad Case of Edward Pitt," *Huntington Library Quarterly* 61 (1998): 223–40.

19. "A Short Memoriall of the Northern Actions," Bodleian Library, MSS Fairfax vol. 36, ff. 9v.–10; J. R. Phillips, *Memoirs of the Civil War in Wales and the Marches 1642–1649*, 2 vols. (London: Longman's, Green, 1874), 2.174–75; *A Diary of the Siege of Colchester by the Forces Under the Command of His Excellency the Lord General Fairfax* (London: 1648). In the anxious summer of 1648 the House of Commons ordered the guard to "keep the clamorous Women from coming up the stairs" and to prevent them from "clamoring in Westminster Hall," *Journals of the House of Commons*, 5.599.

20. John Walter, *Understanding Popular Violence in the English Revolution. The Colchester Plunderers* (Cambridge: Cambridge University Press, 1999), 25, 37.

21. HMC, *Twelfth Report, Appendix. Part IX* (London: 1891), "Beaufort MSS," 27–28. The absence of plunder that so infuriated the soldiers was explained by the

fact that the house had already been gutted in an incident of mob violence early in the war. See Walter, *Understanding Popular Violence*, passim.

22. Edward Hyde, Earl of Clarendon, *The History of the Rebellion and Civil Wars in England*, 3 vols. (Oxford: 1702–4), 2.509.

23. *Parliaments Post*, no. 6 (June 10–17, 1645), 8; *Kingdomes Weekly Intelligencer*, no. 104 (London: June 10–17, 1645), 837; no. 105 (June 17–24, 1645), 841, 844, for exculpatory reminders of past royalist cruelties and a report of a gang rape of the daughter of a fellow royalist by Irish soldiers; *Exchange Intelligencer*, no. 5 (June 11–18, 1645), [33].

24. John Vicars, "The Burning-Bush Not Consumed," in *Magnalia Dei Anglicana: or, Englands Parliamentary Chronicle* (London: 1646), 163–64.

25. Vicars, *Magnalia Dei Anglicana*, 163–64; [G. Bishop], *A More Particular and Exact Relation of the Victory Obtained by the Parliaments Forces Under the Command of Sir Thomas Fairfax* (London: 1645), 4: "many [women] taken, which are every one wounded"; *An Ordinance of the Lords and Commons Assembled in Parliament for . . . a Day of Thanksgiving for the Great Victory . . . Near Knasby* (London: 1645), 4.

26. John Adair, ed., "The Court Martial Papers of Sir William Waller's Army, 1644," *J.S.A.H.R.*, 44 (1966): 205–26.

27. Godfrey Davies, ed., "Dundee court-martial records 1651," in *Miscellany of the Scottish Historical Society*, 2nd ser. 19 (1919): 3–67 (in the third volume of the *Miscellany*). The original record is in Worcester College, Oxford, Clarke MSS, vol. 21, ff. 1–86; Davies printed about five-sixths of the whole; some of his transcriptions require revision. I am grateful to the College for permission to use these manuscripts.

28. Worcester College, Clarke MSS, vol. 21, ff. 32–33 (for Clarke's original shorthand version, see ibid., vol. 20 ff. 17r–v). Davies omitted this case, giving only the verdict; Clarke's transcription both censored and slightly expanded on his original shorthand version. I am grateful to Frances Henderson for her transcription from the shorthand.

29. *Laws and Ordinances of Warre, Established for the Better Conduct of the Army*, (London: 1643), [B3].

30. Worcester College, Clarke MSS, vol. 21, ff. 16–16v. Davies also omitted this case.

31. See the discussion in Michael Braddick, *God's Fury, England's Fire: A New History of the English Civil Wars* (London: Allan Lane, 2008), 428–35.

Chapter 12. "Unlawfully and Against Her Consent": Sexual Violence and the Military During the American Civil War

Portions of this chapter have been published previously as "Physical Abuse and Rough Handling: Race, Gender and Sexual Justice in the Occupied South," in *Occupied Women: Gender, Military Occupation, and the American Civil War*, ed. LeeAnn Whites and Alecia P. Long (Baton Rouge: Louisiana State University Press, 2009), 49–64.

1. The description of this event is from the testimony of witnesses in the trial of Private John Callahan, Co. H, Second New Jersey Cavalry, Case File NN1740 [Mf. M1523, roll no. 1], Records of the Judge Advocate General (Army), R.G. 153, National Archives and Records Administration, Washington, D.C. Hereafter these records will be cited as "[case number], R.G. 153, NARA." A "companion" is a small purse that women wore around their waists and under their clothing.

2. For a discussion of the occurrence of sexual violence in the American Civil War, see Michael Fellman, *Inside War: The Guerrilla Conflict in Missouri During the American Civil War* (New York: Oxford University Press, 1989), 207; Bell I. Wiley, *The Life of Billy Yank: The Common Soldier of the Union* (Baton Rouge: Louisiana State University Press, 2008; originally published in 1952), 205; Joseph Glatthaar, *Forged in Battle: The Civil War Alliance of Black Soldiers and White Officers* (Baton Rouge: Louisiana State University Press, 1990), 118–19. Susan Brownmiller, in *Against Our Will: Men, Women, and Rape* (New York: Fawcett Columbine, 1975), 88, has noted that, while some historians call the Civil War a "low-rape war," she stands "ready to be corrected by some later historians." George Rable notes that "rapes did occur" but points also to the paucity of research devoted to illuminate this subject (p. 416). George Rable, *Civil Wars: Women and the Crisis of Southern Nationalism* (Chicago: University of Illinois Press, 1989), 161, and n. 25, p. 341. Victoria E. Bynum observes that "rape charges were unlikely to reach a courtroom" because of "deeply embedded notions of shame and honor," that "encouraged private vengeance rather than public justice." Victoria E. Bynum *Unruly Women: The Politics of Sexual Control in the Old South* (Chapel Hill: University of North Carolina Press, 1992), 118. Drew Faust maintains that "white females, particularly those of the elite, were rarely victims of rape by invading soldiers" except in the case of guerrillas and other marauders who "were far more likely to challenge the usages of 'civilized warfare.'" Black women, she notes, "served as the unfortunate sexual spoils when Union soldiers asserted their traditional right of military conquest." Drew Faust, *Mothers of Invention: Women of the Slaveholding South in the American Civil War* (Chapel Hill: University of North Carolina Press, 1996), 200; see also n. 6, p. 296. These circumspect references have prompted Ervin L. Jordan, Jr., to call rape "the silent subject of the Civil War . . . alluded to in letters, memoirs, and reports in a cloud of euphemisms." See Ervin L. Jordan, Jr., "Mirrors Beyond Memories: Afro-Virginians and the Civil War," in *New Perspectives on the Civil War,* ed. John Y. Simon and Michael E. Stevens (Madison, Wisc.: Madison House, 1998), 158. See also Jordan, "Sleeping with the Enemy: Sex, Black Women, and the Civil War," *Western Journal of Black Studies* 18, no. 2 (Summer 1994): 55–63. Thomas P. Lowry has published two books that contain detailed descriptions of sexual conduct by Civil War soldiers: *The Story the Soldiers Wouldn't Tell: Sex in the Civil War* (Mechanicsburg, Pa.: Stackpole Press, 1994) and *Sexual Misbehavior in the Civil War: A Compendium* (n.p.: Exlibris Corp., 2006). Martha Hodes's study of wartime and postwar sexual relations between the races is perhaps the most comprehensive study thus far. Martha Hodes, *White Women, Black Men: Illicit Sex in the Nineteenth-Century South* (New Haven, Conn.: Yale University Press, 1997).

3. The Sexual Justice in the American Civil War Project is the first comprehensive study of the response of the Union military to instances of sexual assault

against women and girls by soldiers and civilians during the American Civil War (1861–65). Begun in June of 1998, this research represents the work of Charles F. Ritter and E. Susan Barber, historians on the faculty at the College of Notre Dame of Maryland. At present, the Sexual Justice in the American Civil War Project contains the trial transcripts of more than four hunded courts-martial and military commissions. We, the researchers, are grateful to the College of Notre Dame of Maryland and the Harry Frank Guggenheim Foundation for their generous support of our research.

4. See sec. 30 of "An Act for Enrolling and calling out the national forces, and for other Purposes," 37th Cong., 3rd Sess., Mar. 3, 1863, ch. 75, *12 Statutes at Large*, 731 at 763 (hereafter Enrollment Act of 1863).

5. In her examination of rape and mass rape in the twentieth century and its use as an instrument of war, Rhonda Copelon has suggested that militaries often neither acknowledged that rapes occurred nor prosecuted soldiers for such offenses. Our research indicates that such was not the case in the American Civil War. Rhonda Copelon, "Surfacing Gender: Reconceptualizing Crimes Against Women in Time of War," in *The Women & War Reader*, ed. Lois Ann Lorentzen and Jennifer Turpin (New York: New York University Press, 1998), 63–80, and "Gendered War Crimes: Reconceptualizing Rape in Time of War," in *Women's Rights, Human Rights: International Feminist Perspectives*, ed. Julie Peters and Andrea Wolper (New York: Routledge, 1995), 197–214.

6. Articles of War 1806, Art. 33, in John F. Callan, *The Military Law of the United States* (Philadelphia: George W. Child, 1863), 181.

7. General Order no. 20, sec. 2, Feb. 19, 1847, Records of the Adjutant General's Office, Mexican War, Orders, vol. 9, R.G. 94, NARA. The order is inserted at the back of vol. 9. See also Justin H. Smith, *The War with Mexico*, 2 vols. (New York: Macmillan, 1919), 2: 455–56.

8. Lieutenant Colonel Jody Prescott and Major Joanne Eldridge, "Military Commissions, Past and Future," *Military Review* (Mar.–Apr. 2003): 42–43.

9. Enrollment Act of 1863, 731 at 763. See, for example, Articles of War, 1874, Art. 58. William Winthrop, *An Abridgement of Military Law* (Washington, D.C.: W. H. Morrison, 1887), 350, 361. The criminalization of rape appeared in the 1916 revision of the Articles of War as Art. 92. See Eugene Wambaugh, *Guide to the Articles of War* (Cambridge, Mass.: Harvard University Press, 1917), 33.

10. *The War of the Rebellion: A Compilation of the Official Records of the Union and Confederate Armies* (Washington, D.C.: U.S. Government Printing Office, 1899), ser. III, vol. 3, 148 (hereafter *O.R.*).

11. *O.R.*, ser. III, vol. 3, 153.

12. D. T. Corbin, comp., *Digest of Opinions of the Judge Advocate General of the Army* (Washington, D.C.: U.S. Government Printing Office, 1866), 251.

13. Trial of Private Richard Mitchelson, Co. A, Sixteenth U.S.C.T., NN3037, R.G. 153, NARA.

14. Trial of Private Henry Duncan, Co. L, Fourth U.S. Colored Heavy Artillery, MM2547, R.G. 153, NARA.

15. Trial of Private John Lewis, Co. C, Sixteenth U.S.C.T., MM2774, R.G. 153, NARA.

16. Trial of Private Charles C. Hunter, Co. I, Seventh Kentucky Cavalry, NN1921, R.G. 153, NARA.

17. Trial of Private Thomas Johnson, Co. D, Second New Jersey Cavalry, NN1740, R.G. 153, NARA.

18. Trial of Private John Callahan, Co. H, Second New Jersey Cavalry, and Private Jacob Snover, Co. M, Second New Jersey Cavalry, NN1740, R.G. 153, NARA.

19. Trial of Thomas Mitchell, Company E, New York Engineers, OO886, R.G. 153, NARA.

20. Trial of Thomas R. Dawson, MM792, R.G. 153, NARA; Letter from George H. Patch to his parents, April 28 [1864], Stevensburg, Virginia, in George H. Patch Papers, Mss. 2P2713b, Virginia Historical Society, Richmond, Virginia. See also William Corby, C.S.C., *Memoirs of a Chaplain's Life: Three Years with the Irish Brigade in the Army of the Potomac* (New York: Fordham University Press, 1912), 220–28.

21. See Dorothy Stetson, *Women's Rights in the USA: Policy Debates and Gender Roles*, 2nd ed. (New York: Garland, 1997), 307–9.

22. William Blackstone, *Blackstone's Commentaries*, book IV, chap. XV, 210, ed. George Starswood, 2 vols. (Philadelphia: George W. Childs, 1862), 2: 474.

23. Grace Barnes was vaginally penetrated with sticks and pins by her eight attackers. Trial of James Halon, LL2552, R.G. 153, NARA. The homosexual cases involved accusations that soldiers fondled, danced, or engaged in sexual behavior with other men in their company. See Trial of James Hickey, MM2611, Trial of Philip Dickenhoff, LL18; also Judge Advocate General Joseph Holt to Abraham Lincoln regarding the court-martial of John H. Samon, n.d., in Letters Sent by the Judge Advocate General, U.S. Army, vol. 13, p. 382. All these can be found in R.G. 153, NARA.

24. Act of Congress, Mar. 3, 1863, sec. 30. *Revised United States Army Regulations of 1861 with an Appendix* (Philadelphia: George W. Childs, 1863), 541.

25. *The Revised Statutes of Louisiana*, comp. Ulrich B. Philips. (New Orleans: John Claiborne, 1856), 50–136.

26. *A Compilation of the Penal Code of the State of Georgia*, ed. Howell Cobb (Macon, Ga.: J. M. Boordman, 1850), 35, 85.

27. Act of May 23, 1833, chap. 75, "An Act to amend the criminal laws of this state for the trial of slaves," *Public Acts of the State of Tennessee . . . for the Year 1822*, p. 94, in *State Slavery Statutes* (microfiche edition) (Frederick, Md.: University Publications of America, 1989) The statute also provided that if the defendant were a slave, the owner had the right to appeal the conviction to the county circuit court where the trial was held.

28. Act of Feb. 5, 1842, chap. 193, "An Act to amend the act of 1835," chap. 75, *Public Acts of the State of Tennessee . . . for the Years 1841–42*, p. 231, in *State Slavery Statutes*.

29. Trial of James E. Lee, corporal, First Alabama Cavalry, USA, OO1086, R.G. 153, NARA.

30. Trial of Samuel D. Fitch, captain, Co. C., Sixth U.S. Colored Cavalry, OO789, R.G.153, NARA. Trial of Captain Jacob K. Schuck, Co. E, Fifth U.S. Colored Cavalry, OO1185, R.G. 153, NARA.

31. Trial of Alfred A. Bartholomew, LL2655, and Edward Hays, File E18, no. 31, both in R.G. 153, NARA.

32. Trial of John F. Herd, NN2140, R.G. 153, NARA.

33. Act of Feb. 28, 1852, chap. 174,"An Act to amend the criminal laws of this state," sec. 2, *Public Acts of the State of Tennessee . . . for the Years 1851–52*, p. 251, in *State Slavery Statutes*.

34. *Revised Statutes of Louisiana*, 50, 136; *The Revised Code of the State Law of the State of Mississippi* (Jackson, Miss: E. Barksdale, 1857), 248, 608; Richard H. Stanton, *The Revised Statutes of Kentucky* (Cincinnati: Robert Clark & Co., 1860), 1: 379–80; *The Code of Virginia, Second Edition, Including Legislation to the Year 1860* (Westport, Conn.: Negro University Press, 1970). In 1893 Tennessee added a category of intercourse with females between the ages of twelve and sixteen that was punishable by three to ten years in the penitentiary unless the offense was a rape. The law provided, however, that a defendant could not be convicted on "the unsupported testimony of the female in question," where the female and male were married, where the "female's reputation for want of chastity" was established, and where the female is determined to be "a bawd, lewd, or kept female." R. T. Shannon, comp., *Annotated Code of Tennessee*, citing Tennessee statutes of 1893, chap. 129, sec. 1.

35. Trial of Corporal James E. Lee, First Alabama Cavalry, USA, OO1086, R.G. 153, NARA.

36. Trial of William L. Hilton, LL3201, R.G. 153, NARA. Hilton was sentenced to death, but his case was later overturned because of several technicalities in the trial transcript. Of these the most important was the absence of a statement that at least two-thirds of the court-martial concurred with the finding. This statement was required in cases regarding capital offenses, such as Hilton's, where a sentence of execution was fixed by the determination of guilt. Hilton was subsequently released and returned to duty.

37. Trial of Dudley O. Bravard, OO927, R.G. 153, NARA.

38. Trial of Adolph Bork, private, Company H, 183rd Ohio Volunteers, MM2407, R.G. 153, NARA. On review, Bork's sentence was mitigated to five years at hard labor.

39. General Order 109, Dec. 20, 1862, and General Order 17, Feb. 13, 1863, both in *O.R.*, ser. IV, vol. 2, pp. 248, 395.

40. For example, Jack Bunch's examination of the adjutant and inspector general's Confederate courts-martial ledgers led him to conclude that no cases of rape were prosecuted. See Jack A. Bunch, *Military Justice in the Confederate States of America* (Shippensburg, Pa.: White Mane Books, 2000), 122.

41. For example, Thomas Weatherman, Stanley Isaac, and John Duncan—all privates in the Confederate army—were charged with rape or attempted rape; J. Plantervigne, Joseph L. Crowell, E. M. Anderson, C. L. Hensley, Joseph L. Crowell, and T. J. Dunlap were tried for possible crimes of gender humiliation. However, no trial transcripts have survived. For Weatherman, see Report of Major J. M. Bassett, Seventh Military District, Northwest Missouri for month ending May 31, 1863, entry 183, box 7, folder 678; for Isaac, S.O. 30, HQ Second Corps, Army of Mississippi, entry 97; for Duncan, G.O. 136, Dept. of E. Tennessee, in General Orders, 1863, in chap. I, vol. 3, Adjutant and Inspector General's Office. For Plantervigne,

see G.O. 62, Point Coupee Artillery, entry 95; for Crowell, entry 73, Ashley Dragoons' for Anderson, G.O. 19, Ashley Dragoons, chap. II, vol. 42, p. 131; for Hensley, G.O. 63, Forty-third Tennessee Regiment, entry 95; for Crowell, G.O. 19, Ashley Dragoons, chap. II, vol. 42, p. 130, and for Dunlap, G.O. 175, entry 86, box 2. All of these can be found in R.G. 109 Records of the Confederate Government, NARA, Washington, D.C.

42. G.O. 57, HQ, Army of the Peninsula, Aug. 8, 1861, chap. II, vol. 229, R.G. 109, NARA.

43. G.F.O. 37, HQ, Army of Tennessee, near Columbia, Tennessee, Nov. 28, 1864, entry 86, box 4, R.G. 109, NARA,

44. Special Order [n.n.], HQ, Army of Kansas, Oct. 15, 1861, in chap. 2, vol. 96, R.G. 109, NARA.

45. Circular, HQ 14, 1865, in chap. II, vol. 350, p. 140, R.G. 109, NARA.

46. General Order no. 2, HQ, Departments of South Carolina, Georgia and Florida, Fifth to Seventh Military Districts, entry 73, box 3, R.G. 109, NARA.

Chapter 13. Legal Responses to World War II Sexual Violence: The Japanese Experience

1. Martha Minow, *Between Vengeance and Forgiveness: Facing History After Genocide and Mass Violence* (Boston: Beacon Press, 1998); Mark Osiel, *Mass Atrocity, Collective Memory, and the Law* (New Brunswick, N.J. Transaction Publishers, 2000); Lawrence Douglas, *The Memory of Judgment: Making Law and History in the Trials of the Holocaust* (New Haven, Conn.: Yale University Press, 2001); Eric Stover, *The Witnesses: War Crimes and the Promise of Justice in The Hague* (Philadelphia: University of Pennsylvania Press, 2005).

2. For an overview of the Allied war crimes program in the Pacific region, see Philip R. Piccigallo, *The Japanese on Trial: Allied War Crimes Operations in the East, 1945–1951* (Austin: University of Texas Press, 1979).

3. "Keihō" (Criminal Law), in *Dai roppō zensho* (The Compendium of Laws) (Tokyo: Hōbunsha, 1940), 116, 126.

4. The Marco Polo Bridge Incident, or the China Incident, refers to the armed conflict that broke out between the Chinese and Japanese forces in the outskirts of present-day Beijing on July 7, 1937. Data on courts-martial with respect to rape in China are taken from Kita Hiroaki, ed., *Jūgonen sensō gokuhi shiryōshū dai 5 kan: Tōkyō saiban Ōyama Ayao kankei shiryō* (Secret Documents of the Fifteen-Year War, vol. 5: The Tokyo Trial. Documents Related to Ōyama Ayao) (Tokyo: Fuji shuppan, 1987), 8–9, 14–15, 18–19, 22–23. For the data pertaining to courts-martial in connection to rape in the Pacific War, I relied on Utsumi Aiko, "Senji seidorei-sei to Tōkyō saiban" (Wartime Sexual Slavery and the Tokyo Trial), in VAWW-Net Japan, ed., *Nihongun seidoreisei o sabaku 2000-nen josei kokusai senpan hōtei no kiroku* (The Trial of Japanese Military Sexual Slavery. The Record of the Women's International War Crimes Tribunal in 2000) (Tokyo: Ryokufū shuppan, 2000), vol. 1, 97–98.

5. Eguchi Keiichi, *Jūgonen sensō shō shi* (A Concise History of the Fifteen-Year War) (Tokyo: Aoki shoten, 1986), 117; Kasahara Tokushi, "Chūgoku sensen ni okeru Nihongun no seihanzai: Kahokushō, Sanseishō no jirei" (Japanese Military Sexual Crimes in the Chinese Theater: Cases of Hebei and Shanxi Provinces), *Sensō sekinin kenkyū* 13 (Fall 1996): 9–10; Kasahara Tokushi, *Nankin jiken* (The Nanjing Incident) (Tokyo: Iwanami shoten, 1997); Honda Katsuichi, *The Nanjing Massacre: A Japanese Journalist Confronts Japan's National Shame* (Armonk, N.Y.: M.E. Sharpe, 1999).

6. Kasahara, "Chūgoku sensen ni okeru Nihongun no seihanzai: Kahokushō, Sanseishō no jirei"; Kasahara Tokushi, *Nankin jiken to sankō sakusen: mirai ni ikasu sensō no kioku* (The Nanjing Incident and Three-All Policy: War Memory for the Future) (Tokyo: Ōtsuki shoten, 1999); Ishida Yūji et al., eds., *Chūghoku Kahokushō ni okeru sankō sakusen: gyakusatsu no mura, Hokutan mura* (Three-All Policy in Hebei Province, China: Beituan, the Massacred Village) (Tokyo: Ōtsuki shoten, 2003).

7. Yoshimi Yoshiaki, *Jūgun ianfu* (Comfort Women) (Tokyo: Iwanami shoten, 1995); Yoshimi Yoshiaki and Hayashi Hirofumi, eds., *Kyōdō kenkyū: Nihongun ianfu* (Collaborative Research: Comfort Women of the Japanese Army) (Tokyo: Ōtsuki shoten, 1995); VAWW-Net Japan, ed., *Nihongun seidoreisei o sabaku 2000-nen josei kokusai senpan hōtei no kiroku*, 6 vols.; Yoshimi Yoshiaki, ed., *Jūgun ianfu shiryōshū* (Sources of the Comfort Women) (Tokyo: Ōtsuki shoten, 1992).

8. For the Japanese troop movement in the Philippines in the last year of war, see, for instance, Clayton D. James, *The Years of MacArthur*, vol. 2, *1941 to 1945* (Boston: Houghton Mifflin, 1975).

9. Frank A. Reel, *The Case of General Yamashita* (Chicago: University of Chicago Press, 1949); United Nations War Crimes Commission, *Law Reports of Trials of War Criminals* (Buffalo, N.Y.: William S. Hein, 1997), vol. 4, 1–96.

10. Greg Bradsher et al., *Researching Japanese War Crimes Records: Introductory Essays* (Washington, D.C.: Nazi War Crimes and Japanese Imperial Government Records Interagency Working Group, National Archives and Records Administration, 2006), 9.

11. For details of the prosecution's case on war crimes, see Yuma Totani, *The Tokyo War Crimes Trial: The Pursuit of Justice in the Wake of World War II* (Cambridge, Mass.: Harvard University Asia Center, 2008), chaps. 5–7. For exact wording of war crimes charges, see Counts 53, 54, and 55 of "The Indictment," in *The Tokyo War Crimes Trial*, ed., R. John Pritchard and Sonia Magbanua Zaide (New York: Garland, 1981), vol. 1. For a comparative study of the Yamashita and Tokyo jurisprudence, see David Cohen, "Beyond Nuremberg: Individual Responsibility for War Crimes," in *Human Rights in Political Transitions: Gettysburg to Bosnia*, ed. Carla Hesse and Robert Post (New York: Zone Books, 1999).

12. B. V. A. Röling and C. F. Ruter, eds., *The Tokyo Judgment: The International Military Tribunal for the Far East* (I.M.T.F.E), 29 April 1946–12 November 1948 (Amsterdam: APA-University Press, 1977), vol. 1, 385; emphasis added.

13. Röling and Ruter, eds., *The Tokyo Judgment*, 392–93. "Enforced prostitution" had been recognized as a war crime before World War II. For instance, the

Commission of Responsibilities—established at the time of the Paris Peace Conference in 1919—listed "rape" and "abduction of girls and women for the purpose of enforced prostitution" as recognized types of war crime under international law. UN War Crimes Commission, *History of the United Nations War Crimes Commission and the Development of the Laws of War* (London: His Majesty's Stationery Office, 1948), 34.

14. Röling and Ruter, eds., *The Tokyo Judgment*, vol. 1, 446–48, 453–55.

15. On MacArthur's view of the Tokyo trial, see Totani, *Tokyo War Crimes Trial*, chaps. 1, 3.

16. Mizushima Asaho, *Mirai sōzō to shite no "sengo hoshō": "kako no seisan" o koete* ("Postwar Reparation" for the Making of the Future: Beyond the "Settlement with the Past") (Tokyo: Gendai jinbunsha, 2003), 94–100.

17. Kawaguchi Kazuko, Kawami Kimiko, and Ishida Yoneko, "Sanseishō seibōryoku higai saiban to kanrensuru katsudō: sono seika to kadai" (The Trials Involving Victims of Sexual Violence in Shanxi Province and Related Activities: Achievements and Future Challenges), *Sensō sekinin kenkyū* 47 (Spring 2005).

18. Yamamoto Seita, "Kanpu saiban no keika to hanketsu" (The Progress and Judgment of the Kanpu Trial), *Sensō sekinin kenkyū* 21 (Fall 1998): 47.

19. Hanafusa Toshio, "Kanpu saiban no seika to kadai" (Achievements and Future Challenges of the Kanpu Trial), *Sensō sekinin kenkyū* 47 (Spring 2005); "Kanpu saiban hanketsu yōshi" (Summary of the Kanpu Trial's Judgment), posted at the Shimonoseki hanketsu o ikasukai website (Group in Support of the Shimonoseki Decision), http://www.geocities.jp/ikasukai98. Accessed Apr. 1, 2006.

20. Chūgokujin sensō higai baishō seikyū jiken bengodan (Lawyers' Association for the Reparation Lawsuits by Chinese Victims of War), ed., *Sajō no shōheki: Chūgokujin sengo hoshō saiban 10-nen no kiseki* (Barrier on the Sand: The Ten-Year Trajectory of Postwar Chinese Reparation Trials) (Tokyo: Nihon hyōronsha, 2005), 207–75.

21. Mark Levin, "International Decisions: *Nishimatsu Construction Co. v. Song Jixiao et al.*; *Ko Hanako et al. v. Japan*," *American Journal of International Law* 102 (2008).

22. Matsui Yayori, "Minshū hōtei to shite no 'josei kokusai saiban hōtei' no imi to seika" (The Significance and Achievements of the People's Tribunal: 'The Women's International War Crimes Tribunal on Japan's Military Sexual Slavery'), *Sensō sekinin kenkyū* 32 (Summer 2001). For more information about the Women's Tribunal, see VAWW-Net Japan, ed., *Nihongun seidoreisei o sabaku 2000-nen josei kokusai senpan hōtei no kiroku*, 6 vols. Visit also the VAWW-Net Japan website. http://www1.jca.apc.org/vaww-net-japan/english/index.html. A documentary film of the trial is also available. *Breaking the History of Silence: The Women's International War Crimes Tribunal on Japan's Military Sexual Slavery* (VAWW-NET Japan, 2001).

23. On the Textbook Trials, see Ienaga kyōkasho soshō bengodan (Lawyers' Association for the Ienaga Textbook Lawsuits), *Ienaga kyōkasho saiban: 32-nen ni wataru bengodan katsudō no sōkatsu* (Ienaga Textbook Trials: The Summation of the Activities of the Lawyers' Association for Thirty-Two Years) (Tokyo: Nihon hyōronsha, 1998).

24. Onodera Toshitaka, "Sensō sekinin to sengo hoshō: yoriyoi mirai o kizuki ageru tame ni" (War Responsibility and Postwar Reparation: To Build a Better Future," *Hō to minshushugi* (Law and Democracy), vol. 284 (Dec. 2003), 5. For information regarding the government-level legislative effort to implement restitution measures on comfort women in recent years, visit the website of Digital Museum: The Comfort Women Issue and the Asian Women's Fund. http://www.awf.or.jp/index.html.

25. Chūgokujin sensō higaisha no yōkyū o sasaeru Miyagi no kai (Miyagi Association in Support of the Victims of War in China) website, http://www.suopei.jp/saiban_trend/ianfu/post_475.html. Accessed Apr. 25, 2010.

26. The Yamaguchi District Court ordered an award of 300,000 yen (approx. $3,000) for each of the three former comfort women.

27. The Tokyo District Court recognized the evidence of post-traumatic stress disorder.

28. The Tokyo District Court recommended that the government initiate dialogues for restitution measures.

Chapter 14. Toward Accountability for Violence Against Women in War: Progress and Challenges

This chapter is a more detailed version of my keynote address at the History of Sexual Violence in Conflict Zones Conference sponsored by the University of Iowa Center for Human Rights in April 2006. Thanks to Jo Butterfield for her help in revising the chapter.

1. I addressed many of these questions in "Surfacing Gender: Re-engraving Rape in International Humanitarian Law," *Hastings Women's Law Journal* 5(1994): 243–66.

2. See, for example, Rhonda Copelon, "Surfacing Gender."

3. For example, the debate between Catherine MacKinnon and me on whether to insist on the special character of "genocidal rape" is reflected in Copelon, "Surfacing Gender." See also Karen Engle, "Feminism and Its (Dis)contents: Criminalizing Wartime Rape in Bosnia and Herzegovina," *American Journal of International Law* 99, no. 4 (Oct 2005): 778–816; Beth Van Schaack, "Engendering Genocide: The Akayesu Case Before the International Tribunal for Rwanda," in *Human Rights Advocacy Stories*, ed. Deena Hurwitz and Margaret L. Satterthwaite (New York: Foundation Press, July 1, 2008); http://papers.ssrn.com/sol3/papers.cfm?abstract_id=1154259, accessed Nov. 14, 2008.

4. Dorothy Thomas and Regan Ralph, "Rape in War: The Case of Bosnia," in *Gender Politics in the Western Balkans: Women and Society in Yugoslavia and the Yugoslav Successor States*, ed. Sabrina Ramet (University Park: Pennsylvania State University Press, 1999), 203, 207.

5. Cynthia Enloe, *Maneuvers: The International Politics of Militarizing Women's Lives* (Berkeley: University of California Press, 2000), 299.

6. "Human rights law" refers to the subset of international law that deals principally (with the exception of slavery offenses) with state responsibility for prevent-

ing and protecting persons subject to its jurisdiction from violations and is largely defined today by the Universal Declaration of Human Rights and the various human rights treaties. "International humanitarian law" refers to the laws of war, with focus in this discussion on rules protecting civilians in time of war. "International criminal law" refers to those violations, found in both human rights law and humanitarian law and developed through international criminal tribunals dating from the end of World War II, which warrant international criminal punishment. Today, the Rome Statute of the International Criminal Court (ICC) reflects the latest codification of international criminal law. Rome Statute of the ICC, A/CONF. 183/9; 2187 (July 17, 1998), hereinafter Rome Statute.

7. See, for example, Report of the Secretary General, *In-Depth Study on All Forms of Violence Against Women*, A/61/122.Add.1 (July 6, 2006).

8. Useful histories upon which this section draws include Theodor Meron, "Rape as a Crime Under International Humanitarian Law," *American Journal of International Law* 87 (1993): 424–29; Kelly Dawn Askin, *War Crimes Against Women: Prosecution in International War Crimes Tribunals* (The Hague: Nijhoff, 1997); Patricia Viseur Sellers and Kaoru Okuizumi, "International Prosecution of Sexual Assaults," *Transnational Law & Contemporary Problems* 7 (1997): 45, 47; Patricia Viseur Sellers, "Rape Under International Law" in *War Crimes: The Legacy of Nuremberg*, ed. Belinda Cooper (New York: TV Books, 1999), 159–61; Jocelyn Campanaro, "Women, War, and International Law: The Historical Treatment of Gender-Based Crimes," *Georgetown Law Journal* 89 (2001): 2557–92.

9. Francis Lieber, *Lieber's Code and the Law of War*, ed. Richard Shelly Hartigan (Chicago: Precedent, 1983). On the enforcement of the Lieber Code see Susan Barber and Charles Ritter, chap. 12, this volume.

10. Regulations Respecting the Laws and Customs of War on Land, art. 46, annexed to Hague Convention (IV) Respecting the Laws and Customs of War on Land, Oct. 18, 1907, *entered into force* Jan. 26, 1910.

11. Meron, "Rape as a Crime," 424–45; Patricia Viseur Sellers, "The Context of Sexual Violence: Sexual Violence as Violations of International Humanitarian Law," in *Substantive and Procedural Aspects of International Criminal Law*, ed. Gabrielle Kirk McDonald and Olivia Swak Goldman (The Hague: Kluwer Law International, 2000), 265–77; Patricia Viseur Sellers, "Sexual Violence and Peremptory Norms: The Legal Value of Rape," *Case Western Review Journal of International Law* 34 (2002): 287–89.

12. Geneva Convention Relative to the Treatment of Prisoners of War, art. 3, *entered into force* June 19, 1931.

13. Charter for the International Military Tribunal (London Charter), art. 6(b) and (c), *entered into force* Aug. 8, 1945; Charter for the International Military Tribunal of the Far East, art. 5(b) and (c), Jan. 19, 1946, amended Apr. 26, 1946. Both war crimes and crimes against humanity make common criminal activity an international crime when it occurs in a defined context, that is, when they occur in relation to war, with crimes against humanity, or when they are part of a widespread or systematic attack against a civilian population. The contextual requirements or "chapeaux" for these crimes have changed over time.

14. Askin, *War Crimes Against Women*, 136–39, 142, 162–63; Kelly Dawn Askin, "Prosecuting Rape and Other Gender Related Crimes Under International Law: Extraordinary Advances, Enduring Obstacles," *Berkeley Journal of International Law* 21 (2003): 288, 301–2.

15. Askin, *War Crimes Against Women*, 163.

16. Legal Div., Office of Military Government for Germany (U.S.), Enactments and Approved Papers of the Control Council and Coordinating Committee 306 (1945). Allied Control Council Law no. 10: Punishment of Persons Guilty of War Crimes, Crimes Against Peace and Against Humanity, art. II(1)(c) (Dec. 20, 1945). "Official Gazette of the Control Council for Germany No. 3," (Berlin, Jan. 31, 1946), reprinted in Benjamin B. Ferencz, *An International Criminal Court: A Step Toward World Peace: A Documentary History and Analysis* (Dobbs Ferry, N.Y.: Oceana, 1980), 488. For the failure to prosecute, see Askin "Prosecuting Wartime Rape," 288, 301–2.

17. Askin, *War Crimes Against Women*, 164–203.

18. Iris Chang, *The Rape of Nanking: The Forgotten Holocaust of World War II* (New York: Basic Books, 1997), 49–50.

19. In 2000, Asian women and NGOs, international NGOs, and other human rights organizations sponsored the Tokyo Tribunal (The Women's International War Crimes Tribunal on Japan's Military Sexual Slavery), which finally gave voice to the victims of the "comfort women system." This Judgement of an NGO-created Tribunal (in which I participated as coordinator of the Legal Advisors to the Judges) carries weight as evidence of international law because it involved major international jurists and Judge Gabrielle Kirk-McDonald, the former President of the International Criminal Tribunals for the former Yugoslavia (ICTY), presided. See the Judgement of the International Women's Criminal Tribunal on Japan's Military Sexual Slavery, http://www1.jca.apc.org/vaww-net-japan/english/womenstribunal2000/Judgement.pdf, accessed Nov. 8, 2008, (hereafter Tokyo Tribunal 2000 Judgement).

20. Tokyo Tribunal 2000 Judgement, 29–30; James Sterngold, "Japan Admits Army Forced Women into War Brothels," *New York Times*, Aug. 5, 1993, at A2.

21. Tokyo Tribunal 2000 Judgement, 28. My cousin, now deceased, who was among the U.S. naval soldiers who liberated Saipan, confirmed this. He described finding women, mostly pregnant and "half-crazed," hiding in the caves out of fear that the arriving troops would do the same. He said that the military set up hospitals and maternity wards.

22. Tokyo Tribunal 2000 Judgement, 28. From August 1945 to March 1946, the U.S. command knowingly used organized "comfort women" stations involving Japanese women and perhaps women from other countries, often against their will or based on deception. Eric Talmadge, "A Sequel to Japan's 'Comfort Women'; U.S. Occupation Allowed an Official System of Brothels," *Washington Post*, Apr. 29, 2007, at A13.

23. Geneva Convention (IV) Relative to the Protection of Civilian Persons in Time of War, 12 Aug. 1949, art. 27.

24. Geneva Convention (IV) Relative to the Protection of Civilian Persons in Time of War, 12 Aug. 1949, arts. 146–47.

25. Some have argued, however, that rape was implicit in such grave breaches as "inhumane treatment"; see Viseur Sellers, "Context of Sexual Violence," 296–99; International Committee of the Red Cross (ICRC), Aide-Mémoire (Dec. 3, 1992).

26. Geneva Convention IV, art. 3(1).

27. Geneva Convention IV, art. 3(1)(a & b).

28. Protocol Additional to the Geneva Conventions of Aug. 12, 1949, and Relating to the Protection of Victims of International Armed Conflicts (Protocol I) art. 75(2)(b) June 8, 1977.

29. Protocol Additional to the Geneva Conventions of Aug. 12, 1949, and Relating to the Protection of Victims of International Armed Conflicts (Protocol I) art. 75(2)(b) June 8, 1977.

30. Protocol Additional to the Geneva Conventions of Aug. 12, 1949, and Relating to the Protection of Victims of International Armed Conflicts (Protocol I) arts. 11, 76, 85.

31. Protocol Additional to the Geneva Conventions of Aug. 12, 1949, and Relating to the Protection of Victims of Non-International Armed Conflicts (Protocol II) art. 4, ¶2, June 8, 1977.

32. See Askin, "Prosecuting Wartime Rape," 216–21. Privately inflicted gender violence, including marital rape, has been until recently largely exempt from prosecution on the theory of the male right to dominion and control over the wife; Jane Connors for the UN Center for Social Development and Humanitarian Affairs, *Violence Against Women in the Family*, ST/CSDHA/2, UN sales no. E.89.IV.5 (1989).

33. Rachel A. Van Cleave, "Rape and the Querela in Italy: False Protection of Victim Agency," *Michigan Journal of Gender & Law* 13 (2007): 273, 281–89; Rachel Ginnis Fuchs, *Gender and Poverty in Nineteenth-century Europe* (Cambridge: Cambridge University Press, 2005): 66–67.

34. See Askin, *War Crimes Against Women*, 217–21; Michelle Anderson, "The Legacy of the Prompt Complaint Requirement, Corroboration Requirement, and the Cautionary Instructions on Campus Sexual Assault," Villanova Public Law and Legal Theory Working Paper Ser. 21 (Sept. 2004): 9–14; http://ssrn.com/abstract=555884, accessed Nov. 8, 2008; Kathy Mack, "Continuing Barriers to Women's Credibility: A Feminist Perspective on the Proof Process," *Criminal Law Forum* 4, no. 2 (June 1993): 329; See also Carol Smart, "Feminism and the Power of Law," in *Law and Violence Against Women: Cases and Materials on Systems of Oppression*, ed. Beverly Balos and Marie Louise Fellows (Durham, N.C.: Carolina Academic Press, 1994), 440–41, cited in Askin, *War Crimes Against Women*, 218.

35. See Richard Klein, "An Analysis of Thirty-Five Years of Rape Reform: A Frustrating Search for Fundamental Fairness," *Akron Law Review* 41 (2008): 981, 1048, for a discussion of how race has historically been a factor in the prosecution of rape in the United States and in the implementation of the death penalty. Susan Brownmiller, *Against Our Will: Men, Women, and Rape* (New York: Simon & Schuster, 1975), 210; Sharon Block, "Rape in the American Revolution: Process, Aftermath, and Public Re-Creation," chap. 1, this volume; Sharon Block, *Rape and Sexual Power in Early America* (Chapel Hill: University of North Carolina Press, 2006); Angela Yvonne Davis, *Women, Race, and Class* (New York: Random House, 1981).

36. United Nations Charter, signed June 26, 1945, art. 55(c); Universal Declaration on Human Rights (hereafter UDHR), G.A. Res. 217A, at 71, UN GAOR, 3rd sess., 1st plen. mtg., A/810 (Dec. 12, 1948); International Covenant on Civil and Political Rights, G.A. Res. 2200A (XXI), A/6316 (Dec. 16, 1966), *entered into force* Mar. 23, 1976, hereinafter ICCPR.

37. ICCPR art. 2(1), 3, 4(1).

38. Convention on the Elimination of All Forms of Discrimination Against Women (hereinafter CEDAW Convention), G.A. Res. 34/180, at 193, UN GAOR, 34th sess., 107th plen. mtg., A/34/46 (Dec. 18, 1979). This was definitively corrected in 1992 by CEDAW, General Recommendation no. 19. Committee on the Elimination of Discrimination Against Women, General Recommendation 19, Violence Against Women (11th sess., 1992), A/47/38 at 1 (1993), hereinafter CEDAW General Recommendation 19.

39. Alda Facio, "El androcentrismo de los derechos humanos," in *La mujer ausente: derechos humanos en el mundo* (Santiago: ISIS Internacional, 1991); Charlotte Bunch,"Women's Rights as Human Rights: Toward a Re-Vision of Human Rights," *Human Rights Quarterly* 12 (1990): 486–98. Major studies of the rape of women prisoners were undertaken in the latter 1990s after the establishment of women's projects. See, for example, Amnesty International, *"Not Part of My Sentence": Violations of the Human Rights of Women in Custody* (New York: AI, 1999), http://www.amnesty.org/en/library/info/AMR51/019/1999. Accessed Nov. 15, 2008; Human Rights Watch Women's Rights Project, *All Too Familiar: Sexual Abuse of Women in U.S. State Prisons* (New York: Human Rights Watch, Dec. 1996), http://hrw.org/reports/1996/Us1.htm#_1_25, accessed Nov. 15, 2008.

40. See Deborah Blatt, "Recognizing Rape as a Method of Torture," *Review of Law & Social Change* 19 (1992): 821, 843.

41. Ximena Bunster-Burotto, "Surviving Beyond Fear: Women and Torture in Latin America," in *Women and Change in Latin America: New Directions in Sex and Class*, ed. June Nash and Helen Sofa (South Hadley, Mass.: Bergin & Garvey, 1985) 297, 299–300. Thirty years later the National Commission on Political Prisoners and Torture estimated that most women imprisoned in Chile were raped and sodomized in horrendous ways and identified forced nakedness as among the common elements of torture. See Comisión Nacional Sobre Prisón Politica y Tortura (National Commission on Political Imprisonment and Torture, Santiago, Chile), Informe de la Comisión Nacional Sobre Prisón Politica y Tortura (Nov. 10, 2004), 276–80. Available at http://www.comisionvalech.gov.cl/InformeValech.html, accessed Sept. 27, 2010.

42. United Nations Commission on Human Rights, Report by the Special Rapporteur (Pieter Kooijmans) on torture and cruel, inhuman or degrading treatment or punishment, UN Doc. E/CN.4/1986/15 (Feb. 19, 1986).

43. Inter-American Commission on Human Rights, *Report on the Situation of Human Rights in Haiti* (1995), ¶133: OEA/ser. L/v/II.88 doc 10.rev. (Feb. 9, 1995), chap. IV, 3b(133). The International Women's Human Rights Law Clinic, which I direct, together with Harvard's Immigrants' Rights Clinic and Cambridge-Somerville Legal Services, prepared the petition specifically requesting recognition of rape as torture.

44. Told to author by a member of the Inter-American Commission on Human Rights.

45. The landmark case interpreting the positive obligations of the state to exercise due diligence to prevent, investigate, punish, and protect the victims of nonstate violence was Caso Velasquez-Rodriquez, Inter-American Court of Human Rights, 28 I.L.M. 294 (1989). See also Celina Romany, "Women as 'Aliens': A Feminist Critique of the Public/Private Dichotomy in International Law," *Harvard Human Rights Journal* 6 (1993): 87; Rhonda Copelon, "Recognizing the Egregious in the Every Day," *Columbia Human Rights Law Review* 25 (1994): 352–59; CEDAW Recommendation 19; The Secretary-General, *In-depth Study on All Forms of Violence Against Women*; Convention of Belem Do Para, Inter-American Convention on the Prevention, Punishment and Eradication of Violence Against Women, 33 I.L.M. 1534 (1994), http://www.oas.org/cim/english/Convention%20Violence%20Against%20Women.htm, accessed May 25, 2009; Yakin Ertürk, Report of the Special Rapporteur on Violence Against Women, Its Causes and Consequences, *The Due Diligence Standard as a Toll for the Elimination of Violence Against Women*, E/CN.4/2006/61 (Jan. 20, 2006); The Committee Against Torture (CAT) General Comment no. 2, CAT/C/GC/2CRP.1/Rev.4(Nov. 23, 2007), ¶18.

46. See, for example, Nigel S. Rodley, "Can Armed Opposition Groups Violate Human Rights?" in *Human Rights in the Twenty-First Century: A Global Challenge*, ed. Kathleen E. Mahoney and Paul Mahoney (Boston: M. Nijhoff, 1993), 297, 301; Sir Nigel Rodley (submitted by), *Question of the Human Rights of All Persons Subjected to Any Form of Detention or Imprisonment, in Particular: Torture and Other Cruel, Inhuman or Degrading Treatment*, E/CN.4/1995/34 (Jan. 12, 1995); Sir Nigel Rodley (submitted by), *Report on Torture and Other Cruel, Inhuman or Degrading Treatment or Punishment*, sec. IV(A) A/54/426 (Oct. 1, 1999). It is important to note, however, that Sir Nigel Rodley now accepts that there is human rights responsibility for privately inflicted violence where the state has failed to exercise due diligence or has acquiesced in the violence. For example, he has been an expert member of the Human Rights Committee, which consistently takes this position. See, for example, Human Rights Committee, General Comment 28, Equality of Rights Between Men and Women (art. 3), CCPR/C/21/Rev.1/Add.10 (2000). He also joined the Brief Amicus Curiae on Behalf of Human Rights Experts, Scholars and Advocates (no. 2005 Westlaw 328200) in *Town of Castle Rock v. Gonzales*, 2005, U.S. Supreme Court no. 04-278.

47. See generally, Connors, *Violence Against Women in the Family*; see also Women's Rights Project (WRP), Americas Watch: A Division of Human Rights Watch, *Criminal Injustice: Violence Against Women in Brazil* (New York: Human Rights Watch, Oct. 1, 1991) for the first report on domestic violence by a mainstream human rights organization.

48. CEDAW Convention.

49. Although general recommendations do not have the same force of law as treaties, they acquire it as the interpretation is accepted by ratifying States.

50. See n. 46.

51. World Conference to Review and Appraise the Achievements of the United Nations Decade for Women, Nairobi, Kenya, July 15–26, 1985, *The Nairobi For-*

ward Looking Strategies for the Advancement of Women, A/CONF.116/28/Rev.1 (1986), ¶258.

52. See, for example, the Center for Women's Global Leadership, http://www. cwgl.rutgers.edu/index.html. Accessed Dec. 15, 2008; Charlotte Bunch and Niamh Reilly, *Demanding Accountability: The Global Campaign and Vienna Tribunal for Women's Human Rights* (New Brunswick, N.J.: Rutgers University, Center for Women's Global Leadership, 1994). Conference documents, which generally contain declarations and programmatic priorities, are determined by a consensus of nations. Although the legal weight of these documents, sometimes called "soft law," is debated, conference documents have influenced both international jurisprudence and the negotiation and interpretation of treaties. See, for example, Dinah Shelton, "Introduction: Law, Non-Law and the Problem of 'Soft Law,'" in *Commitment and Compliance: The Role of Non-Binding Norms in the International Legal System*, ed. Dinah Shelton (New York: Oxford University Press, 2000), 1–20.

53. Bunch and Reilly, *Demanding Accountability*.

54. Bunch and Reilly, *Demanding Accountability*, 21–22.

55. Chunghee Sarah Soh, "The Korean 'Comfort Women': Movement for Redress," *Asian Survey* 36, no. 12 (Dec. 1996): 1226, 1233; Tokyo Tribunal Judgement, 2000; Korean Council, http://www.womenandwar.net/english/menu_014.php, accessed Dec. 17, 2008.

56. Tokyo Tribunal Judgement, 2000.

57. See Alexandra Stiglmayer, "Sexual Violence: Systematic Rape," in *Crimes of War: What the Public Should Know*, ed. Roy Gutman and David Rieff (New York: Norton, 1999), 327; Geraldine Ferraro, "Human Rights for Women," *New York Times*, June 10, 1993, at A27.

58. *Vienna Declaration and Programme of Action*, A/CONF. 157/23 (July 12, 1993), hereinafter *Vienna Declaration and Programme*. For a history and analysis of the Vienna Conference, see Donna J. Sullivan, "Women's Human Rights and the 1993 World Conference on Human Rights," *American Journal of International Law* 88, no. 1 (Jan. 1994): 152–67.

59. *Vienna Declaration and Programme*, §I, ¶¶18, 28; §II, ¶¶36–44.

60. *Vienna Declaration and Programme*, §II, ¶38; Declaration on the Elimination of Violence Against Women, A/RES/48/104 (Feb. 23, 1994), §II, ¶40. The Special Rapporteur's reports can be found at: http://www2.ohchr.org/english/issues/women/rapporteur/annual.htm, accessed Dec. 15, 2008.

61. This is notable in the 1994 *Report of the International Conference on Population and Development*, A/CONF. 171/13 (Oct. 18, 1994), ¶4.5. See Rosalind Petchesky and Rhonda Copelon, "Toward an Interdependent Approach to Reproductive and Sexual Rights as Human Rights: Reflections on the ICPD and Beyond," in *From Basic Needs to Basic Rights: Women's Claims to Human Rights*, ed. Margaret Schuler (Washington, D.C.: Women, Law and Development International, 1995); *Report of the World Summit for Social Development*, A/CONF.166/9 (Apr. 19, 1995), ¶79; *Beijing Declaration and Platform for Action*, A/CONF.177/20 (Sept. 15, 1995), ¶29. For a feminist analysis of Beijing see Dianne Otto, "A Post-Beijing Reflection on the Limitations and Potential of Human Rights Discourse for Women" in *Women and International Human Rights Law*, ed. Kelly D. Askin and Dorean

Koenig (Ardsley, N.Y.: Transnational, 1999), 115–35; *Report of the World Confer-ence Against Racism*, A/CONF.189/12 (Jan. 5, 2002), ¶54. See the following for UN directives to incorporate a gender perspective: ECOSOC Agreed Conclusions (July 1997/2); Letter of the Secretary General, Oct. 13, 1997; General Assembly Resolu-tion A/Res/52/100 (Dec. 1997); ECOSOC Resolution, E/Res/1998/26 (July 28, 1998); Twenty-third special session of the General Assembly to follow up implementa-tion of the Platform for Action A/S-23/10/Rev.1 (June 2000); Report of the Secre-tary General, *Integration of the Human Rights of Women and the Gender Perspective* E/CN.4/2002/81 (Jan. 15, 2002); Human Rights Commission Resolution (2002/50), *Integrating the Human Rights of Women Throughout the UN System*. For official UN documents and reports on gender mainstreaming, see also: http://www.un.org/ womenwatch/. Accessed Dec. 17, 2008.

62. See Joanna Kerr, Association for Women's Rights in Development, *The Second Fundher Report: Financial Sustainability for Women's Movements World-wide* 51 (2007). http://www.awid.org/eng/Issues-and-Analysis/Library/Financial-Sustainability-for-Women-s-Movement-s-Worldwide-Second-FundHer-Report, accessed Nov. 20, 2008; Charlotte Bunch, *Women and Gender: The Evolution of Women Specific Institutions and Gender Integration at the United Nations*. http:// www.cwgl.rutgers.edu/globalcenter/charlotte/UNHandbook.pdf, accessed Nov. 20, 2008; Stephen Lewis, *Race Against Time* (Toronto: House of Anansi Press, 2005), 109–44.

63. The Security Council relied on its power established by the UN Charter "to maintain or restore international peace and security." UN Charter, chap. VII, art. 4; see Security Council Resolution 808 (Feb. 22, 1993), Preamble ¶7, deciding to create a tribunal; see Security Council Resolution 827, Preamble ¶6, stating that the creation of a tribunal would "contribute to the restoration and maintenance of peace" in the former Yugoslavia. See also Security Council Resolution 955, (1994), ¶3, establishing the ICTR. See also Arieh Neier, *War Crimes: Brutality, Genocide, Terror, and the Struggle for Justice* (New York: Times Books, 1998).

64. An international alert, "Gender Justice and the Constitution of the War Crimes Tribunal Pursuant to Security Council Resolution 808," outlining prerequi-sites for the court from the International Women's Human Rights Clinic at the City University of New York (CUNY), which I direct, resulted in a meeting with the UN Legal Advisor to discuss inclusion of sexual violence. Document on file with author.

65. Statute of the International Tribunal for the Prosecution of Persons Responsible for Serious Violations of International Humanitarian Law Committed in the Territory of the Former Yugoslavia Since 1991, adopted pursuant to Security Council Resolution 827, S/RES/827 (1993), art. 5, hereinafter ICTY Statute.

66. See ICTY Statute, arts. 2–4.

67. Statute of the International Tribunal for the Prosecution of Persons Responsible for Genocide and Other Serious Violations of International Humani-tarian Law Committed in the Territory of Rwanda and Rwandan Citizens Respon-sible for Genocide and Other Such Violations Committed in the Territory of Neighboring States, Between 1 Jan. 1994 and 31 Dec. 1994, adopted pursuant to S.C. Res. 995, U.N. SCOR, 49th sess., 3453rd mtg., Annex (1994), arts. 3(g) and 4(e), hereinafter ICTR Statute.

68. ICTR Statute, arts. 4(a) and 4(e), respectively.

69. ICTR Statute, art. 2.

70. ICTY Statute, art. 22; ICTR Statute, art. 21.

71. For a detailed account of the process of rule making in the ICTY, see Virginia Morris and Michael Scharf, *An Insider's Guide to the International Criminal Tribunal for the Former Yugoslavia: A Documentary History and Analysis* (Irvington-on-Hudson, N.Y.: Transnational, 1995). See Jennifer Green et al., "Affecting the Rules for the Prosecution of Rape and Other Gender-Based Violence Before the International Criminal Tribunal for the Former Yugoslavia: A Feminist Proposal and Critique" *Hastings Women's Law Journal* 5 (1994): 171–241, which provides the full text of a submission in which the International Women's Human Rights Clinic at CUNY participated. Although mostly strategically based, feminists did disagree on the issue of consent as a defense. In contrast to rules that limited consent defenses, Equality Now and the Coordination for Women's Advocacy argued that consent should be eliminated entirely. For discussion of the competing positions on consent, see, for example, Janet Halley, "Rape in Berlin: Reconsidering the Criminalisation of Rape in the International Law of Armed Conflict," *Melbourne Journal of International Law* 9 (2008): 78–124; Alison Cole, "*Prosecutor v. Giacumbitsi*: The New Definition for Prosecuting Rape Under International Law," *International Criminal Law Review* 8 (2008): 55–86.

72. ICTY: Rules of Procedure and Evidence, IT/32/Rev. 6 (as amended Oct. 6, 1995), see Rules 34 and 96.

73. ICTR: Rules of Procedure and Evidence, entered into force Jan. 29, 1995. The Rule numbers listed in n. 72 are the same for Rwanda. For a comparative discussion of both the creation of the original Statutes and Rules for the ICTY and ICTR, see Catherine Cissé, "The International Tribunals for the Former Yugoslavia and Rwanda: Some Elements of Comparison," *Transnational Law & Contemporary Problems* 7, no. 1(1997): 103–18.

74. Rhonda Copelon, "Gender Crimes as War Crimes: Integrating Crimes Against Women into International Criminal Law," *McGill Law Journal* 46 (2000–2001): 228–29; H. Durham, "Woman and Civil Society: NGOs and International Criminal Law," in *Women and International Human Rights Law*, ed. Kelly Dawn Askin and Dorean M. Koenig (Ardsley, N.Y.: Transnational, 1999–2000), 3: 819.

75. See Human Rights Watch/Africa, *Shattered Lives: Sexual Violence During the Rwandan Genocide and Its Aftermath* (New York: HRW, 1996), http://www.hrw.org/reports/1996/Rwanda.htm (Sept. 1996), accessed Dec. 18, 2008; Binaifer Nowrojee, "Your Justice Is Too Slow: How the ICTR Failed Rwanda's Rape Victims," Occasional Paper. 10, United Nations Research Institute for Social Development, Nov. 25, 2005, http://www.unrisd.org/80256B3C005BCCF9/56FE32D5C0F6DCE9C125710F0045D89F/$file/OP10%20Web.pdf, accessed Dec. 18, 2008; Beth van Schaack, "Obstacles on the Road to Gender Justice: The International Criminal Tribunal for Rwanda as Object Lesson," *American University Journal of Gender, Social Policy & the Law*, research paper 09-02 (Santa Clara Univ. Legal Studies, 2009), http://ssrn.com/abstract=1328370, accessed May 29, 2009; Gaëlle Breton-Le Goff, "Analysis of Trends in Sexual Violence Prosecutions in Indictments by the International Crim-

inal Tribunal for Rwanda (ICTR) from November 1995 to November 2002," Nov.
28, 2002, http://www.womensrightscoalition.org/site/advocacyDossiers/rwanda/
rapeVictimssDeniedJustice/analysisoftrends_en.php, accessed Dec. 18, 2008. See
also website of the Coalition on Women's Human Rights in Conflict Situations,
http://www.womensrightscoalition.org/site/main_en.php, for publications and advocacy dossiers relating to the ICTR record relating to gender violence. Accessed
May 29, 2009.

76. *Prosecutor v. Akayesu*, case no. ICTR-96-4-T, Judgement (Sept. 2, 1998),
hereinafter *Akayesu* Judgement; *Prosecutor v. Kunarac et al.*, case no. IT-96-23-T,
Judgement (Feb. 22, 2001), hereinafter *Kunarac* Judgement; *Prosecutor v. Kunarac
et al.*, case no. IT-96-23-T, Appeals Chamber Judgement (June 12, 2002), hereinafter *Kunarac Appeal* Judgement. For their significance see, generally, Gabrielle
Kirk McDonald, "Crimes of Sexual Violence: The Experience of the International
Criminal Tribunal," Friedmann Award Address. *Columbia Journal of Transnational
Law* 39 (2000–2001): 1, 11–15; Patricia Viseur Sellers, "Emerging Jurisprudence
on Crimes of Sexual Violence," *American University International Law Review* 13
(1998): 1523, 1529; Viseur Sellers and Okuizumi, "International Prosecution of Sexual Assaults"; Viseur Sellers, "Context of Sexual Violence"; Askin, *War Crimes*;
Askin, "Prosecuting Wartime Rape"; Askin, "Sexual Violence in Decisions and
Indictments of Yugoslav and Rwandan Tribunals: Current Status," *American Journal of International Law* 93 (1999): 97–124; Campanaro, "Women, War, and International Law"; Cole, "*Prosecutor v. Giacumbitsi.*"

77. Van Schaack, "Engendering Genocide"; Nowrojee, "Your Justice Is Too
Slow," 3; Copelon, "Gender Crimes as War Crimes," 217, 224–25.

78. Akayesu was the *bourgmeister* or mayor of the Taba commune. For the
documentation see Human Rights Watch/Africa, *Shattered Lives*; African Rights,
Rwanda: Death, Despair and Defiance, 2nd ed. (London: African Rights, 1995) notes
the Human Rights Watch (HRW) documentation of widespread rape during the
Rwandan genocide published before Jean-Paul Akayesu's indictment. The Trial
Chamber recognized the role of misogynist propaganda as incitement to sexualized violence in the case known as the "Media Case," although the indictment and
the proof fell far short of what should have been presented. See Judgement and Sentence, Nahimana, Barayagwiza and Ngeze, ICTR-99-52-T (Dec. 3, 2003), ¶1079.

79. The 1948 Genocide Convention includes, as acts of genocide, "causing serious bodily or mental harm," "deliberately inflicting on the group actions calculated
to bring about its physical destruction in whole or in part," and "imposing measures designed to prevent births within the group." Convention on the Prevention
and Punishment of the Crime of Genocide (Dec. 9, 1948), art. 2(a)–(d). The Tribunal statutes track the Convention. ICTR Statute, art. 2(2)(b)–(d).

80. HRW, *Shattered Lives*; Nowrojee, "Your Justice Is Too Slow"; Van Schaack,
"Engendering Genocide."

81. Van Schaack, "Engendering Genocide," 5–7.

82. Coalition for Women's Human Rights in Conflict Situations, *Amicus Brief
Respecting Amendment of the Indictment and Supplementation of the Evidence to
Ensure the Prosecution of Rape and Other Sexual Violence Within the Competence of
the Tribunal*, http://www.womensrightscoalition.org/site/advocacyDossiers/rwanda/

Akayesu/amicusbrief_en.php, accessed Nov. 8, 2007. I participated in the phone call during which it was reported that there was no follow-up of the witnesses' testimony that led the coalition to prepare the *amicus curiae* brief.

83. Amended Indictment, Akayesu, case no. ICTR-96-4-I (June 17, 1997) as cited in Van Schaack, "Engendering Genocide," 10–11.

84. *Akayesu* Judgement, ¶¶418–38.

85. *Akayesu* Judgement, ¶731.

86. *Akayesu* Judgement, ¶732. The Judgement could not recognize the fact that they were also targeted because of their gender, because gender was not a protected class under genocide. See Copelon, "Surfacing Gender," 261–64.

87. Van Schaack, "Engendering Genocide," 11–12; *Akayesu* Judgement, ¶731.

88. *Akayesu* Judgement, ¶732. For the factual findings of rape and sexual violence suffered by Tutsi women and girls see ¶¶449–60.

89. See ICTR Statute, art. 2, for a description of genocidal crimes; See Askin, *War Crimes*, 338–42; *Akayesu* Judgement, ¶¶507–9.

90. *Akayesu* Judgement,¶687, 690. See also Cole, "*Prosecutor v. Giacumbitsi.*"

91. *Akayesu* Judgement,¶598.

92. *Akayesu* Judgement, ¶686.

93. *Akayesu* Judgement, ¶688.

94. The *Akayesu* Judgement stated: "coercive circumstances need not be evidenced by a show of physical force. Threats, intimidation, extortion and other forms of duress which prey on fear or desperation may constitute coercion, and coercion may be inherent in certain circumstances, such as armed conflict or the military presence [of the enemy]," ¶688.

95. *Akayesu* Judgement, ¶694.

96. Askin, *War Crimes*, 1008; Gaëlle Breton-Le Goff, "Analysis of Trends"; Nowrojee, "Your Justice Is Too Slow"; Van Schaak, "Engendering Genocide," 22–26. Highlighting the positive aspects, see Kelly Dawn Askin, "Gender Crimes Jurisprudence in the ICTR: Positive Developments," *Journal of International Criminal Justice* 3, no. 4 (Sept. 2005): 1007–18; Cole, "*Prosecutor v. Giacumbitsi.*"

97. *Prosecutor v. Tadic*, case no. IT-94-1-T, Amended Indictment, counts 4–6, ¶5 (Sept. 1, 1995). Although rape was common in Omarska prison, a single charge of rape of a female prisoner in the original indictment was dropped when the witness refused to testify. *Prosecutor v. Tadic*, case no. IT-94-1-T, Indictment (Feb. 13, 1995).

98. *Prosecutor v. Delalic et al.*, case no. IT-96-21 (Nov. 16, 1998), hereinafter *Celibici* Case; *Prosecutor v. Furundzija*, case no. IT-95-17/1-T, Judgement (Dec. 10, 1998), hereinafter *Furundzija* Judgement; *Prosecutor v. Furundzija*, case no. IT-95-17/1-T, Appeal Chamber Judgement (July 21, 2000); *Kunarac* Judgement and *Kunarac Appeal* Judgement.

99. *Kunarac* Judgement, ¶¶553–57, 883–90. See also *Prosecutor v. Kvocka et al.*, case no. IT-98-30/1-T, Judgement (Nov. 2, 2001); *Prosecutor v. Mucic et al.*, case no. IT-96-21, Judgement (Oct. 9, 2001); *Furundzija* Judgement.

100. I participated directly in this process through scholarship (Copelon, "Surfacing Gender") and in gender training at the ICTY. See also Meron, "Rape as Crime"; Thomas and Ralph, "Rape in War."

101. ICTY Statute, art. 2 (b) and (c).

102. Letter from Justice Richard Goldstone, Prosecutor, to Rhonda Copelon, Felice Gaer, and Jennifer Green (Nov. 22, 1994) (on file with author). Recognition of the status of rape as torture was included in *Celebici* Case; *Furundzija* Judgement, ¶557.

103. *Kunarac Appeal* Judgement, ¶150–51.

104. *Kunarac Appeal* Judgement, ¶154.

105. *Kunarac* Judgement, ¶542; *Kunarac Appeal* Judgement, ¶119–21. See ¶119 for the tribunal's indica for enslavement.

106. *Kunarac Appeal* Judgement, ¶¶184.

107. *Kunarac Appeal* Judgement, ¶¶58–59. This is also codified the ICC Statute. See Rome Statute, arts. 7–8.

108. The Appeals Chamber agreed with the Trial Chamber's definition of rape. See *Kunarac Appeal* Judgement, ¶127 (quoting *Kunarac* Judgement, ¶460), for the definition.

109. *Kunarac Appeal* Judgement, ¶¶127–33. The *Giacumbitsi Appeal* Judgement, which followed *Kunarac*, sought to narrow the consent issue by declaring that it does not need evidence of refusal by the victim or force. Consent remains ambiguous in requiring that the prosecution prove "the existence of coercive circumstances *under which meaningful consent is not possible.*" See *Prosecutor v. Giacumbitsi*, Judgement, case no. ICTR-2001-64-A, 7 (July 2006), ¶155. Although both decisions acknowledge that consent is highly unlikely in the circumstances that come before the Tribunal, it is not clear what the "impossiblity" of "meaningful consent" will mean. In *Kunarac*, the tribunal described the element as "consent given voluntarily, as a result of the victim's free will, assessed in the context of the surrounding circumstances." *Kunarac Appeal* Judgement, ¶127.

110. Women's Initiatives for Gender Justice, "Gender Integration in the Statute of the International Criminal Court," http://www.iccwomen.org/publications/resources/index.php, accessed May 30, 2009.

111. Rome Statute, arts. 4–8. Certain limits must be noted: ICC jurisdiction is not retroactive and applies only to those who ratify, accede, or commit crimes in the territory of a ratifying State or when the Security Council refers a situation to the Court. Rome Statute, arts. 11, 12, 13. The Court lacks full universal jurisdiction in that a State cannot refer a case where it exercises custody over the perpetrator or because victims reside in its territory, art. 12(2). However, the Prosecutor has *proprio motu* (on her own motion) power to initiate prosecution, subject to judicial approval, and thus must respond to requests by victim groups and advocates, arts. 13(c), 15.

112. Much of what follows reflects my own experience as one of the founders of the Women's Caucus for Gender Justice in the ICC and Director of its Legal Secretariat, which vetted Caucus positions and participated in negotiations as part of an international delegation. Subsequent to the negotiations, the organization was renamed the Women's Caucus for Gender Justice and continues today as the Women's Initiatives for Gender Justice. Its work is available at: http://www.iccwomen.org, accessed Aug. 2, 2008.

113. Rome Statute, art. 9(1); ICC, Rules of Procedure and Evidence, adopted by the Assembly of States Parties, first sess., New York, Sept. 3–10, 2002, U.N.

Doc. ICC-ASP/1/3 (2002), hereinafter ICC Rules; Preparatory Commission for the International Criminal Court, *Report of the Preparatory Commission for the International Criminal Court on Finalized Draft Text of the Rules of Procedure and Evidence*, U.N. Doc. PCNICC/2000/1/Add.1 (2000), hereinafter ICC Rules Annex, http://documents-dds-ny.un.org/doc/UNDOC/GEN/N00/724/06/pdf/N0072406. pdf?OpenElement; International Criminal Court, Elements of Crimes adopted by the Assembly of States Parties, first session, New York, Sept. 3–10, 2002, Official Records ICC-ASP//1/3, art. 9(1), hereinafter ICC Elements Annex, http://www.icc-cpi.int/Menus/ICC/Legal+Texts+and+Tools/Official+Journal/Elements+of+Crimes. htm, accessed July 1, 2009.

114. A discussion of all the debates is beyond the scope of this article, which provides only a brief synopsis. For commentaries from participants in the process see Cate Steains, "Gender Issues," and William Pace and Mark Thieroff, "The Participation of Non-Governmental Organizations," both in *The International Criminal Court: The Making of the Rome Statute—Issues, Negotiations, Results*, ed. Roy S. Lee (The Hague: Nijhoff, 2002), 357–90, 391–98, respectively; Valerie Oosterveld, "The Definition of 'Gender' in the Rome Statute of the International Criminal Court: A Step Forward or a Step Backward for International Criminal Justice?" *Harvard Human Rights Journal* 18 (2005): 55–84; Barbara Bedont and Kathryn Hall Martinez, "Ending Impunity for War Crimes Under the International Criminal Court," *Brown Journal of World Affairs* 6 (1999): 65–86; "Gender Elements" commentary by Eve La Haye on article 8(2)(b)(xxii), "Rape, Sexual Slavery, Enforced Prostitution, Forced Pregnancy, Enforced Sterilization, and Sexual Violence," and Donald K. Piragoff, "Evidence in the International Criminal Court," both in *The International Criminal Court: Elements of Crimes and Rules of Procedure and Evidence*, ed. Roy E. Lee and Håkan Friman (Ardsley, N.Y.: Transnational, 2001), Rules 70–72; Copelon, "Gender Crimes as War Crimes"; Brook Sari Moshan, "Women, War, and Words: The Gender Component in the Permanent International Criminal Court's Definition of Crimes Against Humanity," *Fordham International Law Journal* 22, no. 1 (1998): 154–84.

115. Rome Statute, arts. 7(1)(g) and (h), 8(2)b(xxii), and 8(2)e(vi).

116. Rome Statute, arts. 6–8.

117. Genocide Convention, art. 2; ICC Elements Annex, art. 6(b)(1), n. 3.

118. Rome Statute, and ICC Elements Annex arts. 8(2)(b)(xxii) and 8(2)(e)(vi).

119. Rome Statute, art. 8(1) uses the term "in particular" to ensure that the ICC jurisdiction would not be limited to situations where the crimes were widespread or systematic.

120. Rome Statute, art. 7(1).

121. See, for example, *Kunarac Appeal* Judgement, ¶64, 146–47.

122. See, for example, *Kunarac Appeal* Judgement, ¶78–87.

123. Rome Statute, art. 7(2)(a).

124. *Kunarac Appeal* Judgement, ¶93–101.

125. Proposal concerning the elements of crimes against humanity, submitted by Bahrain, Iraq, Kuwait, Lebanon, the Libyan Arab Jamahiriya, Oman, Qatar, Saudi Arabia, the Sudan, the Syrian Arab Republic, and the United Arab Emirates, U.N. Doc. PCNICC/1999/WGEC/DP.39 (Dec. 3, 1999). For the definition of enslave-

ment and sexual slavery and familial relationships see 7(b), 7(1)(3), 7(1)(g)20(3). For rape see 7(1)(g)(1)(4). For forced pregnancy of "the bearing of children" see 7(1)(g) (6) and 7(1)(g)(4)(4). See also Women's Caucus for Gender Justice, "The International Criminal Court: The Beijing Platform in Action, Part 4" (1999), http://www. iccwomen.org/wigjdraft1/Archives/oldWCGJ/resources/bplus5/part4.htm, accessed Feb. 22, 2009.

126. ICC Elements Annex, Crimes Against Humanity, Introduction, ¶3. Additionally, n. 6 requires, at the least, "a deliberate failure to take action, which is consciously aimed at encouraging such attack."

127. The placement of these limitations in the Introduction rather than as defining elements, coupled with the fact that they are completely inconsistent with culpability criteria under the Statute as well as international law that punishes acquiescence or the failure to exercise due diligence to prevent or stop such violations, argues strongly against acceptance of these nonbinding limitations by the Court. Compare Rome Statute arts. 25 and 28, with the Convention Against Torture, art. 1, and Committee Against Torture General Comment no. 2, Prevention of Torture, CAT/C/GC/2 (Jan. 24, 2008), ¶17–18; see Kamari Maxine Clarke, "Internationalizing the Statecraft: Genocide, Religious Revivalism, and the Cultural Politics of International Law," *Loyola of L.A. International & Comparative Law Review* 28 (2006): 279, 304; Moshan, "Women, War, and Words," 183.

128. Rome Statute, art. 7(1)(g) (crimes against humanity); art. 8(2)(b)(xxii) and 8(2)(e)(vi) (war crimes), and compare "outrages upon personal dignity" as a separate and distinct war crime within the Rome Statute and ICC Elements Annex. Rome Statute, art. 8(2)(b)(xxi); ICC Elements Annex, art. 8(2)(b)(xxi) and art. 8(2)(c)(ii); and arts. 7(1)(c) and 7(2)(c) (enslavement), respectively. For discussion of the statutory negotiations, see generally Steains, "Gender Issues", with the proviso discussed in n. 134, and Bedont and Hall Martinez, "Ending Impunity for War Crimes."

129. For example, the Rome Statute describes the sexual violence crimes as "also constituting" grave breaches and serious violations, art. 7(2)(c). ICC Elements Annex, art. 7(1)(c), n. 11. The Introduction to the Elements Annex also provides that "a particular conduct may constitute one or more crimes," a provision that resulted from the Women's Caucus concern that sexualized violence not be balkanized. Introduction to the ICC Elements Annex, ¶9.

130. Rome Statute, 7(2)(c).

131. A variant on the *Kunarac* definition of rape was preferred over *Akayesu*'s. ICC Elements Annex, 7(1)(g)-1; 8(2)(b)(xxii)-1, and 8(2)(e)(vi)-1; a fierce effort to confine enslavement and sexual slavery to chattel-type exchanges was broadened to include serious deprivation of liberty including traditional slavery-like practices and forced labor, ICC Elements Annex, 7(1)(c) and 7(1)(g)-2. The Elements Annex definition of forced pregnancy required (as does the ICC Statue) pregnancy by rape, confinement and contains a proviso that seeks to exclude abortion laws, Rome Statute, art. 7(2)(f) and Elements Annex, art. 7(1)(g)-4, 8(2)(b)(xxii)-4, and 8(2)(e)(vi)-4. See Eve La Haye, "Gender Elements," 191–92; Steains, "Gender Issues," 364–69.

132. Rome Statute, 7(1)(h), 7(2)(g), and 7(3). See Copelon, "Surfacing Gender," 243, 261–63.

133. Rome Statute, art. 7(3). "For the purposes of this Statute, it is understood that the term 'gender' refers to the two sexes, male and female, within the context of society. The term 'gender' does not indicate any meaning different from the above." Oosterveld, "Definition of Gender," 53; Steains, "Gender Issues," 371–75. It is crucial to read the second edition on this because, quite shockingly, Ms. Steains's original submitted text in the first edition (1999) was redrafted in the editing process so as to come to the opposite conclusion. The second edition restores the original text concluding that the Court could adopt a broad interpretation. See Copelon, "Gender Crimes as War Crimes," 233–39, and n. 60 discussing the distortion of the first draft.

134. Rome Statute, arts. 36 (8)(a)(iii) and (b) (Judges); 42(9) (Prosecutor); and 43(6) (Registry), respectively. Subsequently, rules for voting were adopted to ensure that a minimum of one-third of the judges would be female, and NGOs ensured that experience with and sensitivity to gender issues would be an explicit consideration. Procedure for the nomination and selection of Judges, the Prosecutor and Deputy Prosecutor of the ICC, ICC-ASP/1/Res.2, ¶6. See also Pamela Spees, *A Fair Representation: Advocating for Women's Rights in the International Criminal Court*, Center on Women and Public Policy Case Study Program, Humphrey Institute of Public Affairs, University of Minnesota, http://www.hhh.umn.edu/img/assets/9681/fair_representation.pdf, accessed Dec. 18, 2008.

135. Rome Statute, art. 43(6), http://www.icc-cpi.int/NR/rdonlyres/3B96D3C8-3281-4017-880B-ADD4541D72BC/273436/32243.PDF, accessed Sep. 29, 2010.

136. ICC Rules, 71.

137. ICC Rules, 70 and 72, respectively. See D. K. Piragoff, "Evidence in the International Criminal Court," 369–90.

138. Rome Statute, art. 21(3).

139. For the relationship between Truth Commissions, reconciliation, and justice see Pricilla Hayner, *Unspeakable Truths: Confronting State Terror and Atrocity* (New York: Routledge, 2001). For Truth and Reconciliation Reports, see, for example, *Rapport de la Commission Nationale de Vérité et de Justice* (2001), Digital copies available through the University of Florida: http://ufdc.uflib.ufl.edu/UF00085926/00001?td=haiti+=truth+=commission, accessed Sept. 29, 2010.; *Guatemala: Memory of Silence, Report of the Commission for Historical Clarification* (1999), http://shr.aaas.org/guatemala/ceh/report/english/toc.html, accessed Dec. 18, 2008; *Final Report of the Truth and Reconciliation Commission of Peru* (2003), http://www.ictj.org/static/Americas/Peru/TRC.FinalReport.eng.pdf, accessed Dec. 18, 2008; *Final Report of the Truth and Reconciliation Commission of South Africa* (1998). http://www.doj.gov.za/trc/report, accessed Dec. 18, 2008; *Witness to Truth: Report of the Sierra Leone Truth and Reconciliation Commission* (2004), http://www.trcsierraleone.org/drwebsite/publish/index.shtml, accessed Dec. 18, 2008. Rwanda has established a new form of the traditional Gacaca, involving locally elected committees, which has jurisdiction over the less than grave offenses and therefore excludes rape from this process, although it has sometimes been alleged. See Amnesty International, *Rwanda, Gacaca: A Question of Justice* (2002), http://www.amnesty.org/en/report/info/AFR47/007/2002, accessed Dec. 18, 2008.

140. See Rome Statute, art. 17.

141. See http://www.iccwomen.org/index.php for the current "Gender Report Card" on the ICC, which provides information on state implementation of ICC standards.

142. Security Council Resolution 1325 (Oct. 31, 2000), hereinafter SC Res. 1325; Security Council Resolution 1820 (June 19, 2008) pursuant to UN Charter, art. 39, hereinafter SC Res. 1820. The Women's International League for Peace and Freedom and the Working Group on Women, Peace and Security have been particularly influential. See http://www.peacewomen.org for history and current work, including that related to Security Council resolutions, accessed May 29, 2009.

143. See *Women, Peace and Security*, study submitted by the Secretary General (Oct. 2002), UN Publication, sales no. E.03.IV.1 ¶93–104, 271; Warren Hoge, "Report Calls for Punishing Peacekeepers in Sex Abuse," *New York Times* (Mar. 25, 2005).

144. See Dyan Mazurana and Susan McKay, "Where Are the Girls?" in Rights and Democracy (2004), http://www.dd-rd.ca/site/home/index.php, accessed Dec. 18, 2008.

145. SC Res. 1325.

146. Carol Cohn, "The Rhetorical Construction of the UN's Women, Peace and Security Agenda: From Crafting Documents to Changing Practices," unpublished paper presented at the annual meeting of the International Studies Association, Honolulu, Hawaii, Mar. 5, 2005.

147. SC Res. 1325, ¶17.

148. See, for example, The Secretary-General, *Report of the Secretary-General on women, peace and security*, delivered to the Security Council, S/2002/1154 (Oct. 16, 2002), S/2004/814 (Oct. 13, 2004), S/2005/636 (Oct. 10, 2005), S/2006/770 (Sept. 27, 2006), S/2007/567 (Sept. 12, 2007), S/2008/622 (Sept. 25, 2008). The Secretary-General's reports can be found at http://www.securitycouncilreport.org/atf/cf/ {65BFCF9B-6D27-4E9C-8CD3-CF6E4FF96FF9}/WPS%20S20021154.pdf, accessed May 29, 2009.

149. See Women, War & Peace, "Peace Negotiations" (n.d.), http://www.womenwarpeace.org/node/11, accessed Dec. 19, 2008.

150. SC Res. ¶1 (emphasis original).

151. SC Res., ¶7.

152. Compare SC Res. 1820, ¶¶3, 8, and 12 with the more ample treatment of participation in 1325, ¶¶1–6, 815–17.

153. On November 26, 2008, the Prosecutor appointed Catherine MacKinnon as a temporary gender consultant. This does not, however, fulfill the need to create a permanent high-level position. Women's Initiatives for Gender Justice, *Gender Report Card on the International Criminal Court 2008*, 21 (2008), http://www.iccwomen.org/news/docs/GRC08_web2-09v3.pdf, accessed May 29, 2009. Despite ample documentation of rape, the Prosecutor's first indictment was confined to child soldiers, and his second, while including rape, characterizes it as "outrages against personal dignity" and ignores sexual slavery. See the amicus brief filed by Radhika Coomaraswamy, UN Special Representative of the Secretary-General on Children and Armed Conflict, *Amicus Curiae* in the case of *The Prose-*

cutor v. Thomas Lubanga Dyilo, http://www.un.org/children/conflict/_documents/
AmicuscuriaeICCLubanga.pdf, accessed May 29, 2009; Nicholas Leddy, "The
United Nations Faces Challenges to Effective Action in Darfur," *Human Rights Brief*
13, no. 3 (2006), 59–60; Timothy Webster, "Babes with Arms: International Law
and Child Soldiers," *George Washington International Law Review* 39, no. 2 (2007):
227, 244; for the initial ICC case see *The Prosecutor v. Thomas Lubanga Dyilo*,
ICC-01/04-01/06. See particularly the "Decision on the Confirmation of Charges,"
which indicates the limited nature of the Prosecutor's charges, http://www.icc-cpi.
int/iccdocs/doc/doc266175.pdf, accesses Jan. 29, 2007, ¶9. See also Women's Initiatives for Gender Justice, annual *Gender Report Cards*, http://www.iccwomen.org,
accessed Mar. 19, 2009.

154. See, for example, HRW, *Shattered Lives*, 15–19; Margaret Power, *Right-
Wing Women in Chile: Feminine Power and the Struggle Against Allende, 1964–
1973* (University Park: Pennsylvania State University Press, 2002); Anna Mulrine,
"Unveiled Threat." *U.S. News & World Report* 131, no. 15 (Oct. 15, 2001): 32.

155. Nairobi Declaration on Women's and Girls' Right to a Remedy and Reparation, http://www.womensrightscoalition.org/site/reparation/signature_en.php,
accessed Mar. 19, 2009.

156. Nairobi Declaration on Women's and Girls' Right to a Remedy and Reparation, http://www.womensrightscoalition.org/site/reparation/signature_en.php,
accessed Mar. 19, 2009, ¶3(H).

157. Secretary General's Bulletin (Oct. 9, 2003).

Contributors

E. Susan Barber is an associate professor of history and chair of the History/Political Science Department, College of Notre Dame of Maryland. She is coauthor with Charles F. Ritter of "'Physical Abuse and Rough Handling': Race, Gender, and Sexual Justice in the Occupied South," in *Occupied Women: Gender, Military Occupation, and the American Civil War*, ed., LeeAnn Whites and Alecia P. Long. She is also author of "'The White Wings of Eros': Courtship and Marriage in Confederate Richmond," in *Southern Families at War: Loyalty and Conflict in the Civil War South*, ed. Catherine Clinton (New York: Oxford University Press, 2000) and "Depraved and Abandoned Women: Prostitution in Richmond, Virginia, Across the Civil War," in *Neither Lady nor Slave: Working Women of the Old South*, ed., Susanna Delfino and Michele Gillespie (Chapel Hill: University of North Carolina Press, 2002).

Sharon Block is an associate professor of history at the University of California, Irvine. Her first book was *Rape and Sexual Power in Early America*, and her current scholarship has a dual focus on digital humanities and on the meanings of bodily descriptions in colonial print culture.

Antonia I. Castañeda, a Chicana feminist historian, was born in Texas and raised in Washington state; she received her B.A. from Western Washington State College, her M.A. from the University of Washington, and her Ph.D. from Stanford University. She is the author of numerous articles, including the prize-winning "Women of Color and the Re-Writing of Western History." She is retired and lives in San Antonio, Texas.

Rhonda Copelon was a professor at CUNY Law School, vice-president of the Center for Constitutional Rights, founder of the Women's Caucus for Gender Justice, and cofounder of CUNY Law School's International Women's Human Rights Clinic (IWHR). Copelon was noted for her key role in the landmark human rights case, *Filartiga v. Pena-Irala*, which established that victims of gross human rights abuses committed abroad had recourse to U.S. courts. Additionally, she argued before the Supreme Court in *Harris v. McRae*, in which the Court narrowly upheld the Hyde Amendment, which prohibited Medicaid reimbursement for almost all abortions. Under Copelon's leadership, IWHR's amicus briefs in the International Criminal Tribunals for Rwanda and the former Yugoslavia contributed to the recognition in international law of rape as a crime of genocide and torture. IWHR's work with the

United Nations's Committee Against Torture and other international bodies contributed to the recognition that gender crimes, such as domestic and other forms of gender violence, can constitute torture under the United Nations's Convention Against Torture and Other Cruel, Inhuman, or Degrading Treatment or Punishment. In addition, the IWHR coordinated an effort with partners across the globe ensuring that the Rome Statute was written to take gender into account concerning the crimes, procedure, and evidence and composition of the court and personnel. Rhonda Copelon died in 2010.

Anne Curry is a professor of medieval history at the University of Southampton. Her research focuses on the Hundred Years War and in particular the battle of Agincourt and the English occupation of Normandy (1415–50). She has published extensively in England and France on these topics and also edited the 1422–53 section of *The Parliament Rolls of Medieval England*, a definitive new edition of this key historical source.

Barbara Donagan is an independent scholar. Her publications include articles on aspects of war and religion in seventeenth-century England and a book on the English civil war, *War in England 1642–1649*. She is currently working on the impact of civil war on civilian society.

Kathy L. Gaca is an associate professor of classics at Vanderbilt University. Her wide-ranging research is unified in exploring how sexual norms rooted in antiquity inform current concerns of social injustice. She is the author of *The Making of Fornication: Eros, Ethics, and Political Reform in Greek Philosophy and Early Christianity* (winner of the CAMWS 2006 Outstanding Publication Award) and of numerous articles, including "The Andrapodizing of War Captives in Greek Historical Memory" and "Reinterpreting the Homeric Simile of *Iliad* 16.7–11: The Girl and Her Mother in Ancient Greek Warfare." She is currently at work on her second book, *Armed and Sexual Warfare Against Women and Girls in Classical Antiquity*. She received her Ph.D. in Classics at the University of Toronto and held the Hannah Seeger Davis Postdoctoral Fellowship in Hellenic Studies at Princeton University.

Robert Gerwarth is Professor of Modern History at University College Dublin. He studied history and politics at Humboldt University Berlin and Oxford University, where he completed his Ph.D. in 2003. He is author of *The Bismarck Myth: Weimar Germany and the Legacy of the Iron Chancellor* and editor of several books on modern German and European history. He is currently director of the Centre for War Studies at University College Dublin.

James Giblin has taught African history at the University of Iowa since 1986. He specializes in the history of East Africa. He has published two books on the history of Tanzania, *The Politics of Environmental Control in Northeastern Tanzania, 1840–1940*, and *A History of the Excluded: Making Family and Memory a Refuge from State in Twentieth-Century Tanzania*.

Atina Grossmann is a professor of history in the Faculty of Humanities and Social Sciences at the Cooper Union, where she teaches modern German and European history, and gender studies. A graduate of the City College of New York (B.A.) and Rutgers University (Ph.D.), she has held fellowships from the National Endowment for the Humanities, German Marshall Fund, American Council of Learned Societies, Institute for Advanced Study in Princeton, and American Academy in Berlin. Publications include *Reforming Sex: The German Movement for Birth Control and Abortion Reform, 1920–1950,* and co-edited volumes on *Crimes of War: Guilt and Denial in the Twentieth Century* and *After the Nazi Racial State: Difference and Democracy in Germany and Europe. Jews, Germans, and Allies: Close Encounters in Occupied Germany* was awarded the George L. Mosse Prize of the American Historical Association. She is beginning a research project on trans-national Jewish refugee stories, "Soviet Central Asia, Iran, and India: Sites of Refuge and Relief for European Jews During World War II."

Nicoletta F. Gullace is an associate professor of history at the University of New Hampshire. She is the author of *"The Blood of Our Sons": Men, Women, and the Renegotiation of British Citizenship During the Great War,* which won the 2003 North American Conference of British Studies Book Prize. She is currently working on a book entitled *The Politics of Suffering: How the World Fictionalized War Crimes After World War I.*

Elizabeth Heineman is an associate professor of history and of gender, women's and sexuality studies at the University of Iowa, where she serves on the Executive Board of the Center for Human Rights. She is author of *What Difference Does a Husband Make? Women and Marital Status in Nazi and Postwar Germany* and *Before Porn was Legal: The Erotica Empire of Beate Uhse.* She is the recipient of the 2010 DAAD award for Distinguished Scholarship in German and European Studies awarded by the American Institute of Contemporary German Studies.

Marianne Kamp is an associate professor of history at the University of Wyoming, where she teaches about the modern Middle East, the Soviet Union, and its successor states. She is also the director of the Women's Studies Program and teaches a course on women and Islam. She is the author of a number of articles and a book, *The New Woman in Uzbekistan.*

Charles F. Ritter is a professor of history and director of the Elizabeth Morrissy Honors Program at the College of Notre Dame of Maryland. He is coauthor with E. Susan Barber of "'Physical Abuse and Rough Handling': Race, Gender and Sexual Justice in the Occupied South," in *Occupied Women: Gender, Military Occupation, and the American Civil War,* ed. LeeAnn Whites and Alecia P. Long. He also coeditor with Jon L. Wakelyn of *Leaders of the American Civil War* and *American Legislative Leaders, 1850–1910.*

Yasmin Saikia is Hardt-Nickachos chair in peace studies and professor of history at Arizona State University. She is the author of two published books, *In the Mead-*

ows of Gold: Telling Tales of the Swargadoes at the Crossroads of Assam (1997) and *Fragmented Memories: Struggling to Be Tai-Ahom in India* (2004). She has a forthcoming book entitled *Women, War and the Making of Bangladesh: Remembering 1971* (2011).

Yuma Totani obtained her Ph.D. in history from the University of California, Berkeley, in 2005, and currently teaches at the University of Hawai'i at Mānoa. Her areas of specialization are modern Japan and World War II Pacific-area war crimes trials. She is the author of *The Tokyo War Crimes Trial: The Pursuit of Justice in the Wake of World War II.*

Index

abduction. *See* captives

abortion: as "aftermath" of conflict, 11, 160–61; forced, 12; politics, 250, 316n.31, 321; restrictions, 12. *See also* health

Abu Ghraib, 1, 16, 18–19, 255

Acropolites, George, 79–80

activism. *See* feminist/feminism: activist/activism; human rights: activist/activism

Adomnán, *Law of the Innocents*, 178–79

Africa, German East: patriarchal norms of, 8, 12, 96–97, 99–102; taxation in, 98–100; warfare practices in, 7, 20, 90–93, 100. *See also* captives

African American (free) men: assailants, lynching of, 9; soldiers, 148–49. *See also* slaves/slavery; stereotypes; testimony; witnesses

African American (free) women: rape of, 26, 36–38, 202, 204, 207, 211–14, 296n.2. *See also* slaves/slavery; stereotypes; testimony; witnesses

Agathias, 78

Akayesu Judgement, 244–48, 312n.78, 313n.94. *See also* International Criminal Court (ICC); International Criminal Tribunal for Rwanda (ICTR)

Akiner, Shirin, 57

Albert of Achen, 186

alcohol, use by soldiers, 110, 127, 139, 141–42, 192, 198, 205, 209, 285n.10

Alexander, Isabel, 199

Alexander the Great (Alexander of Macedon), 79, 81, 84, 177, 276n.27

Alexander III (pope 1159–81), 176

Allied Control Council Law No. 10. *See* Nuremberg

Allied Powers. *See* Great Britain; United States; *individual Soviet entries*

Ambrose of Milan, 177

Amedinajad, Mahmoud, 120

America. *See* United States

American Civil War. *See* U.S. Civil War

Americanization, 115

American Revolution, 25–38

Amerindians: political devaluation of, 52; as religious others, 9, 51–53; resistance to missionization, 39–40; societal norms of, 41–42. *See also* Amerindian women; Catholic mission clergy; conversion; Spanish colonial authorities; Spanish conquest of Americas; Spanish military; Spanish soldiers

Amerindian women: attacks on, 17; experience of sexual violence, 41–42; as sexual others, 9, 51–53; status of, 51. *See also* Amerindians; Catholic mission clergy; conversion; Spanish colonial authorities; Spanish conquest of Americas; Spanish military; Spanish soldiers

amicus curiae briefs, 244, 308n.46, 313n.82, 318n.153, 321

andrapodizing, 77–82, 84–86

androcentric interpretations: of human rights, 238; of warfare, 77, 88

Anonyma, 150

Appian, 79–80

Aquinas, Thomas, Saint, 180–81, 183

Aristotle/Aristotelian theory, 51, 81, 176

Armenia. *See under* genocide

army/armies. *See individual military entries*

army-brothel. *See under* prostitution

Articles of War. *See* military code/law/ordinances

Asia, Central, 56, 66, 68. *See also* Uzbekistan (Soviet)

Asia, South, 154, 157–58, 169. *See also* Bangladesh (East Pakistan); India; Pakistan (West Pakistan)

Acknowledgments

From its inception, this book has benefited from intellectual, administrative, and financial contributions from many individuals and institutions. In spring 2006, the University of Iowa Center for Human Rights hosted a conference that provided the inspiration for this volume. Center staff members Amy Weismann and Liz Crooks put tremendous energy into organizing the conference, and student volunteers Ned Bertz, Jo Butterfield, Susan Chang, Katarina Durcova, Monica Foley, Drew Henning, Kelly Jurgenson, Julia LaBua, Aaron Lerman, Girija Mahajan, Andrea McStockard, Aaron Meyers, Megan Vandemark, Emily Shrepf, Leslie Weatherhead, and Meg Zandi ensured that proceedings ran smoothly. Research assistants Amy Braun, Elise Downer, and Woyu Liu, interns Lauren Dana and Bridget Sjostrom, and AmeriCorps VISTA member Kelsey Kramer all lent a hand at important points during our work. Space constraints and considerations of breadth of coverage prevented us from inviting conference participants Tammy Ho, Anna Klosowska, and John Theibault to contribute to this volume, but their comments helped to shape our thinking and their excellent papers informed the final product. I am especially indebted to Jo Butterfield, whose work as a research assistant spanned the life of this project, who composed the index, and whose efforts were critical in bringing the late Rhonda Copelon's chapter to completion.

The Iowa Arts and Humanities Initiative, International Programs at the University of Iowa, the Vice President for Research at the University of Iowa, and the Perry A. and Helen Judy Bond Fund for Interdisciplinary Interaction all provided financial support for this project. Greg Hamot, Director of the University of Iowa Center for Human Rights, provided encouragement and made Center interns available. I am grateful to Peter Agree and Nancy Lombardi for their editorial guidance, and to the Press's anonymous readers for their suggestions for improvements to the original manuscript.

Ken Cmiel and Rhonda Copelon contributed their scholarly and activist energies to human rights—and to this project. Both were inspiring colleagues, and both died before they could see this book completed.

Ken Cmiel, who co-organized the conference, was the Director of the University of Iowa Center for Human Rights and Professor of History and American Studies at the University of Iowa. He was author of *Democratic Eloquence: The Fight Over Popular Speech in Nineteenth Century America* and *A Home of Another Kind: One Chicago Orphanage and the Tangle of Child Welfare*. At the time of his death, he was writing a book on the origins of the Universal Declaration of Human Rights as well as essays on the Genocide Convention and on the contributions of Raphael Lemkin to the field of human rights.

Rhonda Copelon was professor at CUNY School of Law, Vice-President of the Center for Constitutional Rights, cofounder of the Law School's International Women's Human Rights Clinic (IWHRC), and cofounder of the Women's Caucus for Gender Justice. Drawing on Professor Copelon's scholarship on the subject and her collaborations with other activists in the field, the IWHRC submitted amicus briefs to the International Criminal Tribunals for Rwanda and the former Yugoslavia that contributed to the recognition in international law of rape as a crime of genocide and torture. Copelon also coordinated an effort with partners across the globe to ensure that the International Criminal Court codified sexual and gender crimes as being part of their jurisdiction.

This book is dedicated to the memory of Ken Cmiel and Rhonda Copelon. Royalties will be donated to the University of Iowa Center for Human Rights.